CAMELOT'S SWORD

Sarah Zettel was born in California in 1966. She is the author of the acclaimed *Isavalta Trilogy* (*A Sorcerer's Treason*, *The Usurper's Crown* and *The Firebird's Vengeance*), a romantic fantasy based on the folklores of Russia, China and India, as well as *Camelot's Shadow*, her first Arthurian romance. She has also written several science fiction novels and many short stories in various genres. Sarah Zettel lives in Michigan with her husband and their son.

By Sarah Zettel

A Sorcerer's Treason
The Usurper's Crown
The Firebird's Vengeance

Camelot's Shadow
Camelot's Honour
Camelot's Sword

SARAH ZETTEL

Camelot's Sword

HarperCollins*Publishers*

This novel is entirely a work of fiction.
The names, characters and incidents portrayed in it are
the work of the author's imagination. Any resemblance to
actual persons, living or dead, events or localities is
entirely coincidental.

HarperCollins*Publishers*
77–85 Fulham Palace Road,
Hammersmith, London W6 8JB

www.harpercollins.co.uk

Published by HarperCollins*Publishers* 2006

1

A catalogue record for this book
is available from the British Library

ISBN-13: 978 0 00 715871 3
ISBN-10: 0 00 715871 8

Typeset in Meridien by Palimpsest Book Production,
Polmont, Stirlingshire

Printed and bound in Australia by
Griffin Press

This one's for Lydia 'Ford' Kawka, wherever she's gone.

ACKNOWLEDGEMENTS

I'd like to thank Lisa Spangenberg for her expert advice on all things Celtic, as well as the women of SFF-WFS who helped with many small, strange Arthurian questions. As ever, I'd like to thank my very patient, very supportive writer's group, and my loving husband Tim.

Also I'd very much like to thank Vic & Sandy at the Cottage Tea Shop Bed and Breakfast in Tintagel for being spectacular hosts, and for all the great food.

PROLOGUE

My wandering monk returned today.

He found me brooding in the apple orchard where I sat hoping, without really believing, that the meagre sun of this green island would bake some of the pain from my crooked bones.

'You are troubled, Brother Kai,' he said, in his bluff, booming voice.

'Memory,' I said, making room for his broad frame on my stone bench. 'An old man's last and bitterest companion.'

'And what brought on these memories that so darken your brow on one of the finest days God ever wrought?' There was a twinkle in his eye as he said it, letting me know he was attempting to goad me into better humour.

'The market has been here this past week. Some of the brothers helped walk me around it. Not that I have anything to exchange for goods, but they thought to give the old man a change of scenery, and some of the younger brothers find me an amusing and slightly dangerous companion.' I am sure I smiled then, but my monk is not easily shocked, nor is he the sort to scold. These are attributes that make him an easy companion. 'There were all manner of mountebanks and tricksters there, as there are at such gatherings, but there was a harper too. Perhaps the man was a true bard in the old style, I do not know. But as the brothers brought me forward to listen, the harper turned to a lay of Tristan and Iseult. It seemed as if he knew me and had been waiting for me to come.' I am a distinctive figure, prodigiously lame as I am, and such men may be paid well in advance for their songs. After all these long years, the fate of Iseult on Britain's shores still rankles with the men of Eire, and she still has kindred here.

'And did you speak to him?'

I had indeed spoken, demanding to know what pig had taught the man to sing. I mocked his voice and manner until the crowd roared with laughter, and the man sat there, watching me. He took my mocking with a calm that would not be shattered. It is a poor thing to make such a spectacle of oneself, and I was not ready to confess to it.

The monk took my silence as answer enough.

'Did you know them?' he asked after awhile.

'Sir Tristan I knew, a little, the short time he was a knight at the Round Table. A bold youth. A warrior to make his enemies quake in their saddles. Queen Iseult I never knew at all.'

'Is it as men say now, that there was a potion of love drunk between them?'

I laughed a little at this. Let it loose into the world, and how much a history may change! Were there any left on either shore who had not heard this version of the tragedy? Sir Tristan came to Ireland to defeat an Irish king and fell head over heels in love with that same king's wise daughter. But – oh, fell fate! – he must deliver her up to his own lord, King Mark who demands her hand to make the peace and to spite Sir Tristan, of whom he has grown jealous.

The stories diverge after that. Here in the land of Eire one will hear that Sir Tristan arranged for Queen Iseult to be kidnapped so that he might effect her rescue and take advantage of her. On the Britons' strand, you hear that as the lovers crossed the ocean, they accidentally drank a potion given to a servant by Iseult's kin and, by its power fell into an unbreakable passion one with the other. So strong was this passion that when Tristan believed Iseult dead, he died of a broken heart, and then Iseult succumbed herself to the same malady when she saw Tristan in his tomb.

'It makes a fine story does it not?' I answered tartly. 'The potion absolves the pretty pair from having to think about what they're doing. He was a liege man of the High King and she was married to an embattled king, and childless to boot. Oh, yes, a pretty story.'

The monk cocked his head towards me. 'Do you know it to be untrue then? I thought you had never known the queen?'

'Her I did not know, but I knew one who did. A girl sent to Tintagel for fostering. Lynet was her name, and she, to her sorrow, knew far too intimately what befell Tristan and Iseult.' Memories, too many of them old and sour, came to me. 'It is a hard thing to be caught up in the stories of the great,' I said.

He looked at me keenly. 'As it is to be brother to a hero?'

'Just so.' I think he knew how close to my heart he struck, but my monk is not one to apologize for the wounds his honesty brings.

'Well.' He stood, taking up his staff. 'It would seem to me that to exorcise this bitterness of yours, you must draw out that memory with the balm of ink and paper.'

And so I shall. Herewith I set it down. Not the tale of Sir Tristan and Queen Iseult, of which I was, by God's mercy, spared the witness of, but of Lynet of Cambryn who was far less fortunate than I. This is the story she told me, or as much as I can recall through the veil time and hard memory have drawn over those days. Let this tale stand as evidence of the true nature of love, and how the brave soul carries itself in the face of the worst that may come.

Let me begin.

Kai pen Hir ap Cynyr
At the Monastery of Gillean,
Eire

ONE

Lynet Carnbrea stood beside her siblings atop the watchtower in the first light of spring's chill dawn, listening to the bishop proclaim the holy words, and trying not to shiver.

'*For the Lord thy God bringeth thee into a good land, a land of brooks of water, of fountains and depths that spring out of valleys and hills!*' Bishop Austell's voice rang out in the crystalline air of dawn, lovingly drawing out the long and stately Latin. '*A land of wheat, and barley, and vines, and fig trees, and pomegranates; a land of oil, olive, and honey!*'

It was crowded on the watchtower's heights, with Lynet, her brother Colan, their older sister Laurel, Father Lucius to hold the Holy Writ and the bishop to declaim the verse. Laurel tucked a strand of pale hair back under her hood and pressed close to Lynet so they might better share their warmth. The salt winds whipped around their heads, forcing their way under fur-lined hoods, woollen cloaks and even between laces and seams. On the horizon, the sun's light stretched out red and gold above the distant moor. Lynet could just barely make out the glowing remains of the bonfires that had burned all night. Men and women still moved sluggishly around the pools of glowing coals. They stretched, they embraced, some still danced, having trod the fires down to ash already.

Day had come, spring had come. The waters were clear of ice, and all the world would live again. In other places this rite was not held until the first of May. But in the land above the River Camel, they celebrated the thaw when the river ran free of ice and the tinning could begin again.

Every spring, Lynet came up here with her family to greet the dawn and hear the call to work the turning of the year and the quickening of the season.

They were a widely varied group, the children of Steward Kenan and Lady Morwenna. Laurel, the oldest of them, was so pale she might have been a wraith of dawn. Her braid of white-gold hair hung over the shoulder of her substantial brown cloak and the warming morning light shone in her pale green eyes. Colan, Lynet's long-limbed, sparsely bearded brother was darker than Laurel, but not by much. He stood with one foot on the parapet, looking over the rocky country that spread around them. His hair was tarnished brass, and where Laurel's eyes were as green as the sunlit sea, his were like that same sea under a storm cloud. Indeed, there were those who said that it was not Steward Kenan who had fathered these children, but one of the *morverch*, the people of the sea. No one, however, said it where the steward could hear.

Of them all, only Lynet resembled their solid father. Like him, her hair was a rich chestnut, her eyes summer hazel and her skin golden in the winter and brown in the summer.

Steward Kenan did not stand with his children this morning, and Lynet found her gaze drifting towards the west, towards Tintagel where he had gone.

How do you fare, my father? she wondered. *What do you speak of with King Mark? Does he speak to you at all?*

Bishop Austell drew in a final breath and cried, '*A land*

wherein thou shalt eat bread without scarceness, thou shalt not lack anything in it; a land whose stones are iron, and out of whose hills thou mayest dig brass. Amen!'

The prayer shook Lynet out of her thoughts, and she was grateful. She had no wish at all to dwell on what might or might not be happening at Tintagel. Beside her, Colan raised his great hunting horn and blew long and hard, sending the curling note out across the countryside. When the last echo died away, the bishop smote the stones with his crook, and called out, 'Rise up! Rise up! Rise up all you men! Rise up all you women! The waters run clear, and the Lord of all the Earth calls you forth!'

In this fashion, Bishop Austell led them all down the tower's twisting stairs: Father Lucius and the great Bible first, then Laurel, Colan, and Lynet. Together, they marched out into the sprawling cluster of dwellings that formed the *castell* called Cambryn.

'Rise up!' they cried. 'Rise up you men! Rise up you women! The Lord of all the Earth calls you forth!'

Cambryn had grown out of the soil over many generations. The paths between the stone and thatch houses with their little courtyards spread out like old roots. They delved into earth and stone to reach the cellars and storage chambers that were also hiding places in times of war or great storm. Then they pushed up to meet the great timbered hall with its central tower, second storey and roof of pale slate.

Any other morning, if someone had marched through the *castell* bellowing at the top of his lungs, the people would have risen slowly from their beds, rubbed the sleep from their eyes and cursed him mightily. Not this morning. Cambryn's folk surged out of their houses, beating sticks, pots, kettles, stones, whatever might add to the joyful riot of noise. Some wore holly crowns on their heads, or the first of the snowdrops tucked into belts and hoods. Some hoisted leathern bottles of strong drink. Children skipped between their elders, adding their own piping voices to the racket. The bishop's cry was fast drowned out by the song taken up by each and every new voice.

> *'Rise up, all you women!*
> *All in your gowns of green!*
> *Rise up and greet the morning!*
> *Rise up for Heaven's Queen!'*

Another procession snaked down from the heath. This one carried the king and queen of the day hoisted high on two chairs. It was Deane and Nance this year. Both strong and fair, they had been clad in loose robes of red and green. Garlands of holly and ribbons twined in their hair and about their waists. Each carried a stave decked with tin bells that they shook to add to the clamour. They clasped hands over the heads of the crowd, their faces flushed with dance and drink and celebration. There was some noise that they'd been out the night before, not merely treading the fires down to bring luck and health, but observing an older practice which would stretch the bishop's patience to its limit. The thought made Lynet's own spine stiffen, but she prayed they'd come to their senses, and the altar, if that were so.

> *'Rise up all you young men!*
> *All in your tunics red!*
> *Rise up and greet the morning!*
> *Greet the Lord of all the Earth . . .'*

The procession descended the steep river valley. They stormed into the forest, their singing shaking the branches that made a living roof overhead and causing the birds to cry out in angry response. At last they reached their destination. Up ahead, the River Camel ran chattering down the rocky hill-side, as clear and cold as the morning around them. The weirs and sluices waited open and empty. The great kettles of ale that had been warming all night with wrinkled crab-apples bobbing in the amber brew stood on the bank. The ale's smell hung heavy in the air, mingling with the scent of the warm bread that had been brought down from the hall.

Lynet's stomach growled, but she hung back with the others, waiting for Bishop Austell. The sturdy churchman marched into the stream. As the frigid water lifted up his robe's hems and swirled around his knees, he raised his holly-twined crook once more.

'For thou shalt eat the labour of thine hands: happy shalt thou be, and it shall be well with thee,' he cried. 'Thy wife shall be as a fruitful vine by the sides of thine house: thy children like olive plants round about thy table! Behold! That thus shall the man be blessed that feareth the Lord!'

Laurel stepped forward, took up a ladle full of the warm ale from the nearest kettle and passed it to the bishop. He poured a long libation into the river waters, and then drank down the rest himself. When he had emptied the dipper, he lifted up his head, ale still dripping down his beard. Lynet moved to stand beside her sister, who handed Bishop Austell a honeyed cake from the basket of breads. He crumbled the cake into the river.

'In nomine Patre, et File, et Spiritus Sancte.' Bishop Austell drew the sign of the cross over all.

At this sign, the folk of Cambryn surged forward, lowering their festival king and queen to receive their own offerings. Laurel refilled the ladle so they might drink. Lynet popped pieces of sweet, sticky cake into their mouths. With each motion the crowd roared its approval. Deane and Nance kissed, clasped their hands and shook their bells. The folk cheered once more and planted the king's and queen's chairs on the riverside, so 'their majesties' could oversee the work and celebration, and give blessing or pass judgement on what they saw. The rest of the folk danced in and out of the river, barefoot, never minding the cold. They swung their shrieking, giggling children from bank to bank. Lynet and Laurel remained by the massive kettles and baskets, offering food and drink to all who demanded it. The people kissed and laughed and partook eagerly of what was offered.

In the midst of this revelry, the men stripped off their shirts, took up their picks, and began attacking the ragged hillside, loosening great chunks of earth and stone down into the sluices and the baskets. There were not as many of them as there had been in years past. War and raiders had carried off husbands and sons alike. So a number of the goodwives and their daughters waded into the stream beside the men, their hems tucked into their waistbands so they could wield the baskets and the sieves.

Colan stepped briskly up for his ale and his cake. He gave Lynet a broad wink before he stripped naked to the waist and waded into the river with the rest of the men. He'd toil beside them all day, adding his sweat to the libations already offered for the river, the tin and God's blessing.

The great sieves rattled as hands shook them hard, sifting out the dirt and the dust. Then, one woman dipped her hand in and pulled out a rock flecked with silver that glinted in the rising sun. The first of the ore had been found.

Another mighty cheer went up. The festival king and queen kissed long and lustily. Lynet added her voice to the cheering and raised a dripping ladle. Bishop Austell drank deep once more, and Lynet sipped. The brew was warm and welcome, but she had eaten only a mouthful of bread as yet, and she did not need the strong drink's dizziness added to the effects of a sleepless night.

Suddenly, a man's voice rose up over the clamour and the

laughter. The tone of command and warning was so clear and so different from the merry riot about them that all went silent in an instant.

On top of the fell stood a small host of men, ten in number, Lynet counted. Two on horse, the rest on foot. She did not know any one of them. All were dirty and windblown. Their hair stuck out in all directions where it was not braided tight, and travel had heavily stained their dull woollen cloaks. The men on horseback had swords and knives at their belts, and those on foot carried pole-arms that had been used at least as hard as the men.

The two leaders rode their horses forward to the very edge of the hillside.

'We seek the Steward of Cambryn!' boomed the right-hand man. He had the colouring of an autumn fox, dark red hair with keen black eyes. His chin was stubbled by only a traveller's scrubby beard, but his moustaches hung down almost to his waist.

Colan, soaked to the knees, his dripping arms filthy with mud, straightened up. He surveyed these newcomers, and saw, Lynet was sure, how they all went armed.

'Steward Kenan is not here,' he said. 'He has gone to Tintagel to take counsel with King Mark.'

Discreet of you, brother, thought Lynet, half with admiration and half with irony. *Gone to plead more like, and all Mark's other vassals with him.*

'I am Lord Colan, the steward's son, and I stand here for him at this time.' He hoisted himself out of the stream, mustering what dignity he could, filthy, dripping and half-naked as he was. 'I do bid you welcome, Chief Mesek Kynhoem, and you Chief Peran Treanhal.'

Kynhoem. Treanhal. Now she could place these men. Their peoples lived to the north and east of Cambryn's borders. They lived by their kyne mostly, growing some small crops to feed the beasts and themselves. They came up from the moors from time to time, to trade and to reaffirm their loyalties to the steward and the absent queen. There had been trouble between them recently, she remembered hearing. A raiding that had left some men dead. But she thought the bloodprice had been settled before Lord Kenan had left. What brought them here now?

The second man, Peran Treanhal, was the taller of the two. His brown hair was thin on top, letting his speckled pate show through, but still long enough behind to make a stout braid that hung down his back. His hawk-like face had been horribly burned on its right side. The flesh was pebbled and puckered and his eye and mouth both twisted and pulled. The back of one long, raw hand was mottled red and white as well. The whole sight made Lynet wince in sympathy.

'I am here for justice, Lord Colan,' Peran said. His voice was painfully harsh, and Lynet looked again at his burns. *The fire that gave him those burns got its smoke down his throat as well.* 'There has been murder done.'

The word dropped heavily from him, and one of the women behind Lynet gasped. Lynet herself went cold. The charge of murder, of death dealt outside the law of God and man, was as vile an accusation as could be levelled. If it were judged true, far more than bloodprice would be paid. The shame upon family and clan would follow down the generations. The guilty man might even be declared outlaw, a sentence that was the same as death, only more slow.

Mesek sighed. 'It was no murder, Lord Colan. It was the mischance of a young hothead's impatience.' He spoke in a tone far too reasonable for words bearing a clear insult.

'This is for my son's life, and I will be heard!' Peran's raw shout tore from his heart and made the sinews of his neck stand out like knotted cords.

Mesek barked in laughter, as if this was some bitter jest.

At this, Peran's wounded face flushed red and he looked as though he might have struck out, but only just remembered to stay his hand.

'This is no place to hear such hard business,' said Bishop Austell in a voice both quiet and even. 'And no place to make weary travellers comfortable.' He climbed the bank as easily as a much younger man and stopped on the slope before the two chieftains, resting the butt of his crook on the ground before him. It showed his office plainly, and also made a barrier between the new comers and the increasingly uneasy crowd behind him.

Colan moved to the bishop's side and picked up his theme. 'You find us here on our feast day. Will you accept a drink in welcome?' He spread his hands gesturing to the kettles. 'Then let me take you to the hall where you can rest and be refreshed.'

Laurel scooped up a dipperful of the ale and strode smartly up the slope. Lynet did the same, so there would be equal welcome for both men. The crowd parted for them, murmuring to themselves. The elders pushed the children behind them, but none spoke. Misrule might be the game of the festival day, but this thing was out of bounds. All of Cambryn's people saw the pikes and the swords. If it came to blows, shovels, picks and numbers might eventually cause the armed men to give over, but there would be a river of blood shed first.

Mesek's gaze swept over them all, counting, calculating. His fingers rubbed the leather of his reins and his horse danced uneasily under him. Then his thin lips twitched beneath his moustache, as if he did not know whether to smile or frown. But he slipped from his saddle, bowed his head to Laurel and drank from the ladle she offered up to him. It was an informal welcome cup, but it would serve. By accepting the drink, Mesek bound himself to the rules of hospitality and guestship. Colan, acting as Cambryn's lord, must now protect Mesek and his men as he would any of the folk of Cambryn, but Mesek could not now shed blood or offer violence in their home.

'Master Peran?' Colan inquired.

Peran only scowled at the dipper Lynet held out. Fire had made him a fearsome sight. But even beneath the burns, she could tell he had been a hard-bitten man. He did not bother to measure the crowd on the river bank. He instead looked at Lynet, looked and wondered. Lynet bit her lip and made herself hold steady under his gaze.

'I will not drink with my son's murderer,' rasped Peran at last.

'You do not drink with him, Peran Treanhal,' said Colan quietly. 'You drink with me.'

Peran's brows lowered until his eyes were almost lost in their folds, but he did at last dismount to accept the ladle from Lynet's cold hands. He raised it to Colan, who nodded in return, and watched closely as the chieftain sipped the amber liquid. With that single act, the tension that sang in the air eased. Lean Meg, always the quick one, came up behind the sisters with a bucket of ale drawn from the kettle. She and Lynet moved among the other men with their dippers, welcoming and binding them all to the law with each draught.

Lynet tried not to notice how many of them eyed her with the same hard, thoughtful gaze as their chief.

By the time all had drunk, Colan had reclaimed his tunic and his cloak and, although still soaked and mud stained, looked much more the young lord.

'Now, Masters,' he said pleasantly. 'Will you walk with me?'

Mesek looked to Peran, his head cocked and his air so plainly mocking that Lynet shivered to see it.

Who can make mock of murder?

Colan stepped between the two chieftains, careful to take no notice of the hard-eyed men who accompanied them. Those men who shifted their weight, clutched their pole-arms, and eyed each other with the pure and burning anger that came from nothing less than a bloody hatred.

Mesek and Peran both found accord enough to fall into uneasy step with Colan, leading their horses alongside. Their men walked behind, clustering close to their fellows and chieftain and keeping well apart from those of the other clan. Lynet cast a worried glance at Laurel, who only handed her dipper off to Meg, hiked up her skirts and followed their brother.

Lynet, having no other choice, did the same.

Behind them, voices rose and the sounds of work began again, but muted now and more sporadic than before. The arrival of Kynhoem and Treanhal had drained the joy from the celebration, at least for now, and it was a stranger and far less merry procession that trooped back through the empty *castell* to the great house.

Cambryn's great house sprawled on the hilltop, the smaller dwellings spreading around it like a woman's rumpled skirts. Like the rest of Cambryn, it had grown up unevenly over uncounted years. It was by now, Lynet admitted to herself, a strange and ungainly place. Two separate halls thrust out at right angles from a round tower, which looked as if it stood between two disputing neighbours, keeping them from coming at each other. The oldest hall had stood in its place across a hundred generations, being constantly rebuilt on stones laid down in times too ancient to be remembered. The tower at the ancient hall's eastern end had been meant as a defence against the Romans, who never did manage to cross the moors to conquer the Dumonii. Instead, the Romans had sailed around the coast to buy their tin openly, and a flood of wealth had come to Cambryn. That wealth had built the second hall in an imitation of the Roman style with tiled floors, limed walls, many rooms, and many hearths to try to keep those rooms warm and dry against their land's cold and frequent rains.

As they crossed the open fields, Colan kept himself as firmly between Mesek and Peran as their tower kept itself between the two mis-matched halls. Not much talk passed between them, or their men, only black or worried looks. Lynet found herself watching her brother's broad back, trying to divine some hint of what he was thinking from his posture. Something nagged at her, but she could not have begun to say what it was.

Once they passed the first ring of ditches and earthworks, the horse paddock came into view. Colan paused, bowing in apology to Mesek and Peran both. 'I fear our stablemen are down at the tinning,' he said. 'For the moment, you must care for your beasts yourselves. Darney can show you the stables.' He pointed at the lone boy with his withered arm who had come to hang over the slatted gate and gawp at the strangers arriving with the high family.

Mesek grunted his assent and gestured to two of his men who took charge of his mount. Peran did the same. Men and horses followed the stooped and openly curious Darney to the muddy yard and thatched stables. Colan's eyes narrowed. *That much is done,* Lynet could all but hear him think. Four men separated out. The threat, if there was one, had been reduced by that much.

Once inside the second ring of earthworks, Lynet could not help but feel a little more at ease. Cambryn's high house had in its time been home to kings of legend, to Roman traders, and to the lesser kings and greater kings that came in the four generations after the Romans left, and finally to Lynet and her family. This was their place and their people. There was only so much mischief ten strangers could work here.

Colan led the remaining party around to the old hall and pushed back the great, black-timbered door. The hall echoed in its emptiness. Only Russ, Dai and Bram, three greybeard brothers, sat around the central fire. The old men all rose stiffly to their feet and made their bows, their dim eyes and deeply lined faces frankly stunned to see strangers today. Still, Lynet could understand why Colan had brought them all here. Empty or full, this place was the seat of law in Cambryn. The dais stood in the middle of one long wall, with the empty throne waiting on its top stair, and the steward's seat only one step below.

While Laurel directed the brothers to bring extra chairs and benches for their guests, Lynet checked the kettle hanging over the second fire and found there was enough of the milk posset left to share around as a decent warming drink for the men. She sent Bram shuffling off at his best speed to fetch cups, and one of the women who was still at the ovens to help serve.

Peran, however, was in no mood to wait for formalities, or comfort.

'When will the steward return?' he asked bluntly, folding his arms across his chest and nodding towards the dais.

'I cannot tell you,' replied Colan. 'Lord Kenan hoped he would only be gone a week, but it is going on ten days since he left. His last message said he did not know when he would return.'

Mesek shrugged. 'I don't know why you dragged us here, Peran. If Kenan's at Tintagel, then that's where we should go.'

Peran only looked blackly at him. 'Tintagel would suit you well, Mesek, with King Mark's mind so distracted he hasn't spoken sense in a year or more.'

That was not entirely true. Lynet ducked her head to hide her thought, pretending to be engrossed in stirring the kettle.

'So, you'd have us wait here on our steward's pleasure?'
Mesek spat into the fire and wiped his moustache. 'I have
cattle to tend, Peran, and cannot be wasting the spring holed
up here with you.'

Peran's face darkened, his body stiffened and his hands
clenched, not over his sword but near enough. Behind him,
his men gathered, and every one of them still had their pikes
in their hands. Mesek's men moved too, though their master
did not. Suddenly, the guesting laws seemed no more than
idle fancy and Lynet found she could not breathe.

Colan held up his hands. 'Masters, as I told you, I stand
here for my father,' he said, a forced calm in his voice. 'If
judgement is required, I will hear you.'

At this, Mesek smiled, a long, thoughtful, unpleasant grin.
'Lord Kenan's son to judge,' he said, drawing the phrase out,
giving weight and consideration to each word. 'One hears
stories of the sound judgement of the steward's children.'
Mesek looked directly at Lynet.

Lynet froze, rooted to the spot as the blood drained away
from her face. Her heart squeezed painfully and she felt the
old, sick tremors begin.

'Of what do you speak, Master?' Colan inquired. He held
himself too still and too carefully. His hands remained loose
and ready. It was a fighting posture, although he had made
no observable move.

Mesek eyed Colan appraisingly, judging the seriousness,
and the strength of the younger man. Shame twisted itself
deeply into Lynet's belly.

'I beg your pardon, Lord Colan,' he said, although his tone
made it plain he did no such thing. 'I mispoke. It was
nothing.'

'No. Nor was it,' answered Colan pleasantly, relaxing so
far as to sit on the nearest chair, gazing up expectantly at
his guests. One by one, reluctantly and without any sign of

relaxing, they also took their seats. Laurel walked between them to add fuel to the fire, without turning a hair.

Lynet, though, could not move. Mesek was looking at her, his eyes twinkling with knowledge and mischief. Footsteps sounded against stone. Lynet forced her head to turn. Bram came through the tower door, with Jen behind him carrying a tray of wooden noggins. Lynet's hands shook as she filled the cups with the milk posset. She bit her lip and made herself attend to her task. If she could not have pride, at least she could find dignity for her family's sake.

But the ladle slipped from her fingers and fell clattering to the floor, splattering milk across her hems. Shame burned her as she stooped to retrieve it. When she straightened Laurel was beside her. 'My sister, we still have the midday meals and tonight's feast to attend to. Will you go see how the women get on?'

Lynet knew her cheeks were as red as fire, and as ashamed as she was of her inability to govern herself, she was grateful to Laurel. She left the hall and fled through the inner door to the old round tower. The great, curving chamber was hung with tapestries and shields. A mosaic of fish and the *morverch*, the mermaids, had replaced the old flagstone floor in an attempt to bring the tower into better harmony with the other, newer wing. Lynet did not go out towards the garden and the ovens. She strode into that newer wing where the chapel waited.

It was a small chamber, but lovingly painted and above the altar hung a wooden crucifix, a breathtaking work of art. It had been made by Yestin the Joiner, whose hands had also crafted the Round Table for King Arthur. It showed the Son of Man with his eyes turned towards heaven, his mother kneeling at his feet. His anguish and hers had been made to look exactly alike and both were so real Lynet sometimes thought she could hear the distant sound of their breathing when she bowed her head in prayer.

Now Lynet knelt before them at the rail and folded her hands over her breast.

Grant me strength. Grant me strength. Oh, Mary Mother of God, steady my hand . . .

She had hoped after so much time her transgression might have meant less to her family and to the people of Cambryn. But Mesek's sneer told her it was not so, and never would be.

Five years earlier, when Lynet was just thirteen years old, she had been sent to the court of King Mark for fostering. There she was put into the care of Mark's wife, Iseult.

Lynet could still remember the first time she laid eyes on Queen Iseult. She'd heard so many contradictory stories about the red-haired lady from across the water that she'd trembled like a leaf as she was conducted to the solarium. Lynet knew the bones of her history of course. Iseult was part of the peace treaty made between the kings of Eire and those of the Dumonii. King Mark had wrested the Dumonii lands from Eire's overlordship, aided principally by Sir Tristan, who was his nephew and a knight of Arthur's Round Table. In gratitude for the aid given by Tristan and the other men and treasure Arthur had sent for the war, Mark had placed the Dumonii under Arthur's lordship, gaining him peace with Eire by the gesture. To help set the seal on the great and complex treaty, Iseult had been given over to Mark.

But Lynet had also heard that the lady was a witch, that she'd enchanted the king, that she could brew love potions and poisons, or draughts of eternal youth.

What Lynet saw when the door opened for her was a woman sitting on a plain stool. She was so pale she might have been made of snow except for her eyes that shone blue as the August sky when she looked up. Her hands, long and slim but with the appearance of great strength, paused at their needlework. Her hair was the red of late autumn, rich and warm. She wore it looped and braided beneath an embroidered veil as was the style of the great city ladies.

Queen Iscult smiled and rose at once to take Lynet's hands and welcome her in a soft, lilting voice filled with the rhythms of her own distant land.

Between one heartbeat and the next, Lynet fell in love.

Lynet had never known her mother, and Laurel had already been gone a whole year to her own fosterage in Camelot. Lynet's greatest fear at going to Tintagel was finding herself alone among strangers. Queen Iseult seemed to understand her well, for she was more a stranger in Mark's court than Lynet. She took Lynet under her wing at once, teaching her to read in Latin along with the vulgar tongues. She expanded Lynet's understanding of the mysteries of courtesy and proper conduct, and the mysteries of scholarship. The queen was as fair as could be, but she was no fainting, posing beauty for a Romanish city man to admire. She was a physician of such skill that the touch of her hand could find an unseen hurt or detect poison deep within the body. She was quick in laughter and understanding, and she shared what she knew readily.

Lynet also remembered the first time she saw Sir Tristan.

She had thought no one could be so fair as the queen, but the young man was Iseult's match in every respect. He came back to Mark's court about a year after Lynet entered it. Next to him, King Mark, for all his ancient blood and warrior's prowess, looked gruff and clumsy, a figure of dross beside a man of fiery gold.

After the peace with Eire had been concluded, Sir Tristan stayed at Tintagel as Arthur's ambassador to Mark, and his representative to the Eire-landers. Lynet remembered the sweet sound of his harping the night he came back from an errand for King Mark at Land's End. Any accomplishment in music was unexpected for a man of war, let alone such expert skill as he showed. She could still feel the warmth that poured from his bright eyes and his fair voice whenever he so much as glanced at her.

Oh, she remembered well those looks, those secret words and swift touches. She remembered how each time she turned, Sir Tristan seemed to be beside her, beseeching her to bear some word or token to the queen. He pressed her constantly for news of Iseult's manner, her conversation, her very look. It was dizzying to be so sought after by a man of such beauty and fame, even if it was because of another, much greater woman, and Lynet had succumbed to this too.

Succumbed? Mother of Mercy, I drowned.

It was she who ran ahead to make sure their meeting places were empty, and she who stood watch to be sure they remained unobserved. She also bore tokens from Tristan to Iseult, and back again. With a child's heedless and infatuated willingness, she helped to cuckold a king.

The secret was not kept, though Lynet had never knowingly betrayed it. There were no true secrets in any court, especially not about a queen who was not popular with all of the people, despite her beauty and her skill. Too many could not forget that the men of Eire had killed and carried off so many of the Dumonii. As it came to be known that Queen Iseult and Sir Tristan met, it also came to be known that Lynet was their go-between. So, when the whispers finally reached Mark's ears, it was Lynet he followed.

She had checked the cellar. She always did. She was careful. Some part of her recognized the danger in what she did. It was empty, and she ran back, flushed and breathless to the queen, who smiled so sweetly and pressed her hand. The king must have slipped in while Lynet was gone. Lynet took up her station in the drying room, sorting and bundling herbs while Queen Iseult went down the stairs, a wax tablet and stylus in her hand as if she meant to take note of her supplies.

Sir Tristan winked at Lynet as he passed, and whispered his thanks, brushing his fingertips against her shoulder. She could still remember the heat of them, and the blush that rose in her cheeks.

King Mark did not kill Tristan until later, until he found him alone beneath the cliffs. The king of dross beat the golden knight to death with his bare fists. He did not tell Iseult what he had done. He let her find the body when she went that way to collect the seaweed she favoured for some draughts and poultices.

Lynet had not seen any of this, but she did see what came after. It came to her still at night and sometimes even in the day when she caught the scent of blood from the animals slaughtered for the table, or saw the blood on the hands of a man back from the hunt.

She had been with the brewers, overseeing the great steaming kettles in the grey morning air. The wind was heavy with the scents of hops and rain. One of the women had called out, and Lynet had looked up, the great, dripping paddle in her hands, to see Queen Iseult striding across the yard, her hands empty of even the basket she had taken for her work.

Lynet shoved her paddle into the hands of the nearest woman and ran to Iseult. 'Majesty, Majesty, what . . . ?'

But Iseult did not answer or even seem to see her. She strode through the door of the great keep, and there beside the fire, on a plain trestle bench, sat King Mark. His hands, his ochre-red hands, dangled between his knees.

He lifted his heavy head and met Iseult's gaze. And Lynet knew. She knew with a sick and utter certainty what had turned Mark's hands that particular shade of red.

'How could you do this, Iseult?' Mark asked, the tears running down his face. 'I loved you. I gave you all that I had. I treated you with courtesy, with tenderness . . .' His voice broke and he rose up then, a mountain of a man casting his shadow over them. *'How could you do this!'* The raw rage in his shout shook the stones around them.

Iseult made no reply, she just stood there, her eyes cold and glittering. In answer, Mark struck her, knocking her back against the wall as if she were no more than a toy, so that her head cracked sharply against the stone. Lynet ran to the queen, grasping her, trying to support her before she slipped to the floor. The queen staggered, but straightened and managed to stand on her own. As she did, Lynet saw the broad streak on her face where her fresh blood had been smeared with the ochre ash that was Tristan's blood.

Mark looked at Lynet. 'If you want to live, you whore, you'll take her to her room. I'm sending her back to her father, and he can lock her in a plague hut for all I care.' But he did not look at Iseult as he said this, and Lynet saw the way his whole body trembled.

Queen Iseult gripped Lynet's hand, the bruise beginning to darken her white, white face. 'Come, Lynet.'

They went to the queen's private chamber then, the sunny room where she and her women did their weaving and their needlework. Right behind them came Wellan, King Mark's own steward, an ox of a man who stood as solidly beside his master as a cliff stood beside the sea.

The women in the chamber saw their mistress's state and ran up to her, crying and lamenting and wringing their hands. They led her to her stool, but before they had any chance to do more, Wellen said, 'Out, all of you. Any who stays except the little whore will be held to be guilty of aiding treason against the king.'

They stared. They saw the dried blood smeared across Queen Iseult's face, and they all understood. They'd known, or most of them had, Lynet could see that now. She had thought she'd been so crafty, but she'd been deaf to the whispers and blind to the winks and the long looks.

They left the queen then, all the women. Not one stayed beside her. Then Wellan walked out behind them, and barred the door.

Lynet couldn't stand anymore. She collapsed at Iseult's feet, fear overwhelming her. She wailed like the terrified child she was while the queen stroked her hair and murmured soothing sounds. When at last she was able to look up, Lynet saw that for all the time she had sobbed, tears had streamed silently down Iseult's cheeks.

Ashamed, she rose and fetched water and washed the queen's face, dabbing at the ugly bruise that spread across her cheek. All the while, one thought repeated itself in her mind. He could kill them. He had the absolute right of king and husband. He could kill them anytime he chose, and no one would do anything about it.

'What can we do, Majesty?' she asked hoarsely 'What . . .'

Iseult patted her hand. 'Never fear, Lynet. You will be allowed to go home. My lord husband is not cruel in that way.'

'But he will send you away? He said . . .'

'Yes.' Iseult rose, resting her hands on the window sill. 'He will send me to my father for punishment.' Her long fingers gripped the stone ledge as if she meant to break it to pieces. 'Beware your own heart, Lynet. Beware the blindness it can throw over you. Beware . . .' but she shook her head and could not finish. 'Build up the fire, child. The night will be cold.'

The night was cold, and it was long and dark. Lynet huddled on her pallet beside the queen's bed, hungry, terrified, and filled with a sadness so intense it dug its claws into the centre of her being.

Despite all this, or perhaps because of it, she did eventually fall asleep.

She woke befuddled, shivering and parched, to a dead fire and Wellan shouting curses out in the corridor. The door was open. She was alone. The queen was nowhere to be seen.

They found her on the shore beside Sir Tristan who had been left for the carrion birds. She was as dead as he, without a stain upon her. A broken heart some said. Poison said others. It hardly mattered. She was dead, and he was dead, and the whole court was in a frenzy. Suddenly Lynet found herself in the midst of a nest of furies who called her foul names and struck her face, pinched her body, and pushed her into the mud. She hid trembling in the cellars until Wellan found her there, dragged her out by her hair and tossed her down in front of King Mark and his men in Tintagel's hall. She grovelled at his feet, too afraid even to plead for her life.

'Let her go,' was Mark's sentence. 'Let her go back to her father's house and tell him what she has done, and let me never see her face again.'

Wellan himself hauled her to the gates and shoved her through them. Lynet stood outside the keep with no cloak and only slippers on her feet. As she wept, her face pressed against her hands, the rains began. Only the kindness of one of the horsemen saved her from having to make the journey on foot. He loaned her a winded nag that would not be missed too much, so at least she could ride.

But the rain and the blows and the sorrow were too much, and by the time Lynet reached Cambryn, she had a raging fever and could not even stand. For weeks she lay insensible. By the time she woke, her family knew all that she had done.

So too did the rest of Cambryn, and all the lands of Dumonii.

It was this that had been behind Mesek's smirks and sneering slights in the old hall. The judgement of Lord Kenan's children, her judgement, was such that it cuckolded kings and killed queens and knights. And who knew what else she had done? Lynet bowed her head until her brow pressed against the knuckles of her clenched hands. Who knew what favours she had accepted from Sir Tristan to be his errand girl? The rumours ran wide and deep that her virtue was in every respect long gone.

For two years now she had lived with all of this – memory, guilt and shame and the desperate need to protect her family's pride. She had learned to wear a mask of dignity and calm, but sometimes it slipped. And when it did, the pain showed through and there seemed to be nothing she could do but weep a fresh river and hate herself that much more. Her folly had trapped her and she would never be any more than the tainted creature she was now.

So she knelt and she prayed and the stones bit her knees through the cloth of her skirt.

'Laurel thought you might be here,' came Bishop Austell's soft voice.

Lynet opened her eyes and wiped hastily at her tears. Her fingers ached from being clenched so hard and so long. Bishop Austell knelt beside her, crossing himself and bowing his head. His lips moved in silent prayer. Lynet bowed her head once more too, not to pray but to collect herself. By the time the bishop had breathed the 'amen', she was able to stand with him. She brushed her skirts into some semblance of order and faced him with dry eyes and a reasonably composed countenance. This elicited a surprisingly gentle smile from the bishop. Bishop Austell had a hard visage. It was a tinner's face; craggy and pitted, seamed and brown. He'd been a tinner, in fact, before God called him to the monastery. He'd been a little surprised, he told her once. He had thought the Lord predisposed towards fishermen, of which the Dumonii had a gracious plenty. But for all his coarse exterior, there was deep kindness within him, and an understanding of the mercy of the Divine, as well as the wrath.

Today, mercy was plainly in his heart. 'Is there anything you'd like to tell me, child?' he asked kindly.

'Nothing new, good Bishop.' Lynet rubbed her brow and temple. Her eyes ached, and her head felt too heavy for her neck.

'Did one of the men say something to you?'

Not yet. 'Nothing openly, no. They hinted. It was enough.'

Bishop Austell took her hands between his own and gently folded them together in an attitude fitted to prayer. The gesture warmed her, making it somehow easier to breathe at the same time. 'You are of stronger stuff than this, Lynet.'

Which was more than Lynet could bear. She drew away from his kindness, pulling back her hands, drawing down her knotted sleeves as if to hide them. 'No, Bishop Austell, it seems I am not.'

But the bishop was not prepared to let her be. He laid his big, hard hand on her shoulder, turning her so she must face him. 'You have done your penance, Lynet,' he said gently but firmly, ducking his head to catch her eye. 'God has forgiven you. It is a sin not to accept that forgiveness.'

'I know it.' Her voice quavered and her feet twitched painfully at the memory. She did know. She knew in the depth of her heart, but that heart was so frozen in its own darkness that it would not move. 'But until I can forget, how can I forgive myself?'

'We are told the greatest virtue is charity. Spare some charity for yourself.'

Lynet wanted no more of this. 'I will try, Bishop.'

'Will you?' Bishop Austell straightened as far as he was able. Age and prayer had stooped his back. Neither, however, had dulled his wits, and he saw easily that she wanted to make her escape. 'It's also a sin to lie to your confessor, Lynet.'

She turned her face away. It was no help, for now she

looked into the strained and sorrowing faces of the Christ and the Holy Mother, delicately carved to show what true suffering was.

She dropped her gaze to the flagstone floor. 'Should you not be down at the tinning? Lest celebration fall into debauchery?'

With this not so subtle hint, Bishop Austell sighed. 'Father Lucius has a sharper eye for debauchery than I do. He will hold the line. I judged your brother more in need of help.'

Lynet cursed herself silently. All her wallowing in self-pity had left Laurel and Colan alone. 'How is it in there?'

'Calm. Polite, in a rough fashion. Strained.' The bishop looked towards the door, seeing something distant. 'It has been agreed that Colan will hear this plea in the morning.'

Lynet swallowed. 'God help us.'

Bishop Austell nodded. 'That is my prayer. But I think it bears repeating.' He appraised her with his bird-bright eyes. 'Are you ready, Lynet? There will be much asked of you today.'

She straightened her spine. Much asked, and she must meet it. Her only future was in aiding this house and its holders. She had set her feet on the path, and though they ached, she must not turn from it.

'Yes, Bishop, I am.'

Bishop Austell stood aside to let her pass. Lynet walked into the corridor, but even as she did, she felt the weight of his gaze on her back. Not just his, she felt all the Divine that waited there in the chapel watching her, and she shivered.

But Lynet could do nothing except keep walking.

TWO

Lynet found herself able to plunge quickly into the whirl of work that accompanied finding room, food, water, clean clothing, bedding, and space for ten men who had brought nothing but their weapons and horses with them. Even the constant ache in her feet was a welcome distraction. It was far from the first time she and Laurel had fulfilled such duties in their father's house, and their people knew their business as well as the sisters did. Consequently, all was handled with what Lynet judged to be creditable dispatch.

The hardest work was in managing proper lodging and feasting, yet keeping the two peoples apart. Colan busied himself with their chiefs, keeping the men talking peaceably of the prospects for a fair spring and summer, of the health of their cattle and horses, of the latest news and gossip from Tintagel and from Camelot. The Kynhoem and Treanhal, though, had been only partly mollified by the truce their chiefs had struck for the day. They were more than ready to trade blunt glowers and bald insults that could have easily escalated to taunts and blows. Fortunately, both Peran and Mesek recognized the problem, and were not averse to having their men make themselves useful. At Laurel and Lynet's bidding, their guests helped shift stores, work the stables and dig out the cellar that had collapsed under winter's blows.

It was a precarious peace, but it held through the evening meal. In this, they were lucky with the timing of these new arrivals. It was the custom to finish the day's celebrations by feasting the tinners and their folk in the high house, so the old hall was filled to the brim with a boisterous, merry crowd. It was no struggle to keep Kynhoem and Treanhal at separate tables. Lynet herself saw that their trenchers and their mugs were kept equally full, allowing none breath for more than praise or song. Both food and drink were as generous as could be for so early in the spring – soup of salted fish, bacon and lentils, hot boiled goose in a cold sauce of pepper and coriander, a stew of last year's apples and plums, the finest and freshest of the bread, and great quantities of beer to wash all down pleasantly. The feast lasted until well after the sun had gone down. Some among the guests could no longer stand with certainty by its end. Laurel, anticipating this, made sure there were some broad-shouldered lads to lead them gently but firmly to their quarters. Ordinarily, they would have housed most of the newcomers in the great hall for the night, but Laurel judged, and Lynet agreed, that it would be more prudent to keep them well out of each other's sight. So, while Lynet had supervised the feasting, Laurel had dealt with the rearrangement of persons and goods, and the grumbling that must come with that, to make places in the smaller chambers of the new hall for all ten. Mesek and Peran agreed to be conducted to their separate chambers by Laurel herself, and Bishop Austell.

While her sister saw to that important business, Lynet lent hand and eye to making sure the good linens and plate were safely returned to the cellars, that the great fires were banked, and most importantly, that the wine and beer were stored securely back under cork and wax. She kept in motion, for the aches in her feet and back and the fog in her mind told her that if she stopped, she would fall asleep in a moment.

Colan alone remained at the high table, swirling the dregs in his cup, seemingly lost in thought.

Or lost in wine. Lynet mounted the dais and plucked the cup from his fingers. 'Colan, get to bed. You'll do no one any good if you are exhausted in the morning.'

But he only eyed her, lacing his fingers together across his stomach and stretching his long legs out under the trestle table.

'Well, my sister, what do you think of this matter?'

Lynet snorted. 'You ask me? I believed you to be above a woman's counsel.' *Especially this woman's.*

'Come now. You mistook my jokes.' His grin turned rueful as he took the cup back and swallowed the last of the wine. 'My fault, I know. But what do you think?'

His tone was so serious it left her no choice but to answer in kind. She rubbed her eyes, trying to clear them. 'I think you'll need all your wits about you on the morrow. This could easily mean war.'

'Another war,' amended Colan bitterly.

Lynet could not bring herself to answer that. She looked out to the hall below where the folk – those who had not collapsed under the weight of too much beer – laid out their blankets and pallets. Nearly all were women and girls. There were too few men, even when you counted the tinners who stretched out by the fires among the dogs and the little boys bedding down beside their mothers. More wives than their husbands had been up to their knees in the stream this morning, heaving out the great baskets of earth. If things went on as they were much longer, it was they who would be doing the planting as well, and either the stream or the fields would not have enough hands.

Another war, and the Steward of Cambryn gone again.

Gone still.

'You should have made them wait for father, Colan,' she whispered.

'How could I, Lynet?' Colan asked her softly. 'Father will not live forever. Today or tomorrow, it is we who will rule. Our neighbours and our people must come to trust us.'

Trust you, you mean. I am beyond such trust.

'We rule nothing,' she murmured, taking refuge in dutiful piety. 'We hold all in trust for the queen.'

'Aye,' said Colan sourly, setting his cup carefully down on the table. 'And where is she, our good Queen Guinevere?'

Lynet understood it. If in the minds of Cambryn and its neighbours Queen Iseult had been too much present, Queen Guinevere, who had inherited Cambryn from her father, was too long absent. 'Queen Guinevere is where she has ever been, my brother. She is at Camelot.'

'And here we wait on her pleasure, in all things. I tell you, Lynet, she should have come back to us before this.' He spoke not to her, but to the hall. 'These yearly poundings from the raiders, the outrage against King Mark . . . we are battered enough we may soon break. None of the wounds made by her marriage have healed clean in this place.'

Lynet nodded. In the early days of Arthur's rise, before the battle of Badon, few had believed his claim that he was the son of the great Uther Pendragon. One who did, though, was King Leodegace of Cambryn. As part of his support to the young warrior, he gave Arthur his only living child in marriage. His decision nearly split Cambryn in two, and this new feud between Kynhoem and Treanhal was but one outgrowth of that old choice. The fact that Queen Iseult had deceived her lord with a man from Camelot had torn open poorly healed breaks in Cambryn, causing the gall to flow afresh.

None of this was aided by the fact that Iseult's betrayal

and what came afterwards had clearly altered King Mark's reason. For nearly two years he had locked himself into Tintagel like a monk in his cell, riding out hardly ever, speaking even less. Queen Iseult's body had been sent back to her father, and since then the raids on the coast had begun again, and now they were interspersed with those the Saxons made. That was why father had gone to Tintagel along with the other lords of the Dumonii. They went to plead with Mark to take a new wife, to get an heir, to rally himself and his men to the protection of his land. They were desperate. They knew, all of them, that if this went on, Mark would fall, and if Mark fell, the Dumonii would dissolve into squabbling cantrevs and chiefdoms, and the Eirans and the Saxons would pick them off at their leisure. Even Arthur might not be able to stop that work once started.

If Arthur moved at all. Lynet's jaw tightened. There was doubt. Even she had heard it. After all, what recompense did Arthur give Mark for the damage Sir Tristan had wrought? None. Which some said was only to be expected, as Arthur's own mother had also cuckolded her husband at Tintagel. Some now called it 'the place of horns', since so many men had been deceived there. Lynet bore her guilt and she accepted the price. But she could not help wondering whether the High King did the same.

'We are of the queen's blood, and she knows it is our father who keeps her peace and faith, and Arthur's,' said Lynet softly. 'And Laurel says she is an honourable woman.' While Lynet had been fostered with Queen Iseult, Laurel had been sent to Camelot to wait upon Queen Guinevere, and to tie the family more closely to the High King and his court.

'So Laurel says, but what did she see of the queen?' Colan's eyes narrowed, seeing only his own thoughts. 'A woman ruling in a foreign country in a court of riches, surrounded by an army to keep her safe and tribute to keep her well fed. While here we cling to the coast and fight off the Saxons and the Firans and shiver and starve in the winter, watching our wealth whittled away year by year.'

Lynet shrugged, suddenly irritated. She did not want to be reminded of troubles about which she could do nothing. She was tired. Her feet and hands ached. She wanted her bed and the oblivion of sleep. 'Surely the chieftains have brought new troubles enough. Why do you need to bring up these others?'

'Because, Lynet, our father will be home soon. I mean to confront him at last. This accusation of murder is the final sign. We cannot wait any longer for Tintagel or Camelot. If we do, Cambryn will crumble apart.' His words dropped to the barest whisper.

Lynet swallowed, her throat suddenly dry and tight. 'What do you want from me?'

Colan reached out and grasped her hand, a gesture he seldom made. 'Your support, sister,' he said. 'You are the one who is closest to our father. You know his heart. If you stand beside me, I might be able to make him hear. If you do not . . .' he shook his head. 'I do not know what will happen to us.'

Lynet swallowed again, and looked at her brother's hand holding hers. To be needed, to be wanted and reminded that she was still loved by her father, it made her weary heart want to sing. But, at the same time, he was talking about forcing a confrontation that could do nothing but bring more division to Cambryn.

She drew her hand away. 'Get to your bed, brother. Let the morning take care of itself.'

Colan stood. 'Will you think on what I have said?'

'Yes,' she answered, turning away so she saw only the stones of the wall. 'Yes.'

She did not turn back, but she felt him leave. Lynet bowed

her head, all the weariness of the sleepless night and turbulent day washing over her. She swayed a little. She could
not stay here. She could not speak of small matters with so
much filling her head and heart. Meg and the others could
manage very well without her. She lifted the trailing hems
of her skirt, and left the great hall as quickly as she could
without running.

By the time she reached the room she shared with Laurel,
Lynet was shaking. She sat on their broad, low bed and
wrapped her arms tightly around herself. Draughts crept
beneath the shutters, curling around her neck and finding
their way into her slippers to chill her swollen, painful feet.
Angrily, she shuffled to the hearth and poked at the fire,
smashing at the coals to set loose the gouts of flame. She
tossed on bricks of turf and watched smoke and flame rise
together, and then sat down again. Slowly, carefully, she
peeled off her soft slippers and eased down her stockings.

The feet beneath belonged to a much older woman. They
were scarred and knobbled with the toes twisted and splayed.
Any change in the weather made them ache. At the end of
a normal day they were usually so tender and swollen she
had to soak them in cold water and spirits before she could
sleep. She did her best to bear it without complaint, for her
broken feet were the constant reminder of her penance and
her sin.

So many memories, crowding in so fast, but before them
all, the look on her father's face when she came weeping to
him, having risen at last from her sick bed after her exile
from Tintagel. She threw herself at his feet and begged him
to let her enter the convent, to take the veil and spend her
life in repentance.

'No,' he said, laying his great hand on her cheek. 'For then
all men would believe that I blame you for this thing. You
were ill used by a careless man and a heedless woman, and

I will not have you hidden for shame. Go to Bishop Austell for a penance if you must, but when it is done, you will take up your life here.'

It had been a hard penance. She had been charged to walk barefoot fifteen miles to the well of Saint Menefreda, and her wounded feet were the result, although it could have been far worse. She still wondered almost daily at the miracle that let her live through that journey. But even more than the pain, it was the absolution from her beloved father that was the hardest burden to bear. He forgave her, he believed her innocent. He had not changed towards her, nor had Laurel.

Colan, though. Colan did not give the appearance of being one who kept his counsel close, but he did. He hid much behind a smile and a jest. Lynet had always thought this understandable. After all, Colan would inherit the title of steward and rule the land in the queen's name. He was right when he said he must be trusted by the chiefs and lords of all of Dumonii.

But now Colan wanted her to stand with him to sway their father's mind.

Behind Lynet, the door opened, sending a fresh draught creeping around ankles and neck.

'Here you are,' said Laurel. She paused. 'Are you well, sister?'

'No.' Lynet did not look up and wrapped her arms tightly around herself. 'No, I am not.'

'Tell me.'

Lynet turned to face her sister. Laurel stood before her waiting, cool and patient as she ever was. Of them all, it was Laurel who bore the strongest resemblance to their mother. Her pale green eyes all but shone in the dark.

'I fear . . .' Lynet twisted her hands. 'I fear our brother is planning something. Against Queen Guinevere. Perhaps against father.'

Laurel's eyes widened, but only a little. Anyone who did not know her well would have been hard pressed to detect any reaction at all. While her hands twisted together in her lap, Lynet told Laurel all that Colan had said to her.

'Perhaps I have grown too suspicious,' she whispered when she finished her story. 'Perhaps I see conspiracy where there is none. After all, the wise say we judge each other by the measure of ourselves.'

Laurel sat down beside her. 'I think you are right.' She shook her head, her fair face tightening with frustration. 'It is in my heart that Colan knows more of this quarrel between Mesek and Peran than he has said. It may be that he and Mesek are not strangers.'

'And Peran?'

'Of him I am less sure.' Laurel frowned. Her gaze was distant, looking within to re-examine every memory. 'He grieves, deeply. If his son was not murdered, he believes that it was so . . .' She set that aside. 'And he hates Mesek. I had not chance to ask what had happened between them, though. That must come with the morning.'

'But of Colan and Mesek?'

'That too must wait.'

Suddenly, Laurel's calm was too much to bear. Lynet shoved herself to her feet again, anger washing away the day's weariness. 'This is pathetic.' She hobbled across the room. 'I will not wait here in silence while he plots some idiocy.'

'Lynet, no.' Laurel's words stopped her as she laid her hand on the door. 'You will only make matters worse.'

Lynet faced her sister. 'Then I will make matters worse, but I will bring them into the light where they can be seen and dealt with.' *I have had enough of plots and shadows in my life. I will have no more.*

Laurel made no immediate answer to this. Instead, she

took a rush light from the basket by the fire. She thrust it into the flame until it kindled and brought it to Lynet.

'Thank you, sister,' replied Lynet. Her hand closed around the rush stalk, brushing her sister's for the span of a breath. They met each other's eyes but said nothing, and Lynet left her there.

The corridor was both dark and frigid. Lynet could see her breath. She tucked her free hand up into her sleeve, knotting the cloth around her fingers. Where to go? She could not wander aimlessly.

When Colan's chamber proved to be empty, she turned her steps back to the old hall. The room still smelled heavily of beer and meat. Beds and pallets had been grouped around the banked fires and folk were beginning to drowse. She saw Lean Meg hastening by with a leather bottle and stopped her.

'Meg, have you seen Lord Colan?'

She frowned. 'I did. He was out by the ovens. Needed to clear his head from the drinking, was what he told me.'

'Thank you.' That could very well be. Colan had been matching Mesek and Peran drink for drink all night. Despite this, worry ground against suspicion, sharpening both.

Outside, the half-moon hung low over the horizon. Clouds scudded across the darkening sky, carrying the smell of hard rain to come. She looked ahead to the black mounds of the ovens, dark and cold beneath the deepening night. Between them, she saw a man's form, pacing back and forth, trying to keep warm. She recognized Colan's stance, with one hand on his hip and his head thrown back, lord of all he surveyed. She had been right. He was not simply idling there. He was waiting for something, or for someone.

Lynet ducked sideways, putting the bulk of the nearest oven between her and him. She thrust her light into the icy mud, grinding it out. Colan did not check his pacing or make

any motion indicating he had seen her. She slipped into the
shadows of the wall and pressed her back against the stones,
lost in the darkness. She dragged her sleeves down over both
hands now and gritted her teeth to keep them from chattering.

*Ridiculous. Hiding from my own brother. Why don't I go and ask
him what he is doing out here?*

She had no answer for her own question, but neither did
she move.

Boots trod the frost-hardened ground, and a second man
stumped out between the ovens, his square cloak wrapped
tight around his shoulders and his tunic hems flapping around
his knees.

'You've been long enough coming,' growled Colan. 'I was
beginning to think you played me for a fool.'

'Never that, my young lord.' His voice was low and harsh
– the voice of Peran Treanhal. Lynet bit down on her tongue
to hold in her gasp.

'So.' Colan folded his arms, looking the other man up and
down. 'What could not be said in daylight?'

'Well now, my young lord.' Peran was trying to sound
knowing and at ease, but it was a poor act. His shoulders
hunched up as if to shield him from some expected blow,
and every rasping word was tight with tension. 'I thought it
best that you and I discuss certain matters of weight without
extra ears.'

Colan spat. 'I am not here to be riddled, Peran. It's too
damned cold.'

'It is that.' She could not see Peran's face, but she could
see his resolve in the line of his body. His hunched shoulders settled themselves to straighten his back and reveal the
carriage of a fighting man. 'But I thought it would be best
that your young lordship know that you and I share certain
interests, and certain good friends.' Lynet heard the pain in

his words; the physical pain of his burned throat, and the pain of his soul. What he said now cost him, and cost him dear.

Colan was silent for a long moment. 'What friends might those be?' he asked, so softly Lynet could barely make out his words.

Peran hunched closer, all pretence at pride gone. 'A lady of the north, for one.'

Colan drew back. 'What has she to do with this?'

The cold inside Lynet deepened and she pressed against the wall to try to control her shivers. What lady of the north could Colan know? There was no queen, no ally in any of the outlying countries, all the way up into the West Lands. Unless he meant . . .

Fear, cold and sudden as a blade stabbed through Lynet's heart. *Oh, no. No. It could not be. Mother of God, this man does not speak of Morgaine!*

'It's true that my enemy's enemy is my friend,' said Peran.

Colan rubbed his hands together hard. 'Friends don't need to meet in shadows, Peran,' he said. 'What would make me believe what you say?'

Lynet had the idea that Peran smiled at this, and she could only imagine it as the desperate leer of a wolf at bay. 'Why mine own word, and your own good understanding, in which we place so much trust.' The words came out as a sneer. There was nothing of trust here, and much of contempt. Colan's chin lifted. He heard it too. But Peran was not yet done. 'With this comes, say, fifty men with good arms when your time is chosen.'

Colan froze. Lynet's fingers clenched around each other so tightly, her nails dug into her flesh. 'What did you say?' asked her brother.

'You have good ears, Lord Colan.' There was a smile in the harsh words. 'I think you heard.'

'What would you know of my time?' demanded Colan.

Peran did not back away. 'I told you, my lord. We share certain good friends, you and I.'

Colan was breathing hard now, the clouds of steam rising in the moon's light. Lynet's heart hammered against her ribs. For all it was so cold, her face was flushed with a fever's heat.

'Hear me, Lord Colan.' Peran moved closer yet. 'Mesek is a bloody-handed liar. Judge well, and you will know the reward of it.'

Say no. Do not trust this. Colan, do not do this! God, God, do not let him be this much the fool!

But her prayers went unanswered, and Colan said, 'Do you swear it, Peran?'

Peran nodded slowly. 'I do swear, my lord Colan.'

Colan's whole body relaxed then. He bowed a little. 'Then I say you have nothing to fear for the morrow.'

Lynet could easily picture the small smile that must now be on his face. She slumped against the wall, grateful it was there to hold her up. She stared disbelieving at the dim shape that was her brother. *Traitor! Fool and traitor!* She wanted to scream, to wake the world, to have lights brought and this meeting exposed. But all she did was stand where she was and hope she was not seen.

Peran bowed in answer, slowly, haltingly, like an ancient man. 'I knew your mettle when I came here, Lord Colan, and I know too one day I will call you king.'

'I will not forget these words, Peran.' Colan's answer held a promise that he would remember not only these words but their tone, along with that which was not said. This was no pledge of loyalty on Peran's part, and no wish for victory. It was a statement of fact, like storm and winter coming. 'God send you good rest.'

'And you, my lord.' A deep weariness that had little to do

with a long day's ride filled those words. Peran turned and left Colan there. One leg, Lynet now noticed, was stiffer than the other, giving him a slight limp. Was this from the fire that had worked such violence on him and his son? Her thoughts skittered over the trivial idea, refusing to think on what she had just heard. She'd been right. Colan did plan. He planned the overthrow of their father.

And he spoke of Morgaine. Morgaine the Sleepless, Morgaine the Goddess, who held sway in shadows of her own, and who, as a little girl, had lived in Cambryn, alongside Queen Guinevere.

Colan remained as he was for a while, rubbing his hands and looking up at the pattern of the clouds overhead. Was he reading the weather or the future there? Lynet's own teeth were bared now and anger flooded her blood, filling her with its heat and colouring the world red before her eyes. She longed to run out and confront her brother, to demand what devil drove him to such treason. But she held her ground. She had never feared her brother before, but now fear of him and for him pressed against her breast like a stone.

At last, Colan sauntered away, his boots crunching the dead grass, as he headed for the old hall. Lynet stayed where she was until she could no longer hear any sound beyond the ringing in her ears and the pounding of her heart. Then she gathered up her hems tightly in fingers aching with cold and made her slow, stumbling way back to her chamber.

Laurel had built up the fire and was sitting beside the hearth wrapped in layers of coverings. She rose at once as Lynet shuffled in, and flung a fur over her shoulders.

'What is it, Lynet? What happened?' Laurel lowered her into a chair.

Lynet swallowed several times, clutching at the fur over her shoulders. Her mouth had gone completely dry. A draught brushed her ankles, as if warning her of the presence of other ears. Laurel drew her chair close and took up Lynet's hand. 'Tell me, Lynet.'

So Lynet did, her words trembling and stumbling as her feet had in the darkness.

'We must send a messenger for father,' said Lynet when she had told everything. 'He must return with all speed.'

But Laurel just sat back, her jaw set and square. Lynet knew that attitude well. Laurel had seen a difficult choice to be made and would make it now from a heart as hard and as steady as the granite beneath their feet. 'No.'

'But . . .'

Laurel did not let her finish. 'Who could we send in secret? If all is as you say, what would Colan do to us if he found we knew? No.' She shook her head. 'We must wait for father to return, then we will tell him all we know.'

Lynet gaped at her. *Did you hear nothing at all?* She swallowed this angry retort and tried to speak calmly. 'But if we stand together, if we speak before witnesses, what could Colan do?'

Laurel simply cocked her head towards Lynet. 'Who else knows of his plans against our father?'

Lynet closed her mouth. No answer came to her. 'You don't know, and neither do I,' said Laurel. 'What we do know for certain is that many of father's most trusted men are away with him at the coast.'

Lynet raked both her hands through her hair, as if trying to comb out all the fear and fury welling up within her. 'I cannot believe this of Colan. I cannot.'

'You doubt your own ears, Lynet?'

Lynet's hands stilled, and then fell into her lap, their strength utterly gone. 'He never said openly he means to stand against father. We can yet hope I am wrong.'

'But with all he has said, you know that hope is too slender a peg to hang the whole of our land upon,' Laurel whispered. For the first time, Lynet heard how tired she also was. Lynet reached out and took her sister's hand. Laurel gripped her fingers tightly, gratitude plain in her eyes. 'Whatever we may hope, sister, we must not deny what is before us, or we will be in vastly greater danger than we are now.'

Their eyes met, and all the helpless fear Lynet had felt in the shadows returned, and redoubled. 'Why is he doing this?' she asked plaintively.

Laurel was silent, but her hand tightened hard around Lynet's. 'There are rumours in the countryside, sister. You have heard them as well as I have.'

Lynet felt her eyes widen. She had ears, and she knew the art that every high-born lady mastered to some extent, of listening while pretending not to hear. Morgaine. She was stepping up her campaign against Arthur, bringing more folk under her wings, reaching out to other chieftains more openly. 'But is it Morgaine that prods him, or he that reaches out to her?'

Laurel considered for a moment. 'I am not certain it matters. This much we know. Cambryn is set between King Mark's land, and King Arthur's. Morgaine would surely love to make a wedge of her old home between these two.'

'Mother of God.' Lynet crossed herself, but at the same time, hope flickered within her. 'Could . . . could Colan be possessed? Could Morgaine have brought this about?' She let the words trail away.

Laurel was looking at the fire. Her sea green eyes shone in the golden light and the shadows made the fine bones of her pale face stand out sharply. 'No,' she said at last. 'It is his own heart that has done this to Colan.'

Lynet bowed her head, what little hope she held dying in an instant. She did not question Laurel. There were secrets Laurel held close in her own soul, and there were things she could bring to pass that neither of them spoke of openly.

'So, we wait?' Lynet watched her own hands, marked with red crescents where her own nails had cut her flesh earlier.

Laurel put her finger under Lynet's chin and lifted her face so that Lynet must look into her green eyes. The fire flickered in them, and for a moment Lynet was afraid of her sister as well.

'We wait,' said Laurel firmly. 'We keep our tongues still, but our ears busy. If Colan comes to you again, put him off as best you can. Let him believe you are considering what he said before, but are afraid. Father will return soon. Sooner than Colan expects even, and we must be ready. Everything that we know will aid us in making our case.'

She was right, but Lynet found herself desperately wishing she was not. Laurel did not seem to require any answer. She just raised Lynet to her feet, leading her to the bed. 'Rest you now, sister. I will keep watch a little while.'

Lynet made no protest. It was not the weariness that kept her silent while she shucked her dress and drew on the woollen robe for sleeping. It was the knowledge that the sooner sleep came, the sooner the thoughts roiling through her would be stilled. She laid herself down on the feather mattress and let Laurel draw up the furs. Laurel planted a kiss on Lynet's forehead, as if Lynet was a child, and she managed a smile. Laurel smoothed her brow with one cool hand, humming tunelessly. Lynet's eyes grew heavy and she could not hold them open. Sleep covered her over and she sank deep beneath it.

Some time later, Lynet dreamed. She dreamed of her sister standing on the watchtower, tall and pale as a ghost. Laurel faced into the wild sea wind and it blew her shining whitegold hair out behind her. She did not speak, and yet in her dream Lynet knew something was said, and that something was a deep call, and it was heard and, more, it was answered, and Laurel smiled.

THREE

The morning came far too soon for Lynet's liking. She rubbed her eyes hard. She must rise and dress, and go out to the ovens to assist with the breakfast. The tables must be laid, the people must be fed. The tinners first of all so that they might be early to the streams.

It was then that Lynet realized Laurel was not in the bed.

She scrambled out from beneath the furs and coverlets. Her knobbly, scarred feet cringed at contact with the cold floor. She threw on her grey over-dress and shoes and flung open the door. Comically, she almost collided with Laurel, who was reaching out to push the door open from the other side. Lynet gaped for a moment. Her sister was dishevelled and even more pale than was her wont. Laurel met Lynet's surprised gaze briefly, and then walked past her to take a seat in front of the banked fire.

'Mother of Mercy, Laurel!' exclaimed Lynet as soon as she found her voice. 'Did you sleep at all?'

Laurel shook her head and reached for the poker. 'It was better that there be ears and eyes abroad in the house with all that has come to us.' She stabbed at the ashes, looking for coals.

'You should have woken me!'

Laurel looked up at her. Shadows made her eyes seem sunken into her skull. 'I see that now, sister,' she said in a tone that was both bland and over-serious.

Lynet firmly took the poker, stirred the coals, and laid more fuel on the fire. 'By Heaven, sister, you cosset me and exhaust yourself. There will be nothing left of any of us by the time father comes home.'

As soon as the words left her, Lynet wished them back. But Laurel made no remark. She just squeezed Lynet's free hand briefly. They were both tired. They were both frightened. 'You must play hostess this day. I fear I'm done in. Come for me when father returns.'

'Will it be today?' asked Lynet cautiously.

Laurel nodded, keeping her gaze turned towards the young fire. 'And soon. We only need to keep our countenance a little longer.'

Lynet caught up her sister's hand. 'Thank you, Laurel.'

But Laurel drew away. 'Thank me when father is home and we have the truth from Colan. We do not yet know that more may come before then.'

Lynet finished dressing and hurried to the chapel to make her morning devotions. Bishop Austell looked quizzically at her as she knelt alone in prayer, but he did not question her. While he recited the liturgy, she toyed with the idea of telling him all that had happened, but decided against it. Father would be back today. That would be soon enough for the bishop to find out about Colan's scheming.

Outside, the world was wrapped in a blanket of fog. Cold, grey mist rose from the land and descended from the sky. The sun was nothing but a pale blur above them and drops of water covered each surface. Despite the chill that reached down her throat, Lynet welcomed the fog. It was a sign of warmth to come, and of the thaw beginning in earnest.

The fires roared in the ovens and Lynet lingered near them, although Meg had the day's baking well in hand. Those who had spent the night bedded down in the hall were beginning to stir, scratching and stretching, Women poked up the three fires and sent children scampering for fuel and for water. Slowly, the slouching, shuffling folk began clearing pallets to make way for the tables and benches. Some could not manage so much, and hunched in the darkest corners, holding their heads.

Lynet helped with the breakfast. Kettles were hung over the fire to boil the porridge of oats, nuts and dried apple. Malted bread was set on the tables alongside soft, white cheese fresh from the dairy and slabs of bacon and smoked fish. Jorey, the ancient stores master, had an unusually sour face as he saw the bounty filling the boards, with still more coming in the form of crockery jugs of small beer, cider and milk. The roads would be drying soon. They must organize expeditions for trade and tribute as quick as they could, before the raiders organized themselves to take what could be taken from woods and sea.

When Peran came to the hall, he had four men in train behind him. Lynet steeled herself.

'God be with you this morning, Master Peran.' She moved forward to greet him with what she hoped was a placid countenance. 'Will you come to your place?' She gestured towards the high table on its dais. 'The food is laid to break your fast. I hope you will find it to your liking.'

'An' I thank you,' he said, his answer as plain and courteous as her question. 'The hospitality of this house is all that I was led to expect and I am grateful.'

You have good reason to be. Out of the corner of her eye, Lynet saw Peran's men helping themselves from the kettles and settling down peaceably at the lower tables. Reassured, she led Peran to the high table. She filled his cups with cider and ale. Peran raised a cup politely to her, but watched her appraisingly over the rim as he drained it. Lynet felt a furious blush spread across her cheeks. Because of her part in the drama of Sir Tristan and Queen Iseult, she was no longer seen as an honourable maiden. She could be readily considered as something for any man's taking, willing or no.

Lynet set the cider jug down within Peran's reach and returned to the kettles, pretending to concern herself with judging the amounts that remained within them.

Before she could reach any decision, Mesek stumped into the hall. He too had his men with him, but, much to Lynet's relief, Bishop Austell walked beside him, making companionable conversation.

God bless you, Bishop. Decorum and precedence meant she could seat the bishop between the two chieftains, letting him take up the role of diplomat for the table. From the slight smile Bishop Austell gave her she saw that he understood this. She hoped he saw the silent 'thank you' she returned.

'God be with you, Lady Lynet,' boomed Mesek, tucking his calloused thumbs into his belt. 'Are we in time, or are all the dainties gone?' He was watching some point over her shoulder, and she knew he must be looking towards Peran, already seated and served.

The suggestion that their house was poor or miserly left a sour taste in Lynet's mouth. 'I regret our house has only humble fare to offer, Master Mesek,' she said. 'But such plenty as the land can offer, we, by God's blessing, may share with all our guests.'

It was a stiff and overly pious answer, and served only to make Mesek smile. With a wave he dispersed his men to their own meals. 'And your brother, my young Lord Colan?' Mesek's eyes turned to slits as he gazed about the hall. 'He is not here yet?'

'I fear some of our house may be late to rise after our feast day,' Bishop Austell said pleasantly, as he steered Mesek to the table. 'You must forgive us, Master.'

'Must I?' Mesek cocked his brows at Lynet, rather than Austell. He sat in the chair she indicated, stretching out his arms and resting his hands on the table, so that he might claim possession of as much of the board as possible. Peran abandoned all pretence of paying attention to his food and drink and instead watched his enemy make himself comfortable. 'Tell me, my Lady Lynet, what else must I forgive you?' Mesek went on.

'I had not realized you'd taken holy orders, Master Mesek,' said the bishop before Mesek could go any farther. 'Do you turn confessor for my lady?'

'It was the lady I spoke to, Bishop.' A warning note crept into Mesek's voice.

Where are you, Colan? Lynet concentrated on filling Mesek's mug with small beer. She suddenly felt very much in need of her brother's easy smile and quick courtesy. 'Have we offended, Master Mesek?'

'Offended?' Mesek pushed his chair back with an air of mocking surprise. 'Offended? When your brother offers justice with one hand and deals with my enemy with the other? What perfect courtesy is that! Surely learned from that king of courtesy, Arthur himself.' Mesek's grin spread out as broadly as his reach. 'But no, it was from someone else you learned all your ways, was it not, my lady?'

Lynet flinched as if she had been struck. *God have mercy.* She could hear Peran's hard, ragged breathing, but she did not dare turn towards him.

'It does you no honour to insult the blameless lady of the house, Master Mesek,' said Bishop Austell coldly.

'Oh, I would not worry, your eminence.' Mesek leaned back, crossing his ankles beneath the table and his arms over his chest. 'From what I have heard, it has been a long time since honour entered here.'

'You certainly brought none with you,' grated Peran.

'Now then, now then, Peran.' Mesek waggled one thick, dirty finger at the other man. 'You've settled your quarrel. Wait in patience for the judgement you bought.'

'Mesek.' Peran's voice was so low and hoarse, he barely sounded human. 'Do you accuse me?'

'Accuse you!' Mesek let out a bark of angry laughter. 'Aye, I accuse you. Your son's death has driven that weak mind of yours madder than old King Mark's. You know you're a liar, but you won't accept the consequences. You must recruit a boy too drunk with his own little power too . . .'

But Peran was already on his feet, his hand closing around the table knife. Before she had time to think on what she did, Lynet dodged sideways, putting herself between him and Mesek.

'For shame, Master Peran!' cried Bishop Austell who was also on his feet. 'Would you break the laws of God and man?'

The hall around them had gone still. Every line of Peran's wiry form said he was ready to strike. His chest heaved hard with the force of his rage. Behind her, Mesek just grinned.

'Master Peran, you will put down that knife,' Lynet said, her voice low, her hands gripping the crock she carried so tightly she feared she might shatter it. 'You will not break the law here and lose all hope of judgement.'

It was his good hand that clutched the knife and held it ready a handspan above the table. His wounded hand flexed, also ready to block or to shove, or to hold. 'I will not be insulted by the man who murdered my son!'

Lynet did not know what strength kept her there, but she held her place. 'Nor will you turn murderer in front of witnesses.' *Mother of Mercy, keep Mesek silent.*

She watched her words sink into him, watched the anger

and hatred on his face shift to unwanted understanding. Then, slowly, as if it took all his strength, Peran loosened his grip on the knife. It clattered onto the board.

'Well done, my lady,' snickered Mesek. 'But then, you've learned well how to charm a man, haven't you?'

Lynet rounded on Mesek, patience, shame and fear all gone. 'Say what you will to me and of me, Mesek Kynhoem. It is no more than I deserve. But you will not break the peace of this house!'

'Peace.' Mesek stuck his thumbs in his belt and spat out the word. 'How much we hear of peace these days. Mark's peace. Arthur's peace. The whole of the Dumonii united in a great peace with those pirates of Eire. Peace is a woman's skirt to hide behind while men poison those they cannot defeat in a fair fight. Meantimes, our lords and their dogs stand about and say how great this peace is that spreads so wide.'

Peran's breath rasped hard in his wounded throat. The blood drained from Lynet's face and hands. Peran might have come here ready to buy his vengeance, but Mesek came ready to start a war.

'What in God's name is this?'

Every head turned. Relief poured through Lynet. Lord Kenan, the Steward of Cambryn, strode into the hall. He was a tall man, square and broad. His great sword slapped at his hip with each step. Laurel and Colan both hurried behind him, and behind them came a host of familiar faces: Hale, their granite-grey captain, his wiry son Lock, and a dozen men-at-arms, men she had known since childhood and who had followed her father on every campaign only to come back again with new scars and new tales. Lynet was seized with the desire to leap from the dais and take shelter behind their backs, and their blades.

'And here comes the one who sired these pups,' muttered Mesek.

Lynet ignored him. She moved out from behind the table to make a deep curtsey to her father. 'God be praised for your safe return, lord father,' she murmured.

Father rested his hand briefly on her head in blessing, then tilted her chin up, studying her for signs of hurt or fear. If his wife and eldest children were of the sea, Kenan was of the earth. He was solid and craggy as the cliffs and the standing stones, with brown hair, brown beard, brown skin, brown eyes, and hands strong enough to lift a boulder the size of a man's head and hurl it thirty paces. 'And glad I am to be home, Lynet,' he murmured softly. 'I'm sorry you were left to bear this much more.

'Mesek! Peran!' Father raised his voice to carry past her. Lynet, quickly and gratefully slipped aside to take her place next to Laurel. She did not dare glance at Colan.

'I am told there exists some quarrel between you,' their father boomed as he looked from one of the chieftains to the other.

Hearing this blunt understatement seemed to rob both men of their voices. Belatedly, they remembered they owed the steward at least the sign of their obeisance, and both bowed.

'What's the news from Tintagel?' breathed Lynet to Laurel. Father's hands were on his hips, and she could read nothing but annoyance in his stance.

Laurel shook her head minutely and Lynet swallowed a curse. King Mark had been unmoved by the pleas of his lords. He would not break from his self-made cloister.

'Aye, a quarrel there is,' said Mesek as he straightened from his bow. 'And we were promised we would be heard in all fairness.' He stared daggers at Colan, who seemed not to notice.

'That you shall. Clear the hall!' Father called to his men. The men Mesek and Peran had brought with them hesitated, but the men of Cambryn spread out at their steward's word.

Captain Hale moved about the hall, politely but persistently herding those who did not move quickly enough towards the door, reminding some of their work, mentioning to others that they should stay close to Mesek's folk, or to Peran's, to prevent mischief. Lynet's heart was weak with relief. It felt as if after a full day on a storm-tossed sea she stood firm and safe on land again.

'You stay with us, Bishop,' said father as Austell too moved to go. 'It may be we need to hear God's word in this matter.'

The bishop bowed his head in assent, and moved to the end of the table.

'And Colan?' whispered Lynet to Laurel. But she was not quiet enough, for their brother turned towards her, his glance knowing, hopeful, assured. She bent her lips into a smile for him, and could only pray he did not see it was false.

'Our brother greets our father with all joy,' murmured Laurel.

Captain Hale closed the doors with a resounding thump. He and his son Lock flanked the portals while the others ranged themselves about the hall. The fact of their isolation descended onto Peran and Mesek, and that brought a return to proper manners. In movements so perfectly matched they might have been part of a ritual mass, the chieftains descended the dais steps, one on each side, trying to eye each other and the steward at the same time.

Had the situation not brought them so close to tragedy, Lynet would have laughed.

The remains of the food lay everywhere, filling the air with tempting smells, but none moved towards it save father. Apparently satisfied that his authority had been remembered, Lord Kenan mounted the dais and sat himself in the centre of the table. He lifted a cup and Lynet hurried to reclaim her crock and fill the silver vessel to brimming. As she withdrew, he touched her arm in reassurance, and Lynet smiled.

Lord Kenan drank off his cup of cider and set the mug down. 'Now.' He wiped his mouth and beard. 'What business could not wait for my return?'

'Well Peran?' Mesek folded his arms, stepping back so he could view the other man more clearly. 'You've been quick enough to speak before now. Will you tell our lord steward what brings us here?'

The fingers of Peran's good hand rubbed together, searching for the knife left behind on the table, Lynet was sure. 'Lord Kenan,' he said, each word grating against his wounded throat. 'It was in the day of the first thaw that we drove our cattle down to the river to drink. Mesek and the men of Kynhoem fell on us there, and after much fighting they stole the better part of our herd. We left two dead behind us as we pursued them, but darkness prevented our catching them.'

He dragged in a long, heavy breath. The burn on his face seemed to darken as he spoke, growing redder as if his skin was remembering the fire which had wounded it so terribly. 'We went to Mesek next day, not for the return of the kyne, but for bloodprice for those men dead at the hands of his people. He denied us. Denied the raid was his doing, and that the dead were laid low by his hand. He bade us leave without any other answer.

'Honour would not permit such cowardice.' Peran's voice rumbled lower, the words rasping and hissing, like the sea speaking to stones. 'Instead, we followed the trail his men had taken after the raid and in so doing we found the hidden paddock on the moor where they kept the beasts, they thought, from our eyes.' His hands twitched, and he coughed. Lynet felt her own breath grow shallow in sympathy. 'My son led the way to the gate while I and my men circled behind. In the fighting, a fire began, burning the barn, and while . . . and while my son Tam worked beside Mesek's men to save the herd, both ours and those lawfully theirs, Mesek came up . . . he came up behind my son who was trying to save his wealth and he hoisted Tam into his arms and tossed him onto the fire as if he were a faggot for the burning.'

This then was where his burns had come from. Lynet closed her eyes against the image of a desperate Peran diving into the fire, striving to pull his son free, and failing.

Father was silent for a moment, acknowledging the death. Bishop Austell crossed himself, murmuring his own prayer. Lynet glanced at Laurel, and at Colan. Laurel permitted no emotion to disturb the set of her face. Colan . . . Colan was clenched tight and all his attention was on their father.

'This is a foul deed you speak of,' said Lord Kenan seriously. 'If it is true, the angels must weep at it. I wonder you did not take your vengeance at that instant.'

'I wish to God that I had. I stayed my hand.' Peran held up his ravaged and crooked hand. 'I was too wounded to strike back as I should, and more, I wanted all the world to know Mesek was a liar and a murderer. I would have his goods forfeit! His followers driven from their hovels! There is not blood enough in him to pay for this thing!'

Father waited, patient, unmoved. It was only when Peran fell silent, and all could see the tears of pain and loss streaming down his ravaged face that the steward turned to the other man standing there.

'You are quiet, Mesek. What do you say to this charge?'

Mesek shrugged. 'I say it does not matter.'

Kenan raised his brows. Lynet had to work to keep her jaw from dropping. Her skin crept across the back of her neck.

'How is it that this does not matter?' asked father softly.

Mesek shook his head. 'Peran, I wonder that God let you live this long. With that eloquent plea of yours you might have moved our tender lord or his tender son to tears, and you would have had your way and my head. But no.' Mesek faced the steward squarely. 'No. Lord Kenan, Master Peran Treanhal must drag me here because he did not see this thing he claims I did. He must meet with your only son in the middle of the night – where God and any with ears can hear it – and bribe him with the promise of fifty men to aid in your overthrow which has been so long plotted by this true scion of your body.'

God and Mary, does the man have ice water in him? Mesek stood as easy as if he surveyed his own lands while Lord Kenan rose from his chair and stalked around the table. Colan's hands clenched into fists. He made no other move. Lynet wished she could reach for Laurel, but she did not dare move either.

The Steward of Cambryn towered above Mesek. 'Be sure of what you say, Mesek. Be very sure.'

Mesek only tucked his thumbs into his belt. 'I am that, my Lord Steward. I have no need of lies or bribes. There are fools enough here to smooth my way.' He glanced across at Peran, speaking those last words in a tone of utter disgust.

Father stood where he was, and for a heartbeat, Lynet saw indecision in him. Then he remembered duty. He drew his shoulders back and with heavy dignity cloaking him, he walked to stand in front of his son.

'An accusation has been made against you, Colan Carnbrea, son of Steward Kenan,' he said, letting each word be heard plainly so that all would know he did not fear the answer.

'Did you do as Mesek Kynhoem says?' Lord Kenan asked.

Lynet's heart squeezed tight until she felt as if she could not bear the pain. If Laurel felt anything at all, she gave no sign. Colan simply looked at their father. 'No,' he said, flatly. 'Master Mesek is mistaken.' Mistaken, not lying. Colan did not seem ready to say that much in open court. 'It was Lynet I met and talked with,' he went on, and Lynet's strangled heart sank into the floor. 'She was upset by what had been said during the day, and I sought to comfort her.'

Lynet's breath caught in her throat. She saw the plea in Colan's eyes. She saw what he was doing, and she understood it. Here was father, come yet again with no good answer from King Mark. Here before them was plain evidence that Camelot's inattention and Mark's fall were set to split their own land apart, and yet their father would cling to oaths already betrayed.

Beside this, she saw father, tired, aging, angry, alone. What if her words broke him? He might fall under the weight of his son's treachery, as Mark had fallen beneath his wife's. Her lies had brought down one great man. Could her truth bring down another?

Beside them both stood Laurel, her own gaze hard and uncompromising. Laurel knew the whole, long truth and knew the choice Lynet faced. This time, however, Lynet knew her sister would not forgive the lie. Lynet was no child now, run half mad with intrigue and love. If she lied now, she did so for herself and of her own free will.

'Speak, Lynet,' said her father, his voice as stern and uncompromising as Laurel's gaze. 'Is it as your brother says?'

Lynet bowed her head. *Not again, brother. Be your cause so just God himself must smile on it. I cannot lie again.* 'No, my lord father, it is not.'

As she spoke, disbelief welled up in her brother's face, hot rage burning it fast away, but she did not stop. 'I was awake that night, and I was troubled, yes, but I did not speak with my brother. I overheard Colan give his promise to Master Peran that he would rule in Peran's favour, whatever the matter laid before him.' Her throat was dry, her words low and harsh. She wished with the whole of her heart that she could die. 'In return, Peran offered him fifty men for when . . . for when his time came . . .' Lord Kenan's shoulders sagged and Lynet swallowed hard against the bile welling up in her. *God, why, why must it be me?*

In an instant, Kenan reached across the space that separated him from his son, grabbed the young man up by the collar and cast him to the floor.

'Dog!' he shouted. 'I would call you bastard and son of a whoremaster, but I know all too well what flesh sired this treachery.' Though father's hands clenched into fists, only his words struck and they struck hard. 'Dishonour the name you own if you will, but you will not dishonour the office we hold by the grace of God! What answer have you, sir?'

Colan picked himself up from the floor slowly and with a dignity Lynet did not know was his. Barely contained fury smouldered in his eyes. But Colan's gaze was not on their father. It was Lynet he watched. She saw the violent nature of the promise in that gaze, and her heart quailed.

'Since you see fit to ask with such courtesy, my lord father, I will answer,' Colan said. 'Why did I do this terrible thing? What my sister heard,' he made a broad and courtly gesture towards Lynet, 'was nothing more nor less than that I feared you would return from King Mark without answer. And this has happened,' he added as if it were only a small matter. 'But I feared more than that, father.' All pretence at lightness fell away from him and Colan also lifted his voice, to make sure every man there heard all he had to say. 'I feared that with the spring, news of our weakness must wing its way across land and sea. What do the kings of Eire say about the death of their beloved daughter at Tintagel? They have unleashed their raiders already to regain their share of our wealth and make slaves of our bodies. What will they try to regain next?' He spread his hands, the anguish in him rising up to choke at his words. 'We are *abandoned* my father, by those we have served most diligently. We must be ready for the war that is to come. We must find allies who will truly stand with us, not just take the riches of our land and return empty oaths.

'We are cast off and squabbled over because we will not fight back!'

This last word rang through the hall. Colan faced their father, his head held high. In that moment Lynet saw the man he was to become; strong in his own right and no fool, but his blood burned hot in him, hotter than reason and hotter than right.

'So, this is your wisdom?' sneered father flatly. 'The fears and rantings of a miser who would keep all his gold for himself and give none to his master who keeps the house?'

But Colan would not yield one inch. 'You know I speak the truth.'

'I might have once, Colan.' Lord Kenan's shoulders slumped and for the first time that morning, Lynet saw how tired her father truly was. He must have ridden half the night to stand here now, summoned by whatever ghostly cry Laurel had raised. 'But now I know nothing except that you would rise up against me and the lords of this land.' He spoke sadly, but implacably. 'You are no more son of mine, Colan Carnbrea. You bear no name. You have no place in this house nor any claim on that which is mine.'

Disbelief widened Colan's eyes and loosened his jaw. As father stood there offering no other word, no explanation or condition, Colan's face turned slowly white. His hands trembled at his side. 'Father, do not do this,' he whispered. 'I may have acted rashly, but I acted because I feared for our house. I beg you, do not turn away from this.'

Father shook his head. 'It is done,' he said. 'By your own action, and now by mine.'

Lynet expected Colan at least to bow his head in the face

of their father's finality, but he did not. He held his ground, and his pride.

'What action should I have taken?' Colan asked evenly. 'When you leave us to sniff like dogs at Camelot's feast, looking for scraps, to be used like whores for the lust of their men . . .'

At this, all father's rage blazed afresh. 'Enough!'

But Colan was not done yet. 'Would you have been so meek if it had been Laurel or Lynet Sir Tristan seduced?'

'You know nothing,' father grated. 'You are a babe bleating that it has not been fed. Get out before you shame me more.' Father shoved Colan backward, sending him staggering towards the doors.

Colan righted himself, blood showing bright on his mouth where he had bitten his cheek. 'Or having seen them dishonoured, would you have just killed my sisters and gone bowing and scraping back to our false queen . . .'

'Get out!' bellowed father. 'You are no more son of mine! This is no more your house! Get out!'

What happened next came so fast Lynet barely saw it. Colan launched himself at their father. Father turned, quick and graceful, grabbed his son and tossed him aside. But Colan bounced off the wall, and charged again, crashing against father, who threw him back once more. This time, Colan kept his feet, even as the men surged around him, even as Bishop Austell leapt out from behind the table to help grab Colan's arms and drag him backward.

She could not see father. She could not see father anywhere.

Lynet thought it strange that Colan should be smiling when he was held so firmly by father's men. She noted there was murmuring behind her, and that a tight knot of people still stood before her though Colan was in the guard's hands. Then she realized that Laurel was not beside her any more.

While Lynet slowly took all this in, Laurel pushed out of the crowd in front of her.

'Lynet!' When Lynet did not move, Laurel grabbed her hand and dragged her through the press of bodies to their father's side.

He lay on the stones, clutching his belly, and he screamed, a loud ringing scream torn from the depths of pain. Red. There was red everywhere. It fountained out over the handle of the dagger protruding from his belly.

Lynet dropped to her knee. Father screamed again in his agony, clawing at the knife.

'Hold him!' she shouted. 'Get him something to bite on!'

A cloth was pressed into her hands and she tried to mop at the blood and staunch it. Another cloth was twisted into a rope so father could bite down against the pain.

The blood would not be stopped. It flowed thick and salty over the embroidered linen. Worse, with it came a foul stench. The knife had pierced the bowels. Lynet's heart froze within her. She lifted her head, and met her father's anguished eyes, and knew he saw she could not heal this blow.

He reached out one bloody hand to her, and she clasped it, her fingers dripping red with his gore. He choked around the cloth, trying to speak. Laurel, ever swift in her understanding, removed the cloth from his mouth.

'Be strong,' father gasped, clutching Lynet's hand so hard she feared her bones would snap. 'Do not fall to . . . fall to . . .' He shuddered, and his head dropped back. Austell caught father's head before it could thud onto the stones. A groan of pain robbed father of speech and he tried again to tear at his wounds. Two men grabbed his clawed, desperate hands. Lynet looked up to meet her sister's eyes, and saw tears streaming down Laurel's hollow cheeks.

'Is there anything . . . ?' Laurel choked the words out.

Lynet's tongue was slow but the stillness of her hands allowed for no answer but the truth. 'Nothing,' she said hoarsely. 'His belly is breached. Even if I could stop the blood . . .'

Father screamed again. 'God!' he wailed. 'Oh, God! Stop this! Stop this!'

'Lynet.' Laurel said her name so softly, Lynet was not sure how she heard it.

Oh, no. She could not do this. But father was screaming, again and again, his face awash in fearful agony as the floor was awash in his blood. Watching her hand as if she stood outside her own body, Lynet reached out and pulled Colan's dagger from his belly. More blood, so much blood. How much blood could one man lose and still scream for the pain of it? Voices all around her, voices behind and before, and motion she could not understand. There was only her hand and the knife as she pressed the edge against father's throat in the place where the pulse beat. Father looked at her, his brown eyes clear, his reason strong despite the pain, and he, warrior that he was, understood the only help she could give. He wrenched his great hand free of those who held him and grasped her wrist, not to hold her back, but bearing down, helping her break the skin and cut the vein even as he screamed.

More blood spilled, and the scream was cut off in a gargling, drowning sound. Lord Kenan, Steward of Cambryn, sagged onto the floor. His eyes closed for the briefest of moments, and then rolled open, seeing nothing.

Lynet stood. Her father's blood covered her dress. It smeared her cheeks. It dripped from her hands and the ends of her hair. She could taste it on her lips. She was an apparition of blood. She burned with its fire. She turned, raising the dagger she had pulled from her father's death wound and pointed it at her faithless brother.

'Murderer!' she cried. 'Murderer!'

'No!' he shouted, struggling to regain that power of speech and truth that had so briefly compelled them all to listen. 'It was Arthur who caused the murder here! He who betrayed . . .'

She would not let him finish. She would not let him pollute this blood, these stones with his lies. 'False son!' she cried. 'Father slayer! Your hand did this and you would lay the blame on our liege lord! God strike me dead before I ever call you brother again!'

'You are outlaw.'

It was Laurel. She stood as straight and pale as a statue of alabaster. She too had blood spattered on her dress and on her throat, but this flaw only seemed to make her shine more brightly. 'Outlaw,' Laurel said again. 'No law, no protection, no sanctuary.' Her words tolled relentlessly. 'No man may aid you. Any man may strike you dead without penalty and claim bloodprice for the deed. Run Colan, No Man's Son. Run and hide while you can!'

Colour drained from Colan's cheeks leaving them ashen grey. He looked about him, to Peran and to Mesek. Neither man moved. Captain Hale and the others stood back. Laurel had given the traitor leave to run, and they would let him. But they did not relax their vigilance for a moment. Let him make any movement against his doom and he would not live another heartbeat. In the heat of her rage, Lynet prayed he would run, that he would not seek the clean, quick death that Hale and the others would give him. He deserved no such mercy.

Let you envy Cain himself as the wilderness takes you.

Then, he did run, and his motion broke the silence. A roar rose from the throats of the men gathered there, and they surged after him, suddenly a mob, crying out his name, cursing, driving him out the door as a hunting pack drives a deer. But they would not kill him. Lynet was icily sure of that. They'd drive him out to the mile stone, turning him loose in the wilderness. God would take him there, or a man guided by God's hand.

Lynet began to tremble. Her arm dropped to her side and the cursed dagger fell clattering to the floor beside their father's bloody corpse.

FOUR

Lynet looked down at the cold clay remains that had so recently held her father. It was strange, she thought, how fast the colour in a person's flesh fled when life was gone. Was the soul itself red?

In the distance, Bishop Austell was saying, 'Bear him to the chapel. One of you . . . you . . . send for Meg and Father Lucius. He must be washed . . .'

Is the soul red?

Men came forward. They hoisted the awkward weight of their steward's body onto their shoulders. Bearing it well, like the workmen they were, they carried the corpse away, with the bishop walking before them. Where all had been silence, a flood-tide of noise now rose. Voices, running feet, the commotion of bodies rushing into the hall, men and women shouting questions, screams and cries as folk saw the corpse carried past.

All Lynet could do was stand and stare at the blood that was left behind.

'Lady Laurel, what's happened?'

'God above, she's killed the steward!'

Blood. They saw the blood, on her hands, on father's

hands, on Mark's hands, on Iseult's livid face, on Tristan's corpse, so much blood . . .

'No!' declared Laurel. 'This was Colan Carnbrea's work!' *Laurel will not call him brother. No more brother. Never again.* 'He is murderer and outlaw, and so are any who give him aid or succour!'

Laurel was holding her. Lynet recognized her sister's touch. It was as well. Her legs had gone numb, and she did not think she could stand anymore.

There was running and weeping and shouts. She could not make out any of it clearly. The fog had crept in from outside, settling over her eyes and heart. Eventually, hands led her away to another place. They stripped off her bloody dress and sat her down.

After a time, Laurel crouched in front of her. Lynet could clearly see her sister's white, strained face. A clay basin rested on the floor beside her. Laurel wetted a cloth in the basin's clear water and began gently to wash Lynet's face, laving their father's blood from her skin. Slowly, the touch of the water revived her, breaking open her stupor so that the grief could flow.

Lynet's will to move returned in a rush, and she clasped her sister's wrists. They said nothing, just stayed like that for a long moment, both letting their tears fall in silent rivers until the deep wells within them ran dry.

Only then did words return to Lynet. 'Mary, Mother of God. Laurel, what are we going to do?'

'I don't know,' Laurel whispered, wringing the rag out into the basin. 'If Peran and Mesek go to war, I do not think they will spare Cambryn. We can only hold the house if Captain Hale has men enough, and he may not. Folk are scared, Lynet. They may run.' She ran both hands over her hair. Long locks had come loose from her braid and drifted across her cheeks and brow.

Lynet struggled to clear her thoughts. *Think. You cannot weep your way out of this problem.* 'We cannot hold alone.'

'No,' agreed Laurel, lifting her face again. 'We cannot.'

'Then we must get help.' Her mind was not yet completely clear, and she could not say from where this help should come. There was one obvious place to turn, but she hesitated. Despite all he had done and all Lynet had seen, Colan's words from the day before came back, and she could not dismiss the fear of treachery they had planted. That fear kept her from forming any answer for her sister. That fear, and new guilt layering itself over the old.

If she had stood by Colan when he needed her, this would not be happening. Their father would still be alive and Colon's urge to treachery would still sleep undisturbed.

No. I cannot give way to that. She made herself speak. 'We must send for the queen.'

'Must we?' Laurel stood and carried the basin to the small table, setting it there. 'What we know now is that anger against Arthur is running high.' Laurel gripped either side of the basin, watching the wall but seeing memory. 'Bringing Queen Guinevere back may start the war rather than prevent it.'

'Will Arthur abandon his queen to her fate if war does come? If she is here and in danger, his men will follow.'

Laurel stared at her in frank surprise. 'That is a hard bargain.'

'What other one can we make?' asked Lynet, striving for some of Laurel's cold reason.

Laurel said nothing for a long moment. In that silence, Lynet read her sister's thought. 'You cannot be considering going to Morgaine,' Lynet breathed.

Laurel's brows arched. 'I cannot?'

'No,' said Lynet at once.

'Do you remember what Colan said?'

'He lied. How can you believe he did anything but lie?' Lynet's voice took on a shrill edge that resonated inside her ears, making her remember her own shouts. *Murderer! False son!* How could Laurel believe anything he had said? And yet, God help her, she could not forget those few moments before blood and insult had overwhelmed his sense, when he had spoken with such compelling wisdom. Even father had listened to what he had said.

'Do we know he was mistaken about everything?' Laurel asked, her voice both steady and reasonable. 'What if it is the queen who has led us to this place?'

'Queen Guinevere is not responsible for our father's death.'

'Isn't she?' Laurel's calm began to crack. Her breath grew heavier and her words took on a brittle edge. 'Away in Camelot she holds our reins, but forgets our welfare. Sir Tristan commits outrage, and where is she? Queen Iseult is dead and King Mark is weakened and where *is* she?'

Lynet wanted to give way, but she could not. They were all that was left now, the only ones who stood between their land and the ravages of war and anarchy. 'No, Laurel. Morgaine is Colan's friend. Peran spoke of her as friend to him as well. She knew of his rebellion at the very least. She may even have helped. You know as well as I do she works her will by stealth and trickery.'

But Laurel would not relent. 'Yes. Morgaine works by stealth, and she wins.'

'Will you seek the aid of one who supports treason?' Lynet's voice broke on the last word. 'If she is willing to remove one king by stealth, what will she do to another?' Laurel remained unmoved and Lynet's jaw hardened. 'Let me tell you what I know, sister. It is shadows and stealth that breed murder. It is lies and deception. You . . .' her voice shook. 'We cannot do what Colan has done. We cannot look for somewhere else to put the blame for what has happened other than where it belongs. With our family. With Colan, and with you and me.' Lynet swallowed, and forced out the next words. 'And with our father.'

It was the truth and Lynet knew it for the truth, yet even though she spoke it herself, it was almost too much to bear. She felt her throat and jaw quiver, in anticipation of tears to come. 'One of us must go to the queen. We must call on Arthur's aid. If they answer, then all will be right. If they do not . . .'

Weariness drew Laurel's skin tight across her bones, and made each line of her face sharp and hard. 'If not, we are in the right to do whatever we must to keep our folk and our land together.'

Lynet nodded. 'Yes. Whatever we must.'

They met each other's eyes. Laurel's shone with the bright sea fire. She would do as she must. For a terrifying moment, Lynet saw how much Laurel resembled Colan.

'We will call a council, and we will find a way to put these words into action.' Laurel reached out suddenly and gripped Lynet's hand hard. 'We must stand united in this, sister. If any see us divided or indecisive everything will shatter in an instant.'

Lynet could scarce breathe for the enormity of it all. Part of her wanted to hide like a child. Part of her cursed and howled at her parents for abandoning her to this. Part of her wanted nothing more than to send Colan to hell with her bare hands for all she seemed to have taken up his cause. And some small, absurd part was wondering if there was enough beer and cider left to serve such a council as they must now convene. They would have to talk with Jorey, and soon.

'We stand together, sister, and one way or another, our enemies will learn Cambryn does not stand alone.'

*   *   *

And so it was done. Fires and the torches were lit in the great hall. The banners and the shields were all hung. Chairs were set around the central fire and the last of the Spanish wine was brought from the cellar to fill the silver goblets. Captain Hale was there and Lock with him. A full twenty men lined the hall under his charge. Bishop Austell, his strong hand clutching his crook as if it were a holy relic, sat at Laurel's right. Tor, who knew more of the tin and the river than any other man in Cambryn, wrapped both his battered hands around the silver goblet that looked as flimsy as an eggshell in his massive grip.

Mesek sat across the fire from Laurel and Lynet, and Peran a quarter turn of the circle from him. Lynet did not know what persuasion the captain and the bishop had used to get them to agree to the council, but it had not been enough to keep them from coming armed, or interspersing their own men among Cambryn's; a thing that would never have happened had the steward been alive.

Laurel stood. Both she and Lynet had dressed carefully for this meeting, and Laurel was resplendent in her gown of emerald silk embroidered about its hems and trailing sleeves with leaping dolphins. Her cloak was black as midnight, setting off the pallor of her hair and skin. Gold and gems flashed at her throat and adorned her hands. Even Iseult had never looked more the queen.

'It has been decided that Cambryn will send a delegation to Camelot at once,' said Laurel. 'They will return with Queen Guinevere, so that she may settle the disputes between our people, and, if she will not stay, then appoint a new steward to take up the lawful rule of the land.'

'Well, that's done!' Mesek slapped his palms down on his thighs. 'It is a wonder you bothered to call this council. As usual, the children of Lord Kenan will have things their own way.'

'Master, you agreed to hear what our ladies would say,' Bishop Austell reminded him coldly.

Mesek snorted. 'And heard I have. By the time our precious and lawful queen comes to her home again, my men will be dead and my people burned out of their houses by the Treanhal. What then for me and mine?'

Laurel turned ever so slightly towards Master Peran. 'Master Peran? Will you agree to wait for the queen's judgement?'

Peran's burn seemed to pulse in time to the leaping of the flames before him. 'What good has judgement brought me?' he rasped. 'I sought the law. It has brought only more murder, and kept this man alive.'

'Will you blame the law you broke?' sneered Mesek. 'Be grateful *our ladies* are too tender hearted to order your death themselves.'

Lynet heard the sharp note beneath the chieftain's bitterness. She saw the way his hands curled in on themselves and how his teeth bared as he spoke. In that moment, she knew what she had missed before.

Mesek was frightened. His manner was that of a wolf at bay, snarling and lunging at the dogs, knowing that as soon as it ceased to attack it would die. What had been a matter of a few cattle and legal bloodprice had gone terribly wrong. Now his enemy was corrupting what rule there was left in the land. How could he not fear for his own?

Why had Peran even come? His actions showed clearly he was not interested in justice, only vengeance. Lynet remembered Peran had said he wanted Mesek shamed, but if Mesek had done murder before witnesses, shame was already upon him.

What truly drove Peran to this place?

She works by stealth. It was her name that Peran used to bring Colan to trust him. Our land the wedge between Mark and Arthur. The remembered words assembled themselves in a new order.

Oh, God of mercy. Laurel was ready to go to Morgaine. What if Morgaine is already here?

Lynet drew herself up, wishing she could be as cool as Laurel. 'We do not speak of what has been done, but of what must be done next,' she said. 'What good will war bring us? It will prevent the planting and the fishing and the tinning, and that in turn will ensure we all starve when winter comes. War will allow the raiders of all lands to rob us blind and hunt us like deer in the wilderness. Is this better than waiting for the queen and the law?'

Peran blinked, and then he looked away. His hand scrabbled at the arm of his chair, looking for something to hold onto and finding nothing. Lynet did not let her gaze shift from him. *If you are going to deny me, Master, you must do so here and now, before God and all who gather here.*

'Ever the orator, your sister,' remarked Mesek casually to Laurel.

'I bid you be quiet, Master,' replied Laurel evenly.

'So you go to Camelot,' said Peran at last. 'How do we know you will return?'

'That is a simple matter, Master Peran,' said Laurel. 'My sister goes to Camelot, but I remain here, under the watchful gaze of yourself and Master Mesek and all your men.'

That seemed to genuinely take him aback. 'You'd be hostage to your sister's word?'

No trust. All burned away by what has happened, murder or betrayal or something more. Nothing but ash left in your heart.

'Would you accept anything less, Master?' Laurel asked, utterly calm. 'If so, tell us, and we will surely agree to your terms.'

Lynet curled her hands, her fingernails digging into her sweating palms. This was the only throw of the bones they had in this gamble, and if it failed . . . then God have mercy on them, for no one else would.

'God's legs!' cried Mesek suddenly, slamming his cup down. 'I'm beginning to wish you had just killed me, Peran. Let it be done. Let the girl go to Camelot and get the queen. Let her go to elf land and fetch a pot of gold. Just let it be *done*, or the Eirans and the Saxons and every other vulture will find us here bleating like lambs in the pen!'

Peran's face twitched beneath the mask of his burn. 'Very well,' he said. 'Let her go.'

At these words, the bishop bowed his head, and slowly, solemnly began to pray. But Lynet did not join him. She watched Peran Treanhal as he watched her, wary, disbelieving. She thought of Laurel left alone in this man's keeping, and despite all she knew of the depth of her sister's strengths, she shuddered.

God grant me speed, she prayed in her own heart. *God soften the hearts of those I must plead before.*

And God of mercy, God of life, protect my sister from this man, and from the one using him as a shield.

FIVE

Dawn spread out damp and grey, touching Colan Carnbrea with its unkind fingers. Shivering, he crawled out from the rude shelter of his little boat. He'd traded his arm ring to a fisherman for that boat and a satchel of ancient bread and fish smoked to leather. He'd softened each in sea water as he sailed the channel. Four days he'd been on the water. Four nights he'd hid in unfamiliar coves behind rocks and in frigid caves to try to snatch some sleep when he could no longer keep his eyes open. He might have moved faster, but he had no water with him and his thirst drove him repeatedly to shore, searching for some stream or pool that would be his next salvation.

Salvation. Colan's mouth twisted into a grim smile. No. He was beyond that now.

He rubbed his hands and blew on them, trying to breathe some warmth into his icy fingers. It seemed as if he had not been warm since he had fled Cambryn.

Since he had killed his father.

Time and again, he saw his hands reach for the dagger, felt the give of cloth and soft flesh, saw the startled look in his father's eyes. Time and again, he wanted to cry out to his remembered self to stop, to think, to drop the blade, and yet that other self never did. He never could. Colan had come to welcome the thirst and hunger that racked him, as he welcomed the rough seas that rocked and tossed his skin boat. The bone-bare drive of physical need kept all other thought from him. It was the only respite he had left.

Hunched on the little beach, he finished his last piece of bread, licking the crumbs off the bottom of the satchel. The last scrap of fish he stowed away for later. He followed the stream up into the scrub and bracken until he reached the place where the water flowed sweet. There he knelt in the mud and drank as much as he could hold. Then, abandoning the tiny boat that had brought him this far, he hoisted himself up the tumbled rocks and onto the cliffs, scrabbling to reach the level ground at the top. The rest of his journey he would make on foot and he was grateful for it. He could not lose the feeling that he was being followed on the sea. That something far beneath the waters watched and whispered to him.

It frightened him, and he could not make himself believe that he only imagined that unseen presence. As terrible as Lynet had been standing before him drenched in their father's blood, far more terrible had been the merciless white fire in Laurel's fae eyes.

Haunt me over the sea, sister. I will not blame you. But on land, you are no more than I.

The clouds hung low and heavy above him. Colan felt the weight of them with every step over the rough and open ground. He used the line of cliffs as his guide. Below, the sea roared and crashed, shaking the ground. Colan imagined it was Laurel's frustration, and allowed himself a tiny, grim smile. The wind, though, lashed until it felt as if the air around him were ice. Father waited behind that wind, as his sister waited below in the sea. Lynet and her curses surely waited in the numb weariness that settled over his soul. If he stopped, if he faltered, together they would take him.

Colan's boot stubbed hard against a stone. He sprawled onto the heather and muddy grass, crying aloud as another stone banged his chin and scraped the skin he thought had gone numb. Father came closer. Colan shoved himself up onto hands and knees. *No. Not yet. You don't get me yet.*

'Well, now, what's this?'

Above him, two dark blurs against the white-grey sky resolved into the shapes of men in leather jerkins and caps. One carried a spear. One carried a long-hafted axe.

The axe man nudged Colan's arm with a sandalled foot. His elbow buckled and he fell again.

'Can't say for sure,' said the spear man. 'Is it a man or a fish, do ye think?'

The first one stroked his pointed beard with a thick hand covered in swirling blue tattoos. 'Fish, I'd say, and an old fish at that.'

They laughed at their joke, which gave Colan time to push himself back to sit on his heels. He was breathing too hard, and he could not stop the trembling that had seized his limbs. 'I seek the Lady Morgaine,' he said between his chattering teeth. 'I ask you, of your courtesy, to take me to her.'

This seemed to sober them. 'Well now, perhaps it's a man after all,' said the axe bearer.

'Perhaps it is.' The spear man held out his hand. Colan grasped it, and let himself be pulled to his feet.

The axe man circled him, looking for arms, and to make him uncomfortable. Colan endured, concentrating on remaining upright. 'What do you want of the Lady Morgaine, boy?'

What do I want? 'Mercy,' said Colan with sudden, lonely honesty.

The men looked at each other. 'Well, she's but a small store of that.' The axe man stroked his pointed beard again.

'Still, you'd best come and make your case to the Lady herself. She's always ready to speak to any who come openly in her name.'

They flanked him, as much to keep him walking as to make sure he did not make any threatening gesture. The rough, open grassland gave way to stands of trees, and then to the muddy expanse of ploughed fields. Beyond these, they came to a place that was more croft than fortress. Wattle and daub houses stood between wickerwork fences. Folk in rough, plain dress moved about the place, feeding the animals, scolding the children who ran between the houses, setting their hands to all the mending and making that governed life in a harsh country. A few watched curiously as Colan was led past them, but there was no sign of alarm. They were people who knew themselves to be well defended.

Colan's guards led him towards a long, low house with a thatched roof. Smoke rolled out from the hole in that roof, and the scent of a fire came to Colan like a benediction.

The inside of the great house was dim and smoky, but no more so than such a place normally was. There were fewer folk in here, for the day outside was fine, if cold. Some women sat in a circle, carding wool and spinning the thread. The scents of lint and fresh wool mixed with the smoke. Old men sat by the fires, alternately tending them and talking with each other between long pulls from mugs or leathern jacks.

The spear man shouldered some of these greybeards aside with the amiable roughness born of familiarity, clearing Colan a spot beside the fire. No one offered him a stool, but no one seemed to begrudge him a place either, and that was all Colan cared about. He sat on the packed earth, and stretched his hands towards the fire, getting as close to the flames as he could stand. It's warmth spilled over him deliciously.

One of the rough-hewn old men handed him a jack, and

Colan drank cautiously. A sweet, fiery liquid rolled down his throat, and he coughed hard, which made his companions grin knowingly at each other. Not one of them spoke a word and not one of them hid his stares. Colan answered their silence with more of his own. He would not be discomfited by so simple a tactic. Despite the drink he'd just accepted, he did not expect anyone to name him friend or guest until the lady of this house had done so.

Eventually, Colan's clenched muscles eased and he stopped shaking. A bowl of pottage and bread was passed to him. He devoured the plain fare, running his fingers around the inside of the wooden bowl to get every last dollop. When he at last was able to attend to something other than the food in front of him, he looked up and saw the axe man laughing, silently and not in a wholly good natured way.

'Wipe your chin, boy,' the axe man said. 'The Lady will hear you now.'

The man's tone stung Colan's pride, but he held it in check. He carefully wiped both face and hands before he stood, leaving the wooden bowl on the floor. The axe man grunted and led him further back into the hall where the women sat with their spindles and carding combs, creating fine white thread from clots of wool.

Colan bowed courteously to this assemblage and was rewarded with a selection of cold and appraising stares. Not one of the women here looked to be less than a grandmother. Colan remembered his manners, held his tongue and waited.

He waited until his feet began to ache. He waited until his legs and knees remembered their climb of that morning and all the labours they had accomplished over the past days and threatened to begin shaking again. He waited until he wanted to grab one of these silent, ancient women and choke her with her own thread until she swore to show him to Morgaine.

'You are possessed of some patience, Colan Carnbrea, whatever else you may be.'

Colan started and saw another woman sitting in the shadows before him. Like the others, she held a spindle and twisted a fine white thread. She, however, sat in a great carved chair that he would have sworn was not there a moment ago.

It is fatigue and shadow, he tried to tell himself, but he could not escape the understanding that he had not seen her because she did not wish him to.

In Colan's experience, the mark of power in women had always shown itself as the absence of colour. Laurel was the image of their mother, who could call the seabirds down to rest on her hands, and could fill a net with fish in the middle of a hard winter just by wishing it so. Morgaine, however, was raven dark. Her skin was brown from wind and sun. Her long hands were solid and strong from her work, but had such a delicate touch that she spun a thread as fine as any spider's. This woman was as much stone and earth as his father had been, but there was fire there too. Her black eyes shone with it, and they seemed to see all he was and all he had done.

Beside her stood a stripling boy, a brown, lithe whippet of a youth. That boy had his mother's eyes and saw all that she did. He smiled at Colan. The image of a questing hound came to Colan more clearly than ever, as the boy leaned over and whispered something to his mother. She nodded her agreement. Then, she touched his hand, and the boy flashed Colan another mischievous, knowing grin and ran away, vanishing through the hall door and out into the sunlight.

It was a small moment, a single heartbeat of domestic life, but something about it left Colan disquieted. Something too knowing about that gangly boy, something in the fire sparking behind Morgaine's eyes. Colan set these thoughts aside. He was here now, and it was far too late to be disconcerted by so little. He knelt, bowing his head.

Morgaine had clearly finished testing his patience. She turned all her attention to him. He could feel her gaze although he could not see her face. 'You have travelled hard and come alone, Colan Carnbrea,' she said. He could see her long brown hands, her fingers never ceasing to twist the thread. The spindle bobbed and twirled at the end of its thin leash, like a captive insect still weakly struggling for escape. 'I would not expect this of someone of your station. What has happened?'

You know. He was certain of it. Though there was no earthly way for the news to have flown ahead of him, she knew, and she was still going to make him say it.

'I am declared outlaw from my home and people for the crime of murder.'

'Oh?' There was no surprise in her voice, only mild curiosity. 'And did you do this murder?'

'I did.' Memory bit hard. Rage, blinding rage at his so solid father, standing by his word, his useless oath, though he condemn them all to death. Had he really meant to kill the old man? Or only to make him see, finally and forever, that he was *wrong*?

'My men tell me you come begging mercy.' *You mean to taunt me with that word. You will have to poke harder than that, my lady.* 'Tell me, Colan, why I should welcome a hunted man into my home?'

At these words, Colan lifted his head. 'I come, Lady Morgaine, because I have nowhere else to turn, and no other friend who will raise a hand for me. My sisters hold Cambryn now. They will entrench themselves in it, following my father's word though it mean the death of the land itself. You are the only one who understands what Arthur and Camelot truly mean to our land and I beg you not to turn away from me for the mistake I have committed in furthering a cause that is also yours.'

The rhythm of her spinning changed, growing slower, steadier. 'Such flattery.' Was it some trick of the light, or did her eyes grow even darker? 'But even having you in my house is an act of war. Why should I risk my men and myself for you?'

Colan did not shrink before that black gaze. This woman had swallowed up and swatted down great kings. He was powerless and alone before her and he knew it. He had nothing left to lose and that made him reckless.

'Because I offer you Cambryn,' he said flatly. 'Your home of old. It will make you a fortress to stand between Mark and Arthur. Take Cambryn, and Tintagel falls soon after. You hold the coast then, the trade and the tin. You can reach out to the men of Eire for the sake of their old grudges. They will swell your ranks for the time when you are ready to meet Arthur in open battle.'

'Those grudges are older than you know, my young lord.' Morgaine spoke softly, other thoughts running through her spider's mind. Then she sighed, looking modestly down at her spinning as if she were no more than a goodwife in her cot. 'Why do you not do this thing yourself? Why not take charge with those young man's hands?'

He spread his hands. They were filthy, but at least the blood was long gone. No, it would never be gone. Yes. His deeds would wash him clean. No, never clean. He silenced his contradicting thoughts with great difficulty. 'I had thought I would take charge as you say, but none will follow me now.'

'Ah!' she sighed. 'So, you are honest at least.'

His mouth twisted up into a grim smile. 'I hope that much I can be. I tried my hand at deception and because of it I am damned.' His head was beginning to ache. He was tired.

He wanted nothing more than to lie down on this dirt floor and sleep. 'Cambryn is set to tear itself apart. Mark will not help. Guinevere cannot. It is yours to take if you wish to.'

Morgaine watched her thread winding around her spindle for a long moment. Then she shook her dark head. 'Cambryn will not fall to any force of arms I can raise at this time. If it could, I would sit in the great hall now.'

'Then I waste your time, and mine.' Slowly, painfully, Colan stood. His knees ached, and his hands shook with weakness. Where now? What next? There was nothing. Hasty death at his own hand might be best. That was mortal sin. So was murder. Could he be damned twice? He needed the bishop. This was one of those thorny points that Austell loved to chew over.

Behind him, Morgaine spoke again. 'Whether you have wasted your time depends on what you do next.'

He looked over his shoulder at her, sitting in her great carved chair, the white thread dangling from her fingertips making a shining line in the shadows. He met her eyes again. There were depths there, and there was power. A man could fool himself into believing that he might understand that power, that sharp-edged beauty, if only he could get close enough. Perhaps he could even take it into his own hands and hold it for his own ends, if only he dared, if only he came closer.

Colan had taken a step without even realizing it.

'You make me a great offer, but I hear no love in it. No loyalty comes with your handing over the land I know you want for your own.' Her voice was low. He had to strain to hear her. It seemed to move to the rhythm of her spindle that never ceased winding. 'What do you want, Colan Carnbrea?'

'I told you.' Another step towards her. Why did he move? He did not know, he only knew that he did. 'I want my land whole. I want an end to these overlords and their madness.'

'What else? What did you seek when you shed your father's blood, little boy?'

Colan swallowed. He was insulted. He should leave, but he had gone too far and he could only answer. 'Revenge.'

'On who? For what?'

'On Arthur who took our queen away. On the queen for abandoning us to besotted old men and over-loyal fools and then forgetting our tin and tribute make Camelot's wealth.'

'And why, Colan Carnbrea, should I believe you will not seek such revenge on me if I disappoint you as well?'

'I swear you have my loyalty.'

'An oath is air and nothing more without something to bind it. What will you give me, Colan Carnbrea?'

He felt himself poised on the knife's tip, teetering, ready to fall. Could he be damned twice? Looking into her darkness he saw that he could. Twice, thrice, as many times as he chose, but he must choose. Choose here and now. Choose at last and forever. Choose the murder he had done in the raw anger of his heart, choose the bloody future that waited if he tried to reclaim something from the wreckage he had made.

'What will you accept of me?'

She smiled, and it was like the heat of the hidden coal deep within the ash. 'A kiss, Colan. Give me a kiss and your oath is sealed.'

One more step, two, three. She lifted her face to him. Her lips were very red and her eyes so vivid with her power and her secrets he could not look into them any more. He closed his own eyes and leaned forward. His mouth found hers. It was a chaste kiss, as gentle and brief as he might give one of his sisters, and yet he felt something drawn from the depths of his soul. A wave of weakness washed over him. In the next instant, the weakness was gone, and he was standing straight before Morgaine, just as he had been.

She rose. 'Very good, my Lord Colan. Now we will talk.' She stood, holding out her hand. Colan took it and bowed over it with careful courtesy. Morgaine smiled, and led him away, and Colan followed.

SIX

The funeral for Lord Kenan was held three days after his death. It took that long for the grave to be dug in the half-frozen earth and stone. Men brought their picks from the tinning. They worked with a will at the unyielding ground to make a place where their steward could be laid to rest. In all that time, no word of Colan came by land or water.

The bier bearing Lord Kenan's shrouded corpse, along with his sword and shield and the many rings he had won in his life, was lowered into the earth in the early, grey morning. The clouds hung heavy overhead. The wind from the sea carried the smell of salt so strongly they might have stood on the shore. As Bishop Austell read the Book over the grave, Laurel lifted her head and turned her face towards the sea wind. Distracted in her grief, Lynet could only wonder bitterly what the winds told Laurel this time and what fresh disaster would come of it.

All of Cambryn came to stand beside them, to hear the blessed words and say their reverent farewells. All but Colan, and Captain Hale. Hale had gone to Port Yzack to find a ship that would sail Lynet and her small party of protectors up the channel and into Arthur's lands.

Bishop Austell would go with her, and Hale's son, Lock, along with three other men that Lock and his father chose. Meg had wanted to come to wait on her, saying Lynet could not go to the great court without at least one woman in her train, but Lynet had insisted Meg stay at Laurel's side.

'I am going to safety,' she told Meg. 'Laurel stays in danger. It is she who needs all our friends about her.'

She did not say it was vital that they travel lightly. When they came to shore and to the roads again, they would have to ride hard and fast. Meg was many things, but she was no horsewoman. Speed was everything. A great show had been made by Mesek and Peran of each sending out one man to tell their folk what had happened, and how they would be waiting at Cambryn for the queen's arrival. But who could know what messages were passed in the dark, and what secret instructions each man carried in his heart. Already some of Cambryn's folk had begun to slip quietly away. They'd take their chances in the wilderness, or with distant family under a stranger's protection rather than trust that Lord Kenan's daughters could hold Cambryn for even a handful of days.

Bishop Austell was saying the amens. As he closed the great Book, his eyes shone with the tears he held back. Lynet crossed herself and knelt for the final blessing. Then she followed Laurel to the grave's ragged edge, and tossed her share of clay and stones onto her father's shrouded form. It was too early in the year for blossoms yet, so they also threw down holly branches, bright green and shining, to lie among the earth and the relics, and remind all that life was eternal.

Eternal. But not on this earth. Given the damage we do, I suppose it is better that way.

The wind blew hard. For a moment, Lynet thought she smelled spring in it. But then that too was gone, and she turned with her sister from their father's grave.

The funeral breakfast had been as lavish as they could manage. Laurel and Jorcy had already been in conference, Lynet knew. If a war was to come, stores would be the main concern. They had to replenish the cellars, one way or the other. Which would mean sending out yet more men and praying they would return back in time.

She and Laurel passed the feast withdrawn in their own thoughts, eating little, saying less. Fortunately, as they were grieving, this was expected of them. A funeral day was a holy time, and it was treated with respect by all present. Even Mesek and Peran shared the table peaceably. For now.

Lynet stayed in her place as long as she could, but at last she could not stand anymore. She stood, made some excuse, and all but ran to her own chamber. She closed the door, and stood there for a time trying to catch her breath, trying to swallow the tears that threatened to burst out yet again. No more. There was no time. They were to leave as soon as the meal was finished.

The last time she had waited to leave her home it had been to make the day's ride to Tintagel. The night before that adventure, though, she had eaten her dinner beside her father, and Colan had kept her company when she couldn't sleep: singing, telling old stories, and re-reading Laurel's letter that the traders had brought with them from Camelot.

This time there was only Laurel among her blood kin left beside her, and soon even Laurel would be too far away to reach. Lynet slumped onto the bed. Her feet already ached from cold and from standing so long, and her heart ached in anticipation of the loneliness to come. *How will I do this without Laurel?* She bowed her head into her hands.

As if summoned by the thought, Laurel pushed open their door. She carried a small wooden casket with her, and there was an unusual wry smile on her face. As the door swung shut behind her, Lynet glimpsed a man with a spear taking up station outside.

'Whose?' Lynet asked, flicking a finger towards the portal.

'Everyone's,' Laurel replied as she crossed the room. 'No one will trust the others, so I am to be followed by one of Peran's men, one of Mesek's, and one of ours. I am, however, given leave to speak in private with you for this one moment.' She set the casket carefully on the small table. It was plain and flat-lidded but bound in shining brass. 'They are sending for more men, and for some women to watch me when the men cannot.'

An entire flock of uneasy thoughts followed this news. Would Mesek or Peran decide to use Laurel herself to obtain the power in Cambryn? There were ways to gain legitimacy for an ambitious man. A marriage, along with much else, could be forced. Even on Laurel.

'You should be the one to go,' said Lynet hoarsely. 'They know you at Camelot. They will listen to a friend.'

'And that is why I must stay. They know me. I believe the queen cares for me. That will add fervour to the plea you must make.' Laurel's jaw hardened and the light behind her eyes glittered brightly for a moment. 'And I am the eldest, Lynet. I may speak with authority where you cannot.' She lowered her voice. 'And in their eyes I am still a maid and unsullied. It will stay them from turning their hands to the worst, at least awhile.'

Lynet bowed her head. 'Yes, of course.'

'We cannot refuse to speak of these things, Lynet, nor to pretend they do not affect us now.'

'I know.' Lynet's hands still twisted together in her lap. She felt herself to be thirteen years old again, waiting to leave her home for the first time. She was too young for this, too alone, too afraid . . .

'Be easy, sister,' Laurel said gently. 'We are not wholly

without help. I will be among friends as well as enemies. And you . . . I have brought you help should you need it.'

Laurel moved to the brass-bound casket. On its clasp was the smallest lock Lynet had ever seen. While Lynet marvelled at its delicacy, Laurel chose the smallest, brightest key from the ring at her waist and opened the box. She lifted out a piece of clean white linen.

Inside the cloth lay a round mirror about the size of Laurel's palm. It was made of glass so pure and smooth it might have been a pool of water framed with silver.

'What is it?' asked Lynet in the hushed tones that only beauty could inspire. 'Where is it from?'

'It was our mother's.' Laurel handed the precious object to her and Lynet cradled it in both hands. It showed her face more clearly than Lynet had ever seen it before: her hazel eyes sunken into her skull, a glimpse of her brown hair trailing in wisps over her sallow cheeks. The mirror felt heavier than it looked, and quite cool. The silver frame had been worked into the shape of foaming waves so detailed it seemed strange not to hear the sea.

'Mother gave it to me on her deathbed.' Laurel sighed and smoothed her hair back, clearly steeling herself. 'Lynet, there are some things that I must tell you now. Things you must believe before you depart on this journey.'

Lynet tore her eyes away from her own reflection. 'Believe?'

Laurel nodded. Her mouth had tightened into a hard line, as if determined not to let out one poorly considered word. 'You know how it is said we were birthed from the sea?'

'Yes.' It was a jibe, a pleasantry that sprang from Laurel and Colan's pallid complexions. The folk of the Dumonii lands were dark, like their father had been.

'We were not,' said Laurel. 'But our mother was.'

Lynet stared at her, mouth half-open to say this was a

poor time to be joking. But she could already see that Laurel was in absolute earnest, and the words drained away from her.

'Our mother, Morwenna, was the daughter of the *bucca-gwidden*, the White Spirit of the Sea,' Laurel went on. She walked to the shuttered window and laid her hand on it, as if she thought to feel some sympathetic message from the wind outside. 'She told me . . . when our father was a young man, he saw her on the shore, combing her hair in the sun. He fell in love with her in that instant, and came back to the same cove, day after day. She watched him from her place beside her mother, and laughed at the infatuation of a mortal for a being of pure spirit. Then, one day, he did not leave when the sun set. He stayed that night, and the next, and the next. He did not eat, he did not sleep. He did not move, even though he began to waste away. It was watching this devotion that softened her heart towards him. As her kind might sometimes do, she took on mortal flesh and went to him.' Lynet smiled, in soft and sad amazement. 'What you hold is her wedding gift from her mother, our grandmother, who is the Sea.'

Her mother, our grandmother, who is the Sea. Lynet stared at her sister, with her translucent skin and her white-gold hair shimmering in the firelight. She thought of Laurel's detachment, of the witchlights that glowed in her pale eyes when she was angered, or when she spoke with certainty of things she could not have seen.

Lynet swallowed. 'Why did you never tell me?'

'Mother told me not to, not until you were to be married . . . or until danger came.' Laurel's eyes were distant, seeing some memory. Perhaps she saw their mother, lying in the great bed, wasting away from the sickness that came on her after the birth of her last child. Laurel would have been no more than eight then. She would have been very young to be hearing these things and making these promises.

No. Not Laurel. Laurel was never young.

'Mother did not want us pulled away from our father by the other half of our blood, she said,' Laurel went on, coming back to the fire. 'I think if she had lived it would have been different.' She said this last so softly, Lynet could not tell if it was a thought, or a wish.

Laurel lifted her eyes to meet Lynet's gaze. 'Do you believe what I say?'

Lynet did not answer right away. Then a memory came to her, from the penance she had done for her part in Iseult's deception and death, the penance that had ruined her feet, and of a dream of a bright and shining figure that had come to her in the depths of her despair. She had never spoken to anyone of that dream, or of what followed afterwards. She wrapped her fingers around the mirror. Did she believe that moment had been real?

It struck Lynet then how lonely her sister must be. If it were true . . . if it were true that she . . . that they . . . were not fully children of men, but partly of the sea, it was Laurel whom the sea tide pulled most strongly. What would she have been if their mother had lived to teach her its secrets?

Laurel for the sea. She herself for the earth, and Colan suspended between the two.

Oh, mother, what might any of us have been had you lived?

'I . . . I do not know what to think. I am afraid.' *Which is what keeps me silent about what I have seen even now.* 'Bishop Austell speaks of the fair form devils can take.' Even as she said it, she felt the jolt of her disloyalty. How could she believe her sister had been mothered by anything evil?

But what of Colan? And what of me?

Laurel shook her head. 'There are powers in this world that belong to neither God nor the Devil. It is one of our good bishop's few failings that he cannot bring himself to acknowledge that much.'

'What is this thing, Laurel? You surely did not keep a simple mirror secret for so long.'

The corner of Laurel's mouth twitched upwards, acknowledging Lynet's attempt at levity. 'I only know what our mother told me. She said that within the mirror waits a spirit. If great need came to me, she said, I could look into the mirror and I would have help. She warned me though, not to use it too freely, for there would be a price in body and spirit to be paid. She also said that if I came to a time there was no other recourse, I should throw the mirror into the sea, and the sea itself would bring me aid.'

Lynet stared at the mirror again. She saw herself looking back, as plainly as if she were two beings, one facing the other.

'Have you ever used it?'

Laurel ducked her head, and to Lynet's utter astonishment, she saw her sister's cheeks flush red.

'Once. I was curious, or perhaps I was so angry at our mother for deserting me for God that I believed her a liar. I don't know. But one night I did cup the mirror in my hands and looked into it long and hard.

'I do not know how to describe what happened next, but I was no longer where I had been. I was instead in a beautiful garden, such as I had never seen, and there was a man kneeling before me, smiling as if he had never seen anything so wonderful.'

'What then?'

'I was afraid, and I screamed, and it all vanished.' The blush on Laurel's cheeks deepened. 'I never have looked in it since then.'

Lynet swallowed. She could not doubt her sister's word, but belief in it made her palm itch beneath the smooth silver of the mirror's frame, and she wanted badly to cross herself.

'It is all the help I can send with you, sister. I'm sorry.'

With these words, Lynet began to tremble again. 'I cannot do this, Laurel. Not alone.'

If she had hoped for sympathy, her sister offered none. 'You must.'

It was too much to bear. 'How can I?' Lynet cried. 'I know nothing about what's happening! I don't even know my sister or my brother or myself any longer!'

Laurel grasped her by the shoulders, turning her roughly around, stilling her outburst. 'You know all you need, sister,' she said firmly. 'You are Lynet of Castell Cambryn. You are the daughter of Lord Kenan and Lady Morwenna. You are earth and stone, and true heart, as you have ever been.'

The witchlight burned in her sister's eyes, lighting the shadows in Lynet's heart. She saw past it though, and saw that her sister was as frightened, as alone as she was. If she could not be strong for herself, she could not fail Laurel.

Laurel held up Lynet's autumn brown travelling cloak. 'It is time to go.'

Lynet looked at the mirror in her hand and carefully slipped it into the purse she wore on her girdle beside her ring of keys. Once it was secured, she permitted her sister to settle the hooded cloak over her shoulders and lace it tight. Side-by-side, they descended the stairs, ignoring the three men who marched down behind them. Together, they crossed through the old tower, and stepped through its open doors.

Peran and Mesek flanked the steps, with their men around them, backed by a loose but watchful line of the men of Cambryn. Lynet did not permit her eyes or thoughts to dwell on them. She could not let her nerve be shaken again. A short line of lightly burdened horses waited at the foot of the steps. Lock and Bishop Austell were mounted on the lead horses with the three Trevailian brothers – Cam, Stef and Rory – behind. A chestnut mare with white socks, a white blaze and an empty saddle stamped its foot impatiently, waiting for her.

Beyond the horses, the yard was filled with people. A hundred familiar forms and faces stood shoulder-to-shoulder: men and women, ancients and crones and children of every age down to babes in arms. As Lynet and Laurel appeared on the threshold, they all knelt together, the men doffing their hoods and all bowing their heads. It was a pure gesture of loyalty and tears pressed hard against Lynet's eyes.

I will be worthy of this. I swear before God and Mary and Jesus Christ, yes and my father and mother too, I will.

With this vow, a calm descended over her, drying her eyes and lifting her chin. She turned and received Laurel's parting kiss and walked down the steps. Lock came at once to help her into the saddle. As she gathered the reins into one hand, she lifted the other to the folk of Cambryn, and they in turn raised their voices in a mighty cheer. The vibrant noise made itself the wind at their backs as Lynet and her protectors touched up their horses. Without looking back, they rode out towards the west, the coast and all that was to come.

Once out of sight of Cambryn, Lock set a brisk pace. They rode across the rough, low country as quickly as they could. They followed the river valleys, eschewed the heights when possible, and stopped only to rest the horses and themselves when necessary. The way was frequently steep, and even footpaths were few, but it was well known to them all and offered up no surprises. The day, although chill, stayed clear, with the stiff wind blowing all the clouds well before them.

All these elements combined allowed them to reach Port Yzack while the last thread of daylight still burned on the horizon. Its cramped and tiny *castell* backed up against the high cliffs and was watched over jealously by the mottled green bulk of Roscarrock Hill. The great house was not so large as that at Cambryn, being one long, low hall with a slate roof and walls of roughly dressed stone. Still, with Captain Hale there to greet them alongside Lord Donyerth and his wife, Lady Cyda, Lynet felt it to be a palace fit for the Holy Roman Emperor.

Although only in his middle years and still strong, Donyerth was as thin and crooked as a cliff-rooted tree. He was also starved for news, and would have kept them talking over the lavish supper they were served by his four daughters if Lady Cyda had not taken charge. She was a tiny brown bird of a woman who had nonetheless borne nine living children and she would not be gainsaid when she bundled Lynet into the bed set up beside the longest of the fireplaces and shut the heavy curtains around her.

Alone in the warm, dust-scented darkness, Lynet let out the deep sigh she had been holding back for much of the evening. Two flickering slivers of gold slipped in between the curtains, one from the fire, one from the rush lights that lit the hall. By this pale and uncertain illumination, Lynet wriggled out of her over-dress and laid it at the foot of the bed. She did not lay her girdle with it, though. This she belted around her woollen under-dress before she climbed beneath the layers of furs and coverlets.

She had meant to go to sleep at once. Exhaustion lay heavily over her limbs. But her eyes would not remain closed. The gentle pressure of her purse at her hip nagged at her. The mirror waited there, her mother's gift, covered by her sister's warning. She knew that she should let it bide. Despite the reassuring weight of its metal and glass, it was an unearthly thing. Though her ancestors might be spirits of the invisible country, she herself was mortal, and ignorant of such matters. Of all the people that walked God's earth, she should know what dangers lay in acting out of ignorance.

But Lynet's mind strayed back to the mirror again and

again, as it had throughout the day. As the green miles slipped
by, she had not once been able to forget what she carried
with her. She held the horse's reins, but her fingertips tingled
with the remembered feel of the silver waves. While she
worked to keep pace behind Lock, she was aware that she
carried with her a promise of aid that was also the one thing
she had ever known to frighten Laurel.

Lynet pushed her coverings back and sat up, her resolve
wavering.

Holy Mary, Mother of us all, she prayed silently. *Watch over
me now I pray, and give me some sign if what I wish to do is wrong.*

Nothing happened. Outside the curtains she could hear
the infinitely familiar sounds of a hall bedding itself down
for the night. Inside, there was only the harsh sound of her
own breathing and the drumming of her heart.

She crossed herself, opened her purse, and brought out
the mirror.

The mirror was still cool to the touch. The heat of her
body had affected it not at all. The dim light played across
its surface, allowing her glimpses of reflection – one shadowed eye, the curve of her mouth, of her jaw, a lock of hair
that fell across her cheek. Lynet peered into the mirror's shadowed depths and strained to see beyond herself.

A heaviness came over her then, as if flesh and mind both
were turned to stone. She could not support her body any
longer and was seized with the overwhelming desire to shed
it like a damp shift and fly free. But Lynet did not know how
to fly, and so she fell. She fell from her body, fell past shadow
and flickering firelight, fell until there was no more darkness
and pure daylight opened around her.

Lynet blinked. All about her was a place of lush greenery.
Flowers and herbs in profusion bloomed at the feet of beautifully tended trees. The sky overhead was blue and cloud-
less. A warm breeze touched her skin, bringing with it all

the sweet scents of the growing things around her. Somewhere to her right, she heard the chatter of flowing water. The whole of the place promised rest and refreshment and Lynet smiled, her fears banished by pure wonder.

A footstep broke the silence, and Lynet whirled around. A man stood in the shade of a slender birch tree. He was tall and well shaped, like all the other ornaments of this garden. Like them also, there was a reassuring earthliness to him. He was dark of hair and eye, and his craggy face and straight nose were the familiar features of a man of the Dumonii lands. He dressed well but plainly, in brown breeches and an ochre tunic embroidered with blue and yarrow yellow. He was clearly of some rank as well, because rings of braided silver banded his wrist.

But what was such a man doing here?

As if he saw the question in her eyes, he spoke first. 'Be not afraid, lady,' he said as he knelt courteously on the ground before her. 'I am here to serve.'

'Who are you?' she asked.

He lifted his head and she saw in him the strangest melding of happiness and profound sorrow.

'I am Ryol.' He spoke the name slowly, as if it were an exotic spice he had not savoured in many years.

'Ryol of where? Ryol son of whom?' she asked, but the man just shook his head.

'Of nowhere and nothing but here,' he said. 'Not any longer.'

'Are you a ghost, Ryol?' Lynet knew very well she should have been afraid, but in the bright light of this pleasant garden, with a man so thoroughly ordinary in his appearance in front of her, she could not muster the fear. In fact, with her body and her world now elsewhere, there seemed to be a distance between her and all feeling for what existed there, past and present. Even as she wondered at this, she found she welcomed it, for the lightening of the heavy burden of feeling brought her profound relief.

The man, Ryol, smiled a little, but this did nothing to banish the sadness in his eyes. 'I am no ghost. I live, my lady, even as you do.'

'What is this place?'

Ryol paused, as if considering how to answer her question, then said, 'A shadow.'

'A shadow?' Lynet repeated, gazing at the tiny Eden about her. 'What casts such a shadow as this?'

'My lady, if I knew that, I would know all I needed,' he said soberly. Then he shook himself. 'But you have not yet told me how I may serve you.'

'What is it you are able to do?'

His smile grew a little mischievous, as if he were about to show some clever sleight of hand. 'Why, lady, I can do whatever a shadow may do. I can conceal, or I can reveal. I can distort or make clear. I can cover the world between one breath and the next.' He bent his head again. 'Tell me how I may put these skills to your use, and it is done.'

But even as she contemplated this extravagant statement, Lynet felt something wrong, an echo of the tug that had brought her here. It pulled now at the centre of her being, causing the world before her to shudder and blur. She felt sick suddenly and everything before her became nothing but a puddle of melting colour.

She felt her body surround her once more, cramped, aching and cold. She felt hands on her shoulders, shaking her. Someone called her name. She opened eyelids as heavy as lead and crusted with sand. Her rheumy eyes looked up to see Lady Cyda standing over her.

'God of mercy, Lynet,' she said. 'You frightened me. It is morning and I thought you would never waken. Are you well, child?'

Lynet closed her hand around the mirror she still clutched. 'Yes,' she said as clearly as she could manage. 'That I am.'

SEVEN

Colan woke to the persistent prodding of a toe in his back. He tried unsuccessfully to swat it away.

'Come on, boy, shift yourself,' rumbled the axe man he had met yesterday, whose name was Llywellyn. 'The Lady's waiting for you outside.'

Those words woke Colan fully. He'd been bedded down in Morgaine's hall with the other single men. He slept heavily, his belly full and his body safe for the first time in days. That sleep, however, had not been so heavy as to make him forget who he owed for these simple blessings and Colan scrambled to his feet as quickly as he could. None of the other men so much as stirred as he picked his way over their snoring forms. He gave his face and arms a rough wash in the bucket by the fire and accepted the cup of small beer one of the dark-haired women held out for him, remembering to thank her politely. He was only a guest here, and surely watched by many others besides Morgaine.

Outside the iron-banded door, the dawn had barely begun. The morning stars still hung above the brightening horizon. Morgaine did indeed wait for him, sitting on a black horse with a white blaze on its brow. In her black cloak and deep blue gown she might have been a spirit of the night itself. Colan knelt. In return, he received a smile of approval as she gestured for him to mount the bay horse standing beside her black. This he did without question. He touched up his mount as she did hers. Without any further ceremony, they put the dawn to their backs and rode after the retreating night.

The ground was silver with dew and cobwebs. Mist hung heavy in the air, but Colan could tell it would burn away when the sun rose, bringing the first truly clear day of the spring. His heart lifted at this omen, and it emboldened him to risk a few glances at the one he should now properly call his lady. She was regal in her carriage. He had seen this much before, but he had not fully noted the calm dignity of her person. That cool and distant place where Laurel could ascend to from time to time in her anger was the place where Morgaine dwelt. She kept her dark eyes on the way ahead, and Colan could not help but feel she saw much more in the misted world than he did. He felt constrained by walls he had never before known existed.

'You do not ask me where we're bound.'

Her voice seemed richer and fuller to him this morning, as if she were made greater by being out under the open sky.

'I trust you will tell me that when you are ready, my lady,' he answered.

By her smile, he saw that he had answered correctly. 'We go to the sea,' she said. 'Do you know why?'

'My lady, I do not.'

'It is to introduce you to some of your family, Colan.'

That light and simple statement struck Colan dumb. All the fear he had left out on the open water surged over him again. But he mastered himself. He must, for she was watching him.

'If that is my lady's wish.'

She gave him a bare nod, not only to acknowledge his words, he was sure, but to say 'well done', and they rode on in silence.

It was full daylight by the time they reached the cliffs. Colan knew this place. It was the beach where he had come ashore. The brisk ocean wind made his skin prickle beneath his tunic and woollen cloak. He looked out across the pale green waves, remembering their harsh, salt touch, and shivered.

Morgaine dismounted and handed him her horse's reins. 'We must leave them here. They will not stand in the presence of those we go to meet.'

There was nowhere to tether the beasts, so Colan hobbled them both instead. When they were secured, Morgaine led him down a rough and crooked path between the jumbled rocks.

The beach was nothing more than a narrow strip of pale sand scattered liberally with stones. The cliffs' shadows hung over the place, so that they descended into a lingering twilight. Colan's boat was still there, overturned on the sand, looking as if it had washed up lost and empty.

Morgaine stepped around the forlorn object, all her attention on the sea. The waves rushed and roared, splashing their foam onto the rocks. Gulls and terns wheeled overhead, taking advantage of the clear morning for fishing. Morgaine stood as an onyx counterpoint to this mercurial world. The very stones seemed ephemeral compared to her. They could be shifted and changed by wind or sea, but not even the raging gale could move Morgaine.

She raised her arms. Her cloak fell back, and her billowing sleeves slipped down to reveal her strong brown arms. Colan's throat tightened strangely at the sight of her smooth flesh. He wondered if he should turn away. But in the next

moment, Morgaine began to sing, and all thought of movement drained away from him. Her voice was like no other.
It soared to meet the birds overhead. It dived straight to the
centre of his soul. He could not understand a word of her
song, and yet it pulled at him so strongly he thought for a
moment he would be dragged down to his knees. It called
out across the ocean, and he knew that if that call had been
for him, not only would he have understood, but he would
have obeyed whatever command it contained with tears of
joy in his eyes.

When the magnificent song ended, sorrow stabbed Colan.
Perhaps he cried aloud. He could not be sure. All he knew
was that Morgaine lowered her arms. At her feet, the eter-
nally restless sea had gone absolutely still.

From these unnatural waters, the *morverch* rose.

The bards sang of the sea's women as beautiful creatures.
They spoke of long white arms and golden hair. He knew
now that those who created such verses had never seen the
beings that lifted their heads and shoulders before him. He
counted six of them, yet he knew there were others he could
not see. Corpse pale they were, yet life flowed abundantly
within them. Nets of light danced and shimmered under the
surface of their skin as if beneath shallow waters. Soul and
will sparkled in them, creating shadows as well as light in
their eyes which slanted, far too large and far too dark in
their narrow faces. Weeds and flowers tangled in their wet
hair as it flowed down to cover their rounded shoulders and
breasts and then spread out to float in the water. He could
feel the strength of that life pouring out, like the force of the
tide that their presence held so still.

What would it be like to be near one of these women? To
touch her, to know her, to have the tide of his being drawn
up from his depths and mingled with all this strange and
wild beauty? As the thought formed, his flesh crawled. It

was as if he had suddenly entertained carnal imaginings for one of his sisters. With their pale skin and eyes of profound depth, these creatures were very like Laurel, but they were so much more. They were present and immediate, blotting out all other things with the strength of their selves. He knew how their voices would sound once they spoke. He knew if he walked forward and grasped their hands, what their touch would be like.

He knew they were the ones who had whispered to him on the open water.

Welcome, they said to him, though their mouths did not move and not one of them stirred. *Welcome, cousin.*

His heart leapt to be greeted so. Without thinking, he went to them. He strode hip deep into the still salt waters, so that he might grasp their cold, damp hands, and be pulled forward to kiss their shadowed cheeks in peace and welcome. They smelled of salt water and strange flowers, and their chill sank deep into him. The cold did not matter, for it was as familiar to him as human warmth was, even though he'd never felt it before. It was part of him, and he rejoiced in its revelation.

You come in strange company, cousin. The sight of Morgaine standing infinitely patient on the shore flashed through his thoughts, although he did not turn his head away from the *morverch*.

He stiffened a little, but kept hold of the two soft, cold hands. 'That is my Lady Morgaine,' he said carefully. It could not be that these were Morgaine's enemies. He did not think he could bear it if that were so.

Oh, yes. We know Morgaine. The words rang strangely in him, and he was filled with fleeting images, of a distant ship, of a woman in despair on the shore, of a storm heaving up without warning, and a child, a child rolling in the waves and crying out . . .

'Do they speak to you?' called Morgaine..

'You cannot hear?' he asked, surprised. The cousin nearest him just grinned, and he saw her teeth were very sharp.

'It is you they mean to speak with, blood to blood, kin to kin. My ears cannot comprehend such speech,' replied Morgaine, seemingly unperturbed. 'You have a power that I cannot match in this, Colan Carnbrea. There are not many who can claim such a thing.'

The nearest of his cousins drew her hands away and settled back, as if resting on her haunches. The water could have been little more than a yard deep, yet she was hidden in it almost to her shoulders. Did she draw it up around herself like a garment?

Why have you come now, cousin? she asked with that silent voice. *You fled us before.*

Regretfully, Colan knew he had no choice but to tell the truth. 'I did not know it was you, before. I thought I heard my sister, who has cause to wish me dead.'

They did not look to one another as a cluster of human beings might, but kept their unfathomable gazes on him. *Ah!* they sighed. *And why do you return to us now? Why with Morgaine?*

He wavered for a moment. As strong as the welcome he felt among the *morverch* was, the feelings that welled up in him in Morgaine's company echoed through him just as strongly. 'I owe her greatly.'

We know this too, they said, a little sadly he thought. *That is why she brought you here.*

'I do not understand.'

The one nearest to him leaned forward a little. Her hair swayed and curled where it trailed in the water. *She wants something of us, cousin. Of all of us. She never comes but that she is wanting. And because you have made a pact with her, she will have you make one with us.* She stretched out her hand again and laid it on his arm. It was long and slender. The sunlight slipped across and beneath it, as if she were filled with ephemeral light in place of blood.

He laid his warm hand over that cool one. 'If that is how it is, then that is how it must be. I am sworn, cousins.' *And I must finish what I have begun.*

Yes. She sighed deeply. Her free hand moved back and forth through the water, as if judging texture the way a woman might judge the fall of cloth. It occurred to Colan he should be able to see through that water before him to the sea floor, and yet he could not. *Without even knowing what you chose between, you chose the land and the mortal realm, as did your mother.* She paused. *Though she gained much more than you.* She settled back again, resting easily in the waters among her sisters. *Ask your lady why she has brought you to us.*

For the first time since he had seen the *morverch*, Colan glanced back at Morgaine. 'They wish to know why I . . . why we have come.'

'Because your sister Lynet will pass over the water soon, Colan,' said Morgaine, her voice firm but sad. 'She cannot be allowed to reach Camelot.'

For a moment, Colan could do no more than stand there. In his wonder at meeting them, at touching that part of himself that was kin to the *morverch*, he had forgotten their songs. The songs that told of the doom they could bring down on those who sailed their seas.

Down on Lynet who would go to Camelot to try to persuade Cambryn's faithless queen to come to their aid.

He licked his lips and tasted brine. 'Camelot will not answer. They have ignored us in all this disaster.'

'Camelot will answer.' Morgaine's words were dark and they were certain. 'Guinevere will come, and I am not ready for her yet.'

That last word was as cold as the *morverch*'s. It held a deeper threat than any he had ever known, long and old and infinitely patient.

He turned to his cousins again.

He did not have to speak. They had heard and understood, probably more quickly than he. The nearest of them shook her head, in anger and sorrow both.

There are laws, cousin. For each deed and doing, there is a price.

'What price?' asked Colan.

All the *morverch* looked past him, glowering at Morgaine on the shore. Morgaine did not make one sound. Could she see their anger? Of course she could. Morgaine's eyes would not miss such burning resentment.

Come with us, cousin, and no more will be asked of you. By any. His cousin once more lifted her cold hands from the water. A single strand of weed twined around her wrist, dripping silver and trailing down to mingle with the curling locks of her hair. *Come to us and you may do just as you choose.*

He saw their world then; the cool, eternal twilight and the sudden shafts of sun, how they flew free of even the hand of God that pinned man to earth. He felt the threat of death, time and care fall away. Nothing mattered but those who flew beside him through that half-light realm, not life, not soul. That was for the land, and the land was far away.

He strained towards that dream, but as he strained, he felt another tie binding him. It was not duty, not blood or his deeds and damnation. It was Morgaine, there on the shore. It was her will and his oath together that held him there. Anger rose up slowly, swelling like a storm wave. He had not felt the reality of that bond, but now that he knew it was there, he knew he would never lose the touch of it again.

She was using him. With the kiss she had demanded she had bound him to her because she needed what he could do now. He would have cried out to God, but God had made it abundantly clear that He was willing to leave his unre-pentant prodigal to drift in this storm of lesser powers.

Very well.

Suddenly reckless, Colan caught up his cousin's hand. She smiled. *She thinks she has me.*

'Listen to me, cousin,' he said softly so that Morgaine could not hear. 'My sister has broken faith and cast me out. It is because of her I made my pact with Morgaine. Lynet left me with nowhere else to turn. If not for that, I would not trouble you . . . but nor can I join with you.' They had known this when they cast out their invitation. He was sure of it. They tempted him for the same reason Morgaine had tested him, to see what he would do. 'You spoke truly. I have made my choice, and I must be true to word and deed already committed. I know you would not welcome me if I were otherwise.'

He felt the push and pull between his strange cousins, and knew they communicated heart to heart.

We can raise up the seas against your sister, against our cousin, if she comes to us, said the *morverch*. Her voice in his thoughts was flat yet keen, rhythmic as the waves and biting as the winter wind. *But if you would have it done, the price will be another life. If you seek death from us, you must pay for it with yet another life, your own or one bound to you by blood or word. No one who is stranger to you may pay this price in your stead.*

A life. The words pulsed in him. *Another life.* He looked to the woman who stood on the shore, and to those who waited in the sea. He remembered all he had felt this morning. He felt himself leaning towards Morgaine, wanting to prove himself to her, to show his strength and his loyalty. That feeling was true, and it was false. It was true because in his heart he wanted God and all the world to see him lead his land to safety where his father could not. But it was false, for Morgaine had raised that desire with her enchantments and then bent and bound it to her own usage.

'A life for this deed,' he said quietly, facing the *morverch* once more. 'One that is bound to me and mine to give. This I promise you.'

Did they know whose life he thought to deliver up to them? He felt their currents running through him, bemused and shrewd. Oh, they knew. They perhaps had even hoped for it.

His cousin slid towards him. Whether she rose up or he sank down, he was not sure. But now her eyes were level with his own. For a moment, she pressed her cool cheek to his. *Beware of her, cousin. Her plans run deep and long, and her eye sees farther in the dark than yours does at noon. We would not willingly harm you, but the caprice of humans is not ours. We will do as we have said, and take what has been promised.*

'I understand you.'

She glided away again to join her sisters. She smiled at him, and that smile was wicked and wild, sharp and fierce. Then she and all her sisters receded until their white forms mingled with the green and white sea waters, and all the wild liveliness contained within them released itself into the sea again, causing the waves to rise up and rush forward. The surge wetted Colan to his chest and filled his ears with a roar that sounded like nothing so much as laughter.

The dream and the wonder were all gone. With clumsy, heavy strides, Colan dragged himself out of the frigid ocean to stand beside Morgaine.

'What did they say?'

For a confused moment, it was strange to look on her, so colourful and so still. The *morverch* filled his thoughts and senses. It would be a long time before he shook them off. Still, he mustered his attention for the woman in front of him. It would not be good to let his mind drift while he spoke with her. 'They will do this thing, but there is a steep price. I must deliver to them a life, mine or another.'

Morgaine inclined her head regally. 'You have done well, Colan. Do not fear. A life will be found.'

Heart and pride warmed at these words, and his belly knotted to feel it happening. 'I am not afraid, my lady. I knew it would be so.'

'You are learning quickly, my young lord. I am pleased.'

'Thank you, my lady.' He bowed, a gesture which pleased her. She walked past him, and he followed her back up the steep, ragged path. The winds were bitter against his drenched skin and he clenched his teeth to keep them from chattering. When they reached the horses once more, he undid the hobbles and helped Morgaine into her saddle, as befitted a good servitor, before he mounted his own horse.

'Where do we go now, my lady?' he asked, taking up his reins.

As she turned to look at him from one dark eye, Colan realized he had made a mistake. He had asked no questions when they came here; why should he ask them now? 'We go home, since you ask, my young lord,' she answered him, her words holding a subtle edge. 'We go home to wait.'

She wheeled her horse around and rode towards the east and the rising sun.

EIGHT

The cost of the passage was the horses.

The ship's master, a dour man whose four younger brothers plied the oars with him, would not hear talk of gold. It would weigh him down, he said. His eyes glinted at the sight of the horses, though, betraying the fact that here was the answer to some dream, or debt. He was nominally Lord Donyerth's man, and the vessel he worked was nominally Lord Donyerth's ship, but the men who risked their lives on the channel were hard to hold, and could be dangerous if they decided to give their aid to an enemy. For Donyerth to compel the man's service in Lynet's name would mean another rumour and another grudge left behind them. Worse, it would mean more delay, for unwilling men seldom worked quickly. Of course, the master knew all of this, and it made him willing to stick to his original price in the face of all the persuasion Captain Hale and Lord Donyerth used against him. For passage up the channel for the six of them, it would be six horses and nothing less.

'Give him what he asks,' said Lynet when Captain Hale brought her the news. 'Find out from Lord Donyerth if we are likely to find new mounts when we land at Huntspill. If we cannot, then he must spare us some.'

This much Donyerth could do. He provided six fresh mounts to replace the tired beasts now in the shipmaster's hands. Lynet had Hale count out some of their small store of gold as promise against the horses' return. Donyerth did not want to take it, but he did not turn it down either. He knew it was vital Lynet be seen as generous, and he and his lady made deep obeisance to her as they parted. That was a far better story to leave behind her.

The tide turned early that morning, shortly after full light. Bishop Austell celebrated mass with Donyerth's priest and they all took communion before setting out for the bay and their ship, where the shipmaster and his sons waited on the pebbly shore.

Donyerth's horses were experienced sailors it seemed. They did not protest when they were led aboard the low, round craft, nor when they were hobbled together. Lynet and Bishop Austell were bid to make themselves as comfortable as they could in the blunt bow. There they sat among nets, chests and coils of rope, so close together that their elbows bumped when the boat dipped unexpectedly. Hale, Lock and the three Trevailian brothers lent their hands to the work of casting off and plying the oars to pull their ship out into the open waters. There, the master raised the sail to catch the brisk morning wind and took his place at the steering oar.

Cambryn was inland from the coast, but not so far that Lynet had never sailed before. The steady rise and fall of the ship as it ran along the turquoise waves was deeply familiar to her, as was the creak of the wood and the smack and spray of the water. Sea birds trailed in their wake, hoping they'd churn up a fish or two with their passage, and the air smelled of fresh salt and cool water. Lynet inhaled it gratefully. Her head was still clouded and heavy from her strange night, but the cold air speedily cleared it.

If all went well, they would be two days on the water and

another two on the land. Four days' journey altogether, if wind and weather held. Five, or six, or longer if it did not. Her fingers curled around the mirror in her purse. Five or six days to get to Camelot, then. How long to get back? And what help could they gain? She thought about Ryol's tale of his powers. Could he see into the future, her spirit servant? Could he perhaps show her what she would meet at Camelot and how long it would take to accomplish their task? It would surely be worth asking. She itched to try. It would be a fine thing to drag certainty out of the morass of things unknown surrounding her.

'You are quiet this morning,' said Bishop Austell, breaking her reverie. He had wrapped his brown travelling cloak around himself and only the edges of his rich ecclesiastical robe showed. 'Lady Cyda was concerned for your health, you know.'

Lynet chuckled softly. When one was the mother of nine, one could not help becoming mother of all, she supposed. 'Lady Cyda concerns herself unduly. I slept heavily, that's all.'

'That's good to hear,' said the bishop, but there was a hint of scepticism in his voice. 'It would be no wonder if sleep was a stranger after all you have been through.'

Lynet shrugged and pulled her own cloak more closely about herself. The wind was growing colder, or she was. 'We are all in God's hands.'

'Very pious of you, my daughter,' Austell replied dryly. He sat in silence for a long moment, watching the oncoming waves. The wind ruffled his grey hair, and seemed to carve the lines of his weathered face more deeply. 'I've been to many a war with your father. I prayed to God to bring us victory and exhorted the men to believe that He held us in those hands you mentioned. I also gave the supreme unction to those same men as they screamed out for death.' His voice

was so soft the wind nearly carried it off. 'It is a terrible thing
to see a man wounded in war die. They do not go quietly
or well. There were times when I wished God would strike
me blind before I had to witness it again. I still spend sleepless nights from it, and not one of those men I readied for
death was my father, nor had the hand that struck them
down been dear to me.'

Lynet bit her lips and tasted the salt on them. She tried
to push his words away from her. She thought instead of
how she was thirsty already, and of the skins of small beer
and watered wine they had with them. It would do no good
to move away to get one, however. Bishop Austell would be
right here when she returned.

'You are not alone, Lynet,' he went on quietly. 'God and
Holy Mary are with you. I am not your kindred, but such
as I am, I am with you too. You need not carry your burdens
all yourself.'

She bowed her head, more than a little ashamed at her
own reticence. 'I know that, Bishop. I . . .' Words failed her.
She clutched her purse as if it were a human hand. 'I cannot
give over to grieving. Not yet. When we reach Camelot, when
the queen is sworn to aid us, then I can mourn. Then.'

Bishop Austell nodded. 'Be the soldier, Lynet, as you must.
But when your war is over, God will still be here, and so
will I.'

Lynet could not look at him. To do so would be to bring
down tears she did not wish to shed. 'Thank you.'

They sat like that for a while, shoulder to shoulder,
surrounded by wind and riotous water. The understanding
reached between them made their silence companionable,
and Lynet was grateful for it.

Slowly, subtly, Lynet became aware of a change in the air.
The chill of the wind that blew her braided hair back deepened. The sunlight tarnished as a haze covered the blue sky.

The waves that smacked the bow grew irregular, now small, now great enough to splash across the rail and spatter their hems. The haze overhead sagged and thickened into mottled grey clouds.

The shipmaster gazed at the sky, tugging his moustaches and muttering to Captain Hale. Lynet could not hear what he said but she did not need to. There was no one on this ship who could not recognize the signs of an approaching storm. Hale heaved himself off the bench and made his way forward, staggering a little against the unsteady rhythm of the ship. In the time it took him to cross the deck to them, the wind sharpened. It had picked up a sour smell. And then Lynet noticed something else. The birds had gone. They sailed alone on the steepening waters. The horses whickered and shuffled, their hooves clopping and scraping on the unsteady deck, and their ears flattened back against their skulls.

Captain Hale bent close. 'The master wants to take us in!' he bawled in her ear, pointing towards the misted mounds of the coast to their right. Lynet nodded. The thought of delay pained her, but she was in no way inclined to race this sour, darkening wind.

The master had not waited for her assent in any case. He gripped the steering oar and shouted orders to his brothers to shorten the sail and get on their oars, damn them! Did they want to miss the bay and face the cliffs in this?

Hale got himself back to his own bench to grasp an oar with one of the shipmaster's brothers. A wave hit the bow hard, washing over the rail and drenching Lynet's knees with a shock of cold water. The deck tilted beneath her and she gripped the gunwale hard to keep from sliding into the bishop. Another wave washed over her hand and sloshed down to add its bulk to the bilge. A horse whinnied, a high, frightened sound. The master shouted, and the oarsmen strained, and slowly the ship turned its prow towards the land.

The bay was a little ahead of them, lying low, green and deep between the teeth of the grey cliffs. The rising waves slammed themselves against the hidden rocks, creating mighty breakers that caused Lynet's stomach to knot itself up. The wind rose again. Ropes, sails and deck all creaked. Another wave rolled over her arm, and yet another over her legs. The bilges sloshed back and forth, drenching her up to her shins. The prow pointed towards the space of relatively calm water between the nearest breakers.

'Pull!' shouted the master. 'Pull you bastard sons! Pull if you don't want to meet the Devil face to face! Pull!'

One of his brothers hung on the boom, pulling back with all his strength to keep the sail angled towards the wind, but the wind died down in an instant, making the rope go slack, catching the man off balance so he dropped to the deck. In the next breath, the wind redoubled, and the boom swung round. The mast bowed and creaked. The ship flung itself sideways so violently the rail dipped under the water. The waves rolled over them, shoving Lynet down to her neck in icy water. Surrounded by the shouts of the men and the screams of the horses, she thought for sure they must go down.

But they bobbed upright again, so that they were only shin deep in a frigid pool of seawater, ropes and flotsam. The rain started down then, driving as hard and cold as if a second ocean fell from the sky. As Lynet spat the seawater from her mouth and wiped it from her eyes she saw that they were now headed straight for the breakers. The longed-for bay was now too far to the right, and the hidden rocks waited ahead.

Another wave and then another pummelled them. The horses shrieked, and one tried to rear just as a great wave poured down over them. Amid a rush of harsh water and despairing, almost human cries, a rope snapped with a sound like a bone breaking, and every last one of them tumbled out into the ocean. Lynet cried out, and lurched uselessly towards the place where they had been. One panicked brown head lifted above the waters, and then the waves took that last beast down.

The master bellowed, but there was no need. Every man threw himself against the oars, pulling back with all his might while the master fought the steering oar to bring them about. Sea room. They needed sea room. They'd missed the bay and now open water was their only hope. They might be able to ride the waters in their flimsy cask, but if they came up on the breakers they would be ripped open and flung to the merciless waves as easily as their horses had been.

'Bail, Lynet!' hollered another voice in her ear. Bishop Austell shoved a bucket into her half-frozen hands.

The touch of the sodden wood jolted Lynet into action. She crouched down until the bilge was up to her hips and frantically began to scoop water out, pouring it into the sea which only rolled it right back over the sides. The rain drummed down on her back. The wind roared as it pushed and the rocking sea hissed as it pulled, and someone was laughing at her ridiculous efforts with bucket and prayer.

Someone was laughing.

Lynet lifted her head, the bucket dangling useless in her hands. The rain smacked her face, and the bow ducked dangerously low, making her stagger although she was already on her knees. There it was again. Laughter. A pealing, gleeful sound on the roaring wind.

'Lynet!' cried the bishop.

Lynet did not heed him. She dropped the bucket, and it sank slowly. The rough motion of the boat shook her and brought waves of bilge up around her breast. Wind and laughter roared in her ears. Acting on desperate instinct, Lynet tore at her purse strings, thrust her hand into the leather pouch and grabbed onto the mirror.

'Ryol!' She cupped both hands around the mirror, bending over it to shield it from the raging waters as best she could. 'Ryol! I need to see what's in this storm. Show me! Show me what's following us in the storm!'

A solid curtain of rain smacked her in the face. She teetered backward, coughing, struggling to breathe. When her eyes cleared she thought the sheets of rain had thickened. But no. She looked again.

In the grey waters, wearing cloaks of rain, swam the *morverch*. They were grey and black and white like the storm. The flash of lightning was in their eyes as they circled the ship, swimming faster than the surging waves that lifted them up so they could laugh down at the frantic mortals. They grabbed the gunwales of the boat with their long fingers and leaned on it hard, forcing the rail under the water. The master staggered at the oar, almost falling. One *morverch* heaved herself up, and snatched at him while her sisters tipped the ship still further.

Anger propelled Lynet forward. She thrust the mirror into her purse, lunged for the rail and grabbed hold of a pair of slick grey arms. Her fingers dug into the deathly cold flesh. It was too yielding, as if it kept its shape without aid of bone beneath. She hauled backward with all her might. In the space of one gasping breath, Lynet heaved the sea-woman into the sloshing bilge. The pealing laughter turned to shrieks of outrage as Lynet stood over the thing she had captured and stared.

The *morverch* were supposed to be crosses between fish and beautiful women, but this creature was neither. Face and arms and shoulders were akin to those of a human, but her colour was that of an aging corpse despite the fierce life that burned behind her thickly lidded eyes. Below the curve of her ribs she looked more like a seal than any other thing, with a single powerful, sleekly-furred limb ending in a pair of ribbed flippers. Her human-like torso was without feature. It was the teats and slit on her seal's body that revealed her sex.

Her pale hair twined around her neck. Lynet seized on those sodden tresses, knotting them in her fingers, and dragging the sea-woman's head and shoulders out of the bilge waters.

'What are you doing?' she demanded. 'What do you want?'

The creature only grinned at her, displaying a row of teeth as needle sharp as a pike's. The boat rolled and pitched as her sisters leaned on it, scrambling to reach her, screaming some word Lynet did not understand. The sour wind wavered.

'What do you want?' Lynet cried again.

A wave dug beneath the boat, lifting it up and suddenly dropping it sharply down. Men cried out. The creature squirmed in her grip, but Lynet held her fast. The master was shouting again, and the oars made the ship lurch and rock. Wood splintered. It didn't matter. All that mattered was to keep her grip on this loathsome creature.

'What do you want!'

The creature reached out one corpse-cold hand and caressed Lynet's arm.

Fear and nausea swept over Lynet, even as another wave washed over the side of the boat. It knocked her flat, rolled her over, filled her lungs with water, and tore the *morverch* from her hands. Coughing and struggling against her water-logged clothing, she pushed herself up. She found a pocket of air and breathed deep, shoving her hair out of her eyes and cursing inwardly. The *morverch* was surely gone. But no! The sea-woman had been caught by the gunwale and trapped against the wooden side of the boat. She squirmed and wriggled to free herself, and her sisters groped for her. Their flailing hands would find each other in a minute. The *morverch* looked up at Lynet, grinning. Her long-fingered hands wound around Lynet's wrist, the promise of that touch plain. When the next wave came, when she was washed free and the ship overturned, Lynet would be dragged down with her.

'A rope!' shouted Lynet. 'Help me!' She grasped the *morverch*'s tangled hair again, hauling her away from the ship's side.

It was Austell who heard Lynet and waded towards her as the next wave crashed down. The boat rocked, its rail shoved beneath the waters once more. One sea-woman leapt up and grabbed Bishop Austell. In an eyeblink, grey arms wrapped around his throat. In the next, he was gone as if he had never been.

'No!' screamed Lynet and her grip slackened. The *morverch* gave a mighty heave, throwing Lynet back and down into the bilge. A hand jerked her up again, and she saw Stef Trevailian standing over her. He pressed the rope into her hands. Screaming, cursing, more like a she-bear than a woman, Lynet reared up over the *morverch* and threw a loop of rope around her neck. Stef took up the slack, and fought his way back to the mast.

The creature's eyes grew wide with terrified understanding. She was human in this much. She needed her throat to breathe air and water. Lynet felt that breath under her hands. One more wave and they would be overturned. One more wave and they would all be dragged down as the bishop had been. But if that wave came, the sea-woman would be hanged from the wreckage of the boat.

The look of hatred the *morverch* returned hit Lynet with the force of another wave. Lynet jerked backward, but she kept her hands on the rope. 'Let us go,' Lynet demanded. Salt water sluiced off her back and ran down her hair. 'When everyone in this vessel is safe on shore, you will be released.'

'My sisters will save me.'

Lynet wiped at her face, glancing up. Not a single arm overhung the rails anymore, and in place of the wild motion of the boat was now the steadier rise and thump of natural waves. The sea-women had pulled back. Lynet could see a pair of them swimming out into the waves, lifting themselves up to try to see her, and her hold on the rope.

'Perhaps they will save you.' Lynet spat out more brackish water. The ship wallowed like a tub now. If the waters rose again, they could still be swamped. 'They are swift and clever, and we are slow and dull. But will they gamble with your life to get to ours?'

One more wave and they were all dead and cold together. Lynet wanted to pray but she had no strength to do anything but twist the rough rope tighter around the *morverch's* throat.

The wave did not come. The rope twitched and jerked. Stef knotting it tight, probably. Lynet did not dare take her attention from the sea-woman. The boat rocked underneath her. Above her, men called to one another, a bare inch from true panic. They were busy with buckets, ropes and oars. The cold bilge sloshed and splashed. Only she and the *morverch* were still.

Then, the sea-woman dipped her eyes. 'Safe to shore,' she hissed. 'All aboard will be brought safe to shore. It is sworn.'

'When it is done you will be free,' said Lynet, not loosening her grip in the least. 'Not before.'

The *morverch* hissed, her fury plain, but Lynet did not relent. She felt the boat begin to move. No man was at his oar. They sat or knelt on the heaving deck, gripping whatever was closest, staring all about them. Their boat moved as if caught in the swiftest of river currents. No wave buffeted them. The wind had gone completely still, for all the clouds still hung black overhead and the rain pounded down as hard as hail. The only breeze came from the speed of their passage. Looking into the *morverch's* eyes, a vision overtook Lynet. She saw the sea-woman's sisters surrounding the boat, pulling it forward with their hands, propelling it with their strong tails. Did they feel the rope about their own necks these women of the sea, these cold cousins of hers? In the depths of her thoughts, she was surprised at how easily she held that sodden rope, and pronounced the doom. But she would examine that later. For now, she must get her men to shore.

That shore, green, curved and welcoming, approached fast. The boat skimmed over the breakers, lifted on a dozen unseen hands. Its prow cleaved the shallower waves, rushing towards the shore. Then, the waves and their daughters flung the vessel and all its occupants up onto the strand.

The hull ground against stone and sand, and the sound of splintering wood grated against Lynet's ears in the second before the boat jerked to a halt and they were all flung head first into the flotsam.

Lynet dragged herself free of the chaos as quickly as she could, one hand still tangled in the rope. The *morverch* spat at her, but could do nothing more. As the bilge water ran from the split hull, the sea-woman sank backward, panting hard, as if the air itself pinned her to the ruined deck.

Lynet struggled to push herself into a sitting position, retching up yet more sea water, a great green wave curved overhead. She stared up at it in a moment of mute terror before it crashed down on her head. Robbed of sight, of sense, of everything but the horrible roaring of endless water pouring over her, and the frantic, desperate need to breathe.

The waters pulled back, dragging her with them, stretching her out to her full length on the sand, but somehow, incredibly, leaving air behind. Lynet gasped and gagged, vomited water and breathed. She drew air into her ravaged body, fighting against the pain to keep breathing.

After a small eternity, Lynet was able to dig the heels of her hands into the sand and push herself up on trembling arms. A little further inland, she saw the master and his brothers, and the Trevailians, Lock and Hale. She counted them slowly. Yes, they were all there. She knuckled more water out of her eyes.

The boat was gone, and the *morverch* with it. They were safe on this shore, drenched and broken, but safe. She stared out at the restless green ocean.

'Good bishop?' she whispered. A wave slipped up and touched her fingertips. She jerked back at once. Then, out on the open waters, she saw them lift their heads, a crowd of *morverch*, each identical to all the others. They stared at her, all alike in their pure unleavened hatred.

From amid the cluster of her sisters, one sea-woman lifted her head. A red welt around her white throat marked her as Lynet's former prisoner.

You are all that he said, a voice echoed in her thoughts. *We will not forget this. Come to our realm again, little cousin, and you will not leave it.*

The other sea-women closed around her. The waves came up and the rain came down, and they were gone.

Lynet swallowed. She was empty of strength, frozen almost to death, and water-logged to the core. But the men were climbing to their feet, and she must do the same. She must stand. She must not think about Bishop Austell gone and drowned beneath the waves. Another corpse to add to her own charnel yard.

All the men were battered and dripping wet. Stef and Rory both had blood on their hands. Three of the four ship's brothers had bruises and gashes on their heads and arms. There was something wrong with the way the shipmaster held his shoulder.

And there was nothing she could do, nothing at all, except lead them onward.

Stooped with pain and shock and cold, she trudged past them, walking inland towards cliffs and rocks, where there might be some kind of shelter, where they might huddle together to pray for Bishop Austell, and for themselves.

Numbly, all of them followed her, and not even Lynet dared look back.

NINE

Spring's thaw had finally taken firm hold in the vales near Camelot. For Gareth, son of King Lot and nephew to the High King Arthur, that meant freedom. Freedom from a world bounded by snow, ice, cold and stone walls. To be sure, a long winter's night had its pleasures, but for all that, Gareth loved the day, and the wide sweep of the world, especially from the back of a horse at full gallop.

Gareth rode hard. The wind, still touched with winter's spite, slapped his face. Despite that, sweat already dampened his padded leather training armour and ran down from under his banded helm. His shield slapped against his back in time to the drumming of his horse's gallop. Hooves thundered behind him as his fellows, now his rivals, rode fast to catch up with him. His gelding's legs pumped and its sides heaved from its exertions as Gareth bent low over its head. They careened between the well-spaced orchard trees, Gareth guiding the horse with a firm hand and a fast word. Sir Lancelot had taken on a new boy to train, and had declared that all his squires should ride out with him to put the newcomer through his paces. Gareth grinned, and dug his heels into his horse's yielding sides once more so the beast put on a fresh burst of speed. Handling the reins while keeping hold of the flimsy wooden stick he carried in place of an actual spear was difficult, but he kept that toy tucked under his arm as he pressed forward. As first among the great knight's squires, he was not about to let any of the others win this race.

Out of the corner of his right eye, Gareth could just see the new boy, Ewen, pull even with Lionel, and then ease ahead. But he couldn't maintain his lead and fell back with the others.

Not bad, though, Gareth thought, bending lower over his horse's neck. *Come on, Achaius, let's show them what you can really do.*

The edge of the orchard was drawing near, along with a tree that had come down in the winter storms. With knees, reins, and nerve, Gareth sent Achaius hurtling over the trunk and out into the open fields. Mud spattered up from under the horse's hooves as he dug in his heels. Achaius barrelled forward without missing a step. The other hoofbeats fell back and mingled with shouts, and not a few curses.

One last set of hoofbeats, though, thundered nearer. A blur of bronze and red swept easily past Gareth as his knight, Sir Lancelot of the Lake, took the lead of the small troop. He shot across the field towards the next rise. Would he take them over it? No. He checked abruptly, wheeling his great red horse around, and riding straight for Gareth. Achaius spooked at the sudden approach, and danced sideways, but Gareth kept his seat and regained control of his mount as the knight charged into the crowd of boys following him, wheeled, and charged Gareth again. This time, Sir Lancelot had the blunt and flimsy spear down and pointed right at Gareth's chest.

Gareth held his mock spear out sideways and charged, hoping he could slip past the knight's spear and knock Sir

Lancelot from the saddle. It was a chancy move, but if he could just keep on the straight path . . .

But his aim was off and Sir Lancelot's spear struck home first. The hammer force of the blow shattered the light wood, but still bowled Gareth out of his saddle. The world spun until the hard ground slammed against his back and stopped it forcibly. As soon as breath returned to his lungs, Gareth, thankful for the leather and quilting that cushioned him, scrambled to his feet, swinging his shield off his back and yanking his wooden practice sword from its sheath. Lancelot, grinning with a ferocity that made even Gareth's blood go cold, charged again, spear out and down in a way that would have spelled grim death if it had been a real weapon.

Man and horse bore down on him. Gareth stood his ground, shield up and sword ready. He parried the spear, pivoting aside as he did. His vision wobbled dangerously, but he kept his feet, ready for the next pass. The other boys had formed up in a rough line, staring, the youngest of them pop-eyed, obviously not sure how frightened they should be.

The next pass didn't come. Sir Lancelot reined in his horse and turned, the fierce grin still in place. 'Good! That's how it should be done. On your feet and weapon out.' His outland accent made the words tilt and lilt musically. 'The man on horseback always has the advantage, but there's nothing you can do sprawling in the mud crying about your bruises.'

Lancelot dismounted then, and Gareth put up his sword. The Gaulish knight was a fair man. His hair and neat beard shone like brass in the sunlight, and his eyes flashed bright blue. He was not a great man with words, but it was not words that brought such a man fame. Men said that Gareth's brother Gawain was the greatest of the cadre of the Round Table, but it was beyond Gareth's understanding how anyone could say that who had seen Sir Lancelot fight. With sword and shield, none could stand before him. On horseback, he was a storm wind and utterly fearless. No show of force could even slow him down. When he sparred in the practice yard, work stopped so all could watch him dismantle his opponent's defences and drive them to the ground. Not one knight in all of Arthur's host had ever made Lancelot yield. Not Geraint, not Gawain. Agravain had never even tried.

'Now!' Sir Lancelot roared. 'Which of you will stand up to Gareth here! Who will show us what you're made of?' The knight looked expectantly at the ragged line of boys on horses. Gareth thought Lionel or Brendon might step up. But before either of them could move, Ewen had dismounted and stepped forward.

'Ewen! Good,' boomed Lancelot, folding his arms and standing aside. 'Make your try!'

Ewen was a full head shorter and at least two stone lighter than Gareth, but the boy had his shield down and his sword drawn, charging before Gareth had chance to get his own sword up for a proper parry. He had to duck and dance back to buy himself room and time. The boy fought fast and hard, raining down his blows, not prepared to draw breath or give Gareth a chance to draw it, continuing to force him back with sheer speed. Wood creaked and thumped. The blows jolted up his arms to his shoulders as Ewen hammered on him again and again, evidently trying to make up for lack of reach by closing in.

All right.

Gareth turned, angling and curving his path, until he put Ewen's back to the hill. Then, Gareth began to advance, not really attacking, but driving, easing forward with each deliberate parry and short thrust. Ewen, so intent on getting in one clattering blow, and one more, and one more after that, didn't feel what was happening, until Gareth lunged forward under his guard, shoved his shield hard against him and sent the boy hurtling backward over a large white stone. Gareth leapt over that same stone, and stood with his sword at Ewen's throat.

'Do you yield?' Gareth panted.

Ewen, sensibly, lifted his hand off his sword hilt. 'I yield me.'

Gareth sheathed his sword, and reached down to help Ewen up. The boy smiled, and rubbed his shoulder, taking the whole incident with good grace.

He'll do, this one. Do well, in fact.

Sir Lancelot seemed to think so too. 'Not bad, boy.' He clapped Ewen on his good shoulder. 'But you let your opponent take charge of the fight. You had a chance to use that move of Gareth's against him.' Sir Lancelot put himself directly in front of Ewen. Gareth swung his shield onto his back and stepped away so he stood with Lionel and the others.

'Now, see, you stood, so.' Sir Lancelot bent back, raising his arm in imitation of Ewen's previous posture. 'Here. Your balance is gone. All he had to do was this . . .' Sir Lancelot swung around and twisted, slamming his shoulder into Ewen, sending him sprawling once more into the spring mud. This time he was a little slower to rise. 'Stand up, Ewen. You're a man, not a sheep,' chided Sir Lancelot. 'Try on me.'

Ewen stood, but hesitated to obey the rest of the instruction. Gareth couldn't blame him. He knew from experience that trying to shift Sir Lancelot was like trying to shift a standing stone. Before too long, though, the boy showed his spirit. He eyed his opponent's stance before he swung his body and struck, trying to make use of what weight he had. He did make Sir Lancelot, who was grinning over his head, stagger a little.

'Good! Good!' cried the knight. 'You've got the idea. You used your head, and your eyes. But you see, I, your man, stood so . . .' He pushed Ewen into a fighting stance. 'Now, for that, this is where you take him.' Sir Lancelot clapped one great hand on Ewen's shoulder and one on his waist.

The praise had made Ewen daring. 'But a sword . . .'

But Sir Lancelot did not let him finish. 'Didn't that first fall teach you? A sword's a good tool for man and knight, almost as fine as horse or spear, but there will come the day that all has been taken from you. Then all you've got is what God gave you, and you must be ready. Come, get that sword there and you'll see what I mean.'

Ewen swallowed. Gareth grinned down at Lionel, who was already shaking his head in sympathy. Ewen was proving once more he was quick on the uptake, because he'd gone pale. As before, though, he faced it well, reclaiming his training weapons and holding them up and ready. He kept his attention on his opponent and teacher, and tried not to let himself be distracted by the sniggers and quiet bets going on behind him.

Sir Lancelot lunged forward, and Ewen was able to parry, but not to hold. The knight drew his sword back with a hard twist that yanked the blade out of Ewen's gauntleted hands and sent it spinning onto the trampled grass.

'Now what, Sir Ewen?' inquired Lancelot, not even out of breath, and not lowering his guard a single inch as he circled his newest boy. 'Now what?'

Gareth expected the boy to try to feint and run, maybe thinking to get behind the knight. He'd tried something of the kind when he'd been in Ewen's place. But the boy drew back his shoulders and knelt, bowing his head in surrender. Lancelot laughed hard at this and walked up to the boy, sheathing his practice sword as he did so. He slapped Ewen's bony shoulder hard.

'You'll do, boy, you'll do. But you've got to learn not to give up so easy. Come.' He heaved Ewen to his feet easily with a one armed grip. 'Walk with me. Gareth . . .'

But Gareth did not need to be told what to do. As the oldest of Sir Lancelot's current squires, the great red stallion Taranis was Gareth's personal responsibility, and Gareth had studied his duty diligently. Ignoring the laughter and talk around him, he removed the bit from Taranis's teeth and loosened the saddle girth. He gave the horse's legs and hooves a cursory check. Finding Taranis to be in good condition, he turned and did the same for Achaius. The horses were all hot and blown from the wild ride. Walking them back would cool them down and keep them from stiffening up.

Lionel had taken on the duties for the mount Ewen had ridden down and Gareth caught his eye.

'He'll be tough, once my Lord Lancelot's had a little time with him,' Lionel remarked.

Gareth nodded. 'Tough or broken. Seems he knows how to take it, though.'

'Unlike some of us,' said Lionel with an abashed grin. On his first day out in the company of Sir Lancelot and the squires, Lionel had broken a practice spear and sword, and had actually sworn he'd never come back. When Sir Lancelot coolly informed Lionel he could walk back to his father and it would do no damage to knight or king, Lionel had changed his mind. But he'd also had to fight hard to get the knight to take him seriously again. Sir Lancelot had no mercy on those who balked at his training.

Gareth and Lionel fell in behind the younger boys who were leading their own horses back up through the orchards and the earthworks to the town gates. They talked and joked with each other and shouted at the boys, who knew better by now than to jeer back. Gareth breathed deep.

God's legs, it's good to be out again.

By the time they reached Camelot's keep and its stables, Gareth, tired and sweaty, was longing for the dinner that was being laid in the great hall, but the horses came first.

After that, Sir Lancelot would need to wash and properly dress, and his gear would have to be cleaned and stored. There was work in plenty to do. Perhaps he'd just send one of the younger boys to bring him some bread and beef as he'd done the past few evenings. It would be easier than having to get himself presentable as well as his knight.

As he closed the door on Taranis's box, a flicker of bright movement caught his eye. He looked again, and saw a girl standing in the shadow of the stable threshold. She wore her rich brown hair loose around her shoulders and across the full bodice of her otherwise plain dress. It was Rose, one of the fortress's many serving girls. He knew her eyes and her smile, and all that she kept under that plain wool. Gareth felt his own smile shift and broaden as he took in the sight of her. He had pulled off his training coat already, but now he casually stripped off his woollen over-tunic, carefully not looking at her as he did.

The past year had worked a change on Gareth's appearance, and he enjoyed the results. He'd always been tall and lanky as a boy. He had grown taller still over the past summer, but he had also filled out to a man's build, with the broad shoulders and the strong legs of one who worked hard and rode frequently. His raven-black hair fell back in waves from a pleasing face. He'd found all these assets combined with a warm smile and some soft words well-seasoned with lover's honey worked miracles upon the girls, and not a few of the women of Camelot, and he enjoyed that as well.

He had made Rose's intimate acquaintance just the week before, so it was no real surprise to find her lingering about the stables. Everyone knew he was first among Sir Lancelot's squires, and what duties and privileges that work entailed.

Tossing his over-tunic onto a stack of hay sheaves, Gareth gave Rosy a broad wink. She blushed, but returned his gaze boldly. *Perhaps I'm not so tired after all.*

'Make sure Achaius is fed and watered, will you, Lionel?' he said, only half-turning towards the other squire. 'I'll be along shortly.'

'Shortly?' murmured Lionel, earning himself a kick to the ankle, which he neatly dodged.

Gareth did not waste any more time on him. He sauntered towards Rose, and when he reached her, he bowed deeply, in mock courtesy. She smiled, a flush colouring her cheeks prettily, and curtsied in return. When they both stood straight again, Gareth moved closer, taking her hand gently in his own, and running the thumb of his free hand across her cheek, right where the colour was brightest.

A shadow fell across them both. Gareth's head jerked up and he saw Sir Geraint, his nearest brother, standing in the stable doorway, his arms folded. Rose leapt backward, suddenly the very picture of blushing modesty, her fingers knotting in her skirts. Dark-haired and blue-eyed, Geraint looked at Gareth, and he looked at Rosy.

'Now then, Rose,' Geraint said quietly. 'Your mother's looking for you. You'd best go to her.'

Anger hardened Rose's sunny features, but she did not question him. As she whisked around to stomp away, she cast a backward glance full of promise at Gareth. Gareth suppressed a mild curse. Well, it was just a delay. He'd find Rosy later, or she'd find him. But what did Geraint think he was doing?

'God be with you, Geraint,' Gareth said curtly. 'What brings you out here?' It was still strange to be looking down on Geraint, on any of them, for that matter. Of all his brothers, only Gawain could still look him in the eye without having to lift his chin.

'A word with you, sir,' replied Geraint with perfect equilibrium. 'When you've done here.'

'Well, you'll have a good wait. My Lord Lancelot has much for me to do today.' Gareth deliberately turned his back on his brother and started into the stable's cool shadows.

'Is this the answer you give a knight, Squire?'

These words, and the sudden shift to a tone of command, drew Gareth up short. He turned to look carefully at his brother. Geraint regarded him implacably. Gareth swallowed. He'd just made a mistake that too many did. He'd forgotten for a moment the seriousness with which his most quiet brother took rank and respect.

'My apologies, sir.' Gareth bowed his head. 'I will be finished shortly.'

Geraint nodded, satisfied, and walked a little way off to the paddock to watch the young colts and their dams. Gareth stared after him a moment, a hollow feeling forming in the pit of his stomach. Then he heard a horse stamp inside the stables and remembered his duties.

He kept at his work as long as he could, carefully wiping down and brushing both Taranis and Achaius. He inspected every inch of tack and harness and found depressingly little that needed to be cleaned or attended to. Too soon all was in order. Gareth walked back out into the evening sunlight to join his brother at the paddock fence.

Geraint acknowledged him with a nod and a glance, but no word. Instead, he led Gareth out across the yards and through the gates to the wide, sloping green that stood between keep and town. The last of the snowdrifts had finally vanished, leaving behind stretches of mud and mottled patches of sprouting plants. The shadows were already deepening around the town below, turning it black and grey. The early spring twilight was settling and the wind smelled of cold as well as fresh life. The vaguest hint of green lent a hazy look to the distant orchard beneath the leaden sky.

Geraint rested his foot on a stone.

'So, brother,' said Gareth with a sigh. 'What do you want with me?'

Geraint watched him a long moment before speaking, taking in Gareth's stance and features while he considered his words. A long silence was one of Geraint's favourite tactics. It was meant to test the patience of the one who faced him. *But I know you, brother.* Gareth just stood and let Geraint look as long as he chose.

At last Geraint spoke. 'I want, brother, to warn you that your brave deeds with the females of Camelot have not gone unnoticed.'

I should have known. Gareth shrugged. 'So, I've tumbled a few girls. What of it? They were willing.'

Geraint arched his brows. 'A few? From what I've heard, if there's a brace of virgins left for a mile around, it's because their fathers lock them in their dowry chests.'

Which told Gareth exactly how his brother – back from his new lands in the west only a week – had heard how Gareth had spent his winter. His patience snapped. 'Agravain cares only for his own . . .'

Geraint's brows shot up. 'You're very sure my news is from Agravain. Has he spoken to you as well?'

Damn. Gareth found he could not endure his brother's scrutiny any more. Agravain had in fact spoken to him, and lectured, and sworn, and thrown up his hands and declared him too much of a fool to live. But then, Agravain held that opinion of many men.

'Who else have you ignored, brother?'

As soon as Geraint asked the question, another recent speech sprang up in Gareth's memory. *You're emptying that purse of yours fast, nephew. It's the sort of gold that will put you in debt faster than it will buy you out.*

Gareth felt his jaw tighten defiantly. 'My Lord Lancelot says any woman who wants to lie down should be laid down.'

Geraint's mouth twitched, just a little. Gareth was not sure whether his brother meant to smile or frown. Frown probably. Geraint was not fond of Sir Lancelot's matter-of-fact pronouncements, which was strange, as Geraint was everywhere praised for his honesty.

'That is no answer, brother,' Geraint said.

Gareth flushed, but this time he held his peace. Let Geraint wait for his answers, if he had so little to do.

'Mother of God,' murmured Geraint after a tense moment. 'Has the High King spoken to you?'

'No!' cried Gareth. How could Geraint believe he'd disregard their uncle's least word? *What do you think of me?*

Geraint said nothing more, he simply waited, and waited. *Best get it over with.* Gareth would stick on him until Doomsday once he got his spurs in. 'It was Sir Kai.'

Much to Gareth's surprise, Geraint stared for just a moment longer, his face gone slack with disbelief. Then he burst out laughing. 'You brushed off Uncle Kai! God's legs, Gareth, you have lost your mind!' he whooped. 'I'm surprised we've heard nothing of this at board yet. No, I'm surprised I didn't hear it all the way out to the West Lands . . .' he paused, drawing in a great breath and cocking his head towards Gareth as realization dawned. 'But then, you haven't been to board the past few nights have you?'

It was true, Gareth hadn't gone into the hall for the evening meal for the past three or four nights. But, he told himself, it was not Uncle Kai who kept him away. He'd simply been busy.

This truth, as far as it went, was still not enough to give Gareth the strength to meet his brother's clear eyes. 'I have my work to do.'

'That is not what I asked, Gareth,' said Geraint, his voice suddenly stern.

And again, Gareth's temper flared and he set jaw and mind against his brother. 'What business is it of yours?' he demanded. *I've no time for this. My Lord Lancelot is waiting for me . . .*

Geraint's mouth twitched. 'It is my business if you are making an ass of yourself, brother.'

The mildness in Geraint's voice drew Gareth up and he found his chest was heaving. 'How do you get to be pious with me, Geraint? You and Gawain didn't exactly go virgin to your marriage beds. Especially Gawain.' His brother's travels in the king's name had given him a chance to sow his seed far and wide across the isle. If there wasn't at least one little 'ap Gawain' out there, every man in Camelot would be shocked. That Gawain had married his last dalliance was equally surprising.

'Even Gawain was more judicious than you seem to have been,' replied Geraint evenly.

'I told you . . .'

'Yes, you did.' Geraint held up his hand. 'Now, I am telling you.' He levelled one long, work-hardened finger at Gareth's chest. 'You're already in deeper waters than you know. If you keep on, you'll jeopardize your chance at knighthood.'

Temper made Gareth brazen. 'My Lord Lancelot would never forsake me just for sticking a few slatterns.'

At this, Geraint remained quite unperturbed. 'No,' he said. 'Even if more than a few were high-born daughters fool enough to fall for that smile of yours, rendering themselves suspect when it comes time to make good alliances for themselves, their fathers, and our king. Even if one of them might already be married to Lord Jessup who is our first defence against the Saxons to the south of his lands. Even if your knight be willing to disregard all this, you at least should remember it is not my Lord Lancelot who has the final word regarding who may become a knight of the Britons.'

Gareth felt the blood drain from his cheeks. This was the second time Geraint had alluded to the king. What if Arthur had heard something some teary-eyed former maiden had said? Or, God's teeth, what if it was from the *queen* that

Geraint had found out about him and Lady Jessup?

Geraint lifted his foot from the stone and moved closer. 'Listen to me carefully, Gareth,' he said, his voice low but deadly serious. 'You and I are the younger brothers. We have nothing, *nothing* of our own save the good will of our families and our king. We squander that at our peril.

'I know you, Gareth,' Geraint went on before Gareth could find a word with which to answer. 'You're thinking you might marry land as I have. Think on this now. Without the king's blessing, you cannot do even that, and there are others who have the king's ear far more firmly than you.'

Gareth said nothing. His teeth had gritted themselves together so tightly, he was not sure he could have spoken even if he wanted to.

'Come to board, Gareth,' said Geraint. 'Uncle Kai will serve you out a healthy portion of humility as your dessert. You can either face him now and take it like a man, or you can face more bitter condemnation later from every hand. It is your choice.'

With that, Geraint walked away. Having delivered his warnings, he evidently felt no more need to converse with his younger brother. A thousand things he could shout after Geraint filled Gareth's mind, but he held them all back, clutching them tight in his jaw.

Uncle Kai was waiting for him. Uncle Kai whose tongue was sharper than any blade forged by mortal man. He could reduce the whole court to tears of laughter with a single turn of phrase. More than one bard had picked up Sir Kai's quips and added them to songs carried across the whole of the country. Others had been repeated around Camelot for *years*. How could Geraint cold-bloodedly tell him to walk in and face that?

Gareth bit his lip and he realized he was actually contemplating running away.

I've work to do, he reminded himself. *Work to do. It's not my fault if my duties matter more than my dinner.*

Geraint was out of sight, so there was little chance Gareth would catch up to him. He strode back into the keep, heading once more towards the stables, answering those who hailed him with a silent wave. He needed to check Taranis one more time, make sure he was properly bedded down and fed. Then he needed to find Sir Lancelot, help him dress, and apologize for his tardiness. God's legs, what would the knight say about that?

But Gareth found his knight far sooner than expected. Sir Lancelot stood beside Taranis's box, stroking the beast's strong neck. The knight was washed, combed, and dressed in a clean tunic of deep blue with saffron and scarlet embroidery on the chest and hems. Gareth froze on the threshold, but it was too late. Sir Lancelot turned as soon as Gareth's shadow broached the doorway, leaving no chance of retreat. Gareth could only make his bow, and try frantically to think of something to say, some way to explain.

'Sir Geraint tells me he's the cause of your absence, Squire Gareth.' Sir Lancelot gave Taranis a final, firm pat. 'Just what was it your brother had to say to you at such length?'

Gareth stood silent and stared at the tips of his own boots. He felt about ten years old, and a bare yard tall.

Sir Lancelot snorted and leaned his shoulder against the rooftree. 'Been at you about your women, hasn't he?'

Gareth's jaw dropped. Was the whole court keeping track of his dalliances? 'I've taken nothing that wasn't given,' he muttered belligerently, before he remembered who he spoke to, and bowed his head again. Perhaps he should kneel.

But Sir Lancelot only smiled. 'Good,' he said firmly. 'You come out of the shadows then. I'll not have it said one of my men hid from a fight just because it was one of his brothers offered the insult.'

Pride surged through Gareth, lifting head and heart. 'No, my lord!'

Sir Lancelot looked past Gareth's shoulder and then gave him a wink and a grin. 'And you don't forget, a man uses words when there's no sword left under his belt.' A laugh escaped Gareth. He stifled it quickly, but Sir Lancelot made no comment about that. 'It's only fools and weak hearts can't stand up to jibes, whoever they come from.'

'Yes, my lord.'

'Get on then.' Sir Lancelot pushed himself away from the rooftree. 'You're my man and I expect you to act like it. I'll see you at board with the others tonight.'

'Yes, my lord.'

Sir Lancelot strode through the open doors, slapping Gareth's back as he passed. Gareth pulled himself up straight. Yes. His knight would see him at board. So would his brothers, and the rest of court who cared to be there. Some of what Geraint had said nagged at him; about the noble girls rendered suspect, and the difficulty in forming alliances with their marriages. Well, he might be more circumspect in the future, but that was not anything Geraint or Agravain needed to be informed of. They would see how a man carried himself. Sir Lancelot was right. A true man did not hide in the shadows when a fight was offered.

Gareth turned on his heels and followed the path his knight had taken.

Gareth lived at the far end of the barracks with the other squires. By day, they had benches and chairs in front of their hearth. At night, those who did not sleep in the stables beside a sick horse or one in foal, rested in front of the banked fire on pallet beds. Each had a single chest for his spare clothes and few possessions. King's son or Saxon hostage, it was Arthur's declaration that all should be held equal while they learned from his cadre.

Of course that was not how it was. The oldest boys held themselves above the younger, and each knew whose father was a man of worth and whose was not. King's son and High King's nephew, as well as one of the oldest among the squires, Gareth seldom had to fight the others anymore, although before he'd gained his full height he'd nursed plenty of bruises and black eyes.

Upon reaching the barracks, Gareth readied himself with care. He belted his finest green tunic with his best silver. He washed his face hard and slicked his hair back. Feeling about his chin he found no stubble. His beard was not a matter for regular barbering yet, a fact which pained him a little, but tonight was just as well.

I will meet all with dignity, he assured himself smoothing down his sleeves and hems. *I have done nothing wrong and no man can say I have. Not Geraint, not Uncle Kai.*

But as he turned, he found Brendon ap Huel standing in the barracks doorway. Brendon was the third of Sir Lancelot's squires, and, unlike Lionel, was a man Gareth had never been able to like. He had a thin mouth and slitted eyes which always had far too much going on behind them. It was probably he who had washed and dressed Sir Lancelot when Gareth failed to appear, and he'd probably used every moment to talk him down as far as the knight would allow.

Now he was smiling like a cat who'd found the cream unguarded.

'Is something amiss, Brendon?' asked Gareth as coolly as he could.

Brendon shook his head without taking his gaze off Gareth. 'Nothing at all, Gareth.'

'Then what are you standing there for?'

His fellow squire shrugged. 'No reason.' But Brendon was grinning so widely Gareth could see both his missing teeth.

'It's only that I wouldn't be you for a whole kingdom,'

Brendon went on, as Gareth had been certain he would. 'Sir Kai's been working the theme of your absence for days. I think there's not a lady left in the place who isn't permanently red. He almost started a fight the other day when he said you'd tumbled Sir Hayden's Lady Arliss . . .'

'Shut it, Brendon.'

Brendon shrugged. 'I just thought you might want to know how things stand.'

Gareth stalked up to him, letting his shadow fall across the younger man's face. 'You take care with your warnings, Brendon,' he murmured lightly. 'Or Sir Kai might just find out which field you've been ploughing in these past months.'

Brendon blanched. 'You wouldn't.'

But Gareth just turned away from him and joined the loose procession heading across the open yard towards the great hall.

You are my man. My man. The echo of Sir Lancelot's words carried Gareth forward and kept the bite of the evening wind from reaching him.

A wave of warmth washed over him as he entered the hall. Fires roared in both the hearths. As this was not a feast day, the squires were not required to serve their knights at table, but could eat in their own company. Gareth took his place on the bench beside Lionel. Brendon joined them a moment later, but he had sense enough to keep his mouth shut, for now, at least. The youngest boys had the farthest end, closest to the doors and the draughts. Gareth remembered sitting there, his toes just brushing the floor, looking with awe and envy at his older brothers who already rode with the cadre of the Round Table and served the High King in his wars and his peace. Now his three brothers sat at the high tables, Gawain and Geraint beside their wives, and here he sat still looking on.

The difference now was that his own knight, Sir Lancelot,

sat beside them, and Sir Lancelot smiled and raised his cup, just a little, as Gareth caught his eye.

Gareth nodded in grateful reply but had no time to do more. A door at the far end of the hall opened and a voice called out, 'His Majesty Arthur, High King of all Britons!'

The whole company stood at once. In walked Gareth's blood uncle, Arthur the King. Age had begun to silver his hair but it had not sloped his shoulders, dimmed his eye, or weakened his hand. Beside him walked Queen Guinevere. Though nearly Arthur's match for age, she remained one of the most beautiful women Gareth had ever seen. More than one of the squires sighed in their most secret hearts for the warmth of her grey-eyed regard. Arthur held her slender hand in his strong one as he helped her to her seat beside him, and she had no regard at that moment for any but the king.

Behind them came a far different figure; Sir Kai, who was the High King's foster brother, and his seneschal. He was clothed in black except for the golden chain of his office, and stooped over so far that he appeared almost hunch-backed. Sir Kai limped as he stepped up to the high table, leaning heavily on his crutch. One of his legs, thin and twisted, dragged behind the other. One might have thought he was the court fool. Many kings kept some malformed person by to amuse them, and indeed there were some who knew no better who claimed that was Kai's role in the court. Sometimes, Kai even let them think this, though how he could stomach that was beyond Gareth's comprehension.

Now, though, Uncle Kai's keen eyes swept the great chamber, and skewered Gareth down the length of the hall. Gareth lifted his chin and met his foster uncle's gaze. Sir Kai simply smiled as he eased himself into his seat at the High King's left hand.

Gareth ground his teeth together. *I'll not let him play me for the fool. He cannot make anything of me if I do not respond, and I will not. Not until I see my moment. Then, I'll cut him with his own knife.*

The food's arrival put a temporary end to gloomier thoughts. There was roast pork, chickens stuffed with onions, last year's apples roasted with raisins and honey. There was wine, cider and small beer to drink and good brown bread for sopping up the gravies.

The training ride had left Gareth with a good appetite. He helped himself liberally, ignoring the sideways glances from his fellows. Lionel tried to make some talk, but soon gave it up. Everyone was waiting for the meal to finish. Everyone knew what would come. *Well, let it come. I am not afraid. I will not be afraid.*

At last, the meats were only bones and the bread only crumbs. Fortified wines were poured out to the high table, and the talk flowed freely everywhere but at the squires' table. Gareth fought the urge to squirm like a child, and pecked at the crumbs remaining in front of him, avoiding the eyes of his fellows. He was not afraid. But he did wish it would begin, so it could end, so everyone would stop *looking* at him.

Then Uncle Kai took a swallow from his cup, and rested his arm lazily on the table cloth, before remarking, 'I see your wandering squire has returned to us, Sir Lancelot.' His voice was pitched to carry. 'What a relief! Tell us, which bed did you find him in?'

Laughter rippled through the hall. Despite his resolutions, Gareth felt his face begin to heat up. That damnable fact was not missed by Sir Kai.

'Why, you blush, Squire Gareth!' the seneschal cried, ensuring that now every eye in the hall was directed at Gareth. Gareth kept his own gaze fixed on the crumb-covered table. 'Surely, your brother Gawain has told you what a fine thing it is to be so widely welcomed!'

I will not give hint that I hear. His jibes are not worthy of answer.

'And surely, that is enough, Sir Kai,' murmured a woman. The queen. Coming to his aid. This was almost worse than the taunting. What if they said he needed a woman's help to defend himself?

'Enough, Majesty?' repeated Sir Kai, full of surprise. 'There's a word I'll wager young Gareth doesn't often hear!'

Laughter burst out again, including from the boys' end of the table. Gareth glared at the youngsters, who all promptly closed their mouths and tried to look abashed. Not Brendon, though. He just grinned his thin grin at Gareth, relishing each word, memorizing them, and storing them away to repeat later.

You dare to mention this night again, Brendon, and I will make you regret it.

Despite the queen's intervention, Sir Kai was far from finished. 'Of course, the fact that he's gone through so many of our fine ladies so . . . quickly . . . It doesn't say much for his stamina. Is it you that wears your squires out so?' He quirked his eyebrows at Sir Lancelot. Lancelot went very still and his face was thunderous. 'Ah, no, of course not,' Sir Kai went on judiciously. 'It is known that you love only the ladies, and, as the gallant you are, your horse.'

The king was frowning now, but he had not yet made any admonishment. Someone was holding onto Gareth's shoulder. Lionel. Gareth hadn't realized his hands were at his sides, clutching the air where his sword would have been. Let Kai humiliate him if it made him feel more the man, but that he would *dare* turn his vile humour on Sir Lancelot . . .

'Sir Geraint, perhaps you will take Gareth with you into the West Lands when you go,' Sir Kai continued amiably. 'It would be good for him to see more of new places, as it was good for your brother there.' He nodded at Gawain, producing many reminiscent sniggers. Gawain's red-haired wife did not even have the decency to blush at this, and Gawain just looked impassively at his mocking uncle. 'If we keep him here, I'm afraid that we'll soon run out of willing women, and have to begin telling the stable boys to keep their backsides to the wall . . .'

In the roar of laughter that erupted, Gareth shot to his feet. 'Were you a true man I would spill your guts on the ground!'

The shout echoed across the hall. All the rude and outrageous guffaws died away and every eye turned to Gareth. Gareth did not think on any of this. He saw only Sir Kai at the high table, a smug grin on his lean face, another jest ready on his fool's tongue.

Kai lifted his brows. 'Do you say I am no man, Squire Gareth?' He spoke quietly now, but Gareth heard every word. He thought he also heard a murmur that meant caution, but insult burned too deeply for him to understand it.

'I say you are a cripple who gained his seat from my lord king's pity, and who exercises his tongue because he cannot exercise any other part of himself! I say that if you could stand I would make you pay for every word out of your crooked mouth!'

Kai's eyes slid sideways to regard the king for a long moment. *Waiting for my Lord Arthur to save him.* Gareth drew his shoulders back. Arthur was saying something to Kai, and when Kai made a soft answer, the king just shook his head and waved his hand. Then, to Gareth's surprise, Sir Kai slowly rose up until he stood with both hands pressed hard against the table.

'Well, Squire Gareth. Here I do stand.'

Silence filled the hall. It was as if the other company were statues and the only living men were Sir Kai, and Gareth.

He thinks I will back down. He thinks I will not dare challenge the king's brother. That is what makes him so free.

But I too am the king's kindred, uncle.

'Then I challenge you to make good your claims on my body, if you can, Sir Kai.'

Sir Kai cocked his head just a little further, looking like some curious bird. His smile never wavered, and inside, Gareth felt the slightest of tremors. 'Very well then, Squire Gareth. I accept your challenge.'

'Kai . . .' began the king.

But Sir Kai did not let him finish. 'Forgive me, my Lord King, but the boy has spoken before the whole court. Will you, my liege, tell me I may not defend my poor crippled honour?'

The king hesitated. Then, he crooked his two fingers, gesturing for Gareth to come forward.

Gareth did, walking down the central aisle to the foot of the dais. Remembering his manners, and that his knight looked on, Gareth knelt before the king.

Arthur said soberly. 'Gareth, it was a jest, as well you know. Will you, at my request, let this matter be?'

Request, not command. He knows Kai has overstepped his bounds this time. 'I have been sore insulted, my Lord King,' Gareth replied firmly. 'I have a right to prove those insults to be the lies they are.'

King Arthur sighed and Gareth had the impression he wanted to throw up his hands. 'Very well. As neither of you will be satisfied any other way, it will be done at midday tomorrow.'

Gareth bowed his head again. When he stood, he saw Geraint and Gawain staring at him in frank disbelief. But Sir Lancelot gave him the barest of nods, and Gareth felt a flush of warmth run through him. He looked back to Sir Kai, who still stood, and saw how the beads of sweat had begun to form on his brow.

Now we will see who is the man, Gareth thought as he bowed once more and took his leave of the hall.

Now we will see.

TEN

'Have you lost your mind!' bellowed Agravain as he strode across the barracks threshold.

Gareth had been expecting this. He'd stationed himself in front of the hearth so that he would face his brothers the instant they walked in. As he had anticipated, Agravain did not arrive alone. Gawain and Geraint followed in his angry wake. All of them come together to tell him to hide from Kai's insults like a child. Gareth's jaw tightened.

'God be with you as well, Agravain,' Gareth said mildly to his pinch-faced brother. Real anger always left two white dents on either side of Agravain's nose, and they were there now.

'What was that display?' Agravain cried, stabbing backward to indicate the great hall. 'You should be glad the king didn't throw you from the keep.'

Gareth looked past Agravain to Geraint and Gawain. Geraint just shrugged. Gawain quietly closed the door, and leaned his shoulder against it.

As casually as he was able, Gareth sat down on the bench, folding his arms and stretching out his legs. 'I am glad my uncle permitted me to stay. It will give me a chance to make good for the insult I've been dealt.'

At this, Agravain rounded on Geraint. 'You said you spoke to him.'

'I did,' Geraint answered heavily, running his hand through his hair. 'Clearly . . .'

Gareth did not intend to wait for Geraint to finish. 'It is not for Geraint to govern my conduct, Agravain,' he said coldly. 'Nor is it for you. I am not a boy any longer. I am squire to my Lord Lancelot, and if I am doing wrong, it is him I answer to.'

Let all of you think on that a moment. He looked from one of them to the others. His three older brothers. Agravain's face tightened until it looked like his bones must soon snap. Geraint tossed a stick onto the fire, watching the sparks rise, and Gawain – leaning there against the door as if he thought it might pop open – Gawain had a glint in his amber eyes that could have been humour and could have been anger.

'If you are a man, Gareth,' said Gawain at last, 'act like one, and use the sense God gave you.'

'And what do you mean by that, brother?' This time Gareth could not keep the heat from his voice.

'I know my Lord Lancelot is not a great one for strategy, but there are some points of this battle that you should perhaps consider.' Gareth opened his mouth to remind Gawain that Lancelot was a finer warrior than he, but Gawain gave him no time. 'The first is that our Uncle Kai is not, despite what he may sometimes appear, a fool.' He pushed himself away from the door. Gareth snorted. This caused Gawain to raise one eyebrow, but he did not pause in his lesson. 'The second fact you should be pondering,' he held up a finger for emphasis, 'is that it was Sir Kai who taught our other uncle, the High King, to use a sword.'

Gareth found no reply to that. *Sir Kai taught the king?* Uncle Kai was the older of the two. They'd fostered together with Lord Ector, he knew. But Arthur was the best swordsman

among the Britons, greater even than Sir Lancelot. Kai was
. . . Kai was . . .

Geraint must have read the thoughts behind Gareth's hesitation, and he shook his head. 'Kai was not always a cripple,
Gareth,' he said quietly. 'Before his leg was crushed, there
was not a man alive who could touch him when it came to
swordplay. His deeds in the twelve battles are legend.'

Despite all his resolve, a chill crept over Gareth's confidence. 'I've never heard this.'

'That's because you don't listen,' sneered Agravain. 'Do
you think any speak of such things to his face? Would anyone
close to Arthur be so discourteous as to remind Kai of what
he once was?'

Gawain put his boot up on the bench and leaned both
arms on his leg, so that he also leaned over Gareth where
he sat.

'I'll add this for you to think on, Gareth,' he said. Time
had been at work on Gawain. His face had grown heavier,
hardened, and its lines had grown deeper. Gareth found
himself looking at this serious man as if he was a stranger,
and somehow, his words sank in more deeply than words
that came from Gawain ever had. 'There stood Sir Kai racked
by the kind of pain you, if you're lucky, will never know,
and yet, he stood.' Gawain brought his foot down and folded
his arms, in clear mockery of Gareth's own posture. 'He is
not weak, brother, and he is not a fool. If he let himself be
challenged by you, it is *not* because he thinks you can beat
him.'

This bald statement dropped into Gareth's mind like a
stone. He had not stopped to consider that his Uncle Kai
might have been ready in any way for his challenge.

'You will go and apologize,' said Agravain flatly. 'And if at
all possible, stop being a fool before you do yourself a real
mischief.'

Anger, bright and sharp, returned in a rush. Gareth stood slowly, letting Agravain – who seemed to have temporarily forgotten that Gareth was no longer ten years old – see his full height.

'Oh very good, Gareth,' said Agravain wearily. 'You've grown tall. I hadn't noticed. Will you be demanding to fight me next?'

But before Gareth could make his reply, footsteps sounded on the dirt of the yard outside. Sir Lancelot stepped across the threshold. He showed no surprise at finding all the sons of Lot gathered together before the hearth.

'My lords.' Sir Lancelot bowed smoothly. 'I'd have a word with my squire.'

'He is yours,' acknowledged Agravain, but sarcasm tainted the words.

'Thank you, my lords,' replied Lancelot as if he had not heard Agravain's tone. He passed between the brothers to stand beside Gareth. Gareth could not help but notice how reluctantly Gawain and Geraint made way, but make way they did. 'He has duties tonight. I trust you will allow him to be getting on with his work soon.'

'Of course,' answered Gawain. Gareth repressed a smile. Not even Gawain would stand and face Lancelot.

No sooner had he formed this thought than, to Gareth's utter shock, Agravain stalked up to Sir Lancelot. Next to the Gaulish knight, Gareth's lean, dark brother looked like a sapling beside a golden oak. 'Do not think I have forgotten it is your teaching that has brought my brother to this, Lancelot,' muttered Agravain through clenched teeth. 'If he is sore wounded tomorrow, you will answer to me.'

Gareth's jaw dropped. Before Sir Lancelot could make a reply, Agravain marched past the other three, out into the deepening night. Gawain and Geraint glanced towards each other and then towards Gareth. Together they hurried after

Agravain, doubtlessly to try to talk some sense into him.

'Well, he's some fire in him after all, that brother of yours.' Lancelot jerked his chin over his shoulder at Agravain's retreating back.

Gareth nodded, still unable to quite believe what had happened. And Agravain had accused *him* of having lost his mind . . .

But there was no time to think on that. Sir Lancelot faced him squarely. 'You know what I expect of you tomorrow, Squire?'

Gareth drew his shoulders back. 'I do, my lord,' he answered firmly.

'Good.' Sir Lancelot nodded once. 'Then there is nothing more to be said.'

Nor was there. Sir Lancelot kept Gareth by him that night, but there was no mention made of what was to come. Gareth simply went about his duties; making sure his knight's gear and clothes were cleaned and stored, going to the stables one last time to see that Taranis showed no hurt or strain from the day's exercise. Both his fellow squires were reluctant to question or chaff him in Sir Lancelot's presence, and the younger boys only looked on him with a kind of stunned awe. This wrapped Gareth's evening in a strange, almost reverent hush.

It was told around the court that the night before Sir Lancelot was made a member of the Round Table's cadre, he did not sleep. He stayed in the church, praying and fasting, thanking God for this chance to prove himself to the greatest king in the Christian world. The callous, Sir Kai included, said Sir Lancelot was actually waiting for some woman who never showed herself. Despite this envious jeering, some of the younger men had taken to keeping such a vigil in imitation and respect. To Gareth, this night felt like that time, a time apart, as he solemnly readied himself for a great change.

It seemed so even as he lay down on his own pallet by the banked fire, as he did every evening, with the boys and youths all around him, already drowsing and snoring.

Oddly, before sleep claimed him, the last thing his mind's eye saw was lean, furious Agravain standing before Sir Lancelot without a trace of fear.

Gareth did not even consider going to board the next morning, and, thankfully, Sir Lancelot did not order it. He drank his small beer and ate his pottage on his own in the barracks. He cleaned and honed his sword, a plain, but sharp and well-balanced gift from Gawain. It did not really need the attention, but Gareth needed something to do. He was a little surprised that none of his brothers came to rail at him one more time. Perhaps they were with Sir Kai, trying to talk him out of the challenge.

After a time, Lionel poked his head around the doorway, peering at Gareth like a spying child.

Gareth snorted. 'Get in here, Lionel. What did you think you'd find? Agravain hasn't taken my head off yet.'

Lionel sauntered in. 'I knew that much. He's down at the field, looking like he's swallowed an orchard's worth of crab apples.'

'With Brendon right next to him grinning like a hungry hound at the sight of meat, I'll wager,' said Gareth, putting down the whetstone and wiping the blade with the soft, oiled leather one more time.

Lionel nodded. 'You'd best get down there. Brendon's already taking bets that you won't show yourself.'

'Brendon would say I'd run from a crippled man.' Gareth's mouth twisted into a tight smile. 'It's what he'd do.'

The smile Lionel returned was fleeting. 'Gareth . . .'

But Gareth cut him off, shaking his head. 'Don't, Lionel. I've said I will do this thing, and I will.'

'I know. Good luck.'

'Thank you.' They gripped each other's hands and looked into each other's eyes. They had both already fought in pitched battles with their knight and their king. They had the scars to prove it. This was different, though, and Lionel knew it as well as Gareth.

Lionel played squire for him after that. He helped Gareth into his leather jerkin and boots and cinched on his belt. Gareth was hanging his sword on the belt just as Sir Lancelot entered the barracks. Both squires knelt, but he bid them stand at once.

Sir Lancelot surveyed Gareth with a critical eye, and then nodded his approval. Without a word, he turned and marched out into the yard. Gareth, head up and shoulders back, followed, with Lionel right behind, carrying his helm and his plain, square shield.

The day outside was clear though still cold. They crossed the strangely empty keep going out through the gates, and down to the bowl of the practice yard. When the Romans had owned this broad hilltop, they had made an amphitheatre for their sports and assemblies. The round space with its moss-etched stone steps was now used by the High King as a training ground for his men, and for occasional entertainments, most of which were of a merrier sort than this.

Still, it was not a thing that any in the court intended to miss. The people crowded onto every inch of the yard's gently sloping sides, all brightly dressed as for a holiday. Voices shouted and cheered as Gareth passed by, and he found his heart beating fast with excitement, and with fear. The familiar faces seemed transformed into strangers, all watching him not as Gareth, Lot's youngest son, but as a raw contender come to battle for a prize, and they were all eager to see whether he would stand or fall. Despite the solid presences of his knight before him and his friend behind him, Gareth's guts twisted uncomfortably.

Only his brothers seemed unaltered by the coming contest. Geraint and Agravain flanked the High King's chair which had been placed on a red cloth at the field's edge. They watched Gareth as he came down the cracked stone steps. From this distance, Gareth could not tell whether Geraint wished him well or ill, and that made his guts twist all the more sharply. Agravain, however, wore his contempt openly. Seeing this brought a welcome rush of anger. Anger brought back the certainty that walking through this crowd had taken from him.

Sir Kai had arrived at the field first and was now seated on a bench beside the green. He wore the madder red cloak with the gold clasp that showed him to be a knight of the Round Table, an affectation Gareth had never seen on him before. Sir Kai stretched his whole leg out before the bench and tucked his crippled limb beneath it. Both were encased in boots of fine leather that rose almost to his knees. His crutch waited beside him.

For a moment, Gareth felt a twinge of doubt. What would be thought of Sir Kai when he came limping out onto the field on that crutch? Would there really be honour in fighting a man who couldn't even stand on his own? For all his display last night, he'd still needed to lean on the table just to get to his feet. But then the seneschal looked up at Gareth and smiled his mocking smile, making a half-bow where he sat.

'Pay him no mind,' murmured Sir Lancelot as they reached their own trestle bench on the opposite side of the field. 'He is neither the seneschal nor your uncle today. Here, in this place, he is only your enemy.'

Gareth nodded and tried to hold those words close, but he knew that as soon as he looked again at Sir Kai they would fly away.

The rumble of drums heralded the High King's arrival. All knelt, save Sir Kai on his bench. With a procession of musicians and a flag-bearer holding up his scarlet dragon, King Arthur walked down the steps with Gawain following close behind. King Arthur settled himself in to his great chair and the drummers arrayed around him stilled their instruments. With a curt gesture, he bid all assembled there to stand. He then looked to the crowd, and the men waiting beside the field, his face set in a stern frown. With a second sharp gesture, he commanded the combatants to approach.

Gareth obeyed, leaving Sir Lancelot and Lionel behind. His heart hammered harder than he would have wished, and his hands were beginning to sweat inside their leather gauntlets. Sir Kai picked up his crutch and limped across the green to stand beside Gareth. Then, in a slow, careful, fashion, the seneschal knelt before the king, just as Gareth completed the same gesture of obeisance. Gareth tried not to wince as doubt churned in him again. Sir Kai deserved his honour, as did any man. True, he wasn't a blood relation, but the seneschal had been as close as blood family to both Gareth and Geraint when they first came to Camelot. And despite his foolish displays in the hall, Kai was a cunning and trusted advisor to the king. To add to that, if Gawain was right – and this was not a matter about which Gawain would be wrong – he had once been a great warrior and his injury was one come by bravely.

Am I being a true man to put him through this?

'This is a matter of honour,' said King Arthur solemnly, the disapproval of his demeanour not altering one whit. 'Therefore, I will not command either of you to withdraw, though this goes against my better judgement. I will ask, however, as your king, Gareth, and your brother, Kai, will you give up this quarrel over a slighting jest of little courtesy and less import?'

Sir Kai shrugged his crooked shoulders. 'I am the one, challenged, Majesty. It is not for me to end this.'

The king looked to Gareth. An idea came to him, borne on a faint breath of hope. Perhaps this could be ended off the field. 'Were Sir Kai to offer apology, Majesty, honour would be satisfied.'

'Kai?' asked the king.

Sir Kai regarded Gareth for a moment with hooded eyes. His wide mouth twisted into yet another of his store of endless grins. Was it also a pained smile, or was that only Gareth's imagination? 'I too have been insulted, Majesty,' he said. 'If Squire Gareth wishes to make apology for that, and for the challenge, then the matter would be closed.'

'Squire Gareth?'

Gareth struggled for a moment. It would be easy enough. If he searched his heart, he knew had gone too far in the hall, and had spoken from a temper roused when Sir Kai sneered at Sir Lancelot. His uncle's barbs were sharp, and Gareth should have remembered he was being goaded. But then Gareth caught Sir Lancelot's eye from across the green. His knight did not shake his head, or give any such overt signal, but he was frowning as deeply as the king, and Gareth knew what was in his silence. He, Gareth, had committed himself to battle, and if he took the easy way now, Sir Lancelot would not forget, nor would he forgive. Then there was Rosy, and Amanda, and Lady Sabia Jessup in the crowd. It was their honour he defended, as well as his own.

'Squire Gareth?' said the king again. 'Will you give Sir Kai your apology?'

Gareth licked his lips. 'I cannot, Majesty.'

The king blew out a deep and weary sigh. 'Very well. The combat will be to the first blood, or until I judge the matter finished. You will start at my word.'

They bowed their heads once more. From the corner of

his eye, Gareth saw how gaunt Sir Kai's face was, and how the sun shone on the streaks of silver in his brown hair.

If only you were not so stubborn, he thought towards his uncle. *Why are you making me do this to you?*

The moment had come. The king bade them rise and they did so, bowing a final time. Gareth strode out onto the field. Sir Kai, dragging his useless leg behind him, limped slowly across the grass, carrying his shield awkwardly in his free hand. A ripple of high-pitched laughter drifted on the wind at the sight of him, but it was quickly silenced.

Oh, my uncle.

Gareth couldn't watch any more. He kept his attention on Lionel who came forward with his shield. Gareth fitted the strap of his shield to his arm. Then, because he had no choice, he looked up to show the king and Sir Kai both that he was ready. Sir Kai was now directly in front him. He looked Gareth up and down, taking his measure, exactly as he had in the hall the night before. Then, the seneschal opened his hand, let his crutch fall to the ground, and for the first time in his life, Gareth saw his uncle stand up straight.

God's legs!

Gareth knew Sir Kai was called Kai the Tall, and he had seen often that even while he was hunched over, the seneschal's eyes were level with the king's, but somehow, it had never dawned on Gareth what that would mean if Sir Kai no longer had to lean on his crutch. It was as if his opponent had turned suddenly from an old man into a giant. His long, lean shadow fell across Gareth's stunned face. Kai's eyes glittered as he lifted his shield painted with the crossed keys and fitted it to his arm. His very long arm, with a reach that must surely be a full foot longer than Gareth's own.

'Well, Squire?' Sir Kai inquired.

All the world watched him, but most of all Sir Lancelot, wondering what Gareth would do, faced now with this new, straight and terribly alert Sir Kai. Gareth closed his mouth and lifted his blade.

Watch your man. Sir Lancelot's voice came ringing back to him from a hundred practices. *Watch him close! How's he hold himself? Where's his balance? Front? Right? Left? He knows his strengths better than you, he'll lean into them without realizing it. See what he steers away from, and what he pays no heed to. That's where you'll find your way in.*

And Gareth remembered Ewen the day before, charging in, hammering away, letting himself be led. That was a mistake he, Gareth, would not make. Slowly, Gareth began to circle Sir Kai. Kai turned to follow him, pivoting on his sound leg, sword and shield up, beads of sweat already forming at the rim of his helm. Gareth darted in, swinging for Kai's shoulder. The seneschal blocked him swiftly, his blow jarring Gareth's arm up to the shoulder. Shouts exploded, some calling his name, some Sir Kai's. Gareth backed away swiftly, circling again. Kai met his gaze, and he was still smiling.

Kai's great strength was his reach, and from that testing feint, Gareth now knew he had speed. His weakness was his immobility. The question before them both, then, was how long could Kai maintain his readiness? Gareth's other great advantage was the same one he'd had yesterday against Ewen's untrained enthusiasm. Gareth had time.

'Come, come, Squire!' cried Sir Kai. 'It will not do to make yourself dizzy!'

This raised a bark of laughter and Gareth knew coins and bets changed hands behind him. *Not this time, uncle,* he swore silently. *You've goaded me as far as I'll go.*

Gareth darted in again, landing two glancing blows on Sir Kai's shield, and parrying two aimed at head and arm. He backed swiftly out again and kept circling, forcing Kai to turn on his one good leg. Sweat trickled down his uncle's face and the glint in his eyes grew brittle as he turned and turned, not daring to let Gareth get behind him. Kai stabbed forward, but Gareth simply jumped back out of the way, and circled again.

The hissing began then. It was low and soft at first, and Gareth took it only for the wind in the trees. But slowly it grew louder, and a low rumble began. The crowd, those friends turned strangers, were booing him.

'Coward!' shouted one.

'Afraid to face a cripple?' shouted another.

Now Gareth's heart banged against his ribs. The noise broke into his thoughts, crumbling his calm. Kai lunged again, and once again, and Gareth danced back both times, although the second blow caught the edge of his shield. A disappointed roar lifted up above the hissing.

Kai was going pale, but he still managed to grin. His shield hung on his arm a little lower now. 'What are you going to do, Gareth? Dance about until the crippled old man falls over? That will be a famous victory for you.'

Gareth was hot and cold at once. The shouts and the boos robbed him of his ability to think. He stopped, standing still for a moment, trying to catch his breath. When had he started panting? Whistles and cat calls erupted all around, and he couldn't stand it anymore.

Finish this, he told himself as the crowd's bellows throbbed through skull and bone. *Now.*

He ran in sword up, quick forward, quick back, turn again, look for his opening. Quick in, strike hard, let Sir Kai feel his weight as well as his speed, quick retreat. The noise redoubled until the ground trembled. Sir Kai staggered, stumbling backward over his own crutch where it lay, barely catching himself on his good leg as Gareth barrelled in, bringing his blows down hard and fast, pushing with all the force he could manage. But Kai still got in a blow to Gareth's helm, making the world blur dangerously for a moment and forcing him to stagger back. When he could see straight again, Sir Kai was upright, panting hard, his shield and sword both down by his waist. His smile had finally vanished from his face and he took two staggering, trembling steps backward, his knee buckling underneath him.

Now, uncle, let us settle this, thought Gareth grimly, raising his own blade.

He charged in, taking dead aim at his uncle's crippled side. Sir Kai straightened in an instant and swung his blade up in a long, looping motion.

Inviting me in, thought Gareth in the heartbeat before his own momentum carried him beneath Sir Kai's reach and Sir Kai, against all reason, pivoted on his crooked leg, at the same time reversing the motion of his sword to slash the blade sharply across Gareth's face. Gareth flew past, so stunned by shock and swift pain, he barely felt the boot planted in the centre of his back to send him sprawling full length on the grass.

Blood filled his mouth. Pain burned in every nerve of his face. Shouts and laughter rang against his head like more blows. Then, the light faded and something very sharp and very hot pressed against the back of his neck, bringing with it a perfect clarity. The tip of his uncle's sword dug into his bare skin, and his uncle's long shadow blotted out the noonday sun.

'Well, Squire Gareth?' asked Sir Kai pleasantly. 'Do you yield?'

He was bleeding hard. The salt gore filled his nose, making it nearly impossible to breathe. He was flat on the ground. His arm and chest hurt badly, his blade was a foot away, and all the court was shouting for Kai the Tall.

'Yes,' he whispered. 'I yield me.'

But Sir Kai was not yet done. 'And have you learned, nephew?'

'Yes, uncle,' said Gareth with an honesty that hurt far more than the blows he had taken. 'I have learned.'

'Good.'

The hot, dangerous pressure of the sword point lifted from his neck, and the shadow slipped away. Spitting out his blood, and panting hard for breath, Gareth shoved himself into a sitting position. Lionel was running across the green, probably to help him with his helm and shield. But Gareth only watched Sir Kai. Shaking with effort the knight stooped to drop his shield and pick up his crutch and limp off the field, much more quickly, Gareth noted, than he had come on. In so doing, he did not neglect to bow to the king.

Lionel crouched down beside Gareth, saying nothing, but easing off his helm, and slipping his shield cautiously off his bruised arm.

'It's not so bad,' Lionel was saying. 'It looks like a shallow slash across your cheek. Face wounds bleed badly, but it's not torn through . . .'

But nothing he said mattered, because Sir Lancelot had left the crowd that pressed after Sir Kai, and was marching across the green.

Gareth's strength drained away from him as he saw the fury on his knight's face.

'Get me up,' he whispered hoarsely to Lionel. 'For God's sake, get me up.'

Lionel had also seen their knight. He grabbed Gareth by his good arm and helped him haul himself to his feet. Sir Lancelot's face was flushed a deep purple and his eyes were narrowed black slits. Gareth had seen the knight angry before, but never this livid. It was as if a thunderstorm approached, waiting for its moment to break. Sir Lancelot seized Gareth's chin, turning his head this way and that, examining the wound and how it bled. He released him just as abruptly and

Gareth steeled himself for the blow that he was sure must follow.

'You fool!' Sir Lancelot shouted. 'Imbecile! Did I teach you nothing? Are you a babe playing with a stick? He laid a trap for you and you ran straight into it. One of the oldest and feeblest tricks there is, and you fell for it without thinking!'

'My lord,' began Gareth feebly. The cut he'd taken burned badly as he tried to talk. 'I . . .'

'You are useless!' bellowed Lancelot. 'How dare you enter into a challenge that shames me before the king and the whole court!'

For one wild moment Gareth wanted to shout back at his knight, to say that it was not Lancelot who had been kicked to the ground in front of the king, his brothers, and every woman in the court. But of course it was. Gareth was Lancelot's man. His loss was Lancelot's, and Lionel's and even Brendon's.

'You are more fit for wielding a broom than a sword on the battlefield!' Now Gareth wished Lancelot would hit him. The blow would be easier to take than this furious tirade. 'You will get to the scullery where I don't have to look at you, and you will take orders from the lowest maid there until you prove you are fit to take orders from a man!'

Gareth's head snapped up. 'My lord, if you . . .' he began to plead, pain and blood filling his mouth, flavouring his shame.

'You dare question me, sirrah!' Sir Lancelot roared. 'You shame me before all the world and then you have the gall to play dumb?'

'No, my lord,' whispered Gareth. Hanging his head, he turned away. Lionel reached a hand towards him, and Gareth brushed it off. His sword and shield still lay on the ground. He did not dare stop to collect them. Alone, Squire Gareth, son of King Lot, wounded and without help, angled his path towards Camelot's great hall, and the kitchen gardens behind it, swearing with each halting step that he would accept this last and harshest punishment, and that no man would see him cry.

ELEVEN

Over the next few days, Gareth more than once considered taking his own life. Surely God's damnation would be easier to bear than Sir Lancelot's. Word of his punishment was swiftly communicated to the kitchens, and those who served there were more than happy to become his guards and masters. No task was too mean, too long or too dirty to be given him. No taunt was too coarse when the hands he had thought well hardened by sword and leather began to bleed from scrubbing great iron kettles or bleaching yards of linens. He saw Rosy once in the yard as he staggered under a yoke of slop buckets on his way to the pig sty. She turned swiftly away from him. He did not have the strength to pretend he did not see her smirk.

Geraint and Gawain came to sigh over him, and Agravain to scold and to remind him he had been warned. Lionel came once, to say he had Gareth's arms in his keeping. He also told how both Gawain and Geraint had been to Sir Lancelot, and the king, to try to lift Gareth's punishment, or at least set a limit on it, but it was to no avail. Sir Lancelot was within his right, and the king would never violate that.

So Gareth worked himself until exhaustion smothered

thought. He curled up on his hard pallet in the corner of the great hall – creeping in only after all the others had settled themselves to sleep – and tried not to wish himself dead. He had earned this. He would bear it. He would find a way to prove himself. He must.

On the morning of the sixth day of his exile, Gareth trudged out from the keep in the frigid damp of dawn, a birch switch clutched in his hand. Pol, the scullions' master, had woken him while it was still dark. Grinning, Pol told Gareth that the pig-keeper's boy was down, his leg having been torn by one of his own charges, and it was for Gareth to take his place.

So Gareth walked through the town behind the herd of tan and pink swine, breathing in their stench, which matched the stench of their keeper, a mottled brown man named Tiegh. At first it was a bright relief to get away from the stink of the midden and the laundry kettles and out into the fresh air. Tiegh was a silent man, disinclined to taunt or shout. The pigs themselves seemed to know where they were going and as soon as they reached the wood's edge, they scattered eagerly among the trees, grunting with delight and rooting about for any of the previous year's acorns that the squirrels might have hidden.

Tiegh seemed unconcerned that his charges had galloped off. He sat down between the roots of a broad and crooked tree. 'Keep watch,' he said, pulling his filthy hood over his filthy face. With no more than that, the man leaned against the tree trunk and promptly fell asleep.

Gareth sat on a cold stone and dug the butt of his birch rod into the mud. The dappled sun was pleasant and the birds sang loudly overhead, proclaiming love and calling challenges. It was the most peace he'd known in days, and of course, his heavy thoughts thronged to fill the quiet.

He had relived the moment of his defeat a thousand times.

He should have known, should have seen Sir Kai's trick for what it was. He was a fool, and it did not matter if the whole of the court thought so, it was that Sir Lancelot thought it that burned as freshly as it had when he had been ordered from the field.

The other thing that haunted him was the news that had come with Lionel. Gawain and Geraint had failed to get Sir Lancelot to set a limit on his penance. What if the knight did not mean for the punishment to end? What if the humiliation had been too great and he did not intend to recall Gareth to his service?

Leave now, despair whispered to Gareth as he sat in the forest shadows listening to the pigs' distant grunting and Tiegh's matching snores. *Do not beg, or force your brothers to beg for you. Go back to Gododdin, and let that be an end.*

For an end it would be, an exile shorter than death, but no less certain. He would never be admitted to the court of Camelot again if he left it so ignobly.

But what would he be returning to if he went back to the great keep at Gododdin? For him, the place of his birth was a place of vanishings. His mother had gone away when he could barely walk, and had never returned. When he was still a boy, his sister, Tania, had met the most violent of deaths, and she was but a day in her grave when Gawain had set out on the road down to Camelot. It had felt like a miracle when Geraint had shaken him awake in the cold light of dawn a few months later and told him that they were disappearing too, going down south to Camelot to join Gawain. Before that moment, his boy's heart had assumed that like mother and sister, Gawain was gone forever.

Until now, it had always been easier to put memories of his days in Gododdin aside, to look forward to a brave future. He was a city man, and Lancelot's man. But that had vanished now, as surely as his mother and sister, and unlike his elder brother, he might not see it again. Could he make himself walk back into the nightmare that was his only other home?

Hoofbeats drumming hard startled Gareth out of his grim reverie. A company galloped fast from the north, growing nearer with every heartbeat. Before he could stop himself, Gareth ran out through the bracken to see who rode so fast.

They were a battered, mud-stained cadre. Five men, he counted reflexively, pelting hard up the track as if the devil was at their heels. To his surprise, he saw they were led by a woman as pale, battered and mud-stained as any of them. Foam flew from the mouths of their unkempt ponies and for a moment Gareth thought they would tear straight past him.

But no. 'You there!' the woman cried as she reined up sharply beside him.

Gareth bridled at the rough greeting, before he remembered how he must seem standing there reeking of pig with his villein's tunic flapping loose about his knees. But this lady could not throw stones. Her dress was so muddy and salt-stained, he was hard-pressed to tell what its colour had once been. Her hair tumbled in elf-locks around her shoulders and the hands that gripped her nag's reins were swollen and cut by some recent hardship. It was only the gold at her throat and wrists that told him she *was* a lady.

'We are come from Cambryn to Queen Guinevere,' the lady declared. Her voice was harsh with weariness. 'Can any nearby take us to her?'

Cambryn? The heavy accent on her words reminded Gareth of the lilt in the queen's voice. She could well be of the same country. *What news is this?*

Gareth collected himself, and bowed. 'I am of Camelot, my lady,' he said. *Let Tiegh gather in his own pigs.* 'I can take you.'

'Quickly then,' she ordered. 'We cannot be delayed another moment!'

Gareth bowed again. 'Of course, my lady. This way, my lady.' He gestured up the track.

She bit her lip, the skinny pony under her dancing even as it blew hard from its run. 'Can you ride at all?'

Gareth wasn't sure whether to laugh or hurl the question back at her. 'Some, my lady.'

'Up behind Captain Hale then. You can guide us from there.'

Would you'd have me behind you, I might guide you well from there, he thought, stung pride making him lewd. But he reminded himself with one glance that something was badly wrong here and did as he was ordered. He swung himself easily onto the rough blanket that was this Captain Hale's only saddle. Hale saw how practised Gareth's movements were and frowned. But the lady's attention was already on the way ahead. She dug her heels into the pony's side. The beast gave a high whicker of protest, then he too obeyed her.

That they had missed the main road somehow did not give Gareth any good opinion of their skills at direction, but his guidance, shouted into the captain's ear as he took the lead, brought them to it soon enough. The road's stones had been laid in Roman times. They were now cracked and uneven, but they served well enough to bring the ragged troop up to the town's wide open gates.

Many from the country gaped when they first came to Camelot's city. They stared at the great warehouses and straight streets, and the boisterous crowds of people that filled them. Gareth himself had once, clinging then to the back of a horse Geraint had given his silver arm ring to buy. But neither Captain Hale nor his lady seemed to see anything but the way forward. The city turned to field and orchard, and at last the great keep's gates loomed before them.

'God be praised!' the captain breathed. These were the

first words he had spoken that were not Gareth's directions.

'Amen,' answered the lady as she kicked her horse again, trying to urge a little more speed from it. Her eyes were nearly as wild as the beast's by now.

'If my lady permits, I can take you through!' bawled Gareth over the captain's head. 'I am known here.'

The lady reined her pony back just a little, clearly considering whether he was merely bragging, and whether it would cause more delay to believe him or to doubt him. In the end, she nodded. Gareth slipped off the captain's pony with his own prayer of gratitude. His pride was not so far gone that he wanted to be seen coming back to the hall jolting along behind an outland man-at-arms, whatever the emergency.

Striding briskly, Gareth led them up to the iron-banded gates of Camelot's keep.

'The lady of Cambryn to see the queen,' he announced to Shahen and Rafe who stood guard at this hour, helms on their heads and spears in their hands. They gaped at him, and at the bedraggled crowd behind him. But for all his recent humiliations, Gareth was still the king's blood. They raised their spears to salute those who accompanied him and let them all pass.

Gareth and the newcomers crossed the yard, which was alive with folk going about their morning tasks: drawing water, carrying baskets of food and linens to and from the hall's outbuildings. It was another city within these walls, and just as lively as the one outside. Many heads turned to see him back early and in such company.

'Joss!' he shouted to a small boy scattering a pan of crumbs to the chickens. 'Run and find Sir Kai! There are . . .'

But word had flown ahead, and Sir Kai emerged from the great hall. He came down the marble steps, dressed in his customary black, his golden chain gleaming in the midday sun. That Gareth brought these people had clearly not been assurance enough for his uncle, because in addition to the pair of serving boys who followed at his heels, Marcus and Lud came close behind, and they both wore their swords.

'God be with you, my lady, an' you come in peace,' Sir Kai said stiffly. 'I am Kai ap Cynyr, Seneschal to Arthur the High King.'

Gareth, in his servile role, held the drooping head of the lady's over-weary pony so that she might dismount beside her captain.

Gareth wondered if this lady, so tired and so strained, would try her commanding tongue against Sir Kai. But confronted with his dignity and signs of rank on conspicuous display, the lady's manner changed at once.

'My Lord Seneschal,' she said, dropping a deep curtsey. 'I am Lynet Carnbrea, daughter of Lord Kenan, Steward of Cambryn. I and mine have travelled hard these past days to reach the High Queen, Guinevere. We have grave news from her homelands and we beg to be granted audience at once. We have been delayed too long on road and sea already.'

Kai's keen eyes swept over the ragged company, including Gareth standing there holding the halter of a trembling pony. He nodded. 'Huldan, Joss, take these horses and their masters to the stables. See that Carrog is summoned at once that they may be made comfortable. Gareth.' It was no accident that Sir Kai had left off his rank. Gareth opened his mouth to correct it, but his uncle gave him no time. 'As you have brought them this far, will you conduct this lady to the queen's court? I will go at once to her majesty. Please.' Sir Kai swept his free hand back, indicating the entrance to the hall, and bowing as far as his crutch permitted. 'Enter and be welcome to Camelot.'

Captain Hale hesitated, saying something softly to the lady. She shook her head and touched his arm making an equally soft reply. He glowered at the hall's entrance, as if promising that he would tear it apart with his bare hands should any wrong be done there. Only then did he turn and follow the rest of his men as they were led to the stables along with the overwrought horses. Lady Lynet visibly gathered her own dignity around her. She lifted her torn hems and walked up the steps. Gareth caught Sir Kai's eye as he hurried beside her, and saw there both mischief and warning.

What do you think I'm going to do, uncle? It was the wrong question to ask himself. He knew full well what Sir Kai was thinking, and that knowledge rankled. He ducked his head and lengthened his stride to get ahead of the lady in order to conduct her through the hall.

The great keep of Camelot had been raised by the Romans and restored to glory by the High King's father Uther Pendragon. Arthur himself had seen to improvements in both the defences and the decoration. The queen's court, where Gareth took the guests, was in the middle of the keep, open to the sky. The bright sun filled the yard with the light and warmth of spring. Flagged stones paved its floor and graceful pillars supported the arched doorways. A marble fountain made cool and pleasant music in its centre and at its base spread a white and sapphire mosaic of swans. Around the edges, song birds added their own music from airy cages of carved wood and ivory. It was a pleasure just to enter the peaceful place.

Beside the fountain stood the queen's chair of dark oak carved with images of swans with their wings spread in flight, or with their necks twined around those of their mates. On the chair's high back, a swan and a dragon bowed to each other in grave courtesy. Other chairs, less grand, but comfortable, were arrayed before this seat, inviting guests to rest themselves.

The lady did not do so. She paced to the fountain, and stood watching the fall of the water into the polished bowl.

Gareth, still playing his part of good servant, had retired to stand beside an ivory cage filled with finches. In so doing, it seemed he had rendered himself invisible. Lady Lynet did not so much as glance at him. He did not mind. It gave him a chance to watch her. Her face was gaunt, but that was from hard travel, not from nature. Her form and figure were round and full beneath her travel-stained clothing. She looked close to exhaustion in that moment, resting her hands heavily on the fountain's rim. Her boots, he saw below her tattered hems, were torn, and her feet oozed red. Gareth bit his lip, knowing well the intensity of such discomfort from after a hard march.

'My lady?' he said tentatively. 'May I fetch you a blanket or some other wrap?'

But she shook her head in answer. Gareth had the thought that she might not trust her voice. Despite this, she drew her chin back and lifted herself up proudly.

Gareth found himself nodding in approval. He could believe this bedraggled lady was one of the queen's own. For all she had been honed to a sharp edge by some recent disaster, were she dressed for court she would shine.

A parade's worth of footsteps approached from the corridor, and they both turned as the royal party entered. The High Queen, Guinevere, came first, with High King Arthur half a step behind her. Lady Lynet knelt at once. Behind the royal couple came one-handed Sir Bedivere, and Sir Lancelot beside him. Surprise widened Gareth's eyes, and he ducked his head fast, to escape the displeasure in his knight's eyes as Sir Lancelot saw him kneeling there.

But even more surprising was that behind these, walking with slow and measured dignity, came Merlin, in his heavy black robes and carrying his white staff.

With them came a small flood of servants bearing chairs, including the king's dragon-carved seat that was a match for the queen's. They also brought boards and trestles, linens, and platters heaped high with breads, cheeses, a steaming bowl of oaten porridge, jugs of cider and cream. Sir Kai himself carried a jug of wine, and a boy beside him hefted a crock of water for mixing with it. These things were set out efficiently as the queen gestured for the lady to rise.

'Please,' she said, taking her own chair, with King Arthur sitting beside her. 'Sit and be refreshed.'

But Lady Lynet remained on her feet, although she swayed. 'Forgive me, Majesty, but I will not. My news will not wait.'

This seemed to startle the queen, and her face grew even more grave. 'Speak your news then.'

The depth of the lady's weariness told in her hesitation. 'Your Majesty . . . Your Majesties . . . my father, your steward Lord Kenan of Cambryn, is dead. Murdered at the hands of . . . of his only son, my brother Colan Carnbrea.'

Gareth's chest contracted. In a single instant, he was back in the dim hall of his childhood, with Geraint beside him. 'Tania's dead, Gareth. She fell from the heights.'

'He pushed her.' That was Gawain, grim and hoarse from the tears he had shed. 'She was pleading for her life and our father threw her down to the stones.'

The memory of fear, incomprehension, and deep and sudden grief for the sister who had been as a mother to him blinded Gareth for a space of time measured in heavy heart-beats. When he came to himself again, Gareth looked afresh at the lady who stood white with outrage and sorrow before the High King and Queen. His fallen heart went out to her at once in sympathy.

The queen too was pale with shock. 'What you tell us grieves me deeply,' she said softly. 'What occasioned this bloody outrage?'

Lady Lynet swallowed. Whatever memory had risen in her, it caused her to tremble and the skin of her gaunt face drew even more tightly across her bones. 'He feared, Your Majesties, that my father was mistaken in his loyalty to the High King. He feared that nothing would be done to prevent the war that now looms within the heart of the Dumonii lands, because nothing was done to check the outrage Sir Tristan committed against King Mark, nor to compensate for it once it was done.'

Gareth knew he should be infuriated that a bedraggled country woman would accuse his king and queen of neglect to their faces, and then heap shame upon the memory of a knight of the Round Table, but the cold, flat voice with which she delivered these words, the understanding that she spoke them with the last of her strength and nerve, diffused his anger. The silence stretched on so long that Gareth's ears began to ring. Not even Sir Lancelot or Sir Bedivere rose in defence of Sir Tristan.

'We are rebuked,' said King Arthur, at last, inclining his head towards Lady Lynet. 'And it is not unjust. Were I to say there were reasons for what was done and left undone, they would be of little interest and less consolation to you, my lady.' He met Lady Lynet's eyes, and spoke firmly, in a voice that had taken men to battle, and laid down the conditions of peace when that battle was over. 'But you have come to us now and you have been heard. You will not go away without all the aid it is in our power to provide.'

'Nor will you go alone,' replied the queen, her voice full of her own power to command. 'I too hear you, Lady Lynet. It is plain from all you have said that I must return with you to help bring matters to a just and honourable close in the lands of my birth.'

These words seemed to drain the last of the lady's strength. She began to tremble in earnest, groping behind her for some support. Gareth ran forward at once, pushing a chair into place so that she might sit while a servant pressed a goblet of watered wine into her dirty and bloodied hands.

Gareth's heart swelled with feeling too great to be denied. He went down on one knee to the king and queen, and to his own knight who watched his temerity with burning eyes. But he would speak. He could not remain silent anymore.

'Your Majesties, I beg you, let me take up my sword in this lady's cause.'

Lady Lynet stared open-mouthed for a moment, then shoved the cup back into the servant's hands. '*This* is how you honour our plea for help?' she gasped hoarsely. She tried to stand, but she only fell back into her chair. 'By letting your kitchen boy mock me!'

The court erupted at once into laughter. A bright red flush that had nothing to do with shame crept up Lady Lynet's cheeks.

With one hard glance, the queen silenced the laughter. 'Forgive us, Lady Lynet,' she said, as soon as she could be heard. 'This man is my nephew, Gareth, squire to Sir Lancelot, and son of Lot, King of Gododdin.'

Lady Lynet stared, and Gareth bowed his head to her.

She made no apology. She shoved herself back onto her wounded feet, outrage still colouring her cheeks. 'I was told this court had a love of games, but I did not believe Your Majesty would make sport of me when I come on so urgent an errand.'

The queen turned her eyes to Gareth and he saw the flash of steel in her gaze. He understood that to do anything other than retire to his former position beside the finches' cage would be to risk true wrath from her. But as he backed away, he glanced at Sir Lancelot. The knight's unforgiving appraisal seemed to have mellowed somewhat. Gareth's chest constricted with hope.

The queen was on her own feet and crossing the court.

'Be assured, Lady Lynet, no one here mocks you, least of all myself.' She wrapped Lady Lynet's hands around the wine cup again. 'Drink lady, I beg you. Let us give you rest. You have been heard, and will not be misused nor abandoned. I swear it before God most high, and on the memory of my own father.'

Lady Lynet searched the queen's face for a moment, looking for what, Gareth could not tell. The queen released her, stepping back a single pace. The lady then raised her cup, to the queen, and to the king, and drank deeply.

Gareth felt motion behind him. 'I think you'd better take your leave,' murmured a man's soft voice in his ear.

Gareth bristled. He wanted desperately to stay to find out if his plea would be honoured, but he also knew full well he was on a precarious footing. He nodded once, silently, and backed away, slipping sideways across the nearest threshold. He turned, and to his surprise, saw Merlin standing in the corridor, his long, wrinkled hands wrapped around the white staff that never left his side.

'Be careful what you wish for, Squire Gareth,' said the ancient seer. 'You may get it, and I cannot see where it will lead us all.'

Merlin left Gareth there, returning at once to the sunlit court to join the council that would now take place. Gareth gaped after him for a moment, the words tolling in his ears like the echo of doom. Then, all thought of doom cleared away. Merlin, whose eyes saw the future and in whose hands lay the power of the invisible country, had called him *squire*. He would have his place again. He would have his chance to prove himself, to Sir Lancelot, the king, his brothers, and all the world, the Lady Lynet included.

All weight lifted from his heart, Gareth strode lightly back to the kitchen to await the reprieve he now knew would soon come.

TWELVE

By the time Queen Guinevere sought her private chamber, night had fallen. The evening meal had passed without attendance from her or the High King. The time had instead been spent in close council with Lynet Carnbrea over how things stood in Cambryn. So much said, so much left unsaid. Guinevere sat down in front of the fire while her ladies bustled around her.

This was a room of warmth and comfort, furnished both to aid her repose and to show the wealth of her rank. But tonight she might have been a beggar in the meanest hovel for all the ease it gave her. Every word Lynet spoke had seemed an accusation to Guinevere, a condemnation of the careful and patient plans she had helped to lay. Patience cost, never as much as rash action, but as Lynet had testified, the price could still be terribly high.

Lady Sabia, a young matron with chestnut hair and a milk-maid's fair skin, came around her chair and knelt. 'You are exhausted, Majesty. You should come to bed.'

Guinevere smiled a little. 'No, Sabia. Leave me be. I will sit up awhile yet.'

'As you will, Majesty.' Her lady bowed her head and retired

at once. They were all well used to her habits, these wives, daughters and sisters of old friends and new allies. They did not question her when she asked to be left alone. They instead took themselves out of her line of sight so that she could sit in silence.

Guinevere stared into the fire's white and blue heart, and slowly, as if she must peel back the layers of her own mind, she let herself think on Cambryn.

As soon as she had heard Lynet begin to speak, Guinevere had been transported back to the *castell* whose stones had sheltered her through infancy and childhood. She had played in the hills and the yards, cowered with a child's fear from the storms, shivered through the long winters, and celebrated each spring as the thaw freed up the river so the tinning could begin again.

She stood many times beside her father, mother and both her foster sisters in the great hall, where Lynet said murder had been done. She was at their side on that same dais when Arthur first came to them, the moment, though she knew it not, her girl's life had ended and her woman's life began. She stood there again to receive the body of her father, brought home from the great war, and again to have the crown placed on her head and to hear the oath of the chieftains and nobles as their queen. She sat on the throne in that hall when Arthur came back from the battle of Badon, but it was in the makeshift bower by the river that he had asked if she would deign to honour the promise made years before, and consent to become his wife.

She had not been surprised. It was more than an alliance of power and peoples between them, and she had longed for that moment with all her heart. She had prepared for it, causing the Round Table to be built, the greatest addition to a royal dowry that she could conceive. She did this although one of her sisters had warned her not to hope too deeply for the return of a man who had given no promise, and the other . . .

The other had warned her it would mean her death, and it was then Guinevere had first seen the cold glow of madness in Morgaine *verch* Igraine's black eyes.

That threat, that promise, came back to her with the news that her steward Kenan was dead by his own son's hand. Guinevere closed her eyes. She had never met Colan Carnbrea. He had not yet been born when she left Cambryn to become Arthur's wife and queen. It was Kenan's father, Kanasek, who had been her steward then, and all said that Kenan was the image of his father. So, she had thought, who better to entrust oversight of her homelands to? He had done his duty with honour and courage always. How could such a man have fathered a serpent to sting his own heel?

The answer came to her dark as a thundercloud and Guinevere shivered. *That is why my thoughts turn so easily to Morgaine. She is on the move once more. She said she would take my home, and all else that was mine. It would seem she is at last ready to make her attempt.*

She heard a soft tread outside the door, and an equally soft knock. Despite her fears, Guinevere smiled. Sabia went to open the door, but Guinevere did not need to turn to know who it was.

Arthur stood in the doorway, his fond blue eyes shining in the light of the tapers and the fire. Guinevere stood to greet him, marvelling at how, after all this time, the merest sight of this man could still quicken her heart, be it ever so weighted down.

Her waiting ladies did not need to be commanded to withdraw as the king entered. Guinevere had long ago made it plain that unless other orders were given, she alone would wait on her husband. Some took themselves out into the corridor where they might be summoned easily, some retired to the alcove that held the great bed where they might be out of the way and yet still present should there be need.

Arthur came forward, and Guinevere opened her arms to him. For a long time they held each other, and she sighed, savouring the familiar strength of his arms that encased her in a warmth dearer and deeper than the rarest fur could ever bring.

'I am so sorry about Kenan,' Arthur said. 'He was a good man.'

Arthur had met the steward but a handful of times, but he remembered Kenan, as he remembered anyone of good worth. It was one of his many gifts as a leader of men.

'He was,' Guinevere nodded. 'And his elder daughter is a fine woman. I would have kept her here if she would have stayed.' She stood back from Arthur so that he could take the chair beside the fire. Guinevere poured a little of the fortified wine from the graceful jar waiting on the table and handed the gilded cup to him before pouring a cup for herself.

Arthur swirled the goblet and sipped thoughtfully. 'And what of the younger daughter who comes to us now?'

Guinevere said nothing as she resumed her own seat, calling to mind the young woman's hard face and harder words. 'It is pain that makes her bitter, pain and fear. She carries both with good reason.'

'That she does.' He took another sip of the wine and he too looked into the fire. 'I'd say a curse on the head of Sir Tristan if I knew one strong enough.'

'Add one for Iseult on my behalf . . . ah, no. God forgive me.' Guinevere rubbed her brow. 'They suffered enough for their foolishness.'

'And now we suffer for it. You most of all, my wife.' He reached out with his free hand and touched her fingertips.

She smiled at the gesture, but she still shook her head. 'The foolishness I suffer from is my own,' she told him. 'I should have gone home before. But I thought I should be here, keeping the heart of our lands strong for you. Well.' She set her cup down as a wave of illness born of far too much gall swept through her. 'In taking such good care of the heart, I have helped sicken the limbs.'

'It is not so far gone yet, Guinevere,' said Arthur firmly. 'We have time to make this right.'

'God grant it be so.' She could not bear to look at him. She could only watch the fire, searching the patterns of the flame for some better omen than the ones she felt lurking in the shadows at her back.

'What worries you?'

'Do you truly need to ask?'

'Morgaine.' Arthur whispered the word. He who had faced a hundred hosts in battle without flinching feared that by speaking that one word too loudly they might somehow call her up like the Devil from Hell. 'You see her hand in this?'

'Everywhere,' said Guinevere flatly. 'Since Morgause's death, I have known she would return for me. She swore it would be so.'

'And yet you will go to Cambryn?'

'What happens if I do not?' Guinevere set her cup down and spoke bitterly to the fire. 'The Dumonii fall into chaos, and she takes them all. Then, perhaps she makes common cause with the kings of Eire over the matter of Sir Tristan, and they come with their swords and their howling, and then what will be left of Camelot and the Britons?' Guinevere felt nerve and sinew tighten within her. 'She will not destroy all we have built, my husband. God and Mary help me, I will not permit it. Not without a fight.'

She met Arthur's eyes then, and saw a resolve to mirror her own. He feared this particular war, a thing which perhaps only she knew, but he would not fail to fight it. Nor would he deny her part in it, for which she blessed him.

None of this meant he would not try to shelter her all he could. 'Let Merlin come with . . .' he began.

'No.'

'Guinevere . . .'

'No, my lord. I will not.' He did not understand her refusal. He never did. On this one point there could never be agreement between them, and it pained Guinevere that it should be so. She knew it also pained Arthur.

'He can see farther in these matters than those of us with only mortal eyes,' said Arthur gently, reasonably. 'If this is Morgaine's doing, you will need all the forewarning that can be had.'

'Forgive me, my lord, but what good did his sight ever bring?' she replied, also in tones of simple reason. 'To speak with him is to bring disaster. To not speak with him is to pine away for wishing one had, because no matter how great the trouble his visions have brought, we cannot help but say, "This time I will do better if I can but know what will come."' She folded her arms, gripping her elbows tightly, trying to bring some warmth to herself. 'Only God can know enough to see tomorrow in safety.'

There it stood. He would not give Merlin up, and she would not accept him. It was as it had been since the days before their marriage, and would be until the day one of the three of them died.

Thankfully, Arthur made no move to continue his argument. Had he ordered her to take Merlin to Cambryn, she would have done so, but the command and its acceptance would have cost them both something. Perhaps she was being a fool not to take a sorcerer where she knew another lurked. But she had seen too much of the invisible world and the havoc it wreaked upon the lives of mortals. She would not turn to it, even when she must stand before it. Not even to save Cambryn.

God will provide another way. Mother Mary will not desert us in this, she told herself firmly.

'Now that we sit in such perfect harmony,' quipped Arthur mildly, 'I must raise another dull and uninteresting question.'

Guinevere smiled, chuckling softly. 'Speak your dull question, my husband. I am well disposed to hear it.'

He set his cup down, face and posture shifting subtly, and Guinevere knew his mind was turned from their room and the two of them to maps and plans, men and the thousand logistics of even the smallest battle. 'You are certain Lancelot is the one you would have lead your contingent? Gawain will go, or Bedivere . . .'

She shook her head with a small smile. 'I do not flatter myself that my mere reappearance as Cambryn's queen will at once lay to rest all grievances. There may well be challenges to whatever ruling I make, and I will need a champion. I do not like his manners either, but of all your men, it is Lancelot who can best answer such a challenge.'

He did not reply at once. He was weighing options, she knew, carefully considering and discarding other possibilities. At last he nodded, and his gaze turned outward again, seeing her fully once more.

'I wish he was not, but he is.' Arthur leaned forward, and softly traced her cheek with one square-tipped finger. It was a familiar touch that brought with it a kind of aching gladness. 'Will my queen be angered if I beg her to take care?'

She reached up and caught his hand, pressing it to her cheek so she could fully savour the warmth of his touch. 'Never, Arthur.'

After that, there was no more need for words between them for a long time.

*   *   *

Lynet lay on the great bed, afloat on a sea of comfort like nothing she had ever known, and could not rest. She stared up at the unfamiliar shadow of the canopy overhead, her blood thrumming through her veins. She was safe, she was exhausted. She longed for sleep. Why would it not come?

She could not have asked for the audience to go better. Despite the mistake of courtesy regarding the kitchen boy squire, Queen Guinevere and King Arthur had responded fully to her demands. The council had gone on for almost half the day in that courtyard with its laughing fountain. The clouds and sun came and went and the wind blew down bringing promise of rain while Lynet told the whole of her tale to queen and king, knights and the silent, black form of Merlin the sorcerer, whose gaze never left her.

There would be yet more talk tomorrow of strategy and men and numbers. A mass would be said for Bishop Austell by Camelot's bishop. Perhaps then she could mourn properly, and the sight of him vanishing before her eyes would fade.

What was most important though, was the queen's promise. Queen Guinevere would return with them. There was no way to be certain that the queen's presence would bring stability to the land, but should there be those still inclined to war, she would be a far stronger rallying point than the untried daughters of her steward.

Let Laurel be safe, Lynet prayed silently as she lay there in darkness. *Let her be brave. We will come soon.*

She had prayed this same prayer countless times; as they walked across the country, as Captain Hale bargained for the horses with the valley chieftain whom they could barely understand, as they galloped pell-mell up the Roman road, and as they slept in the open huddled together beneath clouds and stars. She had clutched at her pouch and the mirror within, wishing to the depths of her soul that she could be alone for one moment, so that she could summon Ryol. He said he could show her all that was hidden; surely he could show her Laurel.

Lynet blinked. Daere, the maid Queen Guinevere had given her, snored softly in her truckle bed by the fire. She was alone now, or as good as. She did not need to wait anymore.

She fumbled with the purse's ties and brought out the mirror. Even a night beneath the bed coverings had not warmed the metal of its frame. She cupped it in her hands, gazing at her own face in its flawless glass. She was thinner than she had been, and the circles under her eyes had darkened in just these few days. It did not matter. What mattered was to reach for Ryol. She called out with all her strength of mind, and let that call stretch out, unreeling like a ribbon before her until the darkness reached up and pulled her down as if into a deeper sleep.

She woke in the garden. Sunlight poured down on her and the air was sweet and heavy with the summer scents of herbs and blossoms. Those same blossoms bobbed pleasantly in the gentle breeze that caressed her. The grass was soft beneath her slippers, and her feet no longer ached when she stood.

Ryol stepped out from behind his birch tree, looking just as he had before, in his ochre tunic and brown breeches. He came forward swiftly and knelt before her.

'You have returned, my lady.' He took her hand and pressed it to his brow. 'I feared . . .'

This flood of feeling startled Lynet and she gestured for him to rise. 'What could you fear?'

His slight hesitation told Lynet that there was in him a thought he decided not to speak. Instead he said, 'A fine riddle, my lady. What do shadows fear?' He smiled as he stood.

'Have you an answer?' The peace and warmth of the

garden worked on her as before. Her immediate fears were left behind with her body and she could indulge in a small exchange of wit.

'Of course.' Seriousness, as sudden and unexpected as his emotional greeting had been, took him. 'A shadow fears the light, my lady.'

The skin on the back of her neck prickled strangely at these words, and she could find no answer. So it was she who changed the subject now. 'You told me you could show me distant happenings. Can you take me to Cambryn and show me what is happening there?'

'It is a simple matter, my lady. Will you walk with me?' Ryol bowed, holding out his arm.

Lynet laid her hand on his arm. Some part of her had expected his touch to be cool, like that of the *morverch*, or the mirror itself. But he was as warm in his person as any mortal man. Ryol led Lynet between the silver-skinned rowan trees and out into a second garden that sloped up and away from the first. The plants here were homely herbs: fern, tansy, sorrel, sage and rosemary. Their scents were sharp, going straight to her blood and making it course more strongly. The touch of the air around her felt deeply familiar, but she could not have said why.

They passed a hazel tree. Ryol turned abruptly to the left, and all at once before them spread the *castell* of Cambryn. Lynet cried out in gladness before she saw that something was wrong. The stone walls of the cots glittered strangely, as if cut from crystal. She moved forward, and they rippled with each step she took, like a gemstone seen through water. Anything she gazed at directly was solid enough, until she moved. Then, it rippled and receded again.

'What is this?' she demanded. 'What is happening to me?'

'It is not you,' Ryol assured her quickly 'These things are

not real, my lady. They are reflections only. Tell me, what do you want most to see?'

'Laurel,' she answered at once.

Ryol led her forward, sweeping the way in front with his hand, as a man might clear branches from his path. The reflection of her home tore apart like scraps of mist, passing insubstantially by her shoulders, and revealing a new place ahead. Fear rose in her, but Ryol only tightened his grip a little. He pulled her through the fog that had been made of her home. Now she could see they stood beneath the eastern watchtower. The sky was heavy with the clouds foretelling another squall. The grass bent beneath the wind, but this wind Lynet could not feel, nor could she feel the cold that surely must fill the air. To her, it was still as warm as summer, and this made her shiver harder than any natural wind could.

A plume of smoke rose from the tower's open top. Beside it stood a single tall and slender figure. Lynet knew at once that this was Laurel, come out to look over the land for any sign of danger, or hope. Three men stood at the tower's entrance-way, all alert, all eyeing each other. Two were strangers, Peran and Mesek's men. The last was Daveth, a square youth with a thatch of brown hair. He was Captain Hale's eldest nephew, his sister's son, and seeing him there brought a rush of relief to Lynet. He would watch Laurel well. Any danger to her would have to get past him, and would not find that easy.

'Can we see her more closely?'

'Yes . . .' The distraction in Ryol's voice made Lynet look at him. He was casting about like a hound uncertain of a scent. At the edges of her vision, the world glittered and rippled again.

'What is it?'

'I don't know. Something. Forgive me . . .' He reached out his free hand and slashed it through the air, tearing through the glittering whirl of colour. Tower and Laurel and guardsmen all fluttered away like torn silk, and they were inside.

After a dizzy moment, Lynet recognized Father Lucius's chamber. The priest, as well as being Bishop Austell's assistant, was her father's scribe. His chamber was a place for scraping vellum, mixing inks and copying out letters. Tidy stacks of vellum and parchment lay beside stained mortars and pestles and untrimmed quills. It was frigid in the winter, because the brother would not permit a fire in the room. A great wooden writing table and a high stool stood beside the window that had the most solid shutters in the whole of the keep. On it sat an unfinished page of boldly lettered Latin, probably part of his great work to copy out the psalms. It had been meant as a gift for Lynet's mother, but she had not lived to see it finished. Now father had not either.

Father Lucius was not at his work, however. Instead, at one of the two smaller desks, sat Peran Treanhal. She had not known he could write, but he did so now, slowly and carefully, scratching his quill against the vellum, his fire-ravaged face as hard and grim as if he looked over some losing battle.

'What does he write?' Lynet made to step forward, but Ryol held her back.

'Wait,' he said.

The door opened then, and Mesek walked in. Peran looked up, and in the next breath shot to his feet, knocking the bench backward and dropping the quill, which stabbed down onto his uncompleted letter, leaving a great black blot to drown the words he had laid so carefully down.

'How did you know?' breathed Lynet, but Ryol made no answer.

Mesek regarded Peran with contemptuous eyes. 'So, here you are,' he said with his false mildness. 'The priest told me you had squirrelled yourself away in here.' Mesek was, Lynet saw, very careful not to move any closer.

Peran drew himself up, recovering from his shock. 'A wise man might fear to meet his enemy alone.' He nodded towards the corridor. If there were more men outside, they kept themselves out of sight.

Mesek shrugged. 'Wisdom is one crime I've never been accused of.' Deliberately, he turned his back on Peran, and closed the door.

Peran's fingers rubbed together, itching for a weapon, Lynet was sure. The pebbled skin on the back of his burned hand wrinkled and bunched, but he made no other movement. 'What do you want?'

'To offer you compensation,' replied Mesek, sticking his thumbs in his broad belt. 'For all that you have suffered.'

Wariness filled Lynet, and not a little fear.

Evidently deciding Mesek had not come there to do murder, at least not immediately, Peran reached down to pick up the bench. 'Since I doubt you are about to impale your own head on a pikestaff, what compensation could you offer me?'

'Freedom,' said Mesek simply.

Peran froze, his big hand clamped around the bench's board seat. 'What?'

Mesek crossed the room, peered out of the window and pulled the shutters half closed. Peran stood, the bench forgotten, and stared at the other man as Mesek leaned himself against the wall beside the window. 'You've sold yourself to Morgaine the Sleepless and you are finding that she drives a hard bargain. I've been thinking over all that has happened in these past days, and I've come to say I'll help you out of that bargain, if you're willing.'

Hard and bitter laughter bubbled out of Peran's throat. He marched to the window, pulled open the shutter and looked in all directions before he shut it firmly, plunging the room into twilight. 'If you think you can break a pledge made with the goddess, you are mad.'

'Now, now, Peran. If you keep on you will make me angry.' Mesek stuck his thumbs in his belt again. He wore no weapon openly, of course. Lynet wondered if he had concealed one somewhere. She could not believe he had truly walked into this room unarmed. 'I am come with an honest offer that will profit us both.'

Peran wanted to lash out at the other chieftain. Every hard line of his body said so, but he also was unarmed and it took time to kill someone with hands alone. That left him with only words and it seemed he had but a poor store of those. 'Honest offer? You murdered my son!'

This repetition of his charge left Mesek quite unmoved. Lynet expected he would answer with more scorn. Instead, he said quietly, 'Peran, we both know it is Morgaine who killed your son.'

Lynet gaped at this, but Peran staggered as if he'd been struck. He shook his head violently, seeking to scatter Mesek's words. 'No.'

Slowly Mesek pushed himself away from the wall. Slowly, he took a step forward, and then another. 'She is the reason you came to my doorstep, not some half-starved cows. She sent you to test me in some manner. You failed, and it was your son who paid when the word came from the ravens and their mistress that you must take me down.'

'No!' shouted Peran more towards the door than to Mesek. It was as if he willed it to open, for someone, anyone, to enter and save him from these words.

But Mesek did not relent. 'I was not to fall right away, and not by myself. She does not think so small. Cambryn and its family must come with me. So, rather than let you take your vengeance as you so plainly desired, she ordered you instead to drag me to court so that you could goad the young Colan into breaking the steward's family for her. She likes a broad and open road when she travels, does Morgaine.' Mesek was close enough now to grip the work desk with both hands. 'But there are other powers than hers, Peran. Some of them serve in this place.'

Lynet's throat closed. Ryol's hand tightened around hers, but he showed no trace of surprise.

'You knew!' she cried. In answer, Ryol only held up his other hand to motion her to silence.

Peran had jerked his head around and Mesek's mouth curled into his broad axe-blade of a smile. 'Ah, now you look at me like a man.'

The chieftains faced each other, the desk and smeared letter the only barrier between them. Peran's scarred flesh burned red, but the rest of his face had gone white.

'What do you want?' he croaked, so softly that Lynet could barely make out the words.

'What you want,' answered Mesek. 'To be free of outlanders and sorcerers and madmen. We could be if we held Cambryn.'

'Impossible.' Peran did not move. He was waiting to be contradicted, Lynet realized.

Mesek did not disappoint. 'I don't believe so. I've seen enough of the place now, and of our Lady Laurel and her men. It requires only patience and nerve.'

It was Peran's turn to smile, a mirthless, lopsided grimace. 'The steward's daughters are nothing. They are already dead and this place is Morgaine's.'

Anger roared through Lynet. This man had come demanding justice! They had stood in the midst of death and murder to do right, and he meant to repay them by compounding vile treason!

'You can offer me nothing,' said Peran. Beneath the anger

that stormed through her mind, it occurred to Lynet that
Peran sounded sorry.

'Before you say so, ask yourself, why does Morgaine want
this place? If a fortification was all she wanted, she could
have had Tintagel with much less of a fight. Mark's all but
gone now. She could reach out her hand and snap him in
two, and Arthur's oldest ally in our lands would be gone.
She'd have a dozen clans rally to her side in an instant and
she could take Cambryn at her leisure. But she does not do
this. She bends her will to this place. Why?' Mesek spread
his hands, appealing to Heaven itself, but it was clear that
Heaven or Hell had already provided him the answer.
'Because there's power here. Power that she covets, but could
not reach until the keep was split open for her.'

Silence lingered between the two men. The pebbled
expanse of Peran's scar twitched as if it was a living thing.
His burned fingers rubbed together, fast and hard. Mesek
waited, still and patient, ready to let Peran fight his own
internal battle.

At last, Peran found his ruined voice again. 'You say there
is power here that could overthrow Morgaine?'

Mesek nodded slowly. 'It came from the sea with Kenan's
lady, and she handed it to her daughter when she died.' He
spoke carefully, holding the words out to tempt his enemy.
Lynet felt herself grow cold as she realized what power he
must speak of. Beside her, Ryol had also gone utterly still.

A fresh realization dawned in Peran's eyes. 'This is why
you let yourself be brought here, why you agreed to be heard
by the queen.'

'You also are not so ignorant as you seem.' Mesek leaned
forward again, his voice quiet and urgent. 'Come, Peran. This
is our moment. You are no coward. Let your deeds make
your life something other than a fresh slavery.' He held out
his hand.

Peran did not move, he just stared, his eyes bright with pain and fear. What did he see, what did he remember? Lynet was ready to burst with the need to reach them both, to shout loud enough to bring every man in the keep. She would cry out their treachery to Heaven itself and see them die for it.

Laurel! Laurel! Where are you!

At long last, Peran reached out and clasped Mesek's whole hand with his burned one.

'Good,' said Mesek simply.

'What now?' asked Peran, releasing his grip, as if he did not like the touch of the other man's skin. 'She will come, you know, and soon.'

'I thought as much,' said Mesek, nodding judiciously. 'We must watch our lady Laurel closely, until we can find some hint as to this power her mother left her. Her position now is lonely and precarious, and she is wise enough to know it. She will, I think, resort to it before long. After that, the only question will be whether it is better for our ends to lead her to the altar or to the graveyard. Now I'll go. It would not be good for us to be found lingering together. Someone might suspect. We'll talk again later.'

Lynet could stand no more. 'Get me out of here!' she cried to Ryol. The spirit nodded and tugged on her hand, walking her back and away. Walls closed about the room, and they stood instead in the empty and silent corridor.

'You knew!' cried Lynet again. 'You felt this somehow, before it had even begun.'

'I did,' Ryol acknowledged soberly. 'It is part of my service that I must sense the secret threats to those who are my masters.'

A dozen thoughts lanced through Lynet, but only one went straight to her heart. 'Then you knew of Colan's conspiracy, you knew how . . .'

Ryol did not wait for her to finish. 'I did,' he admitted.
'And you did nothing!'

'What could I do?' he asked quietly. 'Your sister would not
come to me, nor accept any service I might give.'

Lynet bit her lip, and felt nothing at all. 'Laurel must be
told what these two plan.' For all she stood surrounded by
the reflection of her home, she felt the distance between
herself and Laurel like a rift in her soul.

Something Lynet could not read shone deep in Ryol's dark
eyes. She did not care, so long as there was a way to give
warning to Laurel. 'It will be difficult,' he told her.

'What must you do?'

Ryol shook his head. 'It is not for me to do, but for you,
lady. You are the one who is still rooted in the mortal world,
and what's more, you are bound to your sister by blood and
sympathy.'

'Then what must I do?'

'You must make of yourself a vision, lady. You must craft
a shape of yourself, and you must send that forth into the
mortal world.'

She hesitated for a single heartbeat. This was strange
beyond words, but if it enabled her to reach Laurel, then she
would do it. 'How?'

Ryol nodded, as if in approval. Still his eyes shone strangely
as he spoke, and Lynet felt something in her clench tight.

'You must will it into being. I will help you. We must go
to your sister first.'

He took her hand again and steered her down the corridor,
sweeping his hand before him. In dizzying succession they
were in the corridor, in the great round chamber of the
central tower, in the kitchen garden, and above the earthworks. Then they stood in the dim recesses of the watchtower at the base of the worn stone stairs.

'Your sister waits above,' said Ryol. 'I am bringing you this close so that you might master your shaping before you try to speak with her.'

'What must I do?' she asked impatiently. Laurel would surely be descending soon, or one of her guards would go up to fetch her. Then she would be surrounded by people until dusk, and by then . . . by then who knew what more might have happened?

Ryol moved to stand behind her. He placed both hands upon her shoulders. 'You must want,' he said simply. 'You must want to be in this place, in the here and now of it, with all your strength. I will help you give that desire shape. Then you must walk up these steps and you will be with your sister.'

Lynet set all doubt and thought of absurdity aside. She faced the steps and she concentrated with all her might.

I must warn Laurel. I must be inside the tower to reach her. She is up above, and I must be here, so I can go to her. I must be in the shadows, and silent, so the guards outside know nothing. I must go quickly, before they come looking. I must be with Laurel. I must warn her. I must . . .

Then she felt the subtle insinuation of some other will around her own. It came like a thread to bind her, tickling and tightening, gently at first, then more strongly. She feared it, but she kept her thoughts formed around her need.

I must warn Laurel. I must be inside the tower to reach her.

It hurt. It hurt as if an iron hook had been thrust into her guts so they might be dragged from her body. What had been vaporous thought was twisted and pulled. It was her thought, and so she was twisted and stretched, and it was unnatural, and it hurt! Lynet screamed aloud and her being shuddered.

'Open your eyes, my lady!' bawled Ryol. 'You must walk! You must see!'

Lynet opened her eyes and she saw the tower around her, but now she felt it as well. The cold thrummed in the air. It filled the stones and they radiated it as a fire did heat. She saw her hand before her, as insubstantial as thought, and she opened her mouth to scream again.

'No!' cried Ryol. She could not feel him, and knew without knowing how that she would not see him if she looked. 'Panic now and I will not be able to hold you here!'

Lynet clamped her jaws shut around her screams and forced herself forward. *I have hands and I have legs. I am myself, and I know these stairs. They are part of my home. I know the touch of their stone. I know every shadow of this place.*

As she concentrated, the pain lessened. Her body was wraith-like, but present. That was all that mattered. She was here, now, in this place, and Laurel was alone above her. She could find her legs and feet and force them into motion. The world no longer flowed around her with the ease of water. She must force herself through it, inch by painful inch. She walked slowly up the spiralling stairs, willing her mind to remember how the stones felt beneath her boots when she had trod them on the morning of the thaw, when she had last climbed this way with Laurel and Colan and Bishop Austell. She put out the shape of her hand and lifted the hatchway above, remembering the feel of the splintery wood, the creak of the hinges. It hurt, it hurt, but the hatchway moved, its hinges strained and lifted and fell back with a bang.

Above her, Laurel jumped and turned at once. Lynet lifted herself out of the hatch. *I have hands, and body and form. I am myself.* With this in her mind, she stood before Laurel.

Laurel saw her, this ghostly form of her. Lynet felt her sister's shock slap against her like the splash of cold water. 'God of mercy, no . . .' she choked.

Lynet held up her hands, tears prickling her eyes. The fear was so cold it added fresh pain to her. *I did not mean to frighten you.* 'Fear not, sister. I am no ghost. I still live.'

'Then what is this?' Laurel's voice sounded small and distant. Lynet could feel the meaning more clearly than she could hear the words. It moved through the air like a song, dark and sombre, yet too quick and off-key for comfort.

'It is the mirror,' Laurel said, answering her own question. 'Mother's mirror.'

This did nothing to quiet the fear. If anything the touch of it grew quicker, more erratic, canting and slanting through the air. It tugged at Lynet, simultaneously pushing her away and drawing her closer. 'Lynet, go back! Now!'

Lynet mustered herself. She reached out with the will that had been shaped to bring her being here, and found the touch of Laurel's fear. Following that fear as if it were a life line, she was able to bring herself closer to her sister.

'Laurel, you must hear me,' she said urgently. 'Peran and Mesek have made a bargain. Peran came here looking to deliver Cambryn to Morgaine. Mesek has turned him against her, or has seemed to. Mesek knows there is power here, and he wants it for himself, so he can stand against Morgaine and whoever else comes.' She swallowed, moving closer yet, wading deeper into her sister's fear and new understanding. 'He means the mirror. That's why you gave it to me, isn't it? To get it away from here?'

'Only in part, Lynet, but yes.' Sorrow at the necessity of burdening her with yet another secret was like summer rain, warm and melancholy and true.

'I understand. It was as well. Now it is safe, but you are not. Mesek means to wed you, or kill you, for the power.'

Laurel's jaw tightened, and the touch of her emotion changed to jagged stone, cutting, forbidding. This was anger, but not at Lynet. For her, there was still the regret of summer rain. 'Is Morgaine coming?'

'Peran believes so.'

Anger cooled and smoothed and deepened, becoming the

pool of dark water that looks so inviting but hides its depths and its danger. 'When?'

'I don't know yet.' As Laurel calmed it was harder to hold on. Lynet's strength and will began to waver. The pain grew, a cramp in her hands and arms, a sharp ache in her back and belly. 'Laurel, I think I cannot stay much longer. I must tell you, Bishop Austell is dead.'

Laurel bowed her head, covering her eyes with her hand. She stayed that way for a long moment before she recovered herself and was able to look at Lynet again.

'I feared as much. God rest his soul. He was a good man.'

Lynet wanted to ask how she had known this, but another cramp cut across her midriff, and sent spasms up her arms. 'Lynet . . .'

Laurel reached her hand out, brushing Lynet's insubstantial shape. A new song, smooth and clear, strong and soaring. Love. Her sister's love. 'I've heard you, sister. I will take care. Trust me when I say I gave away only a piece of power when I gave you the mirror. You must go back now.'

Lynet smiled, stretching out and seeking to form her own song, her own smooth touch to fill the air and find Laurel whom her flesh and bone were too far away to reach. 'I'll come again as soon as I am able.'

Fear and love together now, dark and smooth, painful and healing. 'No, Lynet. This is dangerous.'

Lynet drew her will around that fear and love, suddenly desiring to hold it, to shape it, and return it. *Laurel can I reach you this way?* 'Laurel, they mean to kill you and take Cambryn. How can I wait here for that?'

Love rose over the fear, its soaring tones and healing touch blotting out every other note as Laurel spoke. 'Be very, very careful, sister.'

Lynet was fading, unable to hold this shape that cramped and confined her. 'I will. Pray for me, Laurel.'

Pain spasmed through her as she tried to hold on, to bathe in her sister's love for just one moment more.

'Let go, my lady,' said Ryol, a distant whisper from no source that she could see. 'You have done your work. Let go.'

Her hold broke in a short snap, and as painful as it was, it was a relief, as if she had been set free from a cage. She was beside Ryol once more, in his sunlit garden. He held her hands tightly, but she could not feel it. The whole world around them looked distant, and felt hollow. There was no music of being here to fill the air, not even between her and Ryol. She missed it. Even the pain of it had been strong and beautifully pure.

'You must go back now, lady,' said Ryol. She thought he must be worried, but she could not be sure. She could not feel it, or clearly understand the expression on his face. 'At once. Go.'

Bemused as she was, she saw no reason to argue. She backed away from him, towards the faint but insistent pull that she knew was the call of flesh to spirit. She followed it drowsily, aware that something was wrong in the numbing sensation of distance that swaddled her now.

Then blackness.

THIRTEEN

The touch of morning's light on her eyes woke Lynet slowly. Her body was aching and stone cold. She had curled herself like an infant around the mirror. Every joint protested as she stretched out. Thirst raged in her and pain pounded her head with each heartbeat. She blinked her heavy eyelids. How long had she been away from herself? Daylight now streamed through the shutter slats. Lynet's heart constricted as she saw her waiting maid's empty bed. What if the woman had tried to rouse her and been unable? What if she had gone to fetch help?

How will I explain?

As quickly as she could make her stiff hands move, Lynet slid the mirror back into its purse and tied it to her girdle. To add to the pain in her joints and sinews, her soul already ached to be back with Laurel. She wanted to dog Mesek's and Peran's footsteps. And Morgaine. How could she have failed to make Ryol show her what Morgaine was planning? It would be a grave risk, but they must take it. Surely even Morgaine could not see through all shadows.

Despite these frantic thoughts, all Lynet could do was lie back on the pillows, trying to loosen her breath and find her strength. After a time, a hand scratched at her door.

'Enter!' she managed to croak.

The door opened. Daere came in. The maid carried a tankard of something that steamed, and was followed by a golden-haired girl so thin and bony it seemed her shoulders would poke right through her neat dress. This girl bore a brightly coloured bundle of cloth in her arms.

'It is a tisane sent from the queen,' Daere said, making her curtsey as she handed the silver tankard to Lynet. 'She says you are to drink it all before you come down to join her to break your fast.'

'Thank you.' Lynet made her hands wrap around the tankard. The steam was savoury with herbs and strong wine. She sipped it, tasting sorrel, marjoram, thyme and even a little pepper. It warmed and strengthened her well. By the time she had finished the drink, Lynet found she was able to sit up more easily and watch while Daere laid out the fine garments the younger girl had brought on the foot of the bed. There was an under-dress of rich burgundy linen trimmed at the hem with hawthorn blossoms of white and gold. The over-robe was a brown silk, embroidered with holly branches in red and silver, and with trailing sleeves to be tied to it with red laces. Next to this, Daere laid out a girdle of bronze holly leaves studded with garnets to make the berries. A plain bronze circlet and fawn-brown veil were laid out last.

The sight of so much wealth displayed so casually stunned Lynet. 'These are . . .' she began.

'These are also sent to you by the queen,' said Daere, smoothing out the skirt of the over-dress. 'She asks you of your courtesy to accept this gift as a token of the earnest welcome you are given to Camelot.'

Determined not to play the country maid any more than necessary, Lynet swallowed. 'Of course. I will have to render sincere thanks to her majesty.'

'The queen is a generous and thoughtful mistress,' replied Daere with such an attitude of sincerity, Lynet could not set it down as the empty compliment of a fawning servant. 'I give thanks daily to be in her service.'

There was nothing Lynet could say to that.

Daere and her helper moved about the room, tending the fire, folding back the shutters to let the stiff, fresh breeze in. The wind smelled strangely dry and plain to Lynet who was used to the scents of rain and salt. But the sun was warm and felt like springtime and she was gladdened by it.

Once her other tasks were done, Daere set about the business of dressing Lynet in her new finery. The maid was meticulous about her work. Consequently, the straightening and lacing, buckling, arranging and adjusting took long enough that Lynet's patience strained. Eventually, Daere pronounced Lynet presentable, and she did not protest too much when Lynet insisted she would hang her keys and her purse from her shining new girdle.

Daere conducted her through the maze of wide corridors that made up the keep of Camelot. Laurel had told Lynet that the High King had made a Roman governor's villa into his great hall, and she had tried to describe the beauty of it. Her words, Lynet now saw, had failed. Each window and entry-way was arched and ornamented. The floor was decorated with sparkling mosaics of repeating patterns, or fabulous beasts. Although made of good brown stone, the edifice felt so light and airy, part of her was sure that it must soon float away.

To Lynet's surprise, they passed by the entrance to the great hall. Instead, Daere took Lynet to a smaller door, where she knocked humbly. A waiting lady opened it, a noble woman with rich brown and frankly curious eyes. She curtsied politely to Lynet and stood back so that she might enter what was clearly the queen's private chamber.

Lynet had never seen a more beautiful or luxurious room. The carved furniture alone represented a fortune in materials and skill. She counted five books on the shelf above the writing desk. Carpets that were whole worlds of colour softened the floor.

Queen Guinevere sat before the hearth at an inlaid table spread with a meal whose luxury equalled that of the room. There was cold hare with sorrel and hazelnuts, and a roasted chicken scented with something pungent and savoury Lynet could not name but which nonetheless set her mouth watering. There were white and brown breads, honeyed cakes, and dried fruits soaked in wine.

Lynet began to kneel, but the queen stopped her, raising her up before she could complete the gesture.

'Please sit,' Queen Guinevere said, but she no longer spoke the rolling, formal language of this eastern court. Instead, she spoke the Dumonii tongue of Cambryn, and smiled at the surprise that showed plainly on Lynet's face. As Lynet took the seat that was offered, the queen beckoned to Daere, who came forward at once to pour Lynet both beer and cider.

'Please, break your fast with me now. Help yourself as you wish.'

Whatever words must pass between them, Lynet was more than willing to let them wait awhile. The food was excellent, filling and elegantly spiced. The queen herself ate lightly, but well, sparing Lynet from any anxiety that she was taking too much.

As she ate, Lynet could not help watching the queen, although she tried to be circumspect. She was as beautiful as the bards told, with the bright grey eyes they all praised. She held herself straight and proud, a woman who knew she was watched and measured at all times. They spoke in their common language of nothing urgent, remarks on the meal before them, on the weather. Everything was arranged to set

Lynet at her ease, and indeed she did feel herself relaxing under the gracious influences of comfort and good food. But despite all this, as she regarded the queen from under her properly lowered eyelids, what came back to Lynet again and again was something Laurel had once written to her. *The queen is a gracious woman, in all ways and at all times the soul of polity. One might easily see only the hostess and wise woman and overlook how many secrets she guards and how closely.*

When at last Lynet was able to sit back, both hunger and thirst sated, the queen pushed her own cup aside.

'I thought we should speak privately this morning, you and I,' said Queen Guinevere. Lynet could see she was being watched closely, examined for her reaction.

And can I blame her? She does not know what she is coming to any more than I did when I set out on the road to this place.

'I am at Your Majesty's service,' Lynet replied.

'For which I thank you,' replied the queen dryly, proving to Lynet that she recognized her statement as an empty form. 'But you and I both know that is far from certain.'

That startled Lynet and for a moment she did not know how to reply. But those keen grey eyes told her that only honesty would do. Slowly she said, 'Your Majesty does not trust me.'

The queen considered this for a moment. 'Say rather, I know you do not trust me.' Lynet opened her mouth to attempt to deny this, but Queen Guinevere went on. 'I do not blame you for this, but hope to help amend it.' She spread her hands. They were neat and well kept, which was to be expected, but they were also stained. Some old juice or dye had left its mark there, faintly mottling the white skin. Lynet found herself oddly curious as to what it had been. 'You may ask me any question, speak any concern,' the queen was saying. 'None here now speak our tongue. Only you and I will know what is said.'

Lynet sat in silence, her mind racing, trying to find the correct words. The queen urged frankness, but Lynet could not trust this. Her hand instinctively covered the mirror in its purse.

Queen Guinevere sighed. 'Very well.' She clearly had been prepared for this reaction, although it disappointed her. 'Here is something you should know. Your father knew this much, and perhaps your brother as well. If it did not come to you . . . well only God can see so far.'

Lynet's hand tightened a little on the mirror, and she forced it away to lie in her lap. But the queen was not watching her. She was staring into her wine cup towards some deep memory.

'In the early days, while Arthur was struggling to unite the Britons, it was known that keeping the Dumonii loyalty would be one of the greatest challenges. There were many factors: the distance and difficulty of the crossing by sea, and worse by land . . . not to mention that the Dumonii are so protective of their independence.' She smiled a little at this. 'My marriage to him could only go so far in creating a bond between our people and the rest of the Britons. So, Arthur put all his efforts into cultivating the friendship of King Mark. We had to be careful. Mark laboured under the overlordship of the Eire-landers at that time, and they were not disposed to look favourably on any embassage from Arthur. But we needed Tintagel. Not only because the kings of Eire used it as a staging place for their raids up and down the Dumonii coast, but because Mark's lands joined with my own would provide a road inland, should it become necessary.'

Should the Dumonii rebel, she meant.

'All went well for a time. Mark let himself be persuaded. Arthur swore that once the Saxons had been driven back, Mark would have all the help we could give against the Eire-landers. Mark sent treasure in secret after Arthur, and his best men, in ones and twos, however it could be managed without alarming his outland masters. What lies he told and what risks he ran, I do not know, but he was faithful to his promise, and Mark's wealth and Mark's men helped win the twelve battles that drove the Saxons into the sea.

'It was soon after this that he sent to us a young man . . . a stripling boy, really, named Tristan.'

'King Mark sent you Sir Tristan?' Lynet exclaimed. A memory came to her then, as clear as day. She had been sitting beside Queen Iscult in Tintagel's plain and empty hall. The sea winds howled loud enough they could be heard through the stones. Sir Tristan had agreed to play for them to while away the winter storm. She had been captivated as always by the sweetness of the music, and the fairness of the man, but she had, for a moment, perhaps in guilty conscience, glanced towards King Mark. She had seen in him a mix of love and sorrow so profound she could barely comprehend it. But then Sir Tristan had changed the song to a merry dance tune, and Iseult took up King Mark's hand, urging him to dance with her. He danced like a bear, lumbering and clumsy, but a fresh gaiety took them all, and the moment was over.

Queen Guinevere nodded. 'He called Tristan his nephew, but I had my doubts. He looked far more like Mark himself than like his sister, who was dark as one from the West Lands where Mark was fair, almost a Saxon for looks.'

Lynet had never seen King Mark as anything but a grey old man. She tried to picture him ever resembling the bright Sir Tristan, and failed.

'It happens sometimes that a nephew takes more after the uncle than the father.'

'It does,' agreed the queen, but she did not seem convinced or consoled.

'You think Sir Tristan was King Mark's son?' said Lynet

slowly. A strange realization ran through her mind. Queen Guinevere said King Mark had called Tristan his nephew, but in all her time at Tintagel, Lynet had never heard any mention of a blood relationship between the two.

Queen Guinevere nodded again. 'His son by whom I could not say. Perhaps I am afraid to guess,' she added quietly. 'For Mark had no wife at that time to give him legitimate heirs, so what could make him deny the existence of any son who could carry on the line?'

The implications of this careful statement made Lynet's stomach turn.

'But we did not ask too closely then.' The queen drank a little of her wine, swallowing her own memory, tasting the complexity and bitterness of it. 'Tristan worked hard at his training so that he was able to keep up with the best of the young men, even Gawain. His talents with harp and song were surprising and delightful, and a respite as an entertainment from Sir Kai's jibes.' Her smile turned a little sharp at this, but Lynet did not want to break the tale to ask what made it so. 'We would have kept him here, given him a cohort to lead, but his only ambition was to return to Mark's country and serve him. This seemed not only natural, but desirable. With the lands of the Britons as secure as they could be made, it was time to honour our promise and aid Mark. What better man to send him than Tristan at the head of a century of Arthur's finest? This plan had the added advantage that it would strengthen the ties between Tintagel and Camelot. Mark still had no heir. We needed to take whatever steps we could to make sure his kingdom would not fall into chaos when he died.

'So, with all due ceremony, Tristan was knighted, and he returned home.

'Tristan and Mark together took the war to Eire, and as

you know they brought back both victory and Queen Iseult. It seemed as if no more could be wished for.

'Then, Arthur received a message from Tintagel. It said Mark had heard something deeply disturbing from Tristan. It seemed that the chieftains and nobles near Tintagel were uneasy about Mark's alliance with Camelot. This will not be a new story to you. They were chafing at the idea of a new overlordship replacing that of the Eire-landers. Mark asked that we stay away, leave him free rein until he could sound out his own people, discover for certain who was in favour of things remaining as they were and who would be willing to work for change and how far they would go.'

'This cannot have been true.' The words were out of Lynet before she could stop them. 'No one among the nobles can have been plotting revolt against the king.'

The queen paused, not at all angry at being interrupted, only expectant. 'Why not?'

'Because if it were, Tintagel would have already collapsed. Instead, all the heads of every clan and house have been clinging to one another trying to hold the kingdom together.'

Queen Guinevere let this sink in, considering, evaluating, adding it to her personal treasure store of knowledge. 'I am glad to hear you say this,' she said. 'It makes what is to come that much easier. But you must understand that until this moment, we did not know that much. Our best source of news after Mark was Steward Kenan.'

And after what I had done, he could not go openly to Tintagel, not easily, until that last time when they all went together.

'So, here we have stayed,' sighed the queen, pushing her cup to one side. Daere moved at once to refill it. 'Stifled in our ignorance, waiting to see who would come to us first, if any would come before a war did. We have sent out men in secret, but they have been able to learn little. So few here speak the Dumonii language.' She sighed again, shaking her head. 'And that is one reason why I have not returned to my own lands. I would wager you know the other.'

The queen looked to her and waited. Lynet did know, but she was reluctant to speak the name. That was a road she did not wish to travel, but Queen Guinevere seemed prepared to wait as long as it took for her to take that step.

'Morgaine,' said Lynet finally.

Queen Guinevere nodded. 'Yes. You see, Lynet, I am at heart a coward.'

This admission startled Lynet so badly she could not find a single word to say.

'All know of Morgaine's hatred for my lord Arthur, but she bears me no love either.' She spoke lightly, but the steel in her grey eyes had found its way to her voice. 'She believes that I stole the love of her sister, Morgause, and that it was my fault that Morgause turned against her in the end. Perhaps it was, a little. I do not know.' Anger made a treacherous current under those last words. Anger at her own ignorance, at her inability to find an answer. 'I do know that she purposes my death as well as Arthur's, and while I could face an open fight, I fear Morgaine's home in the shadows and the unseen country.'

The word 'shadows' made Lynet's heart hammer and her fingers reach out for the mirror.

'Now comes your news that she begins to move openly.' Lynet had to work not to shift and shrink under the queen's new gaze. Queen Guinevere examined her now, looking close to see if the words that had passed between them had worked any change on Lynet. 'She must at last feel secure in her following and in her chances of success. Indeed, I would not blame you if you found you must play hostess to her at Cambryn and hear her out. There are few things she desires more than to take the home that was once both mine and hers.'

Lynet's mouth went dry in a heartbeat, and she suddenly found it difficult to breathe. 'If that were true, Majesty, what would you do?' asked Lynet, her voice suddenly unable to rise above a whisper. *If she did not know before, she does now. I'm sorry, Laurel.*

But Queen Guinevere replied evenly. 'You are here and have asked for succour and intervention. This we grant freely as your right. Nothing will change that, as long as no deception is offered.'

She held Lynet's gaze and Lynet held her peace, considering this.

'Has Morgaine spoken with you or your sister?' the queen asked.

'No, Majesty.' Lynet hesitated, afraid to say too much, but at the same time afraid to be seen to hold too much back. 'Laurel has not spoken with Morgaine, but that does not mean she will not. We . . . we believe as you do, that she desires to take possession of Cambryn.' Then, slowly, Lynet began to tell the queen of the sea voyage, and of the *morverch.*

Queen Guinevere listened in silence to these revelations, her face utterly still. If she felt alarm, she concealed it thoroughly. When Lynet had finished, the queen let the silence stand unbroken between them for a long time.

'There are tales that you were begotten not of the land, but of the sea, Lynet. Are they true?'

She spoke matter-of-factly, but Lynet could not forget the queen's confession of a moment before, that she feared the invisible country. But she had also asked for honesty. 'No, Majesty,' said Lynet. 'I am not of the sea. That blessing was my mother's.'

Queen Guinevere nodded once more, after only the briefest of pauses, her face still unreadable. 'I thank you for telling me these things. We must know as much as we can before we go on.'

Lynet hesitated, then made herself ask, 'You will not change your mind now?'

In that moment, the queen's eyes seemed like tempered steel and Lynet hoped never to see such anger turned on her. 'Oh, no, Lady Lynet. Do what she will, she will not have Cambryn of me.' She spoke these words to the air, a promise meant to carry to Morgaine herself, wherever she might be. 'Now then, Lady Lynet, I have my answers from you. What would you of me this day?'

Lynet opened her mouth, and closed it again. *What would you of me?* There were so many things, all of them unreasonable or impossible. 'I would see my men,' she said at last.

'Of course. Your captain and men-at-arms are hosted in the great hall by the knights. Daere will take you.' She rose, and all her ladies were on their feet at once. Lynet also stood, making a deep curtsey. But something was left unsaid, and should not have been.

'Thank you, Your Majesty,' said Lynet, holding her obeisance. 'For all that you have done.'

The queen took her hand, raising her up. She understood, Lynet saw, how much lay under those few words. Understood, and believed. 'You are welcome, Lady Lynet, and know that you have my thanks as well.'

With that, Lynet let Daere lead her from the room. A strange warmth filled her, and it took Lynet a moment to realize it was hope.

The great hall of Camelot's keep was as full, as noisy and as crowded as the new hall at Cambryn would be on any given morning, but it was twice again as large, and more magnificent than her home would ever be. Tapestries that were the work of lifetimes ornamented the walls. Innumerable shields, axes and swords hung over the great hearths. Carpets of red and gold softened the floor where it was not strewn with fragrant rushes. The dais was made of snow-white marble. Atop it waited Arthur's gilded throne of audience flanked by the two golden dragons that were taken by his father Uther from the foul Vortigern, before Vortigern's treachery took that king's life.

As this was the time for breaking the night's fast and not a formal audience, the high table had been set on the dais's first broad step. A number of knights and ladies occupied it, but if the king had been there, he was gone now, so it was not necessary for Lynet to pause there first in acknowledgement and greeting. She could go directly to the trestle table beside the hearth where Hale, Lock and the Trevailians sat with a host of scarred and grizzled veterans. Her passing provoked open glances of curiosity and stories whispered back and forth. But she heard no malice in the susurrus of voices, and hope remained secure within her.

Her men stood as she approached. They were clean and freshly clad, as she was, although less formally, and their hurts had been tended. Hale spoke in praise of their hosts and the comfort of the barracks where they were housed. They were to assist in the preparations for the return journey, he said. The knights Bedivere and Lancelot wanted to speak with them about the land and its conditions, their remaining men and the minute details of their territory and fortifications.

In case Peran and Mesek do not keep their word. In case the land has fallen apart before we return. These thoughts settled uncomfortably in Lynet's mind, but she gazed about her at the strength and the wealth of this place. Lancelot . . . even she had heard that name. He was said to be the greatest among the cadre of the Round Table, come from across the waters, from a people who fled into exile when the Romans came to the island. It was told the other knights looked on him with jealous eyes because of his prowess in battle, although he had not been present for any of Arthur's greatest victories.

Still, that he was to accompany them was a sign of the seriousness with which their claim was taken, and such a famed warrior would pick good men to follow him. They would go back in strength with the queen's justice.

'All will be right, Captain Hale,' Lynet said. 'Give them all the help you can. Keep nothing back.'

He bowed, his eyes bright with the same hope that warmed her within. 'It will be my pleasure, lady.'

'My lady?'

Lynet turned. It was Daere who spoke, suddenly hesitant. A young boy stood beside her, in a neat but plain tunic, shifting from foot to foot, and staring at the floor as he did.

'My lady . . .' the boy said. 'Merlin would speak with you.'

Merlin? The memory of the black-robed cunning man flashed across her vision, how he had watched her without blinking as she spoke.

'Yes, my lady,' said Daere. Her fingers fiddled with her skirt, and Lynet had the odd sensation she would have crossed herself if she could have done it without being seen. *Or perhaps it's just that I would.*

'Very well,' she made herself say. 'Then let us not keep him waiting. You will tell him I am coming,' she said to the boy. He grimaced, bobbed his head and pelted away, leaving Lynet and Daere to follow at a more sedate pace.

Like Cambryn, Camelot was a collection of buildings, sheds, stables, barns, coops and small yards clustered around the square of the great hall. Its people were busy with the thousand familiar tasks that came with spring. Shouts and whistles, snatches of songs and the grunts and squawks of livestock filled the mild air. Daere led Lynet across the yard and under the shadow of the high walls with their wooden palisades. In the northwest corner of the bustling yard, there stood a low cottage with a thatched roof. Its wattle and daub walls had been lime washed to keep them whole. It would have been difficult to imagine a humbler dwelling in the shadow of a great king's court. One wide window faced the yard, its shutters flung open to catch the spring's sun and bright breeze. At a table on the other side sat a grey-headed man bent over a sheet of vellum on which he wrote slowly and carefully with a pen made of a swan's white feather. As if sensing she watched him, the old man lifted his head, and Lynet looked into Merlin's bright blue eyes.

She froze, half-afraid, half-guilty, as if she were a child caught in some act of mischief. He laid his quill carefully down and beckoned to her with one long, gnarled hand. Lynet did not know what to do. She had no desire to come near this man at all, but she could not have clearly explained what repulsed her. He had not yet even spoken a word in her hearing. All he had done at the long council yesterday was listen. Listen to everything and miss nothing.

It seemed to her that her purse grew cold and heavy where it hung from her new girdle and without thinking she covered it with her hand. From his window, Merlin had not ceased to watch her, and to smile with grandfatherly kindness, ready it seemed to wait for whatever her reaction to his gesture would be.

With that complete freedom, it felt oddly as if she had no choice at all. 'You may wait for me here, Daere,' said Lynet. She walked up to the ashwood door that stood open a crack, pushed it back and stepped over the dark threshold.

The inside of the cottage was as humble as the outside. It looked more like a herb wife's home than anything else Lynet might name. Bundles of drying plants hung from the roof beams and filled the air with a thick, pungent scent. The long work tables held mortars and pestles, braziers, scales and weights, earths and ores. Their wood was scarred and stained with inks and dyes and other substances Lynet was sure she would be hard pressed to put a name to. Two things, though, dominated the room even more than the presence of the black-robed cunning man in his plain chair. The first was the books. She counted ten great volumes, each the size of a Bible. The second was the low, round, stone well, covered tightly with a lid that like the door was made of ash. A voice from deep inside Lynet whispered that she truly did not want to know what waters might flow into such a well.

'Lady Lynet.' Merlin stood in welcome. 'Welcome to my home, and thank you for coming.' He pushed out a neatly made chair for her. Lynet stared at it as she had the well. *I am being rude.* But she could only stand there awkwardly. She knew nothing of this man's rank or birth or place. She did not know what gesture of acknowledgement or obeisance to make to him, or even what title to call him by.

'Thank you,' she said because she could think of nothing else. She settled herself in the comfortable chair. The sun streamed through the window, its warmth raising the pleasant smell of herbs, parchment and earth, but she could not free herself of the awareness of the shadows behind her. It was as if they had weight and pressed too close for comfort.

'Did you wish to speak with me, sir?' she asked, as much to distract herself as anything else.

'I did.' Merlin returned to his own chair. 'I am come from telling the High King the thing which you did not tell him, or the queen.'

The shadows crowded closer and the cold bled through from her mirror again. 'What is that, Master?'

'That while you travel with the folk of Camelot, the sea road is closed to them.'

No words came to Lynet. It took all her strength to remain impassive. Merlin's blue gaze never wavered. At last, she was able to say, 'How do you know this?'

His smile was faint and filled with humility. 'If I have a use to the High King it is that I can see such things. What concerns me is that you knew this, and yet said nothing.'

'I have told the queen of the *morverch*,' she said defiantly, like a child caught eavesdropping.

Merlin made no reply. It was not enough. She knew it, and so did he. Lynet could no longer meet his gaze. Her hands knotted themselves together in her lap. The terror and loss and anger of the storm rolled over her. Bishop Austell screamed once before he was dragged down and she could not discern whether that had truly happened or her fearful thoughts added it to her memory now. A lump filled her throat and the cold from her mirror seeped into her heart. 'I made one bargain,' she said weakly. 'I hoped to make another if necessary. We must have speed.'

'Yes,' said Merlin. 'But it will not avail you. You have the enmity of the sea-women. They will not forget the betrayal of one of their blood, nor will they forgive it.'

She did not doubt his words. She had known this in some corner of herself, but she was unprepared for the pain that lanced through her as he spoke this truth aloud. She had done what was necessary. She did not regret it, but it had cost her the connection to her mother through them.

There might be a way yet. If she gave the mirror back to the sea, help would come, Laurel had said. She could open that road again.

But she would have to sacrifice her means of reaching Laurel. She could not do it. Not even to gain a few days.

Merlin still watched her, his gaze as heavy as the shadows at her back. When he spoke, his voice echoed strangely, as if the sound came from somewhere beyond the man sitting before her. 'You carry power with you, in the lines of your blood. You also carry it trapped in silver and in dragon's blood.'

Anger, sharp and unbidden, rose in her. How *dare* he? Spy and thief, stealing the thoughts from her heart and the words from her mouth. 'I mean no harm to any here. What I hold was given to me freely and is mine.'

'I did not say otherwise.' Merlin spoke from within his own frame again. 'Will you let me see this power you bring?'

Lynet suddenly felt as if she had been asked to strip naked. She did not understand why this simple request should affect her so violently, but it did. 'I was told to keep it secret.'

'You were told more than that, I think.'

She bridled. It was too much. The summons, this close quizzing, that he knew things he had no right to know. 'That is my own business.'

He did not relent, nor did his tone lose its mildness. 'You have ignored that other warning, and used the power.'

'That also is my own business.'

'It is, my lady,' he acknowledged. 'But I make it mine to warn you. Accepting such service comes at a price, even though your servant bears you all the love in the world. You have already begun to feel it. The greater the service, the more it will cost you, until you have nothing left to give but yourself.'

'Why do you care?' she demanded.

Once more, Merlin answered the words, and not the tone. 'Because the fate of my king and more hang on such things.'

'Such as myself?'

He nodded once. 'Even so.'

'Then why do you not warn him against me?' she shot back.

If she had hoped to shock or anger him, she was disappointed. Merlin calmly shook his head. 'It is not a warning that would be heard, nor could it be. So, I must do what I can in other ways.'

'And what is it you can do?'

'What I do now, speak of what I know.'

'Then I thank you for your care and your warning, sir.' She stood. She wanted nothing more than to be gone from this deceptively simple cottage.

'You are most welcome, lady.' Merlin inclined his head. 'And will be again if ever you need any aid.'

She half-turned, but froze as these words penetrated the morass of her thought. 'You would help me?'

'I would.'

Lynet opened her mouth and closed it again. 'I will remember.'

Merlin nodded his head once more, and with that, Lynet knew the conversation was at an end. She left, shutting the ashwood door behind her as if she could shut away all that had just been said. She strode swiftly across the yard, barely aware of Daere scrambling to catch up with her. It was only then she realized that she was still clutching her mirror. She lifted her hand away, grabbing her trailing sleeve instead. She moved swiftly, but she realized she had no idea where she wanted to go. Truth to tell, she did not want to return indoors just yet. Perhaps there was a garden where she could go, somewhere, anywhere, where she could be under the sky and breathe the spring's fresh air, and regain once more the feelings of hope to soothe her jangled nerves.

Just as she turned to ask Daere about this, an approaching figure caught her eye. A noble man, one of the knights perhaps, she thought. Then she looked again. No. It was the kitchen boy from the day before. What was his name? Gareth. She only recognized him by the long red slash on his cheek and his raven-black hair. Otherwise he had been transformed utterly. He was clean now, brushed and neatly barbered. Gone were the battered tunic, torn breeches and loose sandals, and in their place were fine linen garments of summer green and goldenrod yellow. A fur-trimmed green cloak streamed from his shoulders, a belt of enamelled bronze circled his trim waist.

'God be with you, Lady Lynet,' he said, making a deep bow. He was taller than she remembered. 'I trust you have been made most welcome among us?'

He had eyes of summer brown that returned to her the first openly cheerful gaze she had seen since she had woken this morning. Something in them soothed and warmed her, even as Merlin's had angered and frightened her. 'That I have, Squire Gareth, thank you,' she said politely. 'And I ask you to accept my apology for my treatment of you yesterday.' She offered a small curtsey. He was the High King's kin, after all, and above her in rank.

'It is I who should be thanking you, my lady,' he answered in a manner both merry and sober at once. 'I know it is tragedy that has brought you here, but you have brought with you my chance at redemption from my own folly. For this I thank you with all my heart.'

He bent swiftly and kissed her hand. Lynet froze, as if he had slapped her rather than saluted her. He straightened, and she could not smooth out her distress swiftly enough.

'Lady, have I offended?'

'No. No, Squire.' She pulled her hand away, letting the fall of her sleeve cover it. 'It is nothing you have done.'

He did not believe her. She did not care, as long as he said nothing of it. Daere was frowning. No, she was glowering. Lynet's feet began to ache. She should go, find somewhere to sit down. Be anywhere but here. 'Is there any way I might aid you?' he asked. 'You have brought about my release from punishment, and my knight has turned me loose for the morning . . .'

'I thank you, but no . . .' She searched hard for some way to make light of this, but none came. 'Thank you.'

'Then, perhaps, if my lady has no other appointment, she

might permit me to walk with her awhile, and show her something of my home?'

Lynet looked up into his face, and his warm, restful eyes. Slowly, it occurred to her that for once, here was a man who did not know who she was and what she had done. The tales they told at Camelot of Sir Tristan and Queen Iseult might not include the name of one gulled waiting lady. She might be able to pass a pleasant hour in simple talk and rest her mind for just this small space of time.

But before she could form a reply, Daere spoke up. 'The lady is needed elsewhere, Squire Gareth.'

Gareth raised his brows at the maid. He plainly did not believe her, but he was not going to call her out in the lie. He only bowed again. 'Perhaps another time, if circumstances permit.'

'I expect the lady will be far too busy for that. Have you no feeling?' Daere sniffed, and turned away. 'Please, my lady, we are wanted.'

Mutely, Lynet turned to follow her maid, who strode off across the yard with a most determined stride. Lynet had to work to keep up with her, and her feet began to twinge in protest. 'Why did you do that, Daere?'

Daere's face puckered with distaste. 'It would not suit my lady's honour to be seen with that one.'

'What has he done?'

'It is not what but who,' replied Daere meaningfully. 'And how often. No, my lady, he is not a safe companion.'

Lynet glanced backward. The squire still stood there, watching the men marching past with their shields on their backs and raising his hand to some acquaintance. The breeze had caught his raven-black hair and blown it back from his fine face. It seemed to her that she could see Sir Tristan's golden shadow beside him. So, Squire Gareth was another one. Another of Camelot's fair men. Her heart hardened within her at this understanding.

But it was not without a little regret that she turned to follow her diligent maid to somewhere else, somewhere safe this time.

FOURTEEN

'Lady Laurel!' Hob Trevith burst into the new hall, his jerkin askew and his breath ragged. 'She is come, and she brings . . .' Hob was panting too hard to finish his exclamation.

Laurel set down her shuttle. Around her, the women engaged with spindles and hand looms looked at her expectantly and uneasily. Laurel regarded her own loom. A bare inch of broad twilight-blue fabric hung completed in the simple wooden frame before her. The draught of Hob's entry set the threads swaying so hard their weights rattled. From the corner of her eye she saw Mesek at his side of the hall and Peran at his. Both stirred uneasily, like dogs who have noticed an unpleasant scent. They had been lounging on their benches with their men about them, tossing the bones, drinking the hall's beer and idling, trying not to look bored, or impatient, or at each other.

Normally, Laurel abhorred the endless work of spinning and weaving. She hated being confined to the dank hall amid the stink and scratch of the wool and the flurry and flutter of constant small gossip. But for the past few days it had been a haven of calm as well as a way to discomfit her captors. The work kept her hands busy and her eyes focused on something other than the guards who hovered so near. It also forced these men to sit still indoors to be by her. She saw no reason why their confinement should be any more comfortable than hers. It was a petty revenge, but for the moment it was all she had.

The guardsmen who flanked them for the purpose of keeping her in her place looked to their masters for instruction and received none. How could they? None of them knew what was happening. Another triumph, as petty as the other, but Laurel accepted this as well.

'How many with her?' Laurel inquired of Hob. The watchman gulped down air and astonishment at her calm. He was, fortunately, remembering her instruction that no name should be given to this particular arrival.

'Ten, my lady, eight men and two waiting ladies, but . . .'

Laurel did not wait to hear anymore. 'Meg.' She turned to the grey-haired woman who had been acting as her chatelaine for the five days since Lynet left for Camelot. Meg stood immediately, passing off her spindle to the girl beside her. 'You and Jorey will see that welcome cups and a good meal are prepared for our guests along with all else that might be needed for their comfort. Hob, you will go and see they are properly escorted to the old hall. I will meet them there.'

'So, Masters,' Laurel said to the chieftains as she brushed the lint from her hands. 'Which of you will come with me to welcome the Lady Morgaine back to Cambryn?'

Her calm declaration was rewarded by the sight of both her captors dropping their jaws.

Laurel swept from the hall. They would follow, or they would not. It did not truly matter. What mattered now was to see how Morgaine chose to present herself, and how she returned Colan.

Laurel had known for three days that the sorceress was on her way. Lynet had brought the news, although she had not been able to tell Laurel much more than that Morgaine had sailed from her home. Even Lynet had more sense than to spy too closely on Morgaine the Sleepless. Guilt moved heavily in Laurel. For all that she had repeatedly warned her sister not to look too often into the mirror, she did not truly try to make Lynet stop. Laurel had her own powers. Her ways of knowing and warding came from the blood in her veins, but none of her arts were as strong as those Lynet now had at her command. If they and Cambryn were to survive this time, they needed what Lynet could learn, and what she could do.

Laurel entered the audience hall with her guards trailing behind. She did not permit herself any hesitation as she climbed the dais to the steward's chair one step below the throne. She sat herself down in the place that had belonged to her father for as long as she had been alive. The strangers among her guard looked at each other uncertainly, but the men of Cambryn took their sign from her and mounted to their places beside her, flanking her with dignity and staring the strangers coldly down.

A heartbeat after they were assembled, Peran entered the hall. He had taken a moment to pull his bronze-clasped cloak onto his shoulders and it billowed out behind him as he strode to the dais, and put his foot on the lowest step.

'No higher, Peran Treanhal,' snapped Laurel.

A kind of smile formed on his scarred face, a warped and devilish grin. 'Who are you to stop me, my lady?'

Laurel felt the witchfires kindle within her. It was a hard light, akin to that which shimmered on the masts and the rails of ships on the sea that were blessed, or were doomed. 'Do you say you are master here?'

He cocked his head just a little. 'Your ladyship has put her keeping in my hands.'

What drives this? You've betrayed your mistress, or said you will.

Why should her coming make you bold? 'Yet I remain who I am, Master Peran, and I have my rank and my birth, and this place is yet mine. Will you take it from me here and now?'

He was able to meet her eyes for a full dozen heartbeats before he relented. Whether that was due to what he saw within her, or to the movement among the men of Cambryn as they stood straight, and changed their grips on spear and pole-arm Laurel could not say and did not care. Peran removed his foot from the dais and stood to the side. For now that was all that mattered.

You are not ready for such a contest yet. Neither am I.

Laurel once again composed her face to the cool mask that she had worn continuously over the past few days. Inwardly, she had never felt more alone than she did at this moment. She told herself she was surrounded by the souls of those who loved her. She knew her men were loyal to her, for her father's sake if not yet for her own. She held the right to be where she was by the laws of God and man. Those truths, though, seemed as fragile as moth's wings as Hob and the other watchmen pushed open the doors and Morgaine entered the hall.

The sorceress was dark of hair and eye, as Laurel had always been told. She dressed simply in a cloak and dress of rich blue, with silver for her girdle and the circlet that held the linen veil over her braided hair. She comported herself with absolute certainty of place and power as she strode up the centre of the audience hall. In her train came two women, dark like their mistress, and like her dressed in rich blue. Behind them, as Hob had reported, marched eight men. These all wore caps and corselets of leather, and all went unarmed, making a peaceful entry into the hall.

The last of them dragged Colan Carnbrea.

Colan's raw hands were bound behind him and rough hemp rope hobbled his legs. His guard thought enough of his rank that they allowed him to find his feet so he could stand as the whole procession came to a halt at the foot of the dais.

Rage filled Laurel at the sight of him. She had thought herself ready for this moment, but the farce of him being hauled before their father's seat in the semblance of a captive burned through her. It was all she could do to keep from ordering the nearest man to impale her faithless brother on his spear so she could watch him die in this place where he had killed their father.

What would you say to that, Morgaine? she wondered, almost idly, towards the sorceress who now made her curtsey at the foot of the dais. *If I removed one of your spies and best barter coin?*

But what Laurel said was, 'Welcome to Cambryn, Lady Morgaine, an' you come in peace.'

Morgaine straightened. 'I thank you for your welcome, Lady Laurel.' Her voice was low and rich, with a lilt to it that Laurel could not place. 'I do come in peace, and to return what is rightfully yours.' She motioned to her men. The two closest to Colan grabbed his arms roughly, half-pushing, half-carrying him forward. When they reached the foot of the dais, they shoved him to his knees so hard that he bit his lip to keep from crying aloud.

Laurel felt one muscle in her cheek twitch.

'He came to me begging shelter,' said Morgaine. 'But the truth of his deeds was soon discovered. I will not shelter one who so betrays his own blood.'

Laurel looked for a moment into Morgaine's black eyes. *In faith, Morgaine, I don't believe you would.* That understanding surprised her, but she kept it deep within herself. Instead she looked down at Colan. He hunched on the stones at her feet with his head bowed. She could see nothing of his face. Her jaw clenched and she held her peace until she was certain she could trust her voice to remain steady.

'Is there anything you would say to me, Colan No Man's Son?' Laurel inquired.

He raised his head and met her eyes, and she saw that there was. There was a wellspring of words within him. Either his own wisdom or Morgaine's counsel kept him silent, however, and he bowed his head once more.

'You may claim the bounty for returning him to us,' said Laurel to Morgaine.

'I will take no such price,' replied the sorceress gravely, as Laurel had been next to certain she would. 'I regard it as enough that the thing is done.'

'Then please accept my thanks for the return of this outlaw,' Laurel replied. *Though, if you truly mean what you say, why you bothered to return him rather than kill him is past understanding.* 'I invite you and yours to reside with us this night before you must begin your journey home.'

Regally, Morgaine inclined her head. 'Thank you, my lady. I do accept.'

That done, Laurel made herself look once more at Colan. He had not made any move. Seeing him crouch there turned her stomach. 'Take him to his chamber,' said Laurel to Hob and Joss. 'Let him be loosed, but make sure a good guard is kept. Let no one save myself speak with him under any pretext. Sentence will be passed in good time.' *Lest you doubt that, Colan.*

If Colan had thought to find any gentleness upon his return, he was disappointed. Hob and Joss hauled him upright and dragged him bodily from the hall before he could get his feet under him. He would, no doubt, find himself in possession of a few new bruises before his fetters were cut, but Laurel could not find it in her to order more care to be taken. She had far greater concerns. She turned her attention back to the patient Morgaine.

'I believe, lady, you know Peran Treanhal.' Laurel turned

towards the chieftain who had waited still and silent throughout.

Morgaine looked to Peran as if noticing him for the first time. She inclined her head to him, as he did to her.

'The Treanhal have been good friends of my people,' said Morgaine. 'I am pleased to see their chief made welcome here.'

'I am come on a matter of law, Lady Morgaine,' rasped Peran. 'Alas the treachery of the outlaw delayed that justice.'

Morgaine looked concerned, but not overly so. *After all, what could the business of such a minor ally matter to you?* 'I am certain the lady will rule soundly in her father's name. I was deeply sorrowed to hear of your father's death, Lady Laurel,' Morgaine was saying. 'Will you, of your courtesy, permit me to visit his grave?'

'Of course.' *Let us keep on with this mummery.* 'After which I trust you will be pleased to rest and take what poor refreshment we may offer you.'

'Again, I thank you, Lady Laurel.'

'If you will walk with me?'

So, Laurel walked the length of the hall beside the sorceress with Morgaine's two silent ladies following behind. Laurel made no remark or attempt at conversation. The fewer words that passed between them, the less likely her rage would betray her. The whole way through the hall and down the corridors, she concentrated on keeping her distance as best she could, not permitting even the hem of her garment to brush Morgaine's.

Outside, the day was chill and the wind brisk. The clouds promised more rain and soon, perhaps another spring storm. *Not all the storms to come are in our hall*, thought Laurel to herself as she led Morgaine out to their father's cairn. The first stones for a proper tomb had yet to be brought. She would send men out for them as soon as this . . . time . . .

had drawn to a close. Until then, Lord Kenan lay like one of the ancients, in his grave beneath a great pile of undressed grey rock.

While her ladies hung back, Morgaine approached the cairn with a reverent demeanour. She stood beside it for awhile, with her head bowed. Laurel tried to compose herself to prayer, to banish thoughts of her brother pacing his old chamber with the guards outside waiting for an excuse to exact punishment from him, of her sister tearing herself apart to keep watch over their home, of herself standing hostage to the plots and plans swirling all around her. But prayer would not come, only more anger and the sick, sad help-lessness that had dogged her since she had watched Lynet ride away.

While Laurel sank beneath her own thoughts, Morgaine reached out and touched her hand as if in friendly sympathy. Startled off her guard, Laurel looked into the other woman's eyes.

'It is a bitter thing to lose a father to violence,' she said. 'I know it well, and I am sorry for you.'

Unexpectedly, a wave of warmth rushed over Laurel. It was such a relief to hear a sympathetic voice. She was surrounded by her folk, but at the same time she was separate and alone. All her family was gone from her, even her beloved sister. What could be worse than that? Although she might be long accustomed to keeping her own counsel, it had been so hard these past days. She was not even mistress in her own home. She had not realized until this moment how desperately she had longed for a friendly voice, to unburden herself to someone to whom she was not mistress but only friend.

As these thoughts passed through her, she felt again the tang of salt on her lips, brought by the hard winds from the ocean that whipped at her cloak and teased her hair.

But I am not alone. Not here, not now. She kept her gaze on Morgaine's without wavering. *I will never be so alone that I need turn to you, not like this, Morgaine. Have you not learned that yet from your dealings with our family?*

Although Laurel spoke not a word of this aloud, Morgaine nodded once, as if she understood, and what was more, approved. Laurel had the sudden feeling she had passed some sort of test, and a fresh spasm of anger shivered through her.

'I have a word I would say to you, lady, while we have this time to ourselves,' said Morgaine.

'What word?'

'Tintagel.'

Laurel did her best not to stare, but some hint of surprise surely showed in her face, for Morgaine smiled, just a little. 'It is a secret to no one that I wish to bring down the murderer and pretender who calls himself King Arthur. Cambryn and Tintagel could be bulwarks in the war that is to come. When it is done, and I and mine have the victory, who better could I ask to hold that great fortress between land and sea? I know your birth and blood well, Laurel Carnbrea, Laurel *verch* Morwenna. That place is naturally yours. I would give it to you.'

Laurel's tongue cleaved to the roof of her mouth. The sea wind blew hard, mingling the scents of rain and salt. She had been to Tintagel, of course. She had stood at the base of its cliffs, revelling in the rush and the wildness of the waves, hearing the song that was the other part of her own self, the part that must remain unknown, because she had promised her mother that she would protect Cambryn.

Tintagel. Could she live there? Be mistress of the land's end, and bring the two halves of herself together? Go every day and take the sea by the hand?

She looked at the woman before her with sudden, sharp

hatred. *How dare you bring me this temptation!* Again, Morgaine only smiled.

'Shall we go, my lady?' Laurel inquired frostily.

'Oh yes,' replied Morgaine. 'We have a long way to go yet, you and I.'

To this, Laurel could find no answer at all.

Laurel presided over the evening meal as best as she was able, seeing to it that her guards and her unwelcome guests were all fed as luxuriously as their remaining stores allowed. She knew from Jorey's worried looks that the extra strain was beginning to tell on the cellars. Provision for the *castell* would have to be seen to before many more days had passed. The idea that she would have to seek permission from Mesek and Peran for this basic duty galled her.

Morgaine, for her part, pretended to a distant acquaintance with Peran, and none at all with Mesek, who had reappeared just as the board was being laid. He did not say where he had been, and Laurel did not ask. She was in no humour to accept any more lies. Meg would be able to find out for her, and if Meg could not, Lynet would. Laurel tried to be grateful that all remained civil and polite, and nearly silent. The rain had begun outside, and its drumming could be heard clearly throughout the meal, there was so little noise in the hall.

By the time Laurel saw her guests settled for the night, a profound weariness dragged at every limb. She wanted nothing more than to seek her own bed, but there was one thing she must do before then. She sent Meg and the girls ahead to prepare her bed, swearing she would be with them shortly. Then, with her guards in tow and little Tag to carry the rush light, she reluctantly climbed the stairs. She travelled the long corridor beneath the roof with the storm's voice battering at her ears and its draughts curling around her ankles, until she came at last to her brother's door.

'I will speak with him,' she said to the guard who had been duly posted.

The young man – Tremere's oldest son, what was his name? – looked as if he wanted to question the wisdom of this, but he remembered himself in time, closed his mouth and stepped aside. Laurel pushed the door open.

A blast of frigid, wet air slapped against her face. Colan stood at his narrow window, the shutters thrown wide. The hiss of wind and rain hid the sound of her entry, and he did not turn.

A sister's exasperation that was older and deeper than her rage snapped into place. 'Are you looking to die of cold?'

Colan turned his head. The flickering firelight left dark hollows on his cheeks. His face was covered with a beard of at least a week's growth, which made him look all the more haggard.

'You do not fear to be alone with me?' he asked. His voice was harsh and lower than it had been when he left.

Laurel sighed. Another game. More sparring with words. 'Should I?'

'You have seen me do murder,' he answered simply. Simply. Nothing was simple now, nor would it ever be again, not even when his head had left his shoulders.

She spread her hands. 'What would my murder gain you?'

He shrugged. 'Why should I scruple at one more death?'

Laurel hung her head. Colan was soaked to the skin. His dirty tunic clung to his chest and he was shivering. He courted illness by his careless behaviour, and somehow this annoyed her more sharply than the fact that she must soon sentence him to die. 'You did not agree to be dragged back here to keep me guessing about whether you purpose my death as well as our father's.'

'You believe I agreed to be bound and thrown at your

feet?' He spoke the words slowly, with every appearance of incredulity.

'I had thought to feign ignorance,' she said almost to herself. 'To let your mistress play out whatever game she has in mind, but now that I see you again, I find I cannot do it.' She folded her arms against the chill wind blowing freely through the chamber. 'This is a failure of cunning which seems to run strong in our family.'

'Sister, I assure you, if I had my way, I would be a hundred miles from this place.'

'I am sure of that.' She was cold, and growing damp. The wildness of the wind streaming in to the chamber cut to her heart, breaking patience and thought. 'But you chose to deal with the wrong mistress. If I knew she could be this demanding of her servants, surely you must have known it as well.'

'Sister . . .' Colan held out his hand, suddenly pleading. He was a pathetic figure, rain-drenched and clearly starved. There was far too much of the boy she had helped raise in his eyes.

'Stop it, Colan,' snapped Laurel. 'Do me the courtesy of believing I can see through this much of the game.'

He dropped his hand, and the rain on his visage took on the look of tears. 'Sister, I swear before God Most High, that you need not fear that I plan anymore with her,' he whispered.

Despair surged around him like the storm winds he had invited in, and, for just a moment, Laurel's certainty wavered. 'Why is that?'

'I failed her.' The words caught in his throat and seemed to rob him of his strength. He sat heavily on the low stool beside the fire. 'When she says you may do as you will with me, she means just that,' he said to the sputtering flames, as if he already saw his fate there.

How could the sight of his defeat still reach her, with all he had done?

Because I failed him. Had I been true to our mother's last charge, he would not have become this thing. 'How is it you failed Morgaine?'

'Our sister reached Camelot.'

So. Heart and understanding snapped back into place at once. 'Should you not say the *morverch* failed her?' she inquired acidly.

He glanced up at her, his brows raised. 'You know of that then? Yes, you would. It does not matter.' He waved his hand wearily. 'It was at my urging they rose to prevent her.'

'Say murder her, Colan. You have not shrunk from the word or deed before.'

Colan picked up a crumb of peat from the floor and pitched it into the hearth. It flared briefly, sending up a scattering of sparks. 'As you will,' he said. 'Perhaps it is only because I can be reached and they cannot. It makes no difference. It was at my urging, and it did not happen. So, by the reckoning of my lady, the fault is mine.' He spoke the words mildly, as if mentioning some small piece of gossip at a feast.

'You seem resigned to this.'

He shrugged again. 'I am damned, Laurel,' he said in a hollow voice. 'I know this. I knew it the moment the knife was in my hand. I thought there might be good result of the evil I committed when I killed our father, much as I thought I had risen above the need I have of Morgaine once I met the sea-women, but there I was wrong yet again.' He turned, lifting his gaze once more to her. 'I ask you only one thing.'

Laurel folded her arms in front of her. 'What is that?'

'Do not give me to the sword,' he said softly, the frightened boy looking out of the man. 'Cast me alive into the sea.'

'Why would you wish such a thing?'

The ghost of a smile flickered about his mouth. 'I promised the *morverch* a life in return for their raising the storm
for my purposes. If I do not give them my life, they will
reach out here seeking another.'

This surprised her, but she was certain he meant what he
said. In this one way he meant to do right. 'Why should you
care?'

He shrugged. 'Believe what you will, sister, but all I have
done is because I do care – for this land, for my kin and all
that we have been and might be. I have been wrong in each
attempt, but it was not because I did not *care*.' His voice broke
on the last word. 'This last debt is mine, and I will pay it as
best I can.'

She had wanted this to be swift. She had wanted the distance
she could put between herself and the world to come to her
aid. She had, of all things, not wanted to feel the tormenting
ache in her heart or to add one more rage against necessity
to her other angers. 'I will consider what you have said.'

'Thank you.'

She could not speak. All her words choked her. She
marched past him and slammed the shutters closed, slapping
the latch into place. Why she did this, she did not know,
especially as she could not look at him as she turned on her
heel and strode out the door.

The small flock of guards stood there in the hall, waiting
for her to make some move or declaration. Stranger and
friend alike she looked at them, and saw only ox-like immobility and mindlessness staring back at her. Her teeth ground
together in seething frustration. How had it come to this?
What sin had she committed that God should punish her
thus? What penance would make it right?

Please, she prayed desperately. *Give me some sign. Any sign.
Thy will be done, only show me what it is!*

A draft from the storm outside curled around the back of her neck, raising the small hairs. A sense of movement turned her head and in the shadows beside the door, Laurel saw the flicker that meant Lynet was nearby.

She swallowed, uncertain as to whether this was the sign she had begged for, or more punishment.

'I am going to the chapel,' she announced. 'I would pray before I retire.'

She swept before them, leading her permanent, personal parade down the empty corridors. The storm had brought night early, and the only reasonable thing to do was to seek one's bed. The very thought of sleep weakened her hands and blurred her eyes, but that blessed oblivion was not yet for her.

Her guards could not go armed into the chapel, and were themselves tired enough of the day and of their duty that they did not seek to follow her inside. Instead, they stationed themselves by the door where they could doze and grumble to each other without committing blasphemy.

Laurel took the failing rush light from little Tag. With a distracted pat, she sent the yawning, blinking child to find his pallet. She used the last of the light to ignite two of the chapel's precious tapers. Above the altar, the light moved the faces of the Saviour and Holy Mother so that their eyes almost seemed to blink, as if to hold back their tears. Lynet turned swiftly from them. She glimpsed Lynet again, beside the altar, so translucent and still she might have been another of the fading images of angels and prophets that adorned the walls.

Laurel knelt in front of the altar rail, bowed her head and crossed herself. She felt Lynet move closer, felt the warmth of her presence that was the warmth of a living body. Despite this Laurel shivered, for that approach was utterly soundless. There was no breath or footfall or whisper of cloth, just the inescapable sensation of another being beside her.

'Laurel.' Even Lynet's voice was a frail ghost. Laurel had to strain her ears to hear her sister speak.

'Lynet. What have you seen?'

'Peran and Mesek have begun to search for the mirror. That is how Mesek kept himself busy while you were receiving Morgaine. He has been asking for tales of the night our mother died.'

I should have guessed it. Laurel's fingers knotted briefly together. *Well, I had a few other things to distract me.* 'Does Morgaine know of this?'

'If she does not now, she will soon. He is less than subtle.' A sort of amused anger weighed down Lynet's words. 'You should know Bess and Jen have both taken bribes.'

Laurel breathed against her icy fingertips. 'I wonder what game she is playing with our chieftains.'

'Her game with them may be done,' said Lynet. 'They have got her what she wanted. Our hall and our family are well and truly breached.'

'Perhaps.' Laurel pressed her forehead to her knuckles. She was so tired. It was so hard to think with Lynet's shade beside her like this. She was forgetting something vital. She knew it. 'Are any of her people abroad now?'

'No. Sister . . . will you look at me?'

Laurel screwed her eyes more tightly shut. 'No, sister, I will not.'

'Why?'

She had only honesty left. Her mind was too crowded and cramped for anything else. 'It frightens me, Lynet.'

'I . . .'

'Yes, I know.' Laurel tried to be brisk and strong. They needed this sacrifice of Lynet. They needed the knowledge she could bring and the watch she could keep. She could carry on telling herself that, and it would still be wrong. She lifted her eyes to the Holy Mother so perfectly carved above her. The wind blew, the candles flickered, and it seemed as if the Virgin's hand moved, as if she wanted so much to reach out to her Son, but did not dare. 'Lynet . . .'

'What is it?'

'Lynet, do not tell the queen that Morgaine is here.'

'Why not?'

Tintagel . . . She would give me Tintagel, sister. She would murder you, but thinks I would accept the fortress. There was something that had been said . . . something Colan had said that was important to this, but her mind was too dizzy with weariness and anger to remember it clearly now. 'Because I do not know enough yet. Because for all our brother firmly believes she came here just to throw him to his death, I do not believe that is the only reason.' Those dark eyes looking at her over their father's cairn, the memory that it was only days ago they were still talking of making an alliance with this woman, the sick nagging feeling that she was forgetting something, the way her sister's presence caught up her fear, touching it, smoothing it, redoubling it until it folded around her like an extra cloak.

'Laurel, this is dangerous.'

'Yes, I know.' *Oh, I do know.*

'I have already told them here of how Morgaine sought to use Peran and Colan, and I have told the queen of the *morverch*.'

Laurel nodded. She clenched her fingers so tightly together pain spread all the way down her hands. 'That is good. She will believe you have told her all there is then.'

Lynet was still for a moment and the fear evened out and loosened, allowing Laurel to breathe more easily.

'Very well. I will hold my silence for as long as I am able.'

'I can ask no more.'

'Be careful, sister.' Love in bright waves rolled around her

now, easing her, embracing her, and yet its intensity frightened her all the more. 'We leave tomorrow, and will be with
you before a fortnight has passed, if all goes well.'

What of this has gone well? 'I will keep watch for you, sister.
God be with you.'

'And you, sister.'

She was gone then, and Laurel was alone save for the
stray wisps of storm wind that snaked across the floor.
Taking up one of the tapers, she walked through draughts,
scarcely feeling the cold. She had felt so much worse this
night. When she reached the corridor, her guards joined
her, stumping along behind. She was too tired and too
worried to care for them. She needed sleep. She needed
desperately to think.

Laurel had given over her chamber to Morgaine's use. She
wanted to isolate the sorceress from Cambryn's folk as much
as possible, and to make it difficult for either Mesek or Peran
to speak with her unobserved. So now Laurel walked down
to the new hall. There was just enough light left in her
guttering candle to show her the sleeping bodies on their
pallets and let her make her way around them to the great
bed that had been set up for her in the place nearest the
hearth. Meg waited for her, drowsing, but she woke herself
instantly when Laurel approached. With the help of her
daughter, the waiting woman removed Laurel's outer dress,
and helped her into the bed, smoothing down the covers to
her own satisfaction so that she could say her duty was done
and seek out her own bed.

The curtains fell into place, and darkness closed over
Laurel. The storm was far away here. Despite this, sleep did
not come. It was buried under a thick blanket of memories.
She remembered the foul smell of sickness that had twisted
her insides. She remembered the swan-white form of her
mother as her women, Meg among them, rolled her gently

onto her side to try to ease her breathing. She remembered the touch of her mother's hands, strangely hot, light as feathers and dry as autumn leaves, as she gave over the mirror and warned Laurel of its promise, and its danger.

'Forgive me, Laurel,' mother had said, her voice a harsh whisper. Her belly was bloated under the layers of her gown as if she were pregnant with another child. 'I meant to stay with you, truly I did.'

Laurel felt the eyes of the women on her, waiting for her to say something pious and comforting to ease her mother's passing. She couldn't say anything. She wanted her mother to talk, and to never stop talking. She wanted to drink in every bit of her so mother would be inside her forever and never leave her, not even for God and Heaven and Judgement Day.

'You are closest to the sea, Laurel. This will be your protection, but it will also mean you must make choices the others do not.' Mother's breath left her then and she was unable to speak for a long sickening moment as her chest wheezed and struggled. 'Choose wisely, my daughter, for there are some choices you will be able to make but once.'

'I will,' whispered Laurel. 'I will try.'

Mother's fingers tightened around hers, so weak, so hot and dry, not like herself at all. It was as if she was already gone. *The soul must be a heavy thing*, Laurel remembered thinking, *if its leaving makes the body so light.*

'Promise me, whatever else you choose, my daughter, my first child, you will protect Cambryn. It is your father's place, and I have loved it always for his sake. Promise me, you will protect this place and your kin within it.'

This was a choice, Laurel had realized then. One of those mother was warning her of. This was real somehow, beyond the speaking of words or the laws of the world. She knew it in the depths of her heart and in the fearful look in her mother's pale green eyes.

'I swear,' she whispered, clutching the cool mirror. 'I swear I will protect this place and my kin within it.'

Mother drew one slow easy breath. She spoke no more, and Laurel held her mother's hand until it slid from her fingers.

Now lying in that same bed, Lynet could only stare into the darkness and think of her promise. She had sworn to protect this place and her kindred in it, but from what? So many powers besieged them, how could she tell which alliance would make them safe, and which would bring them greater danger.

Tintagel. With the sea, her mother's home, spread out at her back, she could keep them all safe, from whatever came. She would never be suffocated inside a house of dead stone again. Lynet had lived through the *morverch*'s attack. If Laurel agreed to help Morgaine, what reason would the sorceress have to try to take Lynet's life again. She would be saving her sister if she gave Morgaine what she wanted. Saving her sister and herself. Morgaine would protect Cambryn, better than Arthur and Guinevere had.

All she had to do was pretend. Pretend that she did not know it was Morgaine who had ordered Lynet's murder. Pretend that it was too late for Guinevere to be of any help to them. She could have the freedom she had always yearned for and still keep the only promise that had ever truly mattered.

It was a staggering choice she was offered. *Some choices can only be made once.*

With her mother's words echoing around her head, exhaustion finally took her, and Laurel slid uneasily into sleep.

FIFTEEN

For the first five days, the journey from Camelot was as easy as could be wished for. The weather held, except for spits and spatterings of rain. The gentle country was well populated and the Roman roads straight and broad. They slept each night on stout beds beneath a roof and hot food, well-prepared and plentiful, waited for them when they rose. The best of everything was brought out for Camelot's queen, and all her people shared in the bounty her presence produced.

After that, though, they came to the edge of inhabited country. The way grew progressively steeper. The lowlands gave way to a country of round hills and sharply creased valleys. They had to dismount and lead the horses so often that Lynet was ready to swear walking would be faster. The trees crowded thick along the ragged tracks, making a loose roof of interwoven branches for the sun to filter through. When there was sun. The weather also ceased to favour them. The overcast sky poured down rain, stopping only long enough for the drenching mists to rise up from the ground. When these got too thick, the rain would fall again, helpfully dampening them down. Their fine and orderly procession turned into a straggling line stretched out across the countryside with not even the waiting women able to keep beside the queen. Cold and damp worked their way into Lynet's boots and wrung enough pain from her feet that she was cursing through her teeth as much to keep her tears back as to give vent to her anger.

They halted while there was still something left of the rain-drenched daylight. Men struggled against mud and weather to raise the pavilion that had been brought. The maids laid out the rugs and set up the cunningly carved furniture and the waiting ladies held an extra cloak over the queen's head, trying in some measure to keep the rain off her. When at last the pavilion was standing and Lynet was able to join the other women in the relative dryness, she was ready to cry a blessing on the weavers of such stout cloth. While the serving women struggled to light the braziers on their tripods, and the waiting women opened wine for warming and stripped the queen of her wet things, Daere found a chair for Lynet to collapse into. She closed her eyes, revelling in the simple sensation of not moving. Daere eased off her sodden boots with extra care. The maid was now fully accustomed to the sight of Lynet's damaged feet and gently but efficiently dried them off and wrapped them in a clean cloth.

After a time, the fires did their work, clothes and carpets began to dry and warmth began to creep back into Lynet. Outside, the rain slowed and stopped, and the noises of the camp rose in its place; men and the very occasional woman calling out, complaining, and laughing. Bread, pottage, bacon and beer were served, and while it was not luxurious fare, it was filling, and Lynet ate with a will. Afterwards, the queen commanded that one of the brandywine jars be unsealed and even the serving women were served a little of the strong and warming drink. As the last of the daylight faded away, stories, jokes and gossip unfolded, mostly about places and people Lynet had never heard of before. She sat with her feet wrapped warmly and her cup of strong wine, and tried her best not to nod off. She was exhausted. She ached. She could not fall asleep. Not yet. She had shared a bed with Daere and Lady Nola every night since Camelot. She must find her way back to Cambryn tonight. She had not spoken to Laurel in days. She did not know what was happening at her home, what Peran and Mesek were doing.

She could not sleep until she knew.

Outside the pavilion, the guard barked a challenge. Lady Sabia was on her feet first, making her way to the door. The loosely laced flap was pulled open and the guard leaned in and murmured something.

'Who is it, Sabia?' asked the queen.

'Lord Lancelot, Your Majesty.'

This answer startled the queen a little, but she motioned to her waiting lady, who opened the pavilion entrance wide enough to permit the knight to enter. He was not alone, Gareth and two other squires – one thinner and slightly shorter, the other broader with narrow, calculating eyes – walked behind him.

'Your Majesty,' said Sir Lancelot, as all four knelt.

'My Lord Lancelot,' said the queen, gesturing for them to rise. 'Is something amiss?'

'Nothing, Majesty.' He bowed to the rest of the company. 'It was only my wish to make sure you were as comfortable as you could be made, and that you had all that you needed. I know well that you and your ladies are not used to such marches as these.'

The queen's face shifted uneasily before it settled into a properly polite expression. 'You are most welcome, my lord,' she said. 'Your care for myself bespeaks your thoughtfulness and loyalty to the throne of Camelot and I give thanks for it.'

'You do me great honour.'

They regarded one another in a silence that grew increasingly strained with each heartbeat, but the knight made no move to go. Lynet found her gaze darting back and forth between Queen Guinevere and Sir Lancelot. She'd seen the Gaulish knight only from a distance before now. He was a handsome man, a veritable statue of knightly virtue, with his strong shoulders and arms, his golden hair, and the fine beard that outlined his chiselled jaw. But there was something cold about his beauty. Involuntarily she found herself comparing him to Sir Tristan. She could not for a moment imagine Sir Lancelot laying his thick fingers to a harp string. This was a blunt man, lacking the lively quickness of a Tristan, or even of his squire, Gareth, behind him.

Gareth, who caught her eye with the barest flicker of his own. In confusion, Lynet dropped her gaze to her hands on her lap. Had she been staring at him? Lord God, she was more tired than she had realized.

'Will you take a cup of wine with me, Sir Lancelot?' asked Queen Guinevere at last, but Lynet could not miss the undertone of reluctance in the invitation.

'Thank you, Your Majesty.' Sir Lancelot bowed. 'You do me yet another honour.'

There then began a complex dance between the squires and the waiting women as another chair was found, a table placed, wine and cups and a bowl of nuts was brought. As Lynet was no servant, she had nothing to do but watch, and she did not miss how, time and again, Squire Gareth seemed to find himself next to Lady Sabia, and how he touched her, softly, secretly brushed her hand or her sleeve, and how she turned away from him each time.

Is this what Daere was shielding me from?

When the flurry of activity settled down again, Sir Lancelot sat beside the queen, his legs stretched out before him, crossed at the ankle. His boots were still crusted with mud, as was the hem of his madder-red cloak, but otherwise the day's hard travel seemed to have had little effect on the knight. He watched appreciatively as Lady Braith poured his wine. She blushed under his regard, and Lady Nola, exiled on the other side of the queen, brushed at her skirt irritably.

The queen missed none of this, and a frown flickered across her face before she could swiftly smooth it away.

'Tell me, Lord Lancelot, how are our men and supplies faring?'

This was clearly not what Sir Lancelot was expecting to hear, and it took him a minute before he was able to answer. 'Tolerably well, Your Majesty. The rain's in nearly everything, but the food casks and the bread are still dry, so we won't be marching on air . . .'

Lynet tried to focus politely on what the knight was saying, but it was difficult. Despite her vow to stay awake, his voice quickly became a monotonous drone. Two of the squires had moved back to chat with the serving maids. Lynet supposed she should tell Daere to help her move closer to the queen, so she could attend better, as she was nominally one of the queen's women for this time. The others listened with every appearance of fascination to Sir Lancelot, except for the queen, who was sipping quickly at her wine, and Lady Sabia, who cast annoyed glances back and forth.

'God be with you this evening, Lady Lynet,' said a soft voice beside her.

Lynet jumped. Squire Gareth had circled round behind her at some point. 'Daere, your mistress's cup is empty,' he said.

Daere opened her mouth to make some tart reply, but Lynet cut her off. 'If you please, Daere.' The maid closed her mouth and glowered again, moving to the wine jar. Lynet did not intend to drink. She just wanted to avoid drawing more attention to herself. 'God be with you, Squire Gareth,' she replied politely.

'I hope you have not found the journey too hard.'

No one was paying particular attention to her, except Lady Sabia, who was staring daggers at Squire Gareth's back, and Daere, who was motioning to the serving girl to hurry and fill the cup.

'I have endured worse, Squire,' replied Lynet. Daere moved across the tent as quickly as she could without spilling the wine. 'Do not alarm yourself on my account.'

'I find I cannot help myself.' He spoke the words soberly, but with a smile in his brown eyes.

'I am well protected, Squire, I assure you,' she answered evenly. She might not be Laurel's match for distant propriety, but she could muster her own dignity when required. When she did not dip her eyes or show any maidenly coyness, the smile in his eyes wavered.

'Right glad I am to hear it.'

Was he giving polite answer to her refusal to banter with him, or did he actually mean those words? Lynet found she could not tell, and that troubled her.

'I thank you,' she said, and could think of nothing else.

He searched her eyes for a moment longer. What he read there she could not say, but he bowed his head and stepped back, making room for Daere who handed her the brimming wine cup, gave the squire a dark glower and began fussily to rewrap Lynet's feet.

As the maid's tacit disapproval did not seem to be shifting the squire, Lynet cast about for some subject of conversation that could not be mistaken for an attempt at intimacy. Her gaze lit on Sir Lancelot sitting beside the queen, much as Gareth now sat beside her.

'So, Squire Gareth, tell me of your knight,' she said. 'How is it a man of Gaul came to be at Camelot?'

She wondered if he would be put off by her interest in Sir Lancelot, but Gareth's face only brightened. He spoke of

Lancelot's father, a king in Britaigne across the water who had sent his son to join the cadre of the Round Table, and how Lancelot had decided to prove himself worthy by facing the hazards of the journey alone.

'It was the most amazing thing,' Gareth said. 'My lord barged through the gates, ignoring the guards. He had a whole string of Saxons with him, a dozen of them, all roped together like horses for sale, and he brought them right up to the door of the keep, declaring he had a gift for Arthur, greatest of all earthly kings.' He swept his hand out, but at the same time glanced behind him, as if to make sure his knight had not overheard him in this brief imitation.

Lynet's brows lifted. 'How did he come by a dozen Saxons as travelling companions?'

'That's the best part of it,' Gareth said eagerly. 'This clot of Saxons had ambushed him and dragged him off to their camp. You see, it is their way, when they wish to take the measure of an enemy, to take one of his men hostage and put him to fight their champion in single combat, so they can gauge his strength and training, and the mettle of the man.

'My lord fought their first champion and slew him. They put forth another, and he slew that one too, and then a third, and a fourth. By then, it became clear to the Saxon chief that Lancelot was prepared to keep killing his men as he kept sending them, and so he surrendered them all and himself with them.'

'A bold tale,' acknowledged Lynet. But while she searched for something more to say, the queen drained the last of her cup, and set it down on the table. 'You must forgive me, my Lord Lancelot.' Queen Guinevere stood, her demeanour all politeness and apology. 'I find I am tired, and would go to my rest.'

The rest of the company got to its feet at once. 'Forgive

me, Majesty,' said Sir Lancelot. 'I forget sometimes that not all are soldiers who can stay awake through the night and still march well in the morning. God be with you.' He bowed deeply.

'And with you,' replied the queen with utmost politeness, but nothing more.

Sir Lancelot nodded to the squires. Gareth bowed to Lynet with his smile all in his eyes. Then he followed his knight as he swept out of the tent, his red cloak billowing behind him.

'There goes one who knows his own worth a little too well,' murmured Daere at Lynet's side, and Lynet found she could not fault her maid's assessment. 'Squire's like the master, it should be no surprise to any.'

It was another of her warnings, and it was well-timed, for already Lynet found herself wondering if that were true. Fortunately, she was spared from having to answer. As soon as the pavilion entrance closed behind the knight and his squires, the serving and waiting women began to dismantle the chairs and tables and in their places unroll beds and coverings. Daere helped Lynet out of her over-dress and left her sturdy woollen under-dress. The maid knew by now to return Lynet's girdle to her, so she could tie it once more around her waist, keeping her purse and its contents beside her.

She lay down on her bed and let Daere pull the covers over her. One by one, the serving women banked and covered the braziers, leaving them all in darkness. Lynet flexed her toes repeatedly, letting the pain help keep her awake. Around her, breathing slowed and the rustlings of the women rolling over and burrowing deeper into their bed coverings gradually stilled. The night sounds outside the pavilion held sway now, and her eyelids tried to close yet again. She could not wait anymore. This was the first time in days she'd had a bed to herself. Who knew where they would be tomorrow night, or what the circumstances would be. She must try now.

Lynet opened her purse and drew out the mirror. She raised herself up on one elbow to lean over it, but there was not even enough light for her to catch sight of her reflection in the surface. She touched her fingertips to the glass. *Ryol. Ryol. Come to me. I need you. Hear me, Ryol.*

Did the glass soften beneath her touch, or was that only another seeming? All Lynet knew clearly was the deep compulsion that seized hold of her once more, pulling spirit from flesh, and she welcomed it, giving herself over to it wholly and falling forward into that deeper darkness.

When her eyes could see again, she stood in the now-familiar garden. Its sunless light poured down on her as a warm and welcome balm. Her weariness had fallen away with the darkness, and she was whole and well again.

She was also alone. 'Ryol?' she called, and for a moment, only the rustle of leaves replied. Then Ryol stepped out from under the birch tree. He passed a wild rose as he came towards her, brushing one of the blossoms with his hip. Three pale petals fell onto the grass, leaving the flower lopsided. It was, she realized, the first imperfection she had seen in this place.

Something was wrong with Ryol as well, although she could not put a name to exactly what it was. He looked as he always did, but she found herself remembering how it was to stand in the old hall and greet her father when he returned once more from helping defend the coast lands. He would look much the same as ever, but little things would be altered: his eyes sunken a little further, his hair a little more grey, a new scar perhaps, but mostly it was in his manner. He came back older from those expeditions, no matter how famous the triumph. His blood, he said, ran a little thinner, and the nights felt a little colder. That was how

Ryol looked, as if the night even in this unending daylight, felt a little colder.

'My lady.' He grasped both her hands, pressing them to his brow.

'Ryol, what is the matter?'

'Nothing, lady. It is fear only.'

'Fear? Of what?'

He licked his lips, as if trying to decide what to say. 'You have been speaking with the sorcerer Merlin.'

Lynet drew back. 'He is Arthur's man,' she said uneasily, remembering the gathering shadows that had hung so heavily over her shoulders in Merlin's house. 'If I want Arthur's help, I must speak with his people.'

'Beware him,' said Ryol softly.

She frowned. She did not want fear in this place. This was a haven from fear and worry, her bright summer garden from which she was free to see and do and act without constraint. 'Why?'

'He trusts no power save his own, my lady, and would bring all under his own heel.' Ryol had not let go of her hands, but only gripped them more tightly, as if he could will his urgency into her. 'He has stolen power before, and far greater power than what you hold.'

'What do you know of Merlin?'

'Enough, lady. I beg you as your loyal servant. Beware him.'

'Be easy then,' she said, in the stiffly reasoned tones she used with Jorey when he was dithering about how much was being laid out for the tinning feast. 'He is back in Camelot. The ladies seem to think the queen does not trust him either.'

'Have you told her anything?'

'I have spoken the truth.' She pulled her hands away. 'Do you say I should lie to my queen?' She said this to prod at him, searching for argument or apology, anything that would give her an excuse to dismiss the worry that was slowly bleeding from him to her.

Ryol would not be drawn. 'You have not told her of the mirror, of myself?'

'No.'

He bowed his head, perhaps giving thanks. 'Pray do not then. She will take me from you.' He spoke with utter certainty.

'She would not rob me of my mother's gift,' Lynet said staunchly. But she remembered the steel flash to those grey eyes. Queen Guinevere would do what she believed necessary, whatever that might be.

'I beg you believe me, lady,' said Ryol earnestly. His face was drawn, and she could see the lines of weathering and age in it. It was, she realized, very like Bishop Austell's. 'While I have waited for your return, I have seen many things, visited many places.'

'You travel of your own will?' It was not something she had considered before, and tales of airy spirits and demons of the night came to her. She shook them back. 'I thought you . . . remained here.'

'This garden is another shadow, lady,' said Ryol. 'It is here for you. When you leave me, there is only darkness and the shifting world around. I can feel the currents and breezes that are the motion of time. I may be anywhere and nowhere at all. The man of me exists only when you are here.'

'What else have you seen?' she asked.

'I will show you.' He extended his arm, and she took it. Lynet walked with her servant through his garden of shadows. They turned beneath the trees, passed the sound of running waters, and walked through the gap in the hawthorn hedge, out onto the open heath, with Cambryn and its keep rising up before them. A black-haired woman in a gown of blue and cloak of black rode at the head of a small procession of ladies and men-at-arms. Morgaine. Lynet shivered at the sight of the smile on the sorceress's face. She looked satisfied, as if at a deed neatly accomplished.

Hoofbeats drummed in the distance. 'My lady!' cried a hoarse voice. 'My lady!'

Morgaine turned to watch Peran, riding so quickly he looked almost comical, with his elbows flapping and his too-small pony's ears laid flat against its skull.

'My lady!' He reined the pony up short to come level with her. He was breathing nearly as hard as his mount. Morgaine regarded all this coldly.

'What is it, Peran?' she asked. 'Why do you follow me?'

'I did not think . . .' he gasped. 'I did not think you would quit Cambryn so soon. I . . . we did not speak before this . . .'

'And why should we speak?'

Peran's face fell and his hands went slack on the reins. In response, his pony shifted back a few steps, snorting its annoyance. Peran did not even seem to notice. He only felt Morgaine's indifference as she sat before him, plainly wishing to continue her own journey. Behind her, her ladies smiled in thin-lipped contempt.

'Because Mesek is searching for the power hidden in Cambryn. He intends to use it to overthrow Kenan's daughters, and deny you the fortress.'

A tiny smile formed on Morgaine's face, growing and spreading before she let out a great laugh, startling her own horse. 'Mesek thinks the power of Cambryn is something you can steal? Oh, he is ten times the fool I thought he was!'

'He thinks I am aiding him, my lady,' croaked Peran.

Morgaine's smile vanished at once. She looked afresh at the Treanhal's chieftain, as if contemplating a stranger before her. 'And are you?'

'I have done all you asked, my lady,' he said, his voice

hitching and rasping in his ravaged throat. 'Mesek roams
Cambryn at will, the Pendragon is returning here, and my
lady will not speak to me. What am I to do?'

Morgaine urged her horse closer to his, so they sat side-
by-side, each facing the other. Morgaine laid her strong
brown hand over Peran's burned and scarred one.

'You have been required to bear much, Peran,' she said
softly. 'I know that. Perhaps it has been too much for you.
I am sorry.'

His eyes were wide and a little wild. He was on the edge
of panic. Even though he was only a shadow before her,
Lynet could feel it swirling through the air. 'Just tell me all
is right, lady. I will believe you. All I ask is that you give me
a little hope.'

'All is right, Peran,' she told him firmly, giving his hand a
small shake, 'You have put us in jeopardy by riding here so
boldly, but it will not matter. You can do nothing more but
wait. Aid Mesek or hinder him, it matters not.' Her smile
grew knowing. 'All goes as it should and all that is wrong
will be made right very soon. Here.' She took up his hand
between both of hers, pulling it close. 'I cannot heal you
fully, but let me give you ease.'

She raised his hand higher, bowing her head over the
mottled flesh as if she meant to kiss it. But instead she blew
out a long breath. Lynet felt it like the lightest of spring
zephyrs. The touch of it brought longing, and a warmth both
soothing and dangerous. Peran hissed in surprise, and a
moment later closed his eyes, all other emotion dissolving
into bliss. Morgaine took his face in both her hands and
kissed him full on the mouth. He answered that kiss ardently,
wrapping his arms about her shoulders, pulling her close as
a man might his lover. Morgaine permitted this, and their
kiss deepened. The heat of it tumbled over and through Lynet.
She became acutely aware of Ryol beside her. She must run

away, do anything but stand here and witness this strange and powerful kiss.

But just as she was sure she could bear it no more, Morgaine released Peran, smiling at the expression on his face that was half-delight, half-disbelief. He touched his throat, and then grasped her hand, pressing it to his brow. In return, she covered his head with her free hand in fond blessing.

'Be patient, my friend,' she said, still smiling. 'You have done all I could ask for.'

'Thank you, my lady,' he murmured. This time there was no jagged edge to his voice. His words were still rough, but they did not strain, and his breath no longer rattled in his chest.

With a nod to her retainers, Morgaine touched up her horse and the procession trotted away down the high road, Morgaine's blue raven banner fluttering in the light breeze.

Ryol's hand lay heavy on Lynet's shoulder, and she felt him warm beside her. For a moment she savoured this. She could do nothing else, her mind was so overwhelmed by the love and the desire that filled all the world as Peran watched his lady ride away. But slowly, all the heat cooled and she remembered blood, and she remembered the face of madness in front of her and she jerked herself away.

'When was this?'

'Yesterday.' Hurt shone in Ryol's newly aged eyes, but Lynet could find no word of comfort.

'We must . . .' she began.

He did not let her finish. 'You must go, my lady,' said Ryol, holding himself very still.

'What?' she frowned. 'No! We must go to Laurel and warn her . . .'

He held up his hand, gazing about him, seeing what she

could not. 'My lady, trust me in this. We have no time. There is danger without and you must go.'

Lynet hesitated, but only for a moment. She must either trust him or not. She stepped back yet further.

'Do not let her take me from you, my lady,' said Ryol urgently, still staring at the empty air. 'Do not let anyone. I cannot reach you if they take the mirror. It would be too much for both of us.' With that, Ryol swept all the shadows away with a gesture. He was gone in a heartbeat, and Lynet was alone in the leaden darkness.

She awoke with a start. She was sprawled on her pallet, the covers in complete disarray, her right hand clutching the mirror tightly. Light flickered across her and leaning close enough to rest a hand on her shoulder was Queen Guinevere.

'You cried out,' said the queen. 'Are you well?' She laid a cool hand on Lynet's brow, checking for fever.

'Yes, Majesty.' Hastily Lynet scrambled to sit up properly, and thrust the mirror beneath the bed covers. 'It was a nightmare.'

But she was not quick enough. The queen caught a glimpse of what she hid, perhaps a sparkle of light on the glass. 'What is that?'

'Oh.' Lynet brought it out again, cradling it in her palm, trying to hide it without seeming to. 'It is a mirror.'

Even in the faint and guttering light of the brazier, Lynet could see how thoughtful the queen's face became.

'May I see it?' Queen Guinevere asked, her voice as smoothly casual as Lynet had tried to make hers.

Lynet desperately cast about for some reason to refuse, but none came and she had to lay the precious artefact into the queen's stained palm.

Queen Guinevere lifted the mirror to the light to examine it better. Lynet clenched her jaw to keep from crying aloud for her majesty to take care. The queen ran her long fingers around the frame, and closely examined the way the fire-light flickered in the flawless glass. With every heartbeat that passed, it became harder for Lynet not to snatch the mirror back again.

'I have never seen one so beautiful,' Queen Guinevere said as she handed the mirror back to Lynet. 'It must be very precious.'

Lynet's fingers folded gently but possessively around the mirror, as if they folded around her own heart. 'It was a gift from my mother, Majesty. Nothing could be more precious.' *Let it be, Majesty. It can mean nothing to you.*

But the queen showed no sign of granting that silent wish. She did not seem to mind her undignified position there on her knees before her liege woman disarrayed in her bed. 'I have never seen a glass so flat and smooth,' she remarked, sitting back on her heels. 'Nor so light. One wonders at the artisan who could make such a thing.'

Lynet managed a thoughtful nod. 'All craft secrets look to be miracles, I suppose.' A thought struck her, a way to divert the inquiry. 'They say the Round Table was joined together by enchantment.'

Queen Guinevere laughed a little at this. 'No, merely consummate skill, but you speak the truth. Still,' she went on musingly, 'that mirror is a lovely thing. If I knew the craftsman, I would surely bespeak him to make me another.'

She looked at Lynet, her grey eyes mild, but full of meaning. The queen was asking for the mirror, and Lynet should give it over to her. That was the way of such things.

But was it for its beauty the queen wanted the mirror, or did she guess something more? *Do not let her take me from you.* Ryol's words rang in her ears. He had known this would come. He had warned her.

'I must beg Your Majesty's forgiveness,' said Lynet carefully. 'This was a gift from my mother, but it was not given to me. It was given to my sister. She lent it to me to carry as the dearest token of our home, but on the absolute promise that I bring it back to her. We have so little left of our mother . . .' She let the words trail off and made herself meet the queen's soft grey gaze.

'I understand,' Queen Guinevere said with a smile that said she knew what it was to be so attached to such a trifle. That smile, though, did not reach her watchful eyes. 'What was your dream?'

'My dream?' she repeated, not understanding.

'You said it was a nightmare that made you cry out,' the queen reminded her patiently. She got to her feet and set the brazier back on its tripod. At the foot of her bed, Lady Nola stirred uneasily but did not wake. 'What was your dream?'

The feeling of being trapped overtook Lynet. She swiftly chose a story that was close to the truth. 'I dreamed I was in Cambryn again. My sister was in danger. I wanted to warn her, but I could not . . .'

'What was this danger?' The queen sat on the edge of her bed.

'I could not be sure,' murmured Lynet, hoping that the catch in her throat would be taken for distress.

'I see.' Queen Guinevere sighed. 'Well, we could ask for a better omen. Still, we move as swiftly as we can and we can do no more.' She picked up the brazier's brass cover. 'Go back to sleep, Lynet. You will soon be home.'

Under the queen's watchful gaze, Lynet returned the mirror to its purse, and laid herself back down on her pallet.

Lynet drew up her coverings. Only then did the queen cover the brazier, blotting out the light. *God Almighty. Could she know?*

This much was certain: Ryol had spoken the truth yet again. Queen Guinevere would take the mirror. She did not believe the story of the dream. She knew something was wrong. Lynet could not risk discovery with it again, but she could not stop keeping her watch over Cambryn. She would have to take greater care. She would have to find another way.

Lynet lay awake a long time waiting for the queen's breathing to slow and soften. Only then could she close her eyes. As she did, she felt a fleeting presence, something swift yet undeniable, like the touch of a shadow's hand on her shoulder.

Ryol? she thought, but her exhaustion overcame her, and both sensation and thought flitted away.

SIXTEEN

'Now!' shouted Gareth, hauling on the ox's halter.

The ungainly creature snorted wetly and lumbered forward as the men behind its cart put their backs to it yet again. The reins creaked and the mud squelched, and with a low sucking sound the cartwheel rolled free of the mud hole and up onto the track again. The ox swung its heavy head as far as the yoke would permit it, annoyed to find its burden mobile. While Gareth held the beast, the carter crawled beneath the conveyance and came out again, all smiles.

'She's sound!' he called up to Gareth, and Gareth nodded in return, giving up a silent prayer of thanks. The last thing they needed was the delay of a broken wheel or axle.

'Pass the word to drive around that swamp!' he called as he mounted his horse again. 'And catch up as quick as you can. We're almost to Lan Nanse, and we need to make it before dark!'

The man touched his brow in salute and set about yelling at the remaining carters. Seeing the matter in hand, Gareth urged his horse into a trot, riding at the edge of the road, skirting between the unbroken fence of trees and the queen's procession.

The springtime woods that surrounded them now would have provided a thoroughly pleasant ride under other circumstances. The haze of green overhead let the sparse sunlight filter through to light up the snowdrops and ferns that poked up everywhere. The first of the herbs had begun to unfurl, softening the countryside and lending their sharp scents to the air that was otherwise overburdened with the pungent smells of working men and beasts. Birdsong was everywhere, and occasionally the rustle and crash of some larger creature. Deer tracks had been seen, and boar, and bear. Sir Lancelot had talked of a hunting party, but the queen would not hear of the delay. If they did not immediately need the meat to feed their people, they were to continue on.

But Gareth did not have much time to admire the wild countryside. His task, along with the other squires, was to ride up and down the length of the procession, being the knights' eyes, and voice where needed, making sure as much as possible that their caravan stayed together and moved at a decent pace. He shouted at stragglers, made peace between quarrelling cousins, and helped pull carts from mud holes, reported to his knight, and then turned around to do it all again.

And this was a good day, when they had a road under them. Not a Roman road to be sure, but it was better than the deer paths they'd been following as they plunged into the great woodland. It would not last much longer. The roads ended at Lan Nanse. After that, they would be crossing the northern edge of Bodmin Moor that lay outside of Cambryn. They would be wishing for those deer runs then, anything to find their way between the bogs and the mists. Gareth shook himself to get rid of the shudder that threatened to creep up on him. Gawain had relished telling him some of the stories Tristan had brought with him of the ghosts and demons that haunted that open wasteland. As a Christian man, Gareth did not believe such tales, but his boyhood was still close enough that he was quietly glad not to have to prove himself in that way. Not yet.

He had almost reached the head of the procession. He could see the backs of the queen and her women on their horses, their cloaks flowing and fluttering in the damp spring breeze. Dark, prim Nola, fair and flighty Braith, who the queen really should see married off before her wandering eyes caught the wrong man, and Sabia, with her brown hair and pale skin, and her smiles full of promises that were somehow never quite fulfilled. Before his disgrace, he'd been more than willing to be patient, certain he'd win through in the end, and with Rosy and the others to take the edge off, why not be willing to wait? But since then, he'd only received the barest of glances, and when he'd tried to touch her secretly yesterday as they had touched so many times before, she had pulled away. Strangely, he'd found himself comparing her, unfavourably, to Lady Lynet.

She would make no promise she did not mean to keep, he thought, and he found himself wondering what she might promise, and to whom, and when. Then he remembered her tale of murder done in her family and her rough shout at the High King himself when she felt herself dismissed. She would never act like Lady Sabia, much less like Lady Braith. For her, flashes of humour were rare. Rarer still seemed glimpses of genuine happiness. No, games of love were not for such a one.

Then why do I keep thinking on her that way? he asked himself, and he found he had no answer.

In front of him, Lady Sabia's horse suddenly stumbled, causing her to fall back behind Lady Nola, who she'd been riding beside. She reined the mare up and looked about her in seeming confusion. Nola also made to stop, but Sabia waved her on, coaxing the horse to the side of the road to let the rest of the procession pass. Cursing under his breath, Gareth urged his own horse forward. He swung down and offered Sabia his hand so that she could dismount with matronly propriety.

'I fear she has taken a stone, Squire Gareth,' said Lady Sabia. 'Will you look?'

As she spoke, Lady Lynet rode past them, watching Gareth as he stood beside Sabia. She should have been up front with the queen and the ladies, but it was her habit to ride back down the line several times during the day to speak with her own captain and his men. Their eyes met and he felt his shoulders straighten a little. He thought to see disapproval or disappointment on her face, but what he saw instead was a weary resignation. She turned her gaze rigidly forward and urged her dapple-grey palfrey into a faster trot.

'Squire Gareth?' said Sabia. 'My horse?'

'Of course, my lady.' Gareth dragged his attention back to the task at hand. The brown mare was a reasonable creature and let him lift her right fore-hoof and rest it on his knee. She whickered, snorted and leaned comfortably on his shoulder while he probed the hoof, especially the soft frog. 'There's no stone,' he said to Lady Sabia. 'It was just a stumble. This road is not so smooth as it would seem.'

'As a man may be less devoted than he seems,' Sabia replied with a strained smile.

Gareth patted the mare's shoulder to warn her she would have to take her own weight now, and set her hoof down. 'What sign of devotion should I have sent you from the kitchens, my lady?' he asked softly. 'When you sent not a one to me?'

Anger flared behind her eyes. Gareth knew that was the sign for him to apologize and pay a compliment. Another day, he would have enjoyed the game. He loved seeing her anger melt away and turn to delight at the merest word from him. But he remained silent, bent double beside her horse, and let her snap at him. 'How could I have done that? The queen watches me so close, I can barely draw breath.'

'Then she is sure to notice you standing here now.' Gently, Gareth felt the mare's ankle and knee, making sure there was no tenderness or sign of swelling. 'Why take the risk now, my lady?'

'Why do you spend your time mooning over that doe-eyed Lady Lynet?' she shot back.

A cold finger touched the back of Gareth's neck. He straightened, laying one hand on the mare's shoulder. 'She is in need of help, and it is my duty as the king's man to offer it.'

'Oh yes, I'm sure she needs a great deal of help from you.' Sabia's words were needle sharp. 'The sort she received from Sir Tristan for helping in the cuckolding of a king.'

Gareth found himself standing very still. 'What?' he asked softly.

'She has so far neglected to mention that, I suppose.' Lady Sabia stepped up in front of him and took the reins he had slung over the saddle. 'It was she who ran messages between the lovers Tristan and Iseult. Perhaps even took money from the king to betray them. A fine lady for you to tip your heart towards.' Ignoring his move to help her, Sabia mounted her horse again. 'Be mindful, Gareth,' she said, her voice suddenly soft. But the needles were still there, only covered over. 'Not all will love you as I do.' She brushed his shoulder fleetingly and smiled her warm smile, still so full of those unkept promises. Then she touched up her horse and trotted away to catch up with the queen and the other ladies.

Gareth stayed where he was, feeling very much at sea. He remembered Lynet standing on her injured feet before the queen, refusing to sit or drink or in any way ease herself until her plight had been heard. He thought of the way she jerked back, so dismayed, when he kissed her hand in a salute of respect. How she had looked at him as she passed a moment ago, with such heartbreaking resignation.

Sabia declared this maiden, this lady, had taken bribes first from Tristan then from the king? No. It was not possible. Such a deed was not the work of one so deeply wounded. There was another story here.

Which meant Sabia had lied to him as well as warned him away from another woman, a maiden, a woman of rank who had no husband to prevent her from being paid honourable attention.

Where in God's name does that *thought come from?*

But before he could begin to answer his own question, he heard Lionel calling his name.

'Gareth!' Lionel cantered down from the head of the procession. 'Gareth! Sir Lancelot is looking for you!'

Gareth swung himself back up into his saddle and followed Lionel, ducking under tree branches and manoeuvring his horse around the larger stones and hump-backed roots. As quickly as he could, he brought himself up to where Sir Lancelot waited, well ahead of the procession, watching it come towards him like some kind of questing beast.

'Blow the signal to halt, Gareth,' said the knight tersely.

'What's happened, my lord?' asked Gareth, reaching for the horn that dangled from his saddle beside his bags and blankets.

'Sir Ruawn hasn't come back.'

Gareth's heart thumped once, hard. Sir Ruawn had been sent out the day before, with three mounted men-at-arms and Brendon, to carry a chest of gold and silver from the queen to present to 'King' Telent of the Rosveare, who held this valley. Telent was not a city man, and his people were not a single clan, said Sir Ruawn, whose people had come from south of this place. They were a loose and quarrelsome group of families who were willing to follow Telent and the council of their patriarchs as long as Telent did not ask much of them in time of peace. As a result, the treasure had to be enough for Telent to share out across a dozen families to keep them pacified long enough for their caravan to cross the valley, and spend the night in relative security, hopefully in the remains of the fortress on the hill.

Gareth felt a sharp prod of guilt. He didn't like Brendon. He didn't like his carping and sneering and non-stop insinuations that the only reason Gareth was back in Sir Lancelot's good graces was because of his uncle's intervention, which hurt all the more because it was very close to the truth. Still, Brendon was also Sir Lancelot's squire and Gareth should have noticed his absence before this, rather than just being grateful for the peace.

Gareth blew three long notes on the horn. The leaders of the procession, the ladies and knights and men on horseback, reined their horses in. The men on foot just stopped where they were, cursing mildly, passing questions back and forth, some taking a moment to lean against trees or carts, or just flop down onto their backsides.

'Come with me, both of you,' said Sir Lancelot. 'We need to tell her majesty. I doubt she'll like what she hears.' He touched up his roan palfrey, and they fell in behind as he approached the queen. Queen Guinevere, in turn, motioned for her ladies to stay behind her. Lynet though, did not seem to be included in the instruction, and she rode up beside the queen to meet them.

'What is the matter, Sir Lancelot?' asked the queen.

While his knight explained, Gareth found himself watching Lynet. She sat her horse well, as he had seen. She wasn't watching the queen, or attending to the conversation. She was looking ahead, as if measuring the miles. He could see her counting hours and days in her mind, wishing there were not so many. Her hand strayed time and again to the leather purse that hung beside her small ring of keys, and he wondered what she kept there. Then, as if she felt his regard, she turned her face towards him. She did not smile or blush or show any sign of surprise, let alone pleasure. Her face held only that same weary resignation he had seen before. It was the face of one who had seen too many battles, and knew there was yet another one coming. What had he done that she should regard him in that way?

Or what has been done to her?

'I will take Gareth, Lionel and three others down to the valley and find out what has happened,' Sir Lancelot was saying and the sound of his own name brought Gareth back sharply to the matter at hand. 'That should be enough to deal with whatever is there.' Sir Lancelot spoke with easy unconcern. There was even a relish to his words. His eyes were lit in a way they had not been since the tedious march began.

'And should you not come back, my lord?' asked Queen Guinevere.

Sir Lancelot grinned at her as he bowed. 'Pray for my soul, Majesty. And Sir Ioan can lead you fast around the valley, or back to Camelot for a larger force of arms.'

The queen clearly did not like that answer, or the knight's grin. She also, however, saw no alternative. 'Then God be with you, my lord,' she said curtly. She turned her delicate palfrey around and rode back to her ladies with Lynet following silently behind her.

Lynet did not look back at him.

'There's a lesson for you, my men,' murmured Sir Lancelot. 'The greater the love, the sharper the tongue.'

Love? The word slapped against Gareth. *What was Sir Lancelot doing speaking of love from the queen, even in jest?*

'Bring me Taranis, Gareth,' said Sir Lancelot. 'And both of you arm yourselves.'

Gareth was glad to obey. The activity drove his knight's strange choice of words from his mind. The ritual of securing his leather and bronze armour, and helping the knight into his steel mail, made it clear to his mind and body that there was to be a battle. Excitement surged into him. He buckled on his sword, slung his shield over his back and mounted Achaius, who danced to show Gareth he was ready to stretch his legs and hoping for a real run. Gareth accepted his spear from one of the younger boys. This was no blunt, light practice stick, but a true spear with an iron tip that could be hurled at an enemy or used to spit him. Lionel met his eyes soberly from the back of his own warhorse, and together they rode to where their knight was waiting with the other armed and mounted men.

Sir Lancelot towered over them both on his great red stallion. He surveyed Gareth, Lionel, and the three men riding with them and gave a nod of approval. Then they rode past the silent stares of the procession, and the queen.

And Lynet. He tried to catch her eye but could not tell if he succeeded. Behind her, though, Lady Sabia looked at him with shining eyes. He managed a gallant smile for her, but nothing of the love or anticipation he used to feel when he looked at her came to him.

The forest thinned quickly as they came to the valley's rim. The clouds overhead had begun to break apart, sending down shafts of warm sunlight to illuminate the lowlands, making it look like a painting of a saint's abode on a church wall. One beam lit up the stone and timber walls of the old fortress that watched them from the opposite side of the valley. Gareth could see no movement up there, no watch kept or signal given. All activity seemed to be centred around a cluster of rude dwellings on the valley floor. They were round and straw thatched and smoke drifted up out of the holes in their roofs. There was not even a proper long house, let alone a hall.

Patches of the valley floor were cleared for cultivation. Cows, black, white and red, grazed where they would. They rode past these unimpeded. In the village before them, they'd finally been noticed. A woman's scream rose up, and she and her fellows ran, snatching up their children and ducking into their houses.

That doesn't bode well, thought Gareth and he set his jaw.

Sir Lancelot continued to canter onward, completely unperturbed, even as they could plainly see the men who gathered in the gaps between the round houses begin to cluster and crowd together, watching their approach. The knight reined up Taranis before this uneasy gathering, and swept them with his gaze: a cadre of unarmed and untrained men, wondering if they should even try to stave off a knight on horseback.

'I seek King Telent,' he announced. 'Who here can take me to him?'

'Telent is dead!' called back one man.

The crowd parted, gladly, Gareth thought, to let the speaker through. He was a small, hairy mountain of a man, with arms and legs equally bowed. The tattoo of a bull ran down his right arm, underneath a quantity of red-brown hair. His beard and hair were both long enough to divide into three braids, and his only clothing was leather breeches and boots, and a kind of loose leather kilt over them. He looked up at Sir Lancelot with a pair of piggish black eyes and folded his arms. A bronze torque had been twisted around his neck, and he wore bronze rings on both meaty, bare arms. Unusually for such an outland chief, a sword hung at his side. With a shock, Gareth realized he knew the blade. It belonged to Sir Ruawn.

'And who are you, Master?' asked Lancelot.

The hairy mountain grinned, showing several black and broken teeth. 'You can call me *King* Enor!' He sniggered as he said it, and several of the men joined in nervously. All of which left Gareth in no doubt at all that Telent had not met his death peacefully.

He watched the houses behind the men, seeing only vague movements inside. He scanned the hillsides. They had been stripped of timber long since, and offered few hiding places. That left the fort. Crumbling as it was, if 'King' Enor was going to conceal his fighting force, there was nowhere else to put them.

'God be with you, King Enor,' Sir Lancelot said, inclining his head politely. 'I bring you greetings from the High Queen Guinevere of Camelot. She sent her emissaries out to you a day since, bearing gifts for the Rosveare king and his men. They have not yet returned. Now I am come to ask if you have seen them.'

'Emissaries?' Enor scratched his chin. 'No , , , no   unless you mean that stringy piece of eastern beef and his boy with the box who come calling yesterday. Hi there, Brengy, bring the boy out.'

Brengy hurried into one of the round houses. Gareth's horse stamped once. Gareth kept his gaze on the ruined fort. He saw no movement, but his hands itched from more than the frightened and hostile gazes of the men around him.

Brengy and another, younger man came back, and between them they dragged Brendon. Gareth's fellow squire had been beaten, and badly. His face was a mass of cuts and bruises and both eyes were so swollen that Gareth doubted he could see. His hands were bound before him with leather thongs that had begun to cut into his wrists and left his hands swollen and useless. They cast him down in the mud at Enor's feet. Brendon groaned weakly and tried to roll over, but could not.

Anger rose up in Gareth. How dare they! How dare this heathen barbarian lay hands on one of the true king's liege men! How dare he rob the queen? He ground his teeth together, barely able to remember he must keep his attention on the fortress. He must not let surprise overtake them.

Sir Lancelot looked down at Brendon lying in front of the valley king.

'Was this done on your orders?' he asked.

'It was!' Enor folded his arms and stood with his feet spread apart, as if daring Sir Lancelot to do anything about it. Gareth's guts twisted, and he felt the blood rise in him, but he could do nothing, nothing but sit there while this barbaric excuse for a man grinned up at the knight.

'And where are his companions?' asked Sir Lancelot.

'Hmm . . .' 'King' Enor made a great show of tapping his chin. 'I think we left them out on the midden heap with Telent.'

'Why would you treat the queen's messenger this way? Did he give offence?'

Enor spat. 'We want none of your queen here.'

Sir Lancelot's face creased in a frown of mock confusion. 'The Rosveare have before this been the friends of Camelot.'

'Telent was Camelot's friend. What has Camelot to give me for that same friendship?' Enor's eyes seemed to shrink back into his skull, growing yet more piggish. 'What that man of yours carries wouldn't do for one of my slaves.'

That's more true wealth than you've seen in your life, you whoreson bastard! Gareth bit his lip and kept his hands knotted around his reins. *Watch the fort. Watch the fort.*

'What is your price then? I will take your words to her majesty and you will hear what answer she makes.'

'My price? Pah!' Enor spat again, this time at Taranis's hooves. The horse stomped once but did not startle. 'She's very anxious to cross my valley. What if my price is her majesty?' He leered. 'I hear these city women are tasty tidbits who like a few real men of a long night!' He let out a huge guffaw, and more of the men joined in this time.

Sir Lancelot slipped off Taranis, handing his spear back for Lionel to take. The knight crouched down beside Brendon, taking closer measure of his injuries. 'Mabus,' he said quietly. One of the men-at-arms dismounted and came forward. Gingerly he lifted Brendon, who groaned again, and half-carried, half-dragged him backward.

'Now, Your Majesty,' said Sir Lancelot, standing directly in front of the valley king. 'You must forgive me. I am from a different shore, and speak a different tongue. I think I did not understand what you said about my queen and my fellow knight.'

Enor leered and spoke slowly. 'I said I think if your queen wants to cross my valley, she'd better be ready to spread her legs for it. Is that plain enough for you?'

So swiftly Gareth could not see the blow, Sir Lancelot lashed out, striking Enor across the ear and sending him reeling. The valley's usurper did not fall, though, and when he found his feet again, he was grinning as if this were what he had been most longing for. His drew his stolen sword and leered at the knight, showing all his dirty teeth.

Sir Lancelot drew his own sword, and swung his shield around to fit over his arm. All the men backed away, some looking terrified, some looking expectant. Back in one of the houses a babe began to wail. One of Enor's men ran forward with his own shield, a great scarred, wooden square bound with bronze.

Oh yes, they'd been waiting for this.

The men circled each other, and Gareth felt his own fierce grin form as he watched the curious relaxation that always overcame Sir Lancelot in combat take hold.

To watch Sir Lancelot with a sword was to watch the hand of God at work. There was no hurry in him, no matter how quickly his opponent moved. He stepped casually from place to place, somehow failing to be where the blow had fallen, blocking only when he chose, and that was only when he saw an opportunity to thrust past his enemy's defences. Shouts went up, jeers and catcalls, reminding Gareth painfully of his own battle with Sir Kai. But this was something different. This would not end with first blood. This was for the valley all around them, and this monstrous creature was a king. What was more, he had already overseen the deaths of one knight and his men-at-arms. After the first of the knight's blows drove him reeling backward, the leer vanished from the valley king's face. He began to fight in deadly earnest, shouting curses and charging in again and again. The knight dodged and circled, bringing down his blows with precise calculation until Enor's shield shattered and the king stood there half-naked, his only armour in pieces. Gareth wondered if he might surrender then. But no. He hung back, Sir Ruawn's sword in both hands, sweat darkening his hair and beard, determined to sell his life dearly. He had a slash on his shield arm, and another cut across his side, bleeding freely.

Movement caught Gareth's eye. Two men from the rear of the crowd had drawn back slowly, hiding behind the bodies of their fellows, hoping to avoid notice. Lionel nodded. He'd seen them too.

Gareth put his heels to Achaius's sides. The horse broke into a fast trot, swinging wide around the crowd shouting for their king. Lionel did the same, circling the other side. The two men spotted them in an instant, and tried to run, pelting away between the houses. Gareth leaned over Achaius's neck and brought down his spear. Behind him rose a fresh chorus of shouts. Before him ran two men in loose tunics and sandals. One carried a horn at his hip, and he was frantically trying to jerk it loose from his hemp belt.

Achaius flew forward. Lightly, swiftly, Gareth manoeuvred horse, spear and self, and rode hard upon the man's heels. He cast the spear down and the man screamed and pitched forward. Gareth rode around in front of him. The man was unhurt, but sprawled on his belly, pinned to the ground by the leather strap of his horn. Gareth glanced up to see that Lionel had already ridden down the second man, who was on the ground and not moving. Then he turned his attention back to the man before him. He dismounted and jerked the spear out of the dirt. The man rolled over, and found Gareth's weapon pointed straight at his chest.

Another shout behind him, and a keening wail.

'When were you to give that signal, villain?' Gareth growled. 'How many men? How armed and where are they?'

'Don't kill me, my lord,' whispered the man. 'Please. I beg you. Don't.'

'Answer my questions, and do not lie,' answered Gareth stonily. His guts twisted. Cowardice on top of treachery. He tried to remind himself he could not expect more from such a one, but if the man had the courage to stand with one who would rise up against his king, however petty, he should have the courage to face the consequences of it.

'Thirty men, my lord, with spears and knives, up in the old fort. We were to blow the horn if it looked like the king would be . . . might be . . .'

More shouts behind them, and another high-pitched wail went up. The man's eyes went wide with panic.

'You've more foresight than your king,' remarked Gareth, stepping back. 'They'll wait for the horn? There's no other signal?'

The man nodded. 'Please, my lord. Don't kill me. I was Telent's man, I swear. I only . . .'

Gareth had neither the patience nor the stomach to hear more. 'On your feet,' he ordered.

Lionel rode up. 'That one's dead,' he reported, his voice hard. 'What's here?'

'Thirty men with spears up in the fort,' Gareth told him. 'Waiting for their signal. We need to get back.'

He slung himself back into his saddle. He and Lionel rode close, driving their prisoner before them, and alternating glances backward. No movement came from the fort, yet. What did they see up there? Not much, he thought. The place had no standing watchtower, and Gareth still could not see any movement.

A scream sounded from the crowd, then a wail and a high ululating cry of grief. Over the heads of the crowd, Gareth saw Sir Lancelot standing over Enor, who lay unmoving in the mud, blood all over his face and chest, his eyes open and dead.

Sir Lancelot was not even breathing hard.

'Is there any other man here who would slander the honour of Camelot's queen?' he inquired. 'Come then. I stand ready.'

No man moved except to cringe backward. The babe was still crying in its house. Gareth wished it would quiet. He prodded his man forward, riding up to Sir Lancelot and reporting briskly what he and Lionel had learned. The knight looked down on their prisoner.

'Who are you?' Sir Lancelot demanded, disgust making his accent more pronounced. For a moment Gareth was not certain the man could understand him.

'Sulmed ap Ros, my lord,' whispered the prisoner at last.

'Which of these is your father?'

'I am, my lord.' A grey-bearded man with a blue sun-circle tattooed on his left cheek came forward. He bore himself more bravely than his son, Gareth thought.

'Do you speak the truth to me, old man?'

Ros nodded. 'I swear it on my son's head.'

'A good oath, old man. Now.' Sir Lancelot raised his voice to make sure the whole of the assembled Rosveare heard him. 'This son of yours stays here with me, as do all your women and your babes. You'll go up to that fortress and tell them how it is your vile kingling came to die. You'll bring them down without their arms, or your son is the first to the sword, and their families will follow.' He spoke steadily and without hesitation. 'You'll be quick, and you will not try to deceive me. I have an army waiting on the hill to come down and take this miserable scrub land and that heap of rocks if I so much as shout. And before I shout, your people will lie spitted on the ground.'

Did they believe him? They looked down at the corpse of their usurper king, still bleeding on the ground, and made their decision. Ros, father of Sulmed, bowed his head, backed away, and all but fled towards the fort.

Sir Lancelot sheathed his sword and swung himself once more onto Taranis's back. He took his spear from Gareth and from that height surveyed the knot of men before him. 'Get the men into one of the houses, and bring out the women and babes. As long as all remain peaceful, no one is to be molested, and nothing taken or compelled.' He glanced up at the hill where the royal procession waited behind its screen of trees. 'Our queen is of a delicate constitution, and would not approve.' He touched up his horse, riding back behind the knot of hostages, to take up a post where he would have the best view of village, fort and men. As he passed by Gareth, he said softly, 'That was well done, Squire.'

Gareth's heart swelled with pride, and with those few words, the nagging aching fear that had dogged him since Camelot fell away.

His own battle won, Gareth set about the business of carrying out his knight's commands.

*   *   *

As easily as that, it was done.

The men holding the fort, upon hearing their usurping king was dead and that their families were hostage to Camelot, were willing enough to lay down their arms and descend in a long line into the valley. One of them even brought Camelot's gold which Enor had sent up into hiding with them.

While these waited under guard beside their women, Lancelot rode up with one of the men-at-arms to inspect the fort for himself. There followed a long hour while they watched the hill, fairly certain all was right, but restless all the same, in case it was not. Then, at last, they saw a flicker of movement and a flash of blue and white on the fortress's sagging wall as the queen's banner was hung out for all to see.

The men of Camelot all cheered and Gareth raised his own horn, blowing two high notes to let the procession they had left behind know it was safe to begin the journey down into the valley that had been so swiftly won. But the celebration was short-lived, for after that came the task of collecting their dead. Sir Ruawn and the other men were laid out straight and wrapped reverently in their cloaks while the priest prayed over them all, seeking God's intercession for the men who had died doing their duty. Then they set some of the Rosveare to digging their graves.

The queen herself had ignored Sir Lancelot's blunt assessment that the council of patriarchs should be put to the sword for leading a rebellion against the High King. She instead gathered them and their families around her, and heard the tale of how Enor had come to power. It was an old, and an ugly story, of a drunken brawl, challenged honour, and a lucky blow, a younger brute overcoming an older leader. No one was willing to come forward with complaints of other crimes, not even King Telent's widow.

Queen Guinevere, holding court from her simple folding chair, urged the council to elect a new leader from among themselves, and ordered that they should go to Camelot to swear their new fidelity to the High King. If they did not, a delegation from the Round Table would be sent to find out why that was. The treasure she put in the council's hands.

'Was that wise, Majesty?' asked Sir Lancelot softly. 'They will only fight over it.'

'Then they will be fighting over the contents of that box,' she replied. 'And not over whether or not they should be coming up to slit our throats and take what we withheld from them.'

They did not linger after this, but proceeded up to the ruined fortress at once. The edifice had been mostly timber, and unlike Camelot, had never been rebuilt. Instead, it had been left to fall apart. But the sun was setting quickly, and the moon was in its final crescent tonight, so there was no going forward from here. There was still a square of stone walls as high as a man's shoulder, and the remains of what had been barracks and stables. It was a defensible position, in case the men of the valley decided to rebel against the queen's mercy and come calling. So, with some difficulty, the tents and the great pavilion were pitched in the yard where the Romans had once marched, trained, fought and lounged. There was plenty of wood for fires, and that which had not rotted was mostly dry.

Even with the dead to think on, the squires would have been fairly cheerful, were it not for Brendon. He'd been cut loose from his fetters as soon as he was in the hands of friends, but the swelling had not eased, and when he did speak, it did not seem he recognized any of them. His breath rattled in his throat, and his face was so much raw meat. Gareth found blankets to cover his old tormentor, and a cloak to make a pillow for his head, but they were in rough camp conditions and there was only so much that could be done. Gareth squatted back on his heels as Brendon groaned and tossed, trying to fight off the blanket. This was not good.

Best tell my Lord Lancelot.

But even as he had the thought, he heard a new voice outside the tent. 'Her majesty has asked that I come see to your squire,' she was saying. 'I have some physician's training. It may be there is something I can do.'

'If it is her majesty's wish,' answered Sir Lancelot. 'I've seen many such a beating. The blood's mostly stopped, and we've made him a bed. Now, time and God will have the healing of him.'

'Then I must crave your patience, my lord, as I am obeying the queen's word.' There was an acid taint beneath Lynet's reply.

Sir Lancelot made no answer, but Gareth could picture him making one of his sweeping bows and stepping back to clear her path. He felt an odd twinge inside him, but he did not understand where it came from or what part of the conversation he had overheard occasioned it.

A moment later, Lynet stepped into the narrow tent. Gareth made as much room for her as he could. She did not even seem to see him. All her attention was on the man lying before her.

'Hold the door open, Daere,' she called to her maid hovering by the entrance. 'I need the light.'

She showed no shock at Brendon's appearance, only rolled back the blankets and looked carefully at him for a long time. She laid her hands on his head, and he groaned in pain, twitching to try to throw her off. She probed carefully through his hair, searching the clots of blood and dirt. She gently touched his swollen face and each eye. Brendon moaned and tried again to struggle.

'Hold him please,' she said.

Gareth put his hands on Brendon's shoulders. 'Now, man, hold still, hold still, it'll be over in a moment,' he whispered.

Lynet continued her deliberate examination of Brendon's hurts, laying her hands in turn on his shoulders, his chest and arms. She picked up his grossly swollen hands one at a time, turning them over and peering closely at the discolouration of the flesh. She touched both legs and even bent close to smell his breath, and his skin.

When all was done, she sat back on her heels, her face grave. 'We'll need clean water, and plenty of it. And you must go to the queen and beg one of her crocks of brandy-wine,' she called to Daere. 'I wish to God we had some of the Eiran's water of life, but that will have to do. Also, if she has a box of wax and cobwebs we need that, and as many clean cloths as can be found, and three needles, and the finest white thread that is to be had.'

Daere bobbed her head, and then looked sideways at Gareth.

'Go!' snapped Lynet. As soon as the maid was gone, she turned to Gareth. 'You'd better find some strong hands, and a stout stick for him to bite on. This will be long, and painful.'

'Yes, my lady.' He scrambled to his feet.

By the time Daere returned with a basket of the things Lynet had ordered, Gareth had found Lionel and Ewen, who each had a strong pair of hands, and Gareth hoped a strong stomach. They repegged the tent to give it more room so they could all fit inside, and twice warned off gathering crowds of idlers. Daere clutched the basket and Lynet knelt beside Brendon. The gash on his face looked green around the edges, and he thrashed and breathed like a man in a nightmare.

Ewen knelt on one side, Lionel on the other, and Gareth by his feet.

'Hold him as still as you can,' said Lynet a little absently.

'I daren't tie him again. Not as he is. If the foul humours are too much constrained, their evil will sink into the bones.'

Then she poured some of the queen's strong wine over a cloth, and set to work.

Gareth had seen men lying on the battlefield, dying of their injuries, while their friends and family did what they could to ease them. He had seen the queen ministering to the sick with her tisane and patience. But he had never seen anything like this methodical work. Lynet washed Brendon with water and wine, a treatment favoured by the Greeks who had discovered the humours of the body, she said. Each movement was accompanied by a long, soft flow of Latin, prayers and, Gareth suspected, older incantations. She packed Brendon's wounds with wax and cobwebs, binding them with the bandages. The light faded. Daere ran for torches and a second brazier. Lynet lanced Brendon's hands with needles heated in the fire, to dry up the water and draw out the bad and sluggish humours. She stitched the gashes over his eyes and in his sides. Sir Lancelot came and stood with the torchmen, watching for a long moment, and then moved away again. Lynet ignored this, as she ignored Brendon's screams as thoroughly as if she had been deaf, until he passed out. That was the only time she broke her stream of Latin prayers to murmur a heartfelt, 'Thank God.'

The air stank of wine and sweat and blood. Lynet's hands were red and black with her work. At the last, she instructed the three men to grab Brendon tight and hold him absolutely still. She wrapped her hands around his right arm, her face grim.

She pulled. Something snapped with a sound like a whip cracking. She pushed and pulled and turned, and bone grated against bone. She was still for a moment, attending only to what her hands told her, and then a soft smile came to her.

'It will heal,' she said. 'If we bind it and splint it tight, he'll have the use of it again.'

She quickly suited actions to words, and soon laid Brendon's bound arm down beside his body. He looked pale, Gareth thought, but his breathing was eased. Lynet laid both hands on his brow. 'The fever's low,' she said. 'If it stays down through the night, he can be carried in the morning, though I doubt he'll enjoy it much.'

'He'll live then?' breathed Lionel.

'That is in God's hands,' answered Lynet, wiping her brow with the back of her hand. She looked pale, and very tired. 'But if he is kept from further hurt and his fever does not worsen, then I believe that he may.'

There was a quiet triumph in her voice, as if for the first time in a long time, she had seen an enemy defeated.

'Let me take you back to the queen, my lady,' said Gareth 'You are surely tired.'

She shook her head. 'I should stay with Squire Brendon. He needs watching in case his fever begins to burn hard.'

'We will do that, my lady,' said Lionel, quickly. 'We've sat beside wounded men before.'

Lynet hesitated, and cast one more long glance down at Brendon, who lay still now, his breathing harsh, but not so fast. The greenish tinge had faded from his swollen flesh, and the smell in the air was clean. 'Very well,' she said, both guilt and relief in her voice. 'But you will come to me at once if he worsens.'

'We swear it.' Gareth got to his feet and held out his hand. For a moment he thought Lynet would refuse it, but she took it in the end and let him help her to her feet. Her touch was strong, he noted. With all he had just seen her do, he should perhaps not be surprised.

Daere glowered at them both, but Lynet either did not notice, or did not care. Gareth held her hand, loosely and properly. Lynet blinked as they left the shelter of the tent, seeming a little dazed to see that night had slipped in from somewhere.

'That was a great thing you did for Brendon,' said Gareth, unable to think of anything else to say, but unwilling to let this stolen moment pass in silence. Her hand might be begrimed, but it was warm against his, and her profile beside him was more comely than he had ever seen it. Work and weariness had relaxed her, making her graceful and strong both at once. At that moment, he did not believe he had ever seen such a fair maiden before.

'I had good teaching,' she murmured. 'And for all he had taken, it could have been much worse. His skull and ribs were left whole.'

'I think no man could fail to heal beneath the touch of your hands.' Gareth smiled and let his gaze slip sideways. 'Such beauty is a fine healer of souls as well as bodies.'

He said it thoughtlessly, almost on reflex. She was so beautiful walking there in the golden torchlight, he wanted to pay her compliments, see her smile at him in that modest and knowing way a maiden could have.

Instead, she stared at him, mouth slack, shoulders slumped, looking anything but complimented. 'Will you never stop?' she cried, throwing up her gore-crusted hands. 'Is this what my land needs? Another pretty man from Camelot to plague us!'

Startled, Gareth pulled back. 'My lady, what . . .'

'What, what, what?' she snapped. 'What have I done to offend? How can I mend matters? And it is all said with a wink and a sly kiss, and there is no intent to amend at all, because you are bent on your conquest and our humiliation! Yes, you learn your lessons well. Did your master also school Sir Tristan in these matters?'

Gareth's temper flared torch bright. 'Sir Tristan was a great knight . . .'

'Sir Tristan has very nearly destroyed a kingdom, and in his dalliance he killed one of the finest . . .' Tears slid down her cheeks and she could not finish. 'Oh yes, the regard of a man of Camelot is such a fine thing that a woman may die of a surfeit of it!'

Before Gareth could make any answer, Lynet whirled around and ran into the queen's pavilion. He stood there, as stunned as if he had taken a blow to the head. His hands flexed a few times while he tried to think what he should do. Nothing came to him. Slowly, he walked back to Brendon's shelter.

'What happened?' asked Lionel as Gareth lifted the canvas flap and ducked inside. 'I heard shouting.'

'I don't know,' said Gareth, sinking to the ground beside Brendon's pallet. 'God and Mary stand witness for me, I don't know.'

'Don't tell me there's a woman out there who was less than delighted to see one of your smiles?' asked Lionel in mock-surprise. 'Or did you go too far for maiden's pride?'

Gareth shook his head. 'I told you, Lionel, I don't know.'

Lionel sat in silence for a minute, then apparently thought the better of pressing the matter. 'Well, get some sleep. I'll keep watch here.'

'No. I'll do it,' said Gareth quickly. 'I'll wake you later.'

'If you're sure . . .' said Lionel, but he was already on his feet. Gareth waved him away, and made himself as comfortable as he could beside Brendon's pallet, adding a few chips of wood to the brazier.

After Lionel left, Gareth sat for a long time, watching the flames, and listening to Brendon breathe. The wounded squire moaned a little and stirred weakly, but he did not wake. Around them, the torches and the fires winked out, leaving only the little blanket of light cast by the brazier.

What had happened? Part of him sneered that she was

only a hysterical maiden, and if she did not properly know how to take a man's compliment, then what was he doing wasting words on her? Then, belatedly, he remembered that it was Queen Iseult who had taught her the healing arts, and that lady must have been very much on her mind at the moment he spoke.

But she cannot blame Sir Tristan for taking what was offered. He pitched another splinter of wood into the brazier. Then he thought on what Sabia had told him before, that Lynet had been the queen's waiting woman, that she had, perhaps, even aided the meetings between her and Sir Tristan. He did not believe the part about bribes or broken honour. That was jealousy. But if Lynet had been so close to Queen Iseult to risk all to accomplish her ends, then she would have been devastated when Iseult took her life.

Whether reasoned or not, she would lash out where she could. And I had to try to speak lover's words to her. Gareth weighed another piece of wood in his palm. *Splendid timing, Gareth.*

But the question came back to him, why did he care? He sympathized deeply with the lady in her troubles. More deeply than he would admit to himself in daylight, or in company. He pitched the wood into the brazier. It rustled as it fell, and sent up a shower of sparks. She was beautiful. But he lived surrounded by beauties, and he'd had his way with more than one who actively courted his smiles. What was it about this lady, what light or shadow in her hazel eyes made him unable to laugh at her contempt?

He scrubbed his head hard with both hands, and suddenly wished Gawain were here, or Geraint. They might be able to tell him. He glanced towards the loosely laced tent entrance and thought for a wild moment about trying to talk with Sir Lancelot. He rejected that idea immediately, without allowing himself to think about why he did so.

Instead, seeing Brendon quiet on his pallet, Gareth crawled

out of the tent and stood up, bending backward until his back popped.

It was a night full of stars. The waxing crescent moon hung low above the valley walls. He could see the torches of the men outside the walls on watch. Gareth stretched his shoulders until they cracked and swung his arms up, letting the chill air clear his head.

Movement caught his eye. While Gareth watched, a figure in a dark cloak made its way down the ragged aisle between the tents, the banked fires and the sleeping bodies. The figure walked with a slightly rolling, limping stride, and Gareth knew it for Lynet. He smiled. Another chance. He'd be courteous and correct. She'd have his apology, and she'd see he understood her worth.

But, abruptly, Lynet turned away. Walking fast, clearly trying not to break into a run, she hurried towards the fortress's far corner, where the remains of a lean-to shed stood.

Gone to relieve herself? Gareth thought, a little dazed. But the lady did not emerge, and worry claimed Gareth, though he did not know of what. He followed her path to the ragged shed and peered inside.

Lady Lynet knelt on a pile of mouldering straw. Her hands were cupped together, and a soft silver light unlike anything Gareth had ever seen before shone up from them. He gasped, then held his breath, lest he be overheard.

But Lynet heard nothing. She only looked at the light in her hands, her face void of expression, her eyes staring. She did not move. As he watched her for a long moment, his own heart hammering hard, Gareth was ready to swear she had ceased to breathe.

Gareth pulled back until he could not see that faint, fae light anymore. He stared at the shed. Then he walked back to Brendon's tent. He sat down beside his fellow squire, and stared at the brazier. There he stayed until the dawn came, not moving, not able to move, only trying again and again to understand what he had seen, and what it could possibly mean.

SEVENTEEN

Peran.

Laurel stood atop Cambryn's westernmost watchtower and breathed in the air from the sea. She tasted the salt like a balm on her lips, and felt the yearning pull. She heard the faint whispers without understanding them and felt the rhythm of the tide in her blood. She needed these things like she needed the beating of her own heart. They gave her strength, taught her secrets, and helped her preserve the distance that let her see clearly enough to keep her promise to her mother.

Peran.

She sent the name out on the wind that was the gift of the sea. That wind wound its way into the yards of the *castell*. It would slip between the very stones of the hall if necessary and find him. It would wake him from sleep and tease at him. It would make him find some excuse for the watchful Mesek, and it would bring him up here to her.

Peran.

She had never done this before, not deliberately, not for such a purpose. Yes, the sea wind had carried her messages, and brought her news when she asked. But the only time she had sought to use the wind to compel a man to her side, it was the searing cry for help she had sent out to their father. The cry that had brought him to his death.

It was no more than a written message would have done, she told herself that morning. No more than as if she'd sent a rider on a fast horse.

But it was more. She knew it then, and she knew it now. But then, as now, she did not know what else to do.

Peran.

She hated the pall of desperation that now stood between her and the calmness of mind she had always believed her special possession. But her thoughts would not still themselves, and – had she not found any certainty since Lynet had come to her last night. It was not just the news she brought – that Peran was indeed fighting both sides of the conflict that squeezed Cambryn – that so disturbed Laurel. It was that Laurel had seen Lynet so clearly. The shape her sister sent forth was growing stronger, and more real. That could only mean the flesh and blood woman was growing weaker, giving more of herself over to this other existence adrift in the invisible country.

It was that which frightened Laurel more than anything she could name. There was only Lynet left. She had failed in every other way to keep Cambryn and her family safe. If she failed Lynet, she failed her mother utterly.

No. She gripped the parapet stones. She was done waiting. Help would not arrive soon enough.

Not from the queen, came the treacherous thought.

That was the worst of it. She knew she could summon help instantly, powerful and willing help. The wind whispered of its passage, getting further away, but still it could be reached. If Laurel just stretched out hand and heart, there was another woman, with a soul very like her own, who would hear her. That one had offered her all the power she needed to make sure she was never trapped again, never so helpless that Lynet must risk herself as she did . . .

Stop. Laurel squeezed her eyes shut. *Stop.*

It had seemed the best idea. Get Lynet out of the keep. Then Laurel could face their enemies without endangering her sister. But what had happened since? She had done nothing. She had sat here, in relative safety, with her shuttle and her needle, with these men breathing down her neck and her own people walking around on tiptoe. She had watched, night after night, while Lynet tore herself in two.

She heard voices below. The wind brought them softly to her.

'Is she still up there?'

'And like to be all morning.'

'I think we've had about enough of this. I'll go pull her down off her perch.'

'Better you than me, Master.'

'You have anything to say about it?'

'If you want to try to compel my Lady Laurel to go when she wishes to stay, then God help you.' That was Taff. She'd sent word to him by Meg that this would come. Good man, he'd obeyed her instructions, although she knew he'd been sharpening his knife, just in case.

She heard the sound of boot soles ascending the steps. The wind swirled around her hems and blew her cloak back from her shoulders.

What are you thinking, Master Peran? Why do you believe you've come?

The hatch lifted and fell open, slamming against the stones. A moment later, Master Peran heaved himself out of the hole. His burns had at last begun to truly heal, she noted. Helped by Morgaine, the angry, mottled redness had begun to fade back to the pink of healthy skin, but it was much more pale than his untouched flesh, giving him a strange patchwork appearance.

'God be with you, Master Peran,' she said.

'You do not seem surprised, Lady Laurel, that I should violate this sacred grove of yours.' He scuffed the stones with his heel.

'Nor am I,' Laurel answered. The sea wind teased her hair ends, circled her waist and drew itself across Peran's healing skin, waiting for her, not patiently, but waiting all the same.

Peran took a step forward, bending to get a closer look at her eyes. She let him, lifting her gaze to meet his. She could feel the sea light kindling within her. That light filled her, fed by the tide and the wind.

'You did this, didn't you?' he breathed. 'You called me.'

'I did.'

His hands opened and closed, once, twice. 'Why?'

'Because, Master Peran, I would know what truly happened to your son.'

'I thought that was what the queen was travelling all this way to discover. You cannot wait another handful of days?'

'My sister is in danger, Master Peran, body and soul. I will not wait.' The wind blew hard, from her to him, carrying word and breath, will and cold fire. 'What happened to your son, Master Peran? You can tell me now.'

This was another deed she had never before committed in cold blood. She knew sometimes that someone before her had spoken only because of her anger, because the cold light and tide within her had reached out, but she had never called on it before. It would be wrong. Mother's watchful spirit would not approve. Still, she had known it was hers and it was real. It was power like Morgaine might wield.

Let us see how it may be used against her slave.

Peran's face slackened and his shoulders slumped. The wind combed his hair back and ruffled his cloak. He turned away to look out over the greening country. It did not matter. Her wind had him now. She had no more need to see his eyes.

'He was a hero, my son,' Peran whispered. Although she could no more see his face, his whole attitude was that of a man laying down a burden that had become too heavy to bear. 'A hero like the bards sing of. He was taller than I, with hands that could bend iron, and a laugh that could make the willow gladden. He would have led our people to greatness. Greatness.' He leaned his hands on the parapet. Laurel made no move. The wind gusted hard, once.

'How does illness take such a one?' he asked plaintively. 'How does the winter's cold take hold of his breathing and turn his face blue and choke him to death? He was so strong, how could that be?'

Laurel made no answer. She was not Bishop Austell to speak of God's plan. She wondered what the bishop thought of that plan where he had gone.

'It was enchantment,' Peran said. 'Poison. I knew it. I saw it in his eyes as they looked on death. And when death came . . . I . . . I carried his corpse to Morgaine. I laid him down in front of her and begged her to redress what had been done, to give my son back his life.'

Laurel could see him, this proud chieftain, on his knees before Morgaine. The body of his son, dead eyes closed at last, lay between them. He did not weep or rage or shout. He pleaded with a father's grief over something too precious to be regained.

'She told me it was not magic that took his life. It was the illness that gripped him. Then she told me that if it was what I wanted, she could bring him back for me.

'She warned me it was a difficult thing, and that he might not live long. It was against the way of things, but it could be done.'

She could see this too, the sorceress, calm and sympathetic, warning with one breath, tempting with the other. She could have chosen to send this man away, to bury his son and mourn him. But she needed him, and so she took up his grief in her clever hands, and she used it against him.

'I told her I would give anything, do anything. She warned me again, and she made me swear. And I did.

'She lit a fire and she burned resins in it until its flame was green as poison, and she heated an iron cup over that fire. What was in it, I could not tell, but she made me lift up my son's head and prise open his mouth, and from that cup she poured three golden drops.

'And in my hands he stirred, and opened his eyes, as if waking from his night's sleep. He was alive. My son was alive, and he called me father, and asked why I was crying.'

Laurel had gone cold. Her wind wavered, blowing hard, then dying suddenly away, as if it too wanted to flee from what it heard.

'But he was not the same, my son, now that he returned. His eyes that had been so warm, that had drunk in life so fully, had gone cold. Now he quarrelled with every man over the smallest slight. He rode into battle like Jove in his chariot, always into the heart of it, where the fighting was fiercest. When there was no fight, he prowled about, looking for something he could not find, looking with those cold, furious eyes.

'When Morgaine sent word that I was to find a quarrel with Mesek, I actually blessed her for it. It would give my son something to do. His restless rages were becoming harder to contain, and men were beginning to whisper.

'So we took some cows to where they would be seen. We left slight guard so that they could be taken. The rest . . . the rest is as I said, except the end. The very end.' His voice went hoarse and halting with remembered pain. 'When he

saw the fire, a great peace stole over my son, there in the
midst of the screaming and the stampeding animals and the
men with their knives and their swords flashing. He just
stood there, gazing at the flames as if he had never seen
anything so beautiful in his entire life.

'He walked into the fire. He did not even look back to tell
me farewell.

'It was my fault, what happened. I did not watch him
closely enough. I did not understand how his death still
haunted him. I must serve her, you understand. I must. If I
serve her well, she will bring him back again.'

These last despairing words Laurel would not have heard
had the wind not carried them gently to her.

Peran's head bowed down and his whole frame shuddered.
Laurel could only stand and watch as he straightened, slowly
and painfully, like a much older man.

'What have I been saying?' he asked heavily. 'What have
you done to me?'

'Nothing, Master Peran,' she whispered. 'You have said
nothing important. I am ready to go with you now.'

The wind fell away to a gentle breeze full of the scents of
salt and spring. The light of the human soul kindled once
more behind Peran's dulled eyes.

'Good,' he said. 'And no more of this, my lady. You want
to talk to God, you do it in the chapel, is that understood?'

'As you say, Master.'

She walked docilely down the steps before Peran, and she
let her guard fall in behind her without comment. She walked
to the hall and took her place at board, eating and drinking
what was put in front of her, and tasting nothing.

Her mind was filled with what Peran had said, and what
Morgaine had done.

She had thought to hear a tale of simple deceit, something
she could threaten him with. Being able to prove him a liar

in public should have been enough to coerce him into some bargain without waiting for the queen. But this . . . what was she to do with this?

And the horror of what she had heard was not the worst of it. The true horror was that from a corner of her heart came a gentle whisper: *Peran was made a fool of by his grief. Colan by his ambition. I will not be a fool when I bargain with her. I know better than they.*

Laurel shot to her feet, startling the whole table, herself included.

'Something amiss, Lady Laurel?' inquired Mesek with his usual wry complacency. 'Or has Peran resorted to putting frogs under your chair?'

Laurel glared at him, hatred rising like gall within her. But at least her tongue remained under her control. 'I go to the chapel, Master Mesek,' she said calmly. 'Would you care to join me?'

'Not if you intend to jump to Heaven,' he said, ignoring the frosty stares of all the Cambryn folk around him.

As he did not mean to prevent her, Laurel strode from the hall, her guard trailing behind. She entered through the wooden door, took water from the fountain, crossed herself, went to the rail and knelt, folding her hands. For a long time she stared up at the carved scene of death and redemption, but she could only see Peran's hungry eyes looking for his own dead son.

Mother of God, what did I think I was doing?

She did not think. That was the problem. Not really. She had not thought properly for days. Not since Morgaine had left behind the lure of Tintagel.

Tintagel. Even now, even with Peran's words still ringing in her ears, it came to her again – the crash of the sea that shook the cliffs, the wind never without the comforting tang of salt. When it had come time for her to be sent for fostering, there had been a question as to whether she, as the eldest, should go to distant Camelot, or to create closer ties with their nearest and most important neighbour. When her father told her he would consider the matter carefully, she had seen a flicker of something in his eyes. Had it been fear? It had been there again when he told her she would go to Queen Guinevere at Camelot. He saw the disappointment she tried to conceal and laid a hand on her head and whispered. 'It is for the best, my child.'

Why the best? What did he fear she would do at that place of sea and stone? What did he fear she would be able to do?

No. No. Laurel rubbed her brow. *I must not think this way. I must remember all that has happened. If not what has happened to Peran, then what has happened to Colan, and to father, and to Lynet. I must not forget.*

But her mind would not clear. She felt as if there was a weight pressing on her thoughts. The stones of her home were suffocating. Even her morning journeys to the watch-tower, to feel the winds and see the birds, were not enough anymore. She could not stay here, not for the rest of her life.

No. Not like this. It will be over soon. Lynet will be here in a matter of days. The queen will come, and it will be over.

She told herself that now as she had told herself before. But she did not feel it, not in the pit of her heart, not as she looked up at Mary, who looked up at her son. She only felt lost and denied.

But how could it be that her heart still wished desperately to believe that the salvation she could not seem to find from the Christ above her might come from Morgaine?

Mother, why? Mother, what is happening to me? she wailed with the whole of her being, not sure whether she prayed to the Mother of All, or to her own mother, dying beside the fire, holding her hand and trying so hard not to let go.

She understood well how Peran felt, for at that moment, she knew she would have given anything, done anything, to have her back.

That realization brought with it a world of understanding, unfolding before her startled thoughts like the wings of some brilliant butterfly.

The temptation that so tormented her was not Tintagel, and it never had been. The temptation was Morgaine herself. That fleeting moment, when she understood there was another being who knew what it was to carry the division between the visible and the invisible within herself, who might teach her what her mother could not, who might help her make peace within herself at a time when all else was threatening war. Who might help banish the knowledge of Colan – locked in his room staring out of his window, pacing his floor, waiting for her to order his death – that never left her, not even in sleep.

Colan had said it. He had warned her with his musings. *I thought I had risen above the need I have of her,* he had said. She had thought the same, and like her brother, it had trapped her.

Morgaine had brought Laurel to this moment, paralysed by her own doubts and impotence. Tintagel was only meant to push her over the edge. The real promise was that Morgaine would stand by her and enable her to embrace her own self wholly.

Above her, the Holy Mother looked up at her Son, who looked up to Heaven. Both in agony, both facing the final loss, the last sacrifice. Had that mother ever extracted a promise from her Son? Made Him swear to protect another? Perhaps those brothers who had waited down below while He sat with his apostles? What did she tell those other children, Laurel wondered, about their oldest brother – their half brother, she supposed – the one who was both more and less than they? What did she tell them when she found out what it truly meant that He was the Way and the Door?

The Door. The open door.

And all at once, Laurel understood. She knew what she must do and what she should have done days ago. It was simple, but it was the one thing she had said she could not do. She needed Lynet's ways of seeing, she had told herself. It was necessary to know what their enemies were doing and thinking.

In leaving open the door for Lynet, Laurel had left open the door for many other things as well, and the result had nearly been disaster.

'Lady Laurel?'

Laurel spun on her knees, her chest heaving with the force of her breath. Behind her stood Father Lucius, his face made white by the violence of her reaction.

'Forgive me, lady,' he said, coming forward hastily. 'I did not mean to startle you. It is only . . .' he stopped, plainly abashed, and she knew what he would say next. 'You have been so long about your prayers, those . . . men . . . have sent me to find you.' He stopped, and then said, far more softly, 'Is there any way I can help you, my lady?'

'Thank you, Father,' she said and she stood, a little stiffly. He was a young man, with a scholar's gentle face and ink-stained hands. His manner was earnest and devout and when Laurel thought of him at all, it was as a kindly, competent servant.

Now she had to hope he was a little more.

'I am glad you are come. There is some help I need. I have an urgent task for you.'

He blinked his round, brown eyes, but said at once, 'How can I serve, my lady?'

'I need you to go to Saint Necturn's well and bring me back a jar full of the holy waters.'

He considered this, glancing up a moment at the crucifix and running his tongue over his lips. 'Should I ask why, my lady?'

She smiled a little at this. He was a fine diplomat, their priest. 'No, Father, you should not. I ask you to be content with the knowledge it is water of a blessed place I need. But if anyone else asks you, say you are going to the monastery at Tintagel.'

He blinked at her several more times, and for a moment she feared he might refuse. But in the end he nodded, his face seeming a little less soft than it had a moment ago. 'I am praying for you, daughter.'

'Thank you, Father.'

'I will go as soon as a horse can be saddled.'

'Thank you, Father.' Laurel stood. Peace took hold in her for the first time in days. Now all that remained was to tell Lynet she must shut the door between them, and pray that her sister was not so far adrift in that other country that she would not understand.

Please, dear mother, be with her.

But both the Mother and her mother remained as silent as ever, and Laurel had no choice but to smooth her sleeves and return to her weaving.

EIGHTEEN

The next evening brought the queen's procession to the edge of Bodmin Moor; mile after mile of rolling, open country with ragged, lonely heights and deep bowl-like valleys. In fair weather it could be deeply beautiful, an unspoiled meadow without end. Once this was part of the great wood that had surrounded them for so many days, but generations had gnawed away at the forest's reach and left this open, treacherous land behind. Even in the clear light of day the moor could not be trusted. What looked to be solid ground could swallow men and horses whole and leave no trace. In foul weather, the mists rose sometimes for days at a time and there were no landmarks or any other means to find direction. A traveller could wander lost in the openness until they died of cold and exhaustion, or the hidden bogs dragged them down.

But on the other side of it waited Cambryn and home. Another day away, perhaps two, since they must go carefully. Three at most. Three days to home, and Laurel, and an end to all this struggle. Three more days.

Lynet had ridden all day beside Brendon's litter. Sir Lancelot had clearly struggled with the decision to bring him.

If they had been more certain of the Rosveare they left behind in the valley, the knight would have shed this impediment to their progress. There was, however, no guarantee he would not simply become a hostage again, and the Rosveare were not kind to their hostages. Lynet felt a pang about moving him at all, but the twin necessities of making all speed to Cambryn, and getting the queen away from an untrustworthy place removed any choice. She did note that Sir Lancelot spent a great deal of time at the rear of the procession rather than the fore today.

So, she trotted along beside Brendon, who, thankfully, spent much of the day asleep, despite the jolting. The fever stayed low and the swelling receded. As often as she was able she gave him bread sopped in watered wine, and it was all staying down. That, as much as his ability to speak the names of those around him during the brief periods when he woke, told her he'd no unseen hurt.

She wore her relief like a cloak all that long day. Since she had left Iseult, she had done such healing as was required in Cambryn. She had closed wounds, set bones, nursed illnesses, but each recovery caused this astonishment in her, and each death raised the fear that her skills had been tainted by her sins. She could still feel her father's blood on her skin, and his belly heaving under her hands as she tried to staunch his wound in the moments before she helped end his life. To know that at least she had not been punished for that act, that her skills were not gone from her, was priceless.

She even regained enough humour to realize that Brendon would likely not be too happy about being the instrument chosen to restore her confidence in her abilities.

The other good the day brought, she told herself over and again, was Squire Gareth's silence. She saw him as he rode up and down the length of the procession, making sure everyone stayed relatively close together, and assisting with any problems, but he did not stop to speak with her. Once she caught his eye as he passed, and he only made her a solemn and silent salute, and rode on.

He had heard her. He had understood. Good. One of them at least understood. She had no business dallying with any man, for no man was a safe companion for her, most especially one of Camelot. He was at least honourable enough to see that.

Such reasoned and goodly thoughts, though, did nothing to ease her heartache each time she saw him ride past, tight-lipped and looking straight ahead.

It will be over soon. We will be home. Matters will be settled. He will go back to Camelot, and I will go about my life.

What life would that be, though, for her and Laurel? What did the queen mean to do? She would have to appoint a new steward, and what would happen to them? Marriage was the most likely possibility, to strengthen the ties between Cambryn and Camelot. Marriage for Laurel anyway. Perhaps there was a man of the north who would take Lynet, or perhaps she would finally be allowed to take the veil.

None of these thoughts brought any more comfort than Gareth's silence did. Yet she could not make herself approach the queen and ask what was in her mind when her appraising grey eyes seemed to know she was concealing so much.

It does not matter. I am doing as I must. I cannot leave Laurel alone. I cannot leave my home unguarded. She touched her purse. The light was fading in the leaden sky. She would be free again tonight, and she would know what was happening. Something nagged at her, something more than the silence and suspicion around her, or even the knowledge that they would be spending the night on the edge of the great moor. It dried out her mouth and made her skin creep under the touch of the gentle wind. She had to get to Ryol, had to leave her confining flesh and know.

Soon. She told herself. *Soon.*

Camp was made on the rise above the empty moor. Lynet saw Brendon, more awake now, a little hungry and very blasphemous, installed in the squires' tent. Lionel swore faithfully to watch over him and to give him only thin pottage and well-watered wine. Stronger food would only strengthen the fever he still carried. Gareth was nowhere to be found, which pleased Daere, and should have pleased Lynet. Instead, it only added to the nagging feeling that grew stronger the closer the sun sank to the horizon.

Something was wrong. Something at home. She was certain of it. Ryol was trying to reach her, to warn her, and she had to sit still under the eyes of the queen and all her ladies in the pavilion. She had to listen to the light gossip and small complaints, trying to concentrate enough to answer their questions. She wanted to scream. She wanted to snatch up the mirror and shout for Ryol, to bring her to his side immediately.

She wanted the queen to stop looking at her.

At last, however, the light began to fade, and the beds were laid out. Daere relieved her of her over-dress, and handed her back her girdle so she could bind it about her, reclaiming her purse and her keys. As soon as her fingers brushed the leather purse, a flood of urgency filled her, rocking her back on her heels.

'Are you all right, my lady?' gasped Daere as she put out a hand to steady Lynet.

The queen turned her head inquiringly. So too did every other woman in the tent.

'Yes, yes, thank you, Daere,' said Lynet hastily, trying to avoid every eye by reaching for her bed coverings. 'My feet ache.'

This they were all willing to believe, her broken feet having been made a public spectacle. Slowly, they all went back to the business of getting ready for their beds, including the queen. Lynet lay still and let Daere draw up the covers so no one would see her grasping her purse so tightly the mirror's edges dug into her hand, even through the leather.

Something was wrong. Lynet closed her eyes, turning over to face the canvas wall so no one could see her distress. Something was blindingly, terribly wrong and she could feel it with each beat of her heart. Light flashed behind her eyelids, like a silent storm of omen. Yet the braziers flickered and cloth and covers rustled, and the queen laughed softly at yet another jest told by one of her useless, gossipy, feather-brained city women.

At last, when Lynet's teeth ached from being ground so hard against the screams that threatened to burst forth, the last light was covered, and darkness fell. She listened to the familiar rustling, sighing sounds of women trying to get comfortable on pallets now damp and lumpy from too much hard travel and not enough airing. Lady Nola dropped off first, as usual. She had a trilling kind of snore. One by one, the others followed her, and last of all, the queen's breath deepened and slowed, and Lynet was able to take one free breath herself.

Carefully, stealthily, she slipped out from under her coverings. No sound of breathing or soft snoring changed. Her groping hand found her cloak and she hugged it close. One cautious, agonizing step at a time she made her way to the door, giving Daere as wide a berth as she could. At last she reached the canvas flap and picked at the knotted lacings with impatient fingers, her ears straining all the while for any change in the sound of restful oblivion behind her.

Since the queen had found her that first night, Lynet did not dare try to use the mirror again inside the pavilion. At least if she were found creeping outside, there might be another explanation. She could buy herself some time concealed in the fringes of the wood, and if she cried out, it was less likely that anyone would hear.

She had to do this, and do it now. Urgency filled her. She had to bite back a cry of gladness as the final knot came loose and she was able to creep out of the pavilion.

Fortunately, the queen did not insist on guards beside the tent. Lynet could see their torches out at the edges of the camp. Soft talking and laughter could be heard here and there, along with stray clanks and clatters. The whole camp was settling to sleep, but not quite there, not yet. That was as well. This way she was only one more carefully moving shadow, just trying to find her bed, or a spot to relieve herself, at the edges of the light. Nothing to worry about. Nothing to question.

'I wondered if you would come out again tonight.'

Lynet whirled around, her fist stuffed in her mouth to stifle her startled scream. A shadow moved out from all the other shadows, and there stood Squire Gareth.

She stared at him. He made no apology for frightening her. He simply stood there, his hands loose at his sides, waiting to see what she would do next.

Lynet lowered her hand. 'Squire Gareth,' she croaked.

'My lady,' he replied gravely, inclining his head. 'What brings you out at this unseasonable hour?'

She swallowed, trying to remember her dignity, and all the plausible lies she had stored up.

'I have asked you a question, my lady,' said Gareth. There was something new in those words. A reminder that he was a man on the verge of knighthood, a man loyal to his knight and his queen and above all to his High King. He had seen something. He was suspicious. This was what had kept him silent and apart from her all day, not her scathing words.

There was not a plausible lie in all the world that he would believe. What was more, Lynet realized as she looked

up at his sad, stern visage, she did not want to have to lie
to him.

You cannot stand here! You have no time to waste!

'Squire Gareth, I swear on the memory of both my mother
and my father, I do nothing that will harm anyone here.
Please, let me pass.'

He flexed his hands. She could hear his breathing, harsh
and uneasy, for a long time before he spoke.

'My lady, listen to me,' he said softly. 'There is something
gravely amiss here. How am I to know that by my silence I
do not jeopardize my comrades, my knight and my queen?
Give me some explanation that I can understand, and I will
hold my tongue. Continue in your own silence, and I must
raise the alarm.'

He meant it. She could tell that easily. He would feel regret,
but he would do exactly as he said.

And for good reason, admitted Lynet to herself

But he was giving her a chance. All of Ryol's warnings
rang in her head, but no lie came to her. She must risk the
truth. If she did not, she was lost already.

'We must not be seen.' She ducked into the nearby copse
of trees and bracken that was surely where Gareth had
watched her progress from before he decided to confront her.
Gareth followed more slowly, and when he did, she saw his
hand was on his sword. He had come to her armed.

When she was certain they were as hidden as they could
be, she drew the mirror from its purse. 'This was a gift from
the sea to my mother,' she told him, holding it out flat on
her palm. It shone faintly in the darkness, as if it carried its
own light within. 'Through this, I may see my home and
speak with Laurel. I do not want the queen to know, that is
why I have tried to hide it.'

She waited for him to laugh, or to cross himself, or to call
her mad. He did none of these. He stretched out one cautious

finger and touched the cool, smooth glass. 'Why should you fear the queen's knowing?' he whispered.

'Her majesty distrusts all things of the invisible country, as well she should,' she added, thinking of Morgaine and all that had been done already. 'If I were not desperate, I would have nothing to do with it.' *Is that true?* She put the question aside hurriedly. 'But my sister is in danger, and the visions I receive from the sea glass are the only aid I may render her while we creep across the country. I beg of you Squire Gareth,' she breathed softly, as she curled her fingers around the mirror. The sight and touch of it was maddening, driving her blood hard in her veins and sending it pounding to her temples. 'Do not give me away.'

He was silent, watching her out of the darkness that cloaked him. 'It is dangerous,' he said flatly.

'Only to myself.'

'How can you know?'

'On this you will have to trust me, Gareth.' She heard the quaver in her voice. 'I am the only one in peril from this glass and what it holds.'

He regarded her for another long moment, his jaw working back and forth. Lynet held her breath, but did not let her gaze leave his. She longed to be able to reach out as she did when she was a shadow. As a shadow she could have gathered up his distrust and returned her own belief and sense of understanding.

Then Gareth said, 'You cannot lie a night out here alone. You will sicken from the cold.'

'It will not be that long this time.'

'You are sure of that?'

She bowed her head. 'No.' It seemed that now that she had begun to tell him the truth, she could not stop.

'Then I will stay with you.'

That startled her. 'No,' she said immediately.

He did not let her speak another word. 'I cannot permit you to come to harm,' he said. 'And if I am to keep my silence about this, I must see for myself what happens.' His lips twitched into a smile for an eyeblink. 'I have been told many strange stories in my life, lady, some by my own brothers. If you want me to believe what you say, you must also let me be witness to it.'

A long and painful history lay beneath those words. She could feel it, even trapped in her separate skin. There was no way around it. Her urgency would burn a hole through her if she did not look into the mirror at once.

Anger sparked in her, but gratitude as well. For she knew that despite all his doubts, he had trusted her as far as he could.

But Gareth mistook the reason for her hesitation. 'My Lady Lynet,' he said solemnly, formally. 'I swear that I will remain to protect you. You will come to no harm while I watch over you.'

'Thank you, Squire Gareth,' she murmured.

He drew himself up with a sigh, acknowledging their strange and awkward circumstances with no more than that gesture. 'What must you do?'

'Sit down,' she said, and she suited actions to words. She brought the mirror up, seeing her own ghostly reflection in its smooth and perfect surface. All thoughts of Gareth, of queen, of any danger, flew away as she saw her other self waiting there.

'Ryol,' she said. 'Ryol!'

Lynet fell into darkness.

The fall this time was short and sharp. The world opened around her almost before she had time to blink, and Ryol was there at her side in the bright sun of the garden. But Ryol had changed yet again. Silver streaked his dark hair, and the petals of the roses and the blossoms lay on the garden's fading grass.

She opened her mouth, but Ryol did not give her time to speak. He grabbed her wrist and pulled her along behind him as he swept out his hand to shift the shadows and change the daylight garden to the dark reflection of Cambryn at nighttime. Clouds gathered thickly, scudding across the half-moon, but as before, Lynet found she could see as well as if the moon had been full and the night clear. Ryol was all but running now and it took all her concentration to keep beside him as the shadows rushed, bent and blurred around her.

When her vision cleared, she found herself standing in Colan's chamber. The fire and the rush lights had both been doused. The room was utterly black. With her shadow sight, she could make out Colan's hunched form crouched on the low sill of his narrow window.

She thought he meant to jump, to kill himself and end his blood-stained life. She felt the guilt in him. It rolled off him like waves of ice water, cutting through the shadow of herself, threatening to wash her away with its strength. It seemed as if he must be wading through it up to his neck. But no. Whether she drifted forward or pulled him close, she neared him, and she found she could feel beneath the guilt, discern its foundations, understand them.

He was going to kill Laurel. He was going to scale the old, time-pitted wall and creep across the roof slates. He could do it. He had done it in secret as a boy. He had waited here quiet and meek, for the men to become bored and complacent, waited for Laurel to become disgusted or distracted so that she did not visit him anymore.

Lynet knew all this, as surely as she knew he had killed their father. He was going to kill Laurel and offer up the death to Morgaine, a sacrifice, to show her he was still loyal, that he was still useful.

That he was still hers and that she could not abandon one of her own.

'No,' whispered Lynet. 'No!'

But he could not hear her, she could not reach him. She was less than shadow now, she was nothing more than witness.

Without even looking to Ryol, Lynet gathered her strength, and reached out for his. It flowed into her like honey, thick and warming. She focused thought and will, and forced herself into being. Pain filled her with its unbearable fire. When her eyes could see again, she turned them on Colan and reached with the shadow that was herself. She caught up her own pain, and that cold, rolling guilt rushing from him, scooping it up like ocean water into a ewer, and with all her strength, she flung it back at Colan where he crouched like some great insect, waiting for his time.

His fingers gripped the stones hard for a moment and he toppled backward, barely catching himself in time to keep from sprawling on the floor. He turned, looking about the room, his face pale as death. His hands shook and he wrapped his arms around himself, doubling over as if suddenly sick. He did not move. Lynet let herself drift a little closer, still solid, still strong, wading through her brother's guilt, collecting it as she went.

'Father?' Colan whispered.

That single word told her what she must do, what she could do. She was an ethereal shape, and shapes could shift. She called up a memory of her father, whom she was said to be so like, the height and breadth and strength of him, the set of his shoulders, the carved hollows of his cheeks, the hard, square hands of a warrior. And the blood, the blood she had last seen pouring from his torn belly.

All this she made herself, and in a final wrenching act of will, all this she showed to Colan. She knew at once he saw and saw clearly, for he screamed in utter horror, throwing up his hands to ward off the bloody ghost before him.

The door burst open, and Lynet let herself vanish, let the pain and the tide of her brother's guilt wash her away, back into the thinnest breath of shadow, as the men of Colan's guard ran into the room to find him crouched on the floor, his head in his hands, trembling and weeping like a babe.

Lynet looked down on her work and felt tears stinging her eyes. 'Take me to Laurel,' she told Ryol.

Gareth sat beside Lynet's body. She lay on the ground, her eyes closed, as peacefully as if she were asleep, save that her flesh was as cold and as pale as death. Only her fingers around the mirror kept their life. The mirror was cold as ice, but her hands were warm, almost fiery. He drew her cloak over her. She did not breathe. Did not stir. He sat back, biting his lip, wondering what he should do.

Watch. Wait. Do as you promised.

The night turned slowly over them. The sounds of the camp gave way to snores and mutters. Cold crept into Gareth. He stood, stretching creaking joints, and paced to the near edge of the woods, as much to try to get some warmth into him as to make sure no patrol or wanderer approached.

Gareth froze. Out in the dark, he saw movement; a black shadow by the soft grey outline of the queen's pavilion. He stared hard. It was Sir Lancelot. Even in the uncertain light of the waxing moon, Gareth knew his knight's form. Sir Lancelot stood beside the pavilion door, leaning in just a little. Was he saying something? Gareth couldn't hear. He glanced down at Lynet lying cold and still. He could not leave her, but what if something was wrong? What if the camp would be roused in another moment?

The flap of canvas folded back from the pavilion's entrance and a woman's silhouette emerged.

It was Queen Guinevere.

Sir Lancelot bowed low. He was speaking. Over the

breeze in the trees, Gareth could hear the soft rise and
fall of the knight's voice, although he could not make out
a single word. The queen answered him, but she was too
far away for him to make out any tone or timbre in her
voice. Sir Lancelot took one step closer, and the queen
drew herself up tall. Whatever she said then, it caused the
knight to step backward and bow again. The queen let the
canvas fall between them. Sir Lancelot stood there a
moment, and then strode away, jauntily, as if well satisfied with himself.

Gareth just stared. The *queen*? Queen Guinevere, wife to
Arthur the High King. The queen and Sir Lancelot!

A state close to panic seized hold of his guts and twisted.
*No. No. It is not possible. I did not see it. It could not be. She would
not. Not even with Sir Lancelot. She would never betray King Arthur.
She would not!*

Memory crashed against him. He was a boy again, his head
tilting up to look at Geraint who looked as sick as he felt.
His hands shook, his voice quavered and tears spilled down
his cold cheeks.

'Why Geraint?' he was asking, his voice high and plain-
tive with a child's pain and confusion. 'Why did he kill her?'

'There was a man, Gareth,' answered Geraint, as gently as
he could. 'She was with child. She would not name him.
Father grew angry . . .' Geraint said no more. There was no
need. They all knew father's anger, his vicious, sudden,
reasonless anger.

Gareth threw himself into his brother's embrace trying to
crawl inside Geraint's very skin, to hide from the confusion
and betrayal, to hide from the truth that his sister was dishonoured, and that his father had killed her for it.

Movement brought Gareth back to himself and he saw the
tent open once more, and the queen emerge again, looking
this way and that. His first broken and furious thought

sneered that she must be looking for Sir Lancelot. Then he realized he was wrong.

She was looking for Lynet.

God's legs.

Gareth crouched beside Lynet where she lay corpse cold, and he shook her. 'Lynet! Lynet!' he called, softly, urgently. He looked over his shoulder. The queen still stood before the pavilion, her hands on her hips. He knew by her stance that worry and anger were at war within her.

'Lynet!'

Slowly, slowly, Lynet began to stir. Her eyes blinked heavily and a low, wordless groan escaped her.

'Lynet, wake up!' He grasped her arms and pulled her into a sitting position. Her face turned towards him but she did not see him. He shook her hard. 'Lynet, Lynet Carnbrea, wake up! See me!'

Animation returned painfully to her face and her gaze, and she thrust her hands between his arms to break his hold. He let go even though she swayed where she sat. He looked back at the queen. They had but moments.

'No!' she moaned. 'No, I mustn't leave, not yet . . .'

'Lynet, hear me!' bawled Gareth in her ear. 'The queen is looking for you! Lynet! Queen Guinevere is awake and she's looking for you!'

Those words brought Lynet all the way back. She grabbed hold of his arm and used it to lever herself to her feet. He was not sure she'd be able to walk, but she squeezed his hand with some semblance of strength, and staggered forward, shoving her mirror into its pouch. Gareth stayed where he was, watching her, his breath coming fast and ragged.

By the time she emerged fully into the moonlight, Lynet was walking normally. Gareth hung back in the trees, watching her move forward with only her usual slight limping.

'My queen!' she exclaimed as she began to kneel.

Queen Guinevere stopped her with a gesture. 'God of mercy, Lynet, where were you! I was thinking you'd wandered off . . .'

'Forgive me, Majesty. I was only relieving myself.' Lynet waved vaguely towards the woods. 'I . . . I do not like to do so too close to the pavilion . . .'

The queen was still for a moment. Because he could not see her face, Gareth could not tell whether she believed Lynet's story or not.

'Well, come inside before you wake anyone else.' The queen held the pavilion door open. Lynet bowed her head meekly and vanished into its shadows.

For a moment the queen stood there alone, looking back towards the main camp, back along the way Sir Lancelot had walked. Then she too retreated inside the pavilion, and all was quiet again.

Gareth put a hand on the trunk of the nearest tree. His breathing would not calm, but instead grew louder, more painful against his throat. Sir Lancelot. Sir Lancelot had come to the queen in darkness, and she had answered him. They had stood there together, so close, spoken so softly.

Gareth pushed his knuckles into his eyes so hard the pain ran back through his skull. *Pluck them out,* he thought ridiculously. *Before you have to see more.*

He swung around, striding away from the camp to he knew not where. Anywhere. Anywhere but back to where Queen Guinevere and Sir Lancelot were.

The queen.

Not the queen.

Never the queen.

The queen.

His foot slipped on the grass and he came back to himself with a jolt. He stood on the sloping hillside. Below him spread the vast, black expanse of the moorland. He threw himself down on the sodden grass, not caring for either damp or cold, and drew his knees up to his chest like a boy. Like a boy who learned far too young that woman's betrayal meant death and madness and vanishing.

There was a mist rising, filling the bowl of the moor valley, as thick and uneasy as the thoughts filling him.

He had not seen it. It was something else. Something different. Some problem or potential danger that Sir Lancelot had to alert the queen to.

But the camp is quiet.

The queen would not betray her king, their king. She loved him.

She was the one to answer Sir Lancelot, not a serving maid . . .

No. No. It had not happened. He was wrong.

Gareth sat hunched there on the hillside, his arms wrapped around himself and his thoughts barging back and forth so that he felt his skull must split open from the force of them. The mist crawled up the hillside. There'd be a real fog soon, all around the camp. He should get up. He should go back, before someone had to come looking for him out here. *How can I face the queen again?* He bowed his head, running both hands through his hair and scrubbing at his scalp as if he could shake loose some new thought from his suddenly too-tight skin. But nothing came, and he stared out at the deepening mist again.

The fog had formed in earnest. It even seemed to reach up to the sky to draw down the clouds and the stars beneath them, for he could now see tiny pinpricks of light shining within the soft grey blanket of mist. No. He looked again. Those were not stars. They moved. What were they? Gareth leaned forward. They were gold. No. Bright white. No. Blue, like the heart of a fire.

Without realizing he had moved, Gareth was on his hands

and knees, leaning forward, his eyes straining into the mist, trying to see the lights. They were blue and green, white and gold. There were four of them. Now five. Now six. They moved in a dance he could not understand or explain, but if he looked a little closer he would see it plainly. It was important. He knew that. He had to understand.

He was on his feet and two steps down the hill. Warning rippled through him with the touch of the cold air on his face, but it was quickly gone, and all that mattered was reaching the lights that moved in their solemn dance. He had to get close enough to understand what it was he saw.

The lights moved away, and Gareth, stumbling over stones hidden by the mist, ran towards them.

NINETEEN

Morning came slowly. Lynet woke to find mist had wormed its way through the pavilion walls, dampening furs and blankets alike. Her cloak was no better, and she shivered as she passed between the complaining ladies to look out on what could be seen.

There was only the deep green grass before their tent, and swirling white beyond. She could make out the dim shapes of men moving back and forth in the fog. She could hear the sounds of the camp, but all were muffled by the thickened air. Men cursed the wood and peat that was too sodden to take any spark. The damp clung like cold sweat to her hands and brow.

The queen came up behind her, frowning out at the mists. 'Well. There is no going forward until this lifts. We may as well be comfortable. Daere, Agnes, light the braziers, if they will light, and see what may be got to break our fast.'

The maids accepted their orders and made their curtsies, setting about on their business. Lynet, though, lingered in the doorway. She had known these fogs from her earliest days, but there was something else in the air, something that made her uneasy. A hundred old stories, things half-seen and half-believed, all crowded into her mind. She touched her mirror through the purse as if it were a talisman to keep them all at bay. Once more she felt the confines of her own flesh, and resented being forced back to herself.

'Will you join us, Lady Lynet?' inquired the queen, who had taken her seat.

The idea of sitting quietly and decorously with the queen's ladies while the mists held the world in suspense sent a shudder up Lynet's spine. She repressed it and bowed her head respectfully instead. 'With permission, Your Majesty, I would like to go check on Squire Brendon. This damp will be bad for his lungs.'

The queen wavered for a moment. She had, after all, sworn to protect her as well as help her, and Lynet had not exactly embraced that protection.

But the queen nodded at last. 'Mind you do not go out beyond the camp. We would lose you for certain in this.'

Lynet made her curtsey and let Daere put her thickest cloak over her shoulders. She left the pavilion acutely aware that the queen watched her walk away.

Worry trembled through her. She would make this a short walk, just long enough to make sure all was right with her people and her patient. Then, she would return to the ladies' pavilion and spend the day at the queen's side sedately and properly occupied in sharing stories, riddles and songs with the others to pass the time until the world reappeared around them.

With this resolve, Lynet turned towards the place where she could see the most movement. The mists gave way for perhaps a yard around her, letting her see just enough of the ground to keep from tripping over the stones and hummocks. She passed the men sitting beside dead fires and staring gloomily out at the fog as they ate bread and beer watered by the thin drizzle. Hobbled horses hung their heads. The mist left silver droplets on their manes. A few of the more spirited shook their heads, scattering a small grey rain of their own making and snorting as if adding a horse-voiced curse to the general gloom. Dozens of familiar, everyday human sounds were all rendered chill and strange because in the veiled daylight she could not see their sources.

After a few minutes of wandering about looking for some landmark, Lynet was beginning to realize she would have to ask if anyone knew the way to the squires' tent. Even in this close encampment, she could not find her way clearly. Then, a gangly young man pelted out of the thicker mists heading straight into her path. Lynet swung around at the same moment he pulled up short.

'Your pardon, my lady!' Lionel cried, making a deep and hasty bow.

'There is no need,' she said, waving the incident away. 'Though you might go a little slower.'

'Yes, my lady.' He shifted his weight, and Lynet stepped a little further aside so that he could continue on whatever his urgent errand was. But Lionel did not move. 'Forgive me, my lady,' he said cautiously. 'But have you spoken with Squire Gareth this morning?'

Lynet felt her spine straighten just a little. 'No, I have not. Why?'

Disappointment creased the squire's face. 'He's gone missing. My Lord Lancelot is most displeased.' Lionel glowered at the fog. 'When we find him, Gareth will wish he'd stayed in his own bed this time.' He caught himself, remembering who stood beside him, and turned pale. 'Forgive me, my lady, I only meant . . .'

'It's all right, Squire Lionel.' Although it wasn't. Now she understood the reason for the cautious tone of his inquiry. Gareth was a rake. If she admitted she had seen him last night, there were very few good conclusions that could be drawn from that.

The other truth sank more slowly into her. Gareth was missing. He had been with her last night, until late. The mists had already begun to rise then. She'd stumbled away, leaving him behind her, and then . . . then what?

'Go on with your search,' she managed to say. 'We do not want Lord Lancelot angry with you both.'

Lionel shuddered. 'No, my lady, we do not.' He made another hasty bow and took his leave.

Lynet wrapped her arms around herself, but it did no good. The cold she now felt came from within her. Where was Gareth? To be sure, on such a morning you could stand quietly beside someone and not be seen, but why would Gareth wish to hide? If he was in another's bed, it was not precisely a matter of shame with him . . .

He'd been upset when she left him, although he would not say why. She had thought it had been because of having to wait beside her, and wake her so suddenly. He was far from easy with what she did. But what if it was more than that? Something she had not seen, or, as bound up as she was in her own troubles, had not asked. She had assumed he had gone back to his fellow squires, but she did not know. He could have gone anywhere.

She stared out at the mists, towards where she thought the moors might be. *No. He did not go that way. Not in the dark with a fog rolling in. You are worrying over nothing.*

But around her voices began to raise themselves above the muted grumbling, chiding, clanging and all the other sounds of the sluggish camp.

'Gareth?' called out a man's voice from somewhere to her right. Then, another, from the left. 'Gaaaaareth!'

Lynet's throat tightened. *Peace. Peace,* she chided herself. *He has only found some warmer bed and is loath to leave it. That's all.*

But what bed could be so warm it would keep Gareth from serving his master at any time? If there was one thing true about Gareth, it was his love for Lancelot and his pride of place. No, he would not wander far away, no matter how upset he was.

Not if he had any choice.

Stop, Lynet. You are only frightening yourself.

But Gareth's name still rang out through the mists, sounded by half-a-dozen separate voices now, and no answer came back. Out there in the unseen camp, conferences, curses and questions shunted back and forth, but she still could not hear the voice she missed.

Lynet felt ill. The mist pressed against her with palpable weight, like Merlin's shadows. She thought of Gareth and how he had stood beside her in the darkness to keep her safe and to keep her secret even when he did not understand what was happening. Perhaps he did it to impress her, rake that he was, but she could not quite bring herself to believe that. He had stayed when he could have left her alone, he had kept his silence when he could have – perhaps should have – betrayed her. Whatever else he was, he was true to his word.

For that alone, she must stand by him. Lynet turned and strode away from the centre of the camp.

Before she had travelled a score of paces, the shadows of tents, pavilion and movement had vanished, taking all the sounds of men with them. Lynet was utterly alone. Her footsteps did not even leave any track on the springy, sodden ground.

A nearby stone made her a seat. As soon as she took the mirror from her purse, drops of moisture formed on its surface. She cupped her hands around the glass, leaning forward, seeing her frightened visage framed in white and spattered with water-like silver tears.

Her soul knew its road well now, and she did not even have to focus her will. The instant she thought of Ryol's name and form, she felt the pull of him. The world of mists was swallowed up and gone in an eyeblink, and Lynet woke once more standing in Ryol's garden.

But the summer sweetness was well and truly gone now. Autumn had come. The flowers were dried on their stalks and the trees' leaves had turned to gold and copper overhead.

Ryol came towards her from beneath the trees. With a shock, Lynet saw his hair had gone completely white, and his shoulders were hunched as if beneath the weight of years. Both hands outstretched to take hers up, his face creased with worry. 'My lady? You come so soon . . .' but just as he reached her, his hands fell to his sides. 'There is danger.'

'Ryol, what has happened here?'

He smiled tiredly. 'Do not concern yourself, lady. It is the consequence of the use of spirit. What has happened?'

'But . . .'

He shook his head. 'What has happened, my lady?' he asked again.

Lynet swallowed her questions. Ryol was right, yet again. There was no time. 'The man, Gareth. He is gone from the camp. The moor is so close . . . did it take him?'

Ryol set his jaw and Lynet saw a flash in his eyes that might well have been anger. A sour scent drifted past on the mild breeze. Despite this, his gaze turned to the distance. She felt his presence travelling from her as he reached out and sought the owner of the name she had given. The garden blurred, as if the fog had found its way in.

'There.' Ryol raised his arm, pointing over her shoulder.

She turned to see. The fog had indeed come, shrouding the garden in its chill and looming mist. As she stared, her eyes seemed to adjust to the watery, grey light, and she saw

Gareth. He was not alone. A crowd of women in white robes belted with silver stood about him. Gareth knelt on the sodden, green ground, his chin held high, his face rapt as he gazed at the woman before him. She was a beauty beyond mortal life. Her hands were long and perfect and she laid them on Gareth's shoulders. Her skin was milk and rose without blemish, her hair a rich red-gold that would have outshone even the beauty of Queen Iseult's. But although she could clearly see every other feature, Lynet could not see the woman's eyes. There were only grey hollows above her cheeks as she looked down on Gareth kneeling before her.

A dozen other maidens, each as beautiful as the first, clustered behind her. With these mist-pale beauties stood a pack of hounds – great, black square-muzzled beasts, with eyes that burned with alert and ferocious life.

Gareth laid his hand over his heart and spoke to the achingly beautiful woman before him, his clear brown gaze never leaving her pure and lovely face. He was swearing something, taking some oath to this woman.

'Gareth!' Lynet cried and lunged forward, but Ryol gripped her arm hard, pulling her back.

'No, Lynet! You are spirit here. If you go among them as you are, they will draw you in and you will be lost.'

'Then I will be a shape.' She steeled herself, concentrating her will. But even as she did so, one of the great dogs lifted its muzzle, as if it had caught her scent. It growled, showing its white teeth. Its fellows stirred uneasily.

'No,' said Ryol again, more gently. She smelled that sour scent again. 'It will not be enough, Lynet. You must believe me.'

The maiden who stood before Gareth took no notice of the dogs. She was smiling. She bent down and laid a delicate kiss upon Gareth's brow.

'What are they?' Lynet whispered.

'The daughters of the moor,' Ryol answered softly. One of the dog's twitched its ears and cold fear took hold of Lynet. 'It was their lights that led him astray.'

Before her, the maiden raised Gareth up, and kissed him again, this time on each cheek. It seemed to Lynet that some of the colour drained from him as he smiled his witless smile at the beauty.

'How can I free him?'

She felt Ryol searching. The push and pull as his spirit ranged forth was like the buffeting winds on the heights. She felt also his reluctance. This she cast aside. It mattered not whether he liked what he did, only that it was done. Whatever fate these creatures might have in store for Gareth, she could not leave him to it. She thought suddenly of Bishop Austell on the deck of the pitching ship, standing strong one moment, and in the next gone down to the merciless embrace of the *morverch*.

No. She would not permit such a thing to happen again.

Ryol sucked in a breath through his teeth. The sour smell around them grew stronger. The maiden took Gareth's hand, and led him to her fellows who all curtsied to him, each smiling, each looking up at him with those strange, hollow eyes. Behind them, the dogs clustered together cutting off retreat, or approach.

'You must go to him,' said Ryol at last, reluctantly. 'In the flesh. You must stand yourself between him and the daughters. Gareth is sworn first to you. As long as you do not release him, they cannot take him.'

I swear that I will remain to protect you. Hope leapt up inside Lynet as Gareth's words rang through her memory. At the time, it had seemed a small reassurance, something to comfort her in the dark. But it was an oath, and in the lands between Heaven and Earth, between life and death, such words bound like bands of iron, as she had good cause to know. 'How can I find him?' There were few trustworthy landmarks on a moor even when the weather was clear. Now the whole world was a blank slate.

'I will guide you. Hold aloft the mirror and fix your will on Squire Gareth. I will find you the proper road.' She looked at him again, this young man turned so suddenly old.

The women and their beasts surrounded Gareth now. She could not see him anymore.

'Thank you, Ryol,' she said, tearing her gaze from the scene. 'We must go at once.'

'Yes.' He hesitated, and then said softly, 'Know this. They will be able to touch you, but not hold you. They are mist. You are stone and sea. You are stronger than they.'

She touched his arm, and he jerked away at once, as if she burned him, but in that single instant, she felt fear and anger spill over her, almost drowning out all other awareness.

'Go,' he said, before she could question him. 'Delay and you condemn him to their mercies.'

His will pushed at hers. With no desire to resist, Lynet let herself be banished back to the mortal realm beyond the mirror.

Lynet woke huddled on her stone, her skin drenched, her whole body shivering. Her head ached. She held the mirror in one numb hand. She pushed herself upright and stood. Her eyes swam from the effort and her knees tried to buckle. She clenched her teeth. All around was an unbroken white cocoon. There was no way to tell how long she had been gone, or if they now searched the camp for her as well as Gareth.

It did not matter. She raised her hand, gone blue with cold, and held the mirror high over her head. She thought of Gareth. She thought of the shape of his face and the sound of his voice. She thought of the startled anger she had seen in him when she took him for the kitchen boy, and of the brilliant smile that could spread a sudden light across his face and up into his summer-brown eyes.

Her palm tingled. Warmth blossomed across her skin. In the next breath, a beam of light, as straight and sharp as a blade, scythed through the enshrouding fog, clearing a path just broad enough for Lynet to walk. Above, the sky was bright blue, below the ground was green and soft, broken only by tiny flowers and lichen-feathered stones. Which direction this road ran, Lynet could not tell. The sunbeams slanted in on to her right, but as she did not know if noon had passed this gave her no help. The path led down into the heart of the moor, and that was all she knew or needed to know.

Lynet knotted her sodden hems in her free hand so that she would not stumble over them, and started forward. She knew without looking that the mists closed behind her. She could feel the cold at her back as surely as she could feel the heat of her unearthly lantern in her hand. She too was now gone, and if she failed, she would not return.

She walked on. The ground beneath her squelched and each footstep brought up a fresh pool of water. The mists dragged at her sleeves and brushed her warm skin with fresh lines of cold. Her body was leaden, and each step felt as if it must be her last, but she kept on. She turned her mind again and again to Gareth, striving to recall each word they had spoken, each moment shared. She thought on the exact shade of golden brown that coloured his eyes, the way his hands gentled his horse and held its reins so easily, how the rapture on his face when he looked at the daughters of the moor had been so close to how he looked when he spoke of Lancelot's deeds.

There was no time here, no direction or true sense of place.

Hunger and thirst nagged at Lynet. Her sodden clothing clung to her body, an icy drapery that provided no screen from the elements. The ground beneath her was so drenched, she could as easily have been wading through a stream as walking on the land.

Then the wind blew hard to her left and the way in front of her opened wide. There she saw Gareth lying on a stone. Lynet gave a wordless cry of gladness and ran forward. The wind blew again, bringing the mists back down, cold and close. The mirror's light blinked out, and she was alone.

Lynet stopped short. Fear closed over her, but she held firm against it. She carefully placed the mirror in its bag. It would not do to lose it now. Slowly, she turned in a circle, staring hard at the whitened world around her. Through the thin veil at the edge of the fog, she saw movement. Then she saw Gareth again, stretched on his back on the flat, age-speckled stone. She hiked up her skirts and ran to his side.

Gareth lay on his cold bed, unmoving and pale as death. Only his open eyes and small, witless smile showed him to be alive. If he knew she was there, he gave no sign even though she was panting hoarsely by the time she reached him. Over him, the mists swirled, every shade of grey blurring together and separating out again.

'Gareth!' Lynet laid her hands on his chest, feeling for breath and beating heart.

Her touch seemed to reach him as her voice could not. Gareth turned his pale face towards her. Slowly, recognition came to him, and the smile fell away, replaced by sick despair. But he made no move to rise. Around them, the wind blew again, tugging at the mists, and reforming them. With it came something else.

Sorrow.

It rode the wind, thick and choking. It came down in the

soft rain and soaked through her skin, until Lynet could barely draw breath.

There were shapes in the mist. No. She looked again. The mist formed the shapes – the white women in their gowns of pale grey. Here in the world of flesh, what little colour they had was gone. Their unbound hair was white and hung loose down to their feet. The daughters of the moor came forth from the fog as a great and solemn parade of beauties with the sorrowful wind blowing before them. Some of them carried torches that flickered white in the white world that cut them off from all creation. At the end of their slow, sad procession came the one who had taken the oath from Gareth and given him her kiss in return. Lynet knew her by the plain band binding her ivory brow. She held a sword in her perfect hands now. Its blade was dove grey and the milky lights of the torches played along its length.

The dogs paced beside them. Of all this ghostly procession, only the beasts had colour. They were solid black. Water beaded on their coarse fur and bristling hackles and the swirling mists were reflected in their bright eyes.

You must stand yourself between him and the daughters. Gareth is sworn first to you, and as long as you do not release him, they cannot take him.

Lynet rose from her knees. She swallowed hard against the lump that filled her throat and blinked back her tears. She rounded the stone, putting her back to Gareth so that she faced the moorland's daughters and their black hounds.

One of the lead dogs growled a warning, and the daughters halted their stately progress. Only then did the sword-bearer look towards Lynet. Her eyes were as hollow and indistinct as they had been when Lynet saw them in the mirror, and yet that gaze seemed to pin her down with its weight. The sorrow grew still more keen, as if this woman breathed it out from herself.

Frozen, frightened, and with anger swelling inside her, Lynet drew herself up to her full height. With an effort, she shook the sorrow off. She knew the touch of such feelings by now. She knew they could be taken up or allowed to pass. She would not let it distract her.

'I am Lynet of Cambryn,' she declared. 'Daughter of the Lady Morwenna of the sea. I am come to take this man back to his people.'

A low, rippling growl passed among the hounds. One stepped forward, baring its white teeth as it pressed next to the woman who carried the sword. She did not make a move or speak a word to control the animal.

The man is ours.

The words sounded within her thoughts rather than in her ears, passing straight to the centre of her in the same way that the sadness did.

'He is not yours. He belongs to his own people who search for him even now.'

The sword-bearer did not stir, but the shadows hiding her eyes deepened and the sorrows grew stronger, turned colder. *He made his vow to us.*

Lynet remained unmoved. 'He made his vow to me first. I have the prior claim.'

He gave his word willingly.

It cannot be I must stand here and argue over Gareth like a fish at market, Lynet thought, half-despairing, half ready to laugh at the absurdity of it. But that thought led to another. An argument at market led to a bargain, but many such a bargainer resorted to deception.

'You lied to him,' she assayed this softly. It was a guess, nothing more. But when the sword-bearer made no answer, Lynet felt a spark of triumph catch. For the first time that whole cold, shrouded morning, she felt herself smile. 'A vow made to falsehood cannot bind. The only reason you can hold him is that you have made him too weak to move.'

The woman stepped forward. She was fully as tall as Lynet. Her face was lean and sharp, as distinctly formed as the sword she carried, and Lynet still could not see her eyes.

Do not do this thing, sister. Do not invite death where it is not needed. The man has given his life freely.

Lynet did not back away. She stood against the voice in her mind, against this strange woman with her shadowed eyes, and all her sisters and the great black dogs crowding close to those silent maidens and she knew down to her marrow she was right. 'I am no sister of yours,' she said. 'I am a steward's daughter. What you may be I know not, but I know the law. If you lied, he was coerced and you may not justly claim him. And you did *lie*!' The last word burst from her as a shout.

One of the black dogs barked, a single commanding noise, and the woman before Lynet flinched. Lynet frowned, confused. The dog growled, and the sword-bearer's perfect face grew taut.

Do not make us take you as well, she repeated and a new note sounded in her voice.

Fear.

Instinctively, Lynet lifted her hand. She passed it between them, the gesture she had seen Ryol make so many times to change and wipe away the shadows of his garden.

Let me see you, she willed the woman before her. *Let me truly see you.*

For a moment, the veil cleared. For a single heartbeat, Lynet looked into the sword-bearer's eyes. They were pale blue and ancient, and exhausted from looking out on all those years without rest or respite. Those eyes were wracked with a sorrow that cut so deeply Lynet could not begin to comprehend it. The sorrow she felt around her was but the smallest fraction of what was contained within this pale lady.

In that moment she understood these were not like the sea-women. These were not the free and heartless fae. They had no wish to make this sacrifice. They were trapped here, even as Gareth was. For how long, for how many lifetimes, it was impossible to say, nor was it possible to guess how much blood they had shed.

'God forgive you,' she whispered. 'Whatever your sins. God and Mary and Jesus Christ grant you rest, but I cannot let you pass.'

She had the briefest hope the holy names would bring some aid or succour, but the veil closed again over the woman's ravaged eyes, and once more a dog barked. The beast nearest to Lynet raised its hackles impatiently, and the low growl it gave trembled through the earth.

Belatedly, the true source of her danger finally became clear to Lynet.

They will be able to touch you, but not hold you, Ryol said. *You are stronger than they.* But he had spoken of the daughters of the mist, not their great dogs. They were living creatures, massive and fierce, and she stood there with nothing but her bare hands.

The nearest dog bared its teeth and stepped forward another pace.

Bow down, said the sword-bearer. *Bow down and accept judgement for interrupting the holy rite.*

The sorrow blew away on the wind and in its place came outrage, towering and terrible. Lynet was small and alone, weak and far from home. She was an ignorant child who knew nothing of the glory she had challenged, of the importance of what the man behind her did.

Lynet felt it all, and she trembled, and she let it pass over her. But it would not do to let these maidens, and their masters know that. So Lynet forced her tremors to grow as if the false guilt they poured over her had truly sunk into her soul. She bowed her head as if in the gravest of shame. She made her hands shake and, slowly, she knelt onto the sodden ground.

The very air around her sang. She did right. The sword-bearer came another step closer, to accept her surrender and bring relief to her for her repentance.

In a single, swift motion, Lynet leapt to her feet and snatched the sword from those white hands. The hilt was solid and heavy. Holding the gleaming silver blade in front of her, she backed away until she felt Gareth's stone at her heels.

'Hear me,' she said, her heart beating so hard it caused her hands to shake. 'None of you shall pass here.'

The lead hound lifted its head and howled. In answer, the daughters wailed. It was a sound like the ending of the world. It beat against Lynet, robbing her of breath and sense. The daughters surged forward, throwing themselves against her, battering her with sorrow and the terrible, terrible sound of their weeping. She could barely feel their blows but the confusion of their crowding, the deafening noise of their weeping, threatened to bear her down.

You are stronger than they. You are stone.

Gritting her teeth, Lynet moved. She shoved her way forward and all the maidens fell back until she faced the lead hound. The creature snarled, unleashing a burst of fear, and Lynet raised the sword, and swung it down onto the dog's neck.

The blade jarred her arms as it contacted flesh and bone with a strangely dull thud. All other sound ceased to be.

The hound gave a rough bark that sounded disconcertingly like laughter and fell back until it stood beside its fellows. The entire pack faced her now, all burning eyes and white fangs, and the maidens cowered behind them.

The dogs began to stalk forward, coming together in a

mass. Lynet retreated, circling to draw them off Gareth. They wanted her. They would come towards her. She must hold them off somehow, lead them away, give him a chance to come to himself. She could not even see him anymore, but she had no time to spare a thought for that. She must not be distracted from the pack.

The dogs came on, each pressing close to his fellows to make a solid wall. Then, one-by-one, like inky shadows they melded into one another. Each remaining beast stretched and reformed as their flanks swallowed their fellows until there were only two the size of black elkhounds, grinning at her from their wide muzzles. Then, in an impossible blurring of flesh, there was only one hulking, swollen monster towering over her. It no longer looked like a hound. This was a massive black bear, with a bear's clawed paws and heavy shoulders and blazing, beady eyes.

Absurdly, Lynet wished Colan were here. He knew how to hunt the bear. Holding the sword up and out before her, she retreated but her feet banged against a stone behind her.

The demon bear before her gave a chuckling growl and lowered its heavy head. Its teeth gleamed as white as the mists, as white as the skin of the maidens behind it, and slowly, leisurely, it ambled towards Lynet and her stolen blade.

'Hey!' cried another voice. 'Hey!'

Gareth?

He had come to, as she'd hoped. He had at some moment got himself to his feet and circled behind the monster. Now he waved his arms, as ridiculous as any boy trying to chase a pig from the garden.

'Hey! You great black puppy! What are you doing there?' He reached down and grabbed up a muddy stone. 'Are you only strong enough to attack a woman? Puppy! Coward!' He tossed the feeble missile at the monster. It thumped faintly against its pelt. 'Face a man if you want a fight!' He scooped up dirt clods and a handful of pebbles and hurled them to smack and clatter against the beast's muzzle. 'Where's your bitch of a dam, puppy? Maybe she can fight! Where're your teeth?'

The monster snapped at the air, bristling and swelling to twice its size. Gareth dodged, putting a listing boulder between himself and the demon, but there were none big enough to shelter him. The sword shook in Lynet's hands.

You are stronger than they . . . But he meant the maidens. Did he? He did not say that.

'Come on, puppy!' cried Gareth. The tremor in his voice drove Lynet into action.

Lynet lunged. Her movement caught the monster's eye. It whirled around, and hurled itself forward, its fanged maw blocking out all other sights. Lynet brought up the blade and thrust it down the monster's throat. Its teeth grazed her arms as it jerked itself backward, gagging and choking and ripped itself from off the sword, nearly tearing the blade from her hands. Lynet hung on for grim life as she stumbled backward. The monster staggered after her, blood pouring from its muzzle, but it still did not fall. Gareth rounded the creature until he reached her side, and could take the sword that now dangled limp in her hands. He was still sickly white, and shaking at least as badly as she was. The beast clawed the ground and swung its body back and forth. Gareth lifted the sword so he held it by the hilt and the weapon made the shape of the cross before him. She thought he whispered the holy names as he drove the blade down into the monster's neck. More blood, an impossible fountain of blood, spurted up to the sky as if to colour the mists themselves scarlet.

Finally, finally, the beast collapsed onto the waterlogged ground, and died.

Gareth took two trembling steps backward. Lynet lurched forward two more so that they stood side-by-side.

As they stood, shaking and panting, fearing that the thing before them might move again, a new sound broke across their awareness. A wordless cry lifted up, but not of horror this time. This shout was of unspeakable gladness. Lynet raised her blurring eyes and saw the daughters of the moor once more. They shone now, so white that to look at them was like looking at the sun. All of them lifted their hands to the heavens, the sound from their throats a single reverberating note of joy.

And they were gone, gone in an instant, and Lynet knew without question that they were free, each and every one of them.

Lynet looked up into Gareth's face, and incredibly, not only did Gareth smile at her, but Lynet felt herself smile in return. Around them, the mists melted away, and they could plainly see the honest shape of the world and how the land rose towards the height where the camp waited for them.

Gareth reached out his free hand and Lynet took it gratefully. But they could do no more. Slowly, almost gracefully, they collapsed together beside the hulking carcass of the monster they had slain. Blessed darkness took hold of Lynet then and she fell into it as easily as if Ryol waited at the end.

TWENTY

Colan Carnbrea dreamed.

He dreamed he pressed through a great wood to an open place. A broad meadow surrounded a lake that lay like a still, dark jewel in the autumn-brown grass. All about, the tall trees stood guard, and they were filled with mighty ravens, their keen eyes and their sharp beaks gleaming. There were so many that it seemed that each leaf in the forest had turned into a great, black bird. They all looked at him, and the clamour of their croaking was like raucous laughter.

Then, the grey surface of the lake quivered. It trembled and it broke, and a mare as black as the ravens charged forth. Panic surged through Colan and he tried to run, but the mare made straight for him, tossing its gleaming black mane and baring its white teeth. The ravens shouted their carrion cries, urging the wild beast on, and no matter how Colan ran he could not reach the shelter of those terrible trees. At last, he tripped and sprawled onto the grass. The mare reared over him, and all the ravens laughed to see him throw up his hands as a feeble guard against the hooves that flashed so brightly.

But the hooves came down beside him, and as if this were

some signal, the ravens all took flight, rising up in a cloud
to darken the sky. The clapping of their wings deafened him,
and in their blur of motion they stretched and changed,
turning the grey sky to midnight black. The peaceful stars
shone down as if through the gaps in the ravens' wing
feathers.

Colan gaped, his heart hammering hard in his chest, and
beside him, a familiar voice spoke.

'Do you know me, Colan?'

Colan scrambled backward on all fours. The mare had
spoken, and in the way of dreams, the mare was Morgaine,
was the mare, was Morgaine. She was both and neither and
he could not make a single sound.

At last, he croaked, 'Yes, my lady, I know you.'

'And do you know why I am come to you?'

'No, my lady.'

'Because last night I saw you boldly try to prove yourself
to me, and I accept that deed.' She was Morgaine alone then
for a moment, and he saw her smile.

'I failed,' he whispered.

'You were sore prevented.'

The ghost. He saw it again, his father's bloody shade
standing before him, its great hands spread wide. Fear stabbed
through him, but Morgaine reached out her hand and
touched the ghost with one brown finger.

The shade shrank, shrivelled, and changed, and it was
Lynet who stood before him. Just Lynet, and all the fear was
gone.

Slowly, Colan sat up. 'How can this be?'

Morgaine sighed and lifted her hand. The image of Lynet
melted away 'Your youngest sister has done more than I
expected. It was the elder I feared; the younger I passed over.'
She shook her head in annoyance. 'She found you out, and
she moved as she could to save her sister's life.'

Anger flooded him, the sharp and sudden emotion of one who has been lied to.

Morgaine smiled on him and he felt bathed in warmth. All would yet be right if she could still smile on him. 'It is she you must kill, Colan.'

And for all the anger in him, for all he had been ready to murder Laurel who was so much stronger than he would ever be, the idea of striking Lynet down with the same blow repelled him. It was reasonless and he knew it. He'd been ready for the *morverch* to take her, but she had survived to fight back, as he had. She was so much like him, his little sister. He remembered her as an infant toddling after him as soon as the nurse loosed her from her leading strings. She had frightened him, that was all. Of course she had, for she also loved Laurel. But was that any reason to turn on him yet again? He shook his own head now, unable to reconcile the two colliding needs boiling up within his breast.

'Why? Why must I kill her?'

For the first time, something like pity crept into Morgaine's voice. 'Because, Colan Carnbrea, it is the path you have started down. There was a moment when you could have chosen otherwise, but you did not. Now death is the only choice you have.'

'Why me?'

'Because your sister moves to bar me from this place. Soon I will not be able to enter here. Indeed, I may not be able to touch a one of you. It must be done, and it must be you.'

Colan bowed his head and squeezed his eyes shut against the tears that threatened to spill down. He had thought himself protected against her because he was no longer amazed. He did not know how long he had been snared in this web, nor how much he had spun himself.

'How?' he asked. 'I cannot leave this room.'

She showed him. She poured the knowledge into him like

wine. It was heady and bitter and it filled him with a reeling
drunkenness of power that in turn filled him with fear of
her and of himself and of all that must come after.

Colan woke.

The mattress ticking was soaked with his sweat and more
poured down his icy skin. He lay there, his eyes straining to
see in the absolute darkness. For a dozen heartbeats, he tried
to pretend his dream had not been real.

But it was, and he knew it. He also knew that he would
do as Morgaine commanded, and that by the time he came
to it, thought would have driven the fear and regret away,
and he would understand it was the only right way.

For that understanding yet to come, Colan Carnbrea began
slowly and painfully to weep.

Pain throbbing in her arms woke Lynet. She lifted her head,
gazing about her. She lay on her pallet in the queen's pavilion,
dressed in a dry shift of white linen. Both her arms rested
atop the bed coverings, swathed to the elbow with white
cloths.

'She wakes, Majesty!' called Daere, coming into Lynet's
range of vision. 'God be praised!' The maid laid a rough hand
on Lynet's forehead and gazed with real concern into her
eyes.

Lynet tried to speak, but her raw throat seized shut, and
she could only cough. Daere at once lifted a cup to Lynet's
lips. The watered wine felt like the balm of Heaven as it
moistened her parched mouth, and Daere gave her a little
more.

'You frightened us so, my lady,' she admonished gently. 'I
think the Holy Mother must be getting tired of the sound of
my voice and your name by now.'

Lynet gave the maid a wavering smile, but still could not
find her voice. Daere tipped the cup for her once more. While

she sipped, Queen Guinevere came up beside the serving woman.

The queen's face was impassive. She felt Lynet's head for fever. Finding none, she lifted first one of Lynet's arms, then the other, examining the bandages and Lynet's hands, presumably for signs of swelling, pus, or corruption of the flesh. When satisfied there were no signs of these dangers, Queen Guinevere glanced at Daere, who set down the cup and hurriedly brought a stool that the queen might sit, and then withdrew.

Lynet tried to ease herself up into a sitting position, but it was of no use. The least motion of her arms was painful and there was no strength left to her. She gazed down at her own distant hands. Between the pain and the tension that filled her, it was all Lynet could do to maintain the silence that courtesy required. She wanted to explain, or for the queen to start shouting. Anything, so long as it began now so it could be over with that much sooner.

'So,' said Queen Guinevere at last. 'You come to me, demanding my help and protection for you and yours, as your right. Then when I give you that protection and help, I find you've lied to me, that you carry with you an object of mystical power about which you've said nothing, and that you wilfully leave my protection so that I must risk more of my own to find you.'

'I am sorry, Majesty,' Lynet murmured. 'I . . .' She lifted her gaze just long enough to see the depth of the anger burning behind the queen's eyes.

'Well?' inquired Queen Guinevere coldly.

'I could not stand and wait,' Lynet whispered. She tried to put some strength into her voice, but failed. 'I knew something was wrong and that I must try to help him any way I could.'

'Him.' The queen repeated the single word. 'Your lover?'

'No! No. He isn't . . . he hasn't . . .'

The queen rubbed her brow. 'I'm glad of that at least.' She regarded Lynet for another long moment, but the tide of her anger had ebbed a little. 'Why did you not tell me what you meant to do?'

'I did not think you would permit it.'

A corner of the queen's mouth twitched. 'Perhaps not,' she said calmly. 'But had I all the facts in the matter, perhaps I would have decided differently. You did not consider that.' It was a flat statement, and, Lynet could not deny, a true one.

'No, Majesty.' But even as she spoke the words, Lynet bridled at them. She had faced so much that it seemed suddenly insupportable to have this woman, whatever her rank, harangue her. 'I did what I felt I must to save a good man.'

Queen Guinevere was not impressed. 'And in so doing, you risked your life as well as Gareth's, and your life at the moment is infinitely more valuable. Did you stop to think what your sister would do if I came to her bearing your corpse and a strange story of losing you in the fog?'

Lynet's mouth closed.

'Who will listen to my judgement over another dead Carnbrea?' the queen continued. 'What vengeance would be sworn in your name? Your person is of great worth, and it is not for you to risk it! God's legs, girl!' she cried. 'I would think you'd had enough of starting wars!'

Lynet could say nothing. She just bowed her head.

'Why did you not tell me of your magics?'

'I was bound to secrecy,' said Lynet to her finger ends where they protruded from her bandages. 'By my sister and my mother's memory.'

'Do you think your mother meant that you should keep this secret from your queen?'

'I do not know.'

'Nor do you. What else have you not seen fit to tell me?'

Lynet bit her lip, hesitating. She did not want to speak, but in the pit of her soul she knew she risked all with her silence. If one more omission were discovered, Guinevere would not forgive. To lose the aid and succour of Camelot was to lose everything. 'Morgaine the sorceress has been to Cambryn.'

While Lynet watched, the blood drained from Guinevere's cheeks until she was as pale as one of the moor's daughters. Behind her, the women who had been pretending not to listen raised their heads. One, Nola, crossed herself hastily.

Guinevere ignored all this. Her hands knotted in the cloth of her skirt. She held her silence, her jaw working itself back and forth. The moment stretched out until Lynet felt as taut as a bowstring.

'Is she there now?' asked Queen Guinevere

'No.'

'What reward did she offer for helping her?'

'None. She returned my brother to us, she says for justice.'

'Justice.' The queen gave one hard laugh. 'It is at least an original reason.'

Gritting her teeth against the pain, Lynet managed to sit up a little straighter. Daere saw her efforts and came forward with another pillow. The queen watched impassively, waiting until Lynet could gasp out her words. 'I ask you to understand, Majesty,' Lynet pleaded. 'We did not know if Camelot would aid us, or what form that help would take.'

'You did not know if you could trust me after so long an absence, you mean,' replied Queen Guinevere, her neutral tone returning. She rubbed her brow once more. 'Ah, God of mercy, there are so many . . .' she cut herself off, waving away her own words. 'Very well, you have told me what I asked. Is there anything more?'

'No, Majesty.'

They sat in silence again. The queen, Lynet was sure, was giving her time to carefully consider that answer. Suddenly, outside the pavilion, a mighty cheer shook the air. Men's voices rose up not once, but again and again, in praise and ringing laughter. All the women left their places, running to the pavilion entrance to see.

The queen rose more slowly and joined her ladies, peering over their heads. Lynet tried briefly to crane her neck, but she saw nothing except the folds of their gowns.

Queen Guinevere looked back and nodded to Daere. The maid slipped her arm under Lynet's shoulders. With difficulty, because Lynet could not grip anything, and her legs were weak, Daere stood her up and supported her to the doorway. The other ladies made way for her so she could stand beside the queen and look out.

On the sloping green, the men of the encampment had gathered in a great crowd, and clearly they had been busy. The monster must have been carried back with her and Gareth, for now its head stood on a pike planted in the ground, and Gareth, pale and blood-streaked, but grinning ear-to-ear all the same, was hoisted up on burly shoulders. He held aloft a great black drape of fur that, Lynet realized a moment later, was the beast's skin.

As they watched, the cheering men set Gareth on his feet, and the crowd of them parted. Up the aisle they had created strode Sir Lancelot. He stood, hands on his hips, smiling just a little, every inch a golden, noble figure. Gareth, his face shining, knelt before his knight and lifted the skin up. The knight received it from him, ignoring how the blood stained his hands. With a nod, he gave Gareth permission to rise, and Gareth did. Lancelot, Gareth, and the whole encampment marched towards the queen's pavilion. The cheers and the shouts of Gareth's name filled the air and for all she wanted to be glad for him, the whole cacophony made Lynet's head throb.

With great and stately ceremony, Sir Lancelot and Gareth both went down on their knees before the queen. Together, they laid the skin at her feet. Its black fur shimmered in the sunlight. Lynet could smell the fresh blood and her hands twitched as she remembered it spattering on her arms and her face.

'I beg Your Majesty to accept this trophy won by my squire Gareth in great battle with the beast of the moors,' boomed Sir Lancelot.

Lynet looked over the knight's shoulder at Gareth. His hands and battered tunic were red, his face flushed and triumphant with the praise of his fellows. His head was bowed, but all the same he stole a glance at her. He saw the bandages on her arms and his face twisted into a mask of concern.

Above them all, the queen changed. She seemed to grow in stature, drawing the invisible cloak of royalty about her as she lifted up her arms. 'So perish all enemies of God and the High King Arthur!'

The answering cheer was deafening. The women joined in with their own shouts. Only Lynet held herself silent.

'My Lord Lancelot,' cried the queen. 'You will tap a cask of strong ale so that all may drink to the might of Squire Gareth, to the glory of the knights of the Table Round and all who follow them!'

Lynet had not thought it was possible for the cheers to grow louder, men now shouting the queen's praises as well. For a moment she thought her head would split open and she swayed on her feet. Daere leaned close to help steady her. Despite all this, Lynet marked how Lancelot's eyes lingered on the queen's before he bowed his head and stood, bending from the waist and backing away until he could properly turn and relay the order for the ale to be brought. Gareth knelt where he was a little longer, looking towards Lynet until Lionel shook his shoulder roughly and hauled him to his feet to rejoin the celebrations.

Guinevere watched the crowd go, one hand resting on the pavilion rope.

'Majesty?' said Lady Nola quietly. 'What should be done with . . . ?'

The queen looked down at the grisly trophy. 'Let it be scraped and cleaned as best as can be done now. It will make the king a cloak for the winter.' She eyed the crowd gathering around Lancelot, who now hoisted an ale keg high to a fresh chorus of cheers. 'Despite the fact that the weather is now with us, I think we will not be moving this day.' She paused, considering. 'So, my ladies, you may as well go down and enjoy the festivities. I will stay here and wait on the Lady Lynet.'

A chorus of thanks rose from the ladies and their servants. Only Daere hesitated, but she moved quickly enough once she saw Lynet settled into a chair. When the last of them had gone, Queen Guinevere let the canvas fall, cutting off the sight of the celebration if not its boisterous noise.

'Well, Lady Lynet, you have helped win a famous victory.' The queen turned back towards her. 'And there is nothing my lord Lancelot loves so well as victory,' she added softly. Then, she shook herself. 'Are you well enough to while away the time and tell us the full tale?'

It was no polite request and Lynet knew it. She mustered her wits and spoke, telling how she had walked the mirror's road to find Gareth, and what had happened on the moor. When she faltered, the queen held out a cup so that she might drink a little.

Queen Guinevere listened to all in silence, as Lynet now knew was her way, asking no questions, making no interruptions and likewise, showing no feeling. Lynet could well understand why some called her cold who did not know all she held beneath the surface.

When at last she was done, the queen spoke softly. 'This mirror you carry, what is the price of its use?'

'I don't understand, Majesty.'

'Come, Lynet,' she said impatiently. 'All such things demand a price of the one who wields them. The older and stronger they are, the greater the price. What is the cost of the hire of this thing for you?'

'It tires me . . .'

'And that is all?'

Lynet meant to answer 'yes', but something stopped her. She thought of Ryol and his fading garden, of the pull against her soul the last time she entered that place, of how even now as she thought of him, part of her wanted to reach for the mirror. She wanted to be there again, to know what might be learned in that place apart.

'No,' she whispered.

'No.' The queen repeated. 'You will give it to me.'

'What!'

The queen only looked at her with cool eyes.

'It is mine!' Lynet said, aware she was pleading like a child for a toy. 'It belongs to my family,' she amended.

'Lynet of Cambryn.' The force of the queen's voice cut across her thoughts like a knife. 'Do not force me to remind you once more who I am, or that all that is yours is by right mine.'

Lynet shrank back. Her hands trembled. She had no strength left to resist, however much she wanted to. 'No, Majesty.'

The queen rose and took the purse from Lynet's belt. She did not open it, but instead tucked it into her own broad woven girdle. When she turned again to Lynet, she was no longer the cold queen. She was a simple woman of middle years, weary from her endless chores.

'I am sorry, Lynet,' she said, running her hand across her brow. 'For everything.' Queen Guinevere fell into her own chair as if she suddenly lacked the strength to stand. 'I wanted this to be easier. I wanted . . . ah, Mother of God.' She shook her head once more. 'I should not have left matters so long. You see . . .' she paused, uncertain, and then went on. 'You see, beyond all the reasons of loyalty and pride and peace between the Dumonii and the rest of the Britons, I had my own reasons for leaving Cambryn as it was.

'I had thought by now to have children of my own to return to Cambryn and take up the rule there, so that the right order and fealty might be preserved.'

She spoke calmly, practically, but Lynet saw the tears glittering in Guinevere's eyes. Those tears did not fall. They remained shimmering in her eyes like a false promise, shining bright but never becoming true. 'But God, it seems, has declared it is not to be, unless he means to make a second Sarah of me.' She smiled a little at her own jest.

'So. Clearly, the rule in Cambryn must be settled. I would that you had not decided to back up your bets by hazarding Morgaine. It will make things much harder.'

'Yes, Majesty,' was all Lynet could say.

'We can delay no more tomorrow. I will not let Morgaine steal more of a march on us than necessary.'

'Yes, Majesty.'

Queen Guinevere got to her feet. 'Now, I too must put in an appearance at the festival outside. I had also better make sure no more than one cask has been drained.' She smiled sourly at the noise that had not ceased for a moment throughout their solemn talk. 'Come, let us get you to bed.'

As deftly as any lady's maid, the queen rose her to her

feet and supported Lynet back to her pallet. Lynet lay down and the queen arranged the coverings over her.

'Let your mind be at ease, Lynet. We will make things right. Try to rest and gather your strength.' The queen touched Lynet's brow once, briefly. Then, she drew herself up, once more becoming the High Queen of Camelot, and walked out of the pavilion, leaving tired Guinevere behind.

Lynet stared up at the wavering ceiling of canvas overhead and tried not to cry. She did not wish to rest. She wished to be about some business, any business. But her hands ached too deeply to move of their own accord, and the few strides she had taken before had left her weak. Above all, though, she felt the absence of the mirror like the loss of a limb.

What will I do? She bit her lip. *What can I do? Laurel doesn't know about Colan. She won't know anything until it is too late*

Then came the sound of a step outside, and a man's soft voice. 'Lynet? My lady?'

Light spilled across her as the canvas opened. She tried to sit up, but could only turn her head to watch Gareth cross the soft carpets that made the pavilion's floor. He looked down on her. He had thought to wash the blood off himself, but he was still haggard and there were dark circles under his eyes. He was breathing hard, as if he had run some great distance.

Slowly, he knelt beside her, as he had knelt to the queen. There was no mockery or irony in him now, only his soul laid bare behind his eyes. He reached out, hesitantly, plainly fearing to cause her pain, and touched his fingertips to hers.

No word passed between them. There was nothing but that touch, so light against her hand. Yet in that moment, certainty came to her and the understanding that opened one human heart fully to another.

A thousand thoughts occurred to her then. This could not

be real. It was only the relief of finding herself alive when she should be dead. She could not love; she was condemned by her own actions. This man could not want her as she was, nor was he the kind to wish for one woman only when there were so many others to be had.

Lynet set all that aside so she could look into Gareth's eyes.

'I came to thank you,' he said softly. 'Once more you have saved me.'

She smiled, and tried to speak lightly, remembering him dancing about and throwing dirt clods to chase off the demon. 'Well, you more than repaid me out on the moor.'

Humour shone in his summer-brown eyes. 'I had become used to being in your debt, my lady. I don't know what I shall do with my freedom.'

A ringing began in Lynet's ears, and her heartbeat grew slow and heavy. 'What do you wish to do with it?'

'I wish to show you that Sir Tristan does not stand for all men of the Table Round,' he whispered. He spoke the words as if he had held them long inside. 'I wish to show you the faithfulness of one man of Camelot.'

He kissed her then, softly, a brush of the lips and nothing more. It might have been a chaste gesture, a kiss of peace, save that it left within Lynet a burning so fierce that the sea itself could not have quenched it, but it was so sweet, so infinitely, impossibly sweet.

'Gareth . . .'

'No, Lynet,' he said, and from the ache in his voice she knew he felt that same impossible sweetness. 'Let it bide. Accept it. Whatever may come next, for this moment, let it be real.' He rose then, and her throat closed to see him move away. 'Daere saw me come,' he told her with his smallest smile. 'I do not want her to think I had time to commit any dishonourable act.' He bowed, and was swiftly gone.

In the wake of his leaving, Lynet no longer felt uneasy.

She lay, content to rest, and to feel the echo of his lips against hers. *Let it bide. Accept it.* She had heard such words before, and she had never forgotten where.

It had been in the blackest time, when she had returned home from Tintagel, when her father had refused to send her to the convent, but instead had sent her to Bishop Austell to confess and receive penance.

She remembered the bishop's face as she knelt before him in the chapel, telling him all she had done. She had thought at the time it was stony anger and disappointment at her that had carved the lines so deeply into his face. Now she understood he was trying to keep himself from crying aloud. When she finished, he bowed his head for a long moment, and his lips moved in prayer, for guidance, she thought, perhaps for strength and patience. Even after he breathed an inaudible amen, he stayed as he was, looking at the stones beneath his feet, both his calloused hands wrapped about his crucifix.

At last, he looked up and met her eyes. *He'll release me,* she thought, wild with hope. *He'll tell me I must go to the sisters and spend my life in cloistered penance.*

But he did not. 'You will walk barefoot to the well of the blessed Saint Menefreda, and you will thank God aloud every step of the way for your life and your repentance.' His voice was hard, but his gaze did not leave hers, not even as her face fell. 'There you will wash in its waters and pray three times.' He made the sign of the cross over her head. 'And may God and the Holy Virgin walk with you, my child.'

Although it was not the cloistered escape she'd longed for, it was God's word, and Lynet undertook her penance with a will. Barefoot, she walked across the stony countryside, wearing only a rough grey woollen shift and carrying only a pilgrim's staff, her hair unbound and her head uncovered. As she walked she cried out to God, until her voice was no more than a whisper. The rough-spun wool rubbed her skin raw, covering her with bright red weals. Her feet, though, took the worst of it. By the time she reached the well, her feet were utterly raw. Stones had cut and worn down the skin and frost-hardened earth had torn them and coated them with filth.

The holy well was in a green and sheltered grotto. The wind did not come here. There was only the rush and chatter of the stream where it bubbled from the hillside. The last of summer lingered here, with the ferns and bracken still green and the earth still soft. But she saw little of this beauty. The pain in her feet all but made her swoon as she knelt beside the stream where it trickled down its well-worn channel.

As prescribed, she bathed three times in the water, and with what little was left of her voice, she prayed. Night fell and the cold was unbearable. She crept beneath a mound of fallen leaves, seeking warmth like a wild animal. Shivering from the cold, hunger and pain, she fell into a stupor neither waking nor sleeping, and yet it seemed to her she dreamed. For with her blurred eyes, she saw a shining form step out of the well that slowly resolved itself into a woman. White hair cascaded down her shoulders and a gown of white covered her. Lynet sat up, open mouthed in her awe, and in the next moment she prostrated herself on the ground.

'Holy Mary, Blessed Virgin, Mother of God . . . .' she babbled and croaked, her mind so stunned she could only gasp out the torrent of titles. But gentle hands raised her up, and lifted her face so she must meet a pair of eyes as tranquil and grey as the sea at rest.

'Such names are not for me, my daughter. Save them for their proper owner.'

'But . . . but then who . . .'

'One who cares for your mother's children and answers their call when she can.' The lady smiled a smile of love and deep sorrow. 'You will learn my name when you are ready to hear it.'

She knelt then, and touched Lynet's wounded feet.

'I can heal you, but I cannot make you whole. It is your heart alone that can make that miracle. But accept this much child. Accept it and let it bide. The rest will come when you forgive yourself.' She laid her cool hands against Lynet's feet, and she kissed Lynet's brow with a brush like the touch of sea foam, and she was gone.

With her the pain was gone. Lynet's feet were sound, but as the lady had said, they were not whole. They were toughened, mottled and scarred, and the toes splayed and curled under. But it was blessing unlooked for and Lynet gave thanks. On her healed feet she walked home, and though they pained her badly, there was no sickness this time.

Accept this. Let it bide. She knew now who that shining woman was. It was not God's mother, but her own grandmother, the *bucca-gwidden*, the white spirit of the sea who had come to her then.

Accept this. Let it bide. This touch. This kiss. This moment, whatever comes next. This much is blessing.

With a sigh, Lynet slipped into dreamless sleep.

TWENTY-ONE

Lynet's peace did not last beyond the blessedly clear dawn.

From the time she woke, she felt the pull of the mirror. While Daere dressed her and helped her to eat when her trembling hands and aching arms refused to hold bowl and spoon any longer, Lynet watched the queen. Guinevere carried herself as she always did, with ease and grace. She laughed at her ladies' jokes, and dispensed orders calmly, lightly. Lynet tried to find some shade of the tears she had seen the day before, some crack that she might be able to reach through to beg for the mirror back. But there was nothing. The weary woman had been laid away with the over-dress from the day before. There was only the queen.

But Queen Guinevere had the mirror with her. Lynet could feel it tucked in her girdle. It sang to her, and it pulled at her, restless as a child tugging at her sleeve. She needed to reach within it, to find out what was straining for her attention. Something must be wrong, and she needed to know what it was.

It only grew worse when Daere changed her bandages and the queen came over to inspect her wounds. The flesh was healing cleanly without smell or sign of putrefaction. Lynet felt the mirror like a piece of ice being brought near her skin. It burned coldly without even touching.

'Can you grip my hand?' the queen asked.

Dutifully, Lynet squeezed Queen Guinevere's fingers as tightly as she could before the pain became too much. 'Majesty . . .' she murmured.

Queen Guinevere looked at Lynet, her cool, grey eyes making a far different kind of mirror. There was no getting past that surface now that it had hardened. The queen knew full well what she wanted to ask, Lynet was sure, and she would not relent.

'Thank you,' Lynet said, the words ringing fragile and hollow.

'You'll ride with Daere today,' said the queen as she straightened up. 'You will not be able to work the reins with those.'

Lynet bowed her head, unable to find the polite words of obedience to answer with. *All will be right,* she told herself, biting her lips against her pain and her fear. *I will be home tomorrow. The queen will not refuse Laurel when she asks for the mirror back.*

Holding firmly to these thoughts, she was able greet the anxious Captain Hale when he came to her, telling him truthfully that she was well and growing stronger, and send him back smiling to reassure the rest of Cambryn's men. She was able to stand on her own feet to leave the pavilion with the other ladies, to stand in the clear morning light while the serving women helped the soldiers strike their tent and load it into the carts.

'My lady?'

Gareth. Lynet opened her eyes, which she did not realize she had closed. The squire stood behind her, leading the steady brown mare she had ridden this whole long, weary way. He was trying to smile, but worry prevented that smile from reaching his eyes.

'Thank you, Squire Gareth,' she managed to say. 'I will need some assistance today I fear.' She lifted her bandaged arms.

He bowed and made to help her, but Daere somehow got there first, shooing Gareth back to hold the mare's bridle. They shared a smile over the maid's head as she bent down and with a surprisingly strong motion, hoisted Lynet into her saddle. Daere then firmly took the reins from Gareth to tie to her own horse's saddle. Gareth bowed to the maid with such solemn courtesy, Lynet had to duck her head and suck on her cheeks to keep from laughing out loud.

It was to be the only relief she had. As she could not ride for herself, she could not move about the procession as she was used to do, going back to talk with Captain Hale, or to check on Brendon. Daere, perhaps afraid Lynet might slip in a word or two to Gareth, kept her firmly in the middle of all the ladies who rode behind the queen as their slow, deliberate procession crossed the emerald-green moorland. Every step brought her closer to home, but never closer to what she needed. She needed the mirror to find out what was happening to Laurel, to know what happened in Cambryn. Maybe they would be home tomorrow, but there might easily be another day's delay. Mesek, Peran, Colan and Morgaine could bring an end to everything in another day if she were not there to give warning. There was nothing she could do without the mirror. Not even Gareth, riding up beside her whenever he could find an excuse, could aid her. He could not rush this endless march, and he could not bring to her the mirror the queen had stolen.

She tried to continue telling herself it didn't matter, that she would be home tomorrow, that Laurel would be well and all would be right. This chorus chanted hourly into the halting chaos of her thoughts helped stave off the worst of the fear and longing, until they came at long, long last to the heights of Rough Tor. Lynet surveyed her own country with a relief that flowed like honey in her veins.

Then, Sir Lancelot turned his horse slowly down the northern slope, and all the procession made to follow, the queen included.

The blood drained from Lynet's face. 'Daere, I must speak with the queen!' she cried.

Daere obediently urged her mount forward and Lynet's horse followed, until they walked beside the queen's tall grey mare. Queen Guinevere looked down at her, calm and expectant.

'This is not the road to Cambryn, Majesty,' she said, forgetting all courtesy in her confusion. 'We need to turn south.'

Queen Guinevere cocked her head, but did not rein her horse in. She continued down the slope, holding her mount to a careful pace so it would not step in a hole or turn its hoof on the rough ground. 'We do not go to Cambryn, Lynet,' she said. 'We go to Tintagel.'

The last word dropped into Lynet's understanding like a stone and for a moment all she could do was stare. The queen did not look back, she watched the way in front of her. Lynet's mare stumbled and snorted hard before righting itself.

'Why, Majesty?' Lynet cried at last. Her heart shattered to jagged pieces. They were not going home. They were not going to Laurel. They would leave Laurel alone for two more days, and she could reach out and snatch the mirror and shout a warning that would carry all the way to Cambryn . . .

'Because before any other thing can be done, we must make sure that King Mark stands strong,' the queen was saying.

'But . . .' Lynet stammered. Pain lanced down her arms as her hands strained to move, to tear the girdle from the queen's waist, even as her mind recoiled in horror from the thought of such an act.

'But what, Lady Lynet?' asked Queen Guinevere.

'Why did you not tell me?' she asked weakly.

The queen only looked at her, and it seemed to Lynet that every word she had spoken, and everything she had done flashed between them. *Because I cannot be trusted. Because I have made one mistake too many.*

Because I begin to run mad.

'I must ask you to bide in patience and trust me, Lynet,' said Queen Guinevere. 'It is for the good of Cambryn and all the Dumonii that I do this now.' For the briefest moment, Lynet saw a trace of the sympathy that had overcome Queen Guinevere yesterday, but then it was gone, locked away inside the casket of the queen's heart. Queen Guinevere nodded to Daere, who in turn let them fall behind, and Lynet could only watch the queen descend the wrong side of the rolling green tor behind Sir Lancelot.

They were returning to Tintagel. She had not imagined such a thing. In her mind's eye, she saw the fortress on its island rising cold and hard-edged over the sea. She saw the *castell* and croft that sprawled across the rolling headland. And she saw Colan and her father riding before her, leading her to meet Queen Iseult, to begin her fosterage, and end the life that she had known.

She saw the gates swing shut in the rain. She saw King Mark with his red hands dangling between his knees.

Why are you doing this? she cried within her mind. *Why?*

The mirror would tell her. Ryol would show her. That was why the queen had taken the mirror. She did not want Lynet to know what was happening, what was wrong. Ryol cried out to her now, getting further away with every step, and she could do nothing. Nothing at all.

No. That was not true.

'Bring us close again, Daere,' she ordered.

'But my lady . . .'

'Do as I say!' she snapped.

Daere closed her mouth, pressing her lips into a thin and disapproving line. Nonetheless, she obeyed, leading Lynet forward so that once again they rode beside the queen, who was plainly not pleased to see them there.

'Majesty, at least let me send two of my men back to Cambryn, so my sister knows what is happening and where she can get word to us.'

The queen considered this. Shadows that were all of her own making shifted behind her grey eyes. 'Yes,' she said in the end. 'You may send word to Cambryn that we are to be found at Tintagel. That would suit well.'

Lynet bowed her head and ordered Daere to take them back along the procession. She met Captain Hale coming up to consult with her. He had, of course, noticed the change of direction as soon as she. After a certain amount of wrangling, they agreed that Lock and Stef Trevailian would go to Cambryn and warn Laurel. Lynet watched her men riding fast towards her home and thought her heart would break. But she could not go that way, not yet. She must try to find a way to endure.

Lynet passed the rest of the day in the fog of her own despair. They moved in and out of woods she knew, passed the huddled stone houses of clans who had held their lands for generations. Folk ran out to hold up their hands, or kneel, or just stare, as the procession rode past. But none of it could reach her heart. Her uncertainty teased and whispered, providing a feast of horrors for her imagination to gnaw on while her anger at the queen simmered. But above all, she felt the mirror. It pulled at her without ceasing. She felt Ryol within it hovering, stretching but unable to reach her. The pain in her arms, which had subsided, now redoubled as if drawing strength from her unrest.

Then, as the sun began to sink towards the horizon, the wind blew hard, and Lynet smelled salt. She lifted her head and clearly saw the sloping rise before them, dotted only here and there with trees, but sprouting stones as thickly as if they had been sown there. She knew the shape of the land like she knew the shape of her chamber walls. When they topped that hill, they would look out across Tintagel's headland.

The queen, however, did not mean for them to do so tonight. She ordered a halt, despite Sir Lancelot's frowns, and said they would pitch camp where they were. The only reason Lynet could fathom for taking this course was that despite her refusal to send out advance messengers, the queen did not truly want to surprise Tintagel. She wanted Mark to know that she was come, and that she was unconcerned about him and what he might think to do about that coming.

So once more the pavilion rose, and Lynet was shepherded inside with the other ladies. She looked about for Gareth, but could not find him among all the activity of readying them a place to sleep for the night. There was more than a little grumbling about having to do this within an hour's ride of a *castell* that could have taken them all in, but nothing that might come even close to rebellion. All here trusted the queen and were willing to serve her pleasure.

All save Lynet.

In the pavilion, the ladies made preparations to eat their evening meal. Lynet sat in her chair, her throbbing and useless hands in her lap. Her eyes strayed again and again to the queen, as if hoping to catch a glimpse of the concealed mirror. She still carried it in her girdle. Lynet could feel it as the queen moved to and fro.

I will find a way to speak to her. I will find a way to make her understand it is mine and I have need of it.

'My lady?' whispered Daere in her ear. 'My lady, you must wake up. You must eat something.'

Lynet opened her eyes. Once more she had drifted away without realizing it, and this added yet one more worry to her growing tally. Daere stood before her with a bowl of steaming broth. It smelled delicious, full of meat and wine and herbs. Her mouth watered and yet her stomach twisted inside her. The queen sat with her ladies at her table, so far away. Her hands twitched and her fingers curled.

'My lady?' said Daere again.

'Yes, Daere,' she managed to say. 'Yes, I will eat.'

The maid helped Lynet hold the bowl to drink. She tasted nothing as she swallowed. There was only a trail of warmth trickling its way down her to a void that did not want to be filled. Queen Guinevere glanced towards her once, and their eyes met. *Do you feel it?* she wondered towards the queen. *Do you feel the weight of what you've taken from me? Give it back, give it back. It's mine, and I cannot abandon my sister!*

If the queen divined any of these thoughts she did not show it. She only looked at Lynet with a calm that reminded her sharply of Laurel. Laurel alone in Cambryn, waiting for her to come back, to tell her what was happening within their home so she could know how to keep herself safe.

Daere's bowl bumped her lips and Lynet turned her face away. 'No more,' she said.

It seemed for a moment Daere might argue. In the end she only said, 'As you will, my lady,' but she was clearly both disappointed and disapproving. It didn't matter. Daere helped Lynet to her pallet. She sank back down on her pillows. Nothing mattered but that there must be a way to reach the mirror again, to reach through to Ryol and to Laurel. There must be.

The light was fading around her. The talk growing softer in here, although out beyond the thin cloth wall it was still lively. The noise pounded against her ears, intolerable because it was not what she wanted to hear. She wanted to hear Ryol's voice, and Laurel's. She gritted her teeth to keep from crying out. Bootsteps came close to the pavilion, and for one wild moment, Lynet hoped it was Hale. She could order Hale to take the mirror back for her, to put it into her useless hands . . .

The violence of her thoughts froze Lynet. *What is happening to me?*

'My lady, what is it . . . ?' said Daere. Lynet knew she had gone white. She felt it. The pain pulsed hard in her arms.

I'm going mad. Oh God and Mother Mary. That's what the matter is. But she could not say that. She could not say anything, even to ease the worry creasing Daere's face. Beyond her, there was movement around the door, and Lynet looked up mutely, half-afraid now that it would be Captain Hale, and she would not be able to stop herself from telling him to take back what the queen had stolen, to give her back the door to Ryol who was too far away.

Stop!

But it was not Captain Hale. It was Sir Lancelot, with Gareth behind him once more. Knight and squire knelt before Queen Guinevere, and did not seem to see the consternation in the queen's face as she bade them rise. What was she really thinking? Lynet itched to know, to reach out with the force of her will and pour her understanding into the queen. Sir Lancelot took up a cup of wine for himself without, Lynet was sure, having been bid to drink. The queen frowned, but settled back with a cup of her own.

Lynet's hands itched. Only weakness kept her still.

Help me, she cried out in her thoughts, to God and to Ryol and Laurel. *Help me!*

'My lady,' said a voice. Her whole body jolted and she saw Gareth standing over her.

Help me! Her hand scraped across the bed coverings, but her voice would not come, because she could not find which word she wanted to speak: the polite words of greeting she must say to keep back the glances and whispers of the ladies around her, or the plea for succour that was rising over the swirl of need and madness that filled her.

Gareth glanced at the ladies and the frowning queen, and back at Lynet's straining form. Daere, for once not sniffing or disapproving, brought him a stool.

'I thought you would wish to know that Brendon is doing well, and if his curses are anything to judge by, gaining strength steadily,' he said as he sat. This was for the benefit of the ladies around them. More softly he added, 'What is it, Lynet? What pains you?'

Lynet licked her lips. Gareth, just a little faster than Daere, picked up a cup from beside the pallet and held it for her so she could drink the small beer. The tang of it steadied her a little. Or perhaps it was the urgency and care in Gareth's brown eyes. She could not tell. 'The queen has taken the mirror,' was all she could say.

Gareth set the cup down. 'Daere, my lady is warm, I think. Perhaps a cloth for her head?' Daere, worried enough to accept a recommendation from the squire, retreated. What did Daere see? What did any of them see? She didn't know, she couldn't know, and it terrified her.

'We are but two days' from your home, Lynet,' he said soothingly. 'You have done enough. All will be well. The queen will return the mirror as soon as we reach Cambryn.'

'No, you don't understand.' She shook her head frantically. 'I mustn't . . . I can't . . .' *Mustn't what? Can't what?* She didn't know herself. She only knew that this skin she wore was too tight, that it separated her from too much. She could not remain here, helpless and ignorant, while Colan plotted against Laurel, while Mesek and Peran between them decided how to plunder Cambryn. A few days was more than enough time.

Gareth glanced over his shoulder and then leaned close. 'Lynet, listen to me,' he whispered urgently. 'You are weak. You must regain your strength before you can think of taking that mirror up again. Please.'

'I cannot, Gareth. I feel it within me now and I cannot escape it.' Fresh fear gripped her as she spoke. It was true, though she had not fully understood it until now. She could not turn her mind away, could not shut the need off. 'Talk to me a little,' she said suddenly, grasping at straws. 'Give me something else to think on.'

So, Gareth talked. While his knight sat beside the queen and told a long story of some campaign or the other, with all the other ladies sitting around him openly fascinated by the tale or his presence or both, Gareth spoke softly to her of life at Camelot. Daere came with the cool cloth and more of the queen's tisane. Lynet tried to focus attention on these things, and on Gareth's gentle stream of words that lit his eyes as he told her of the life he loved. He talked of work and play, of small jokes and hurts, of his three elder brothers, all of whom were members of the cadre of the Round Table.

And yet there was a yearning under all his words, a feeling beyond simple ambition that she could not understand, and she wanted to, because it would tell her of the man behind the summer eyes, and his love of his knight and his brothers, and her. She would understand then, and she wanted so much to understand, so she could believe, so she could somehow find a way past her fear.

Once more she cursed her isolation, her confinement. If she could only reach out. If she could only find Ryol once more. She felt him, she was sure, in the invisible country, separated from her by the thinnest of veils, by the finger-nail-thickness of a piece of glass.

Then, soft as an infant's touch, she felt him. He stirred just beyond her. *My lady?*

Ryol! She reached out eagerly, straining at the confines of her body. He was there. He was with her.

Lady Lynet, what are you doing?

The queen's taken the mirror. She could almost see him now, a veil of colour and shape behind and beyond the confines of the pavilion. *You were right . . .*

Lynet go back.

What? The world around her had gone grey, leaving only a narrow tunnel of vision where Ryol's shadow hovered. Gareth was whispering to her. He touched her, but someone took his hand away. She should care for this, but could not. All that mattered was that Ryol was here and the door to Laurel and to home would soon be open.

But that was not what Ryol said. *You must not do this. It is too much for mortal flesh.* She could see him more clearly now. He held up his hands in warning. He was old again, stooped and weathered and sagging, his strong arms thin and his face drawn tight. She felt his fear spill over her. *Go back!*

I cannot! She's taken the mirror! I cannot leave Laurel!

Desperate, tearing need made her reckless and Lynet propelled herself forward into darkness. There was no sensation save that of rushing movement, of flying faster than any bird of the air. Elated, Lynet stretched out, though she knew not how. She had no form, no limit, no boundary to herself. She was what Ryol had once spoken of being. She was everywhere and nowhere, all things and nothing at all.

Laurel! She called out with her silent voice. *Laurel!*

Light came, and colour and sense, but it was not like when Ryol walked beside her. She did not feel as if she stood on her feet and saw with her eyes. It was more that she simply knew all things and knew them all at once.

She knew that Mesek sat in the old hall, talking amiably

with the old men, passing a leather jack of strong beer around, reaching down now and then to scratch the ears of the nearest hound. She knew he watched them all as they yarned away, deciding which one knew the most truth, and it was to this one he'd pass the beer.

She knew that Peran stood outside the hall, talking with his own men. They were growing impatient, and he was reminding them that since they had entered into the game, they must play. One of them, tall Laveen whose ear had been half torn off in an old fight, shook his head, saying that it was Peran who had entered in the game. In the back of his mind he thought his chief had gone mad, and wondered if tonight he would finally muster the nerve to steal away. Lynet reached towards that thought, breathing her will on it as she might breathe on a flickering coal. *Yes, leave. Yes, he is mad. You need not stay. Go home to your own and tell them he is mad. Tell them that.*

She knew Colan stood before his window. Death was in his thoughts, winter-cold, implacable death.

She knew Laurel was bathing. She stood naked in a basin of water brought to her by Father Lucius from Saint Necturn's well. She'd seasoned it with salt harvested from the sea and she'd prayed over it three times. She would take the water left from the bath and sprinkle it around her bed, and over each threshold of the hall, and she would be safe. Morgaine could no more reach her here.

Good. That is good. But sister, I am here and there is so much you should know.

She reached for her sister, as she had reached for this place, to bring her close and know her and be known and tell her all she had learned.

And she could not. It was as if she pressed her hands against a brick wall, or a carving of stone. She knew Laurel was there, she could feel where she had been, but Laurel herself was closed and silent before her as she finished her bath and pulled a drying sheet around herself to go stand before the fire.

Laurel, no! You cannot mean to shut me out too! She beat against her sister's closed self with all her will. But Laurel did not even lift her head.

She had come all this way to find Laurel, to protect her and tell her all she knew, and she could not even speak to her. Despair rolled over her, and Lynet fell back, all the way back into the long rushing darkness. But now she was without anchor, without goal or destiny, there was only movement without purpose and she could not still herself. Nor could she find herself. Her body was nowhere. She was lost.

Ryol! She cried out. *Ryol!*

Direction came to her, and purpose to her motion. Light and colour unfurled around her to become a ragged, sloping green hill running down into a black and raging sea. Rain poured down from a fury of lightning-filled clouds. A man knelt on the ground, staring out at the angry waters. His mind was filled with the images of a great city – round towers of gleaming stone, streets paved with mosaics and marble. Beautifully tended trees hung with strange fruits that filled the air with a sharp perfume grew beside great obelisks of granite and basalt covered with runes and elaborate carvings and painted bright red, green and blue. People in gowns of white wool and blue linen went to and fro about their business amidst the peace and untold beauty.

Gone. All of it gone and only him left to see. Only him left because he had run away.

'I thought you might be here.'

Ryol. He was with her. She could not feel her own shape or shadow clearly, but she was aware of him, his warmth and his sorrow enveloping her the way the rain enveloped the weeping man before her.

'Why here?' was all she could ask. The memory of the shining city, lost to the waters, would not leave her. Through him she saw the dead tossed and tumbled in the darkness.

'I hoped you would be able to call for me. This is the place where I was last and most myself.'

The weeping man was Ryol as he had been, servant to the prince of that great and shining city. He had warned his prince, who dallied with the affections of one of the sea-women, only to abandon her. He'd had a great wall raised all about his island home so that the waters could never touch him, but it had failed, and so the sea claimed his life, along with the whole of his city.

The angry sea would not release the souls of the dead. It was for them that Ryol bargained himself. He would become the protector of the sea's children on land, if the sea released the drowned to their rest, to wait in peace for Judgement Day.

It was this that brought him to her. It was for this reason that her grandmother had given Ryol's prison, his garden, himself, to her daughter. It was for this reason that mother had refused to look into the mirror. She feared he would draw her back to the sea, away from her husband and her children. Lynet knew all this in an instant, and it was too much. Her voice vanished and her vision thinned, letting all the darkness show through the veil of the raging scene before her.

Ryol drew closer, and she felt the edges of herself grow clear again.

Her voice too returned, reed thin and shaking. 'What has happened to me, Ryol?'

He was a long moment answering. Beyond them, his other, far younger self huddled beneath the punishing rain and remembered his old mother sitting in her garden, humming as she spun her thread and tended his sister's children. 'You have reached too far, Lynet. You have pressed past the boundaries that flesh allows.'

'And you?' she whispered.

'I also have reached too far. You needed so much, I had waited so long to fulfil my promise, to pay for those souls freed long ago . . . I gave too much, and now I fear there may not be enough left.'

She could not find her body. She could not reach Laurel. She barely knew herself from the darkness. Oh, yes, she had gone too far. 'How am I to return?'

So softly her insubstantial self could barely take in the words, Ryol said, 'I do not know that you can.'

Lynet felt herself go very still. She had been warned. She had been warned so many times and by so many who should know, and she had ignored them all. *And here I came so desperate not to be the fool any more. Oh, God save me, is there no end to my own folly?*

'I must try,' she whispered. 'Please help me.'

'I will do what I can, my lady. Come with me.'

As he had so many times he led her forward, away from the rain and the storm of his own life. He swept the shadows before them, a thousand coloured blurs of light and life that sought to wind their tendrils around her and pull her from the path, but she clung tightly to her guide, and somehow remained whole. At last she saw the queen's pavilion become strong and solid about her. With the unnatural clarity of her night vision, she saw herself lying upon her pallet as if she had been laid upon a bier.

'What must I do?'

'You must want,' said Ryol. He hovered just beyond the edge of her vision, looking on her as she looked on herself. 'You must want your life and self again.'

Want? Want what she had rejected so many times, the confines she had raged against. Anger billowed out of her, and the pavilion and her other self on its pallet began to recede.

Stop. Stop, Lynet. You will be lost.

She wanted to close her eyes, to fold her hands in prayer, to make some other gesture, but she had neither eyes nor hands nor knees.

I want my eyes, she told herself desperately. *My heart. My body wrapped around me. I want my hands so that I may tend my patient again. I want my voice so that I can speak to my sister, and my queen, and to Gareth.*

Gareth. I want to look on Gareth again with my own eyes. I want to feel his hand brush mine and hear his jests again.

I want to go home. Please. I want to go home.

She felt the leaden, aching self that she hated. She felt the broken feet and the wounded arms and the isolating flesh, and she cringed and it faded, and she knew what she must do.

I want to go home. She pulled herself closer to that clay-cold mortality that was also herself, and she embraced it with all the warmth she could summon. *Home. Home and self. This is mine and I accept it. I let it bide.*

The darkness rushed up again. Ryol was gone. Clay and earth and pain encased her, and she felt blood and breath and heart. Her eyes flew open, and reflex tried to sit her up, but she fell back onto her pallet, her mouth gaping and gasping but unable to form any word.

'Lynet?' whispered a voice. 'Are you awake? Lynet?'

Gareth. Gareth was there beside her but she could not see him. Her weak, bandaged hand flailed out and found only the canvas pavilion wall. But then she felt it, the pressure of his palm, flat against hers. Understanding came. He was outside the pavilion, on the other side of the cloth wall. Waiting for her to wake.

She saw him then, clear as day, crouched on the grass, his

face drawn and white with worry. He was thinking of her, not believing she had simply fallen asleep. He was thinking also of other women, of one named Morgause and another named Tania, and of how he had lost them and lost his father and could not bear to lose her as well.

With a shock, Lynet realized she knew all these things though she could feel the weight of her own flesh all around her. Then, that knowing was gone, and there was only the press of his palm and his voice. 'Lynet? Speak to me, Lynet. Please.'

'I am . . . I am here,' she managed to say.

'Thank God,' he said fervently. 'What happened?'

What happened? The urge to laugh tickled her throat. 'I tried to reach the mirror,' she said.

Silence. She felt his hand tremble through the cloth that separated them. 'Lynet, why?'

Because I am a frightened fool, Gareth. Because I would not listen. Because I do not want my sister to die and my home to fall. 'It is done, Gareth. I will not do it again.'

'Thank you,' he breathed.

'You must go,' she told him, and it took almost as much strength to form those words as it had to return to her aching body. 'You cannot be found here.'

'I will not be the one who takes any harm if I am,' he answered simply. 'For that reason I will go. I'll come to you in the morning.' His hand pressed once more against hers, and she heard the shuffle and rustle as he stood and walked away. She bit her tongue hard to keep from calling him back.

Carefully, Lynet lay back down. She felt as if she was made of both stone and glass. She was too heavy to move, and so fragile that if she did she would shatter in an instant. Thirst nagged at her and she could not seem to make herself close her eyes. She'd had enough of darkness, and although the moonlight filtered only dimly through the canvas, it was better than blindness.

As she stared, she thought she saw images in the thin
sheen of the moonlight. She saw rain, and walls, and tangled
lovers, she saw brown eyes and blue, the flash of swords and
a long, green trail that led to nowhere but urgency. And she
understood what these were, but she still could not make
herself close her eyes.

Watching the dreams of other women, Lynet lay on her
pallet and waited for daylight.

TWENTY-TWO

Laurel woke to the spring dawn. She sat up in her bed, and breathed deep. The world opened before her eyes and her heart rejoiced. Her sleep the night before had been sound, deep and dreamless. Her defences had proven true. She was not safe, not completely, but she had shelter for her soul now, and Morgaine could trouble her there no more.

The knowledge that she held that much secure made the thought of yet another day's confinement easier to bear. Or perhaps it was only that an outside will was no longer eroding her patience. It did not matter. It was so, and she was grateful.

In token of that gratitude, she crossed herself and bowed her head in thanksgiving to all the powers that come to aid those in need. She would have to find some good gift for Father Lucius when all this was over. She regretted that she could not go to the watchtower this morning and take what news was to be gathered from the sea winds. But if she opened the door of herself wide enough to take in that knowledge, Morgaine could easily slip in.

Laurel swung her feet out of bed. *And I will have to explain to Lynet, too. She will be stung by this.* Worry touched her. *What if it was more than that? There is nothing I can do for her. I must trust her to find her way. I have left too many things undone here.*

Now that she could reason clearly again, she saw the one thread she had dropped from the pattern, which had almost unravelled all the rest. She had been focusing on Master Peran, as had been Morgaine's desire. She had not seen that the time had come to trust Master Mesek.

Laurel dressed herself in her green over-dress and plaited a green ribbon in her hair, making herself plain but presentable. She had sent Meg and the other waiting women out of the chamber last night, carrying with them the basin she had bathed in. Clearly, they had obeyed her strange orders to sprinkle the water over the hall's various thresholds. She would also have to find a way to thank them.

Her guards, as ever, waited outside her door. She noted that Peran's man was not the same one who had been there the night before, and she wondered at that.

Down in the new hall, the boards were laid, and the breaking of the fast had begun. The scents of bread and pottage, meats and cheeses, rose invitingly. She was able to meet the eyes of her people easily this morning, stopping to talk and answer such small questions as had arisen overnight. She knew those around her saw the worry lifted from her, and felt the hope it sparked in them. Perhaps this thing would be over soon, they all thought. Perhaps they would be free of the strangers watching their lady, and squatting outside the walls of their *castell*, and all would end in a return to peace.

She found Meg fetching another crock of cider and stopped to speak to her about the state of the cellars.

'You should know what is left in the cellars, my lady,' said Meg abruptly. 'Jorey is most concerned.'

'As he has been for days.' Laurel saw an urgency in Meg's eyes and worry crept in to her. 'But tell me how we stand.'

Meg began a litany of casks and tubs and loaves. Satisfied

Laurel was engaged in domestic concerns, her guards split off, with two heading to the pottage kettles and the third, Peran's new man, hurrying to join his fellows.

As soon as they were gone, Meg said, a little more loudly than necessary, 'Here is my tally.' She unlooped a wax and wooden tablet from her belt, and opened it to show Laurel.

A few words had been written there: CAMELOT COMES TODAY TO TINTAGEL.

Laurel did not lower the book until she was certain she could school her face into the properly banal expression and hand the closed tablet back to Meg.

'Tell Jorey I'll be with him after breakfast, and tell our other cellarers that we have received the tally and will give out what is needed, as it is needed.'

Meg made her curtsey. 'I will do that, my lady.'

They stood side-by-side there for a moment, Meg giving Laurel time to think whether there was anything else that needed to be done in regards to the message she had just been given. Laurel surveyed the scene before her without really seeing it. Camelot comes to Tintagel? Why there? They were supposed to come here, to relieve her, and save their home.

What is the queen playing at?

Playing at securing the greatest power here, she answered herself. *Betting it will be easier to take first Tintagel then Cambryn, rather than the other way around.*

Oh, Lynet, you must be going mad with impatience.

Laurel looked at her people, her guests and her captors. She saw Mesek sitting back at the table, wiping his moustaches while he reached out to spear yet another hunk of white cheese on his knife. But his opposite was nowhere to be seen.

'And where is Master Peran?' she asked Meg.

'He was talking to his men there.' Meg nodded towards

the dispirited group that huddled at the end of one of the long tables. Mesek's men on the other side of the hall eyed them, grinning as they chewed their mouthfuls of bread and pottage. 'Then he up and left. I have not seen him since. They say one of his men crept off in the night. Perhaps Peran's gone to find him.'

'Perhaps,' nodded Laurel, keeping her thoughts to herself. Peran's madness would not let him leave so easily, not before he had gained Morgaine her victory and shown himself to be her true servant. No. There was danger in Master Peran still, especially if his men who camped outside the earthworks had thought to set watch on the heights. The path of a queen's progress from Camelot would not be hard to track. By noon, it would be common knowledge where that procession was going. She had but a little time to use this. 'Find some of our men to keep him in sight. I do not want him to lose his way wandering about the *castell*, nor getting into the cellars.'

'I understand, my lady,' said Meg sagely. Laurel took the crock from her. Meg made her curtsey and went off to find those who could be trusted with Laurel's errand. Laurel took the cider to the high table, and without a word refilled Mesek's cup. The chieftain watched her with raised brows, stroking his long moustaches thoughtfully.

'And to what do I owe this courtesy, Lady Laurel?' he inquired as she took her seat.

'My need to speak with you, Master,' she replied conversationally as she helped herself from the platter of salted beef and fresh bread.

His brows shot up again. 'And here I thought that was a privilege you were reserving for Master Peran. Shall the two of us lock arms and venture up to your tower?'

'I would as soon spare us both.' Little Ama ran up to fill her cups, one with beer and one with cider. Laurel waited until she was gone to speak again. 'If nothing else, we will attract far less notice as we are.'

'That is the truest thing you have said since the beginning of this mummery.' Mesek took a healthy swig of his cider and stared down the hall, seeing his own men, and his enemies and all those in between, Laurel was certain. Seeing too, his own plans, and wondering about what was happening back among his own kindred. 'What is it then, my lady?'

Where to begin? she wondered briefly. 'You are being used, Mesek.'

Mesek tipped up his cider cup, considering the dregs of it. 'That is where you are wrong, my lady,' he said softly. 'I and mine will not be used anymore.' He spoke firmly, and with a conviction that was absolute. Laurel found herself wondering what she would have seen had it been him she called to the tower rather than Peran.

'You think you are rebelling, even against the Sleepless One, but you are doing what she wants,' Laurel told him flatly. 'You are staying here and maintaining this show of an appeal to the law. You are helping to keep me trapped here. Peran lied to you, Mesek. He is coaxing you along so that you will stay and continue to play their game. When the judgement comes, if it comes, it will be made to fall apart.' This last was intuition alone, but given all that had happened, she did not doubt it.

'How?'

'I do not know,' she admitted. 'Yet.'

Mesek set his cup down and pushed his chair back, sticking one broad thumb into his worn leather belt. 'How is it you know any of this?'

Laurel felt a small and mirthless smile form. 'You are bribing and interrogating my people about my powers, and yet you do not believe I might have my own ways of knowing and seeing?'

Mesek considered this, fingering his moustache. 'I think you fear me, lady,' he said. 'I think you want to keep your place and your power, and let no person save yourself hold these things.' He waited to hear her denial, to find what bluster or anger she had in her.

'Yes, Mesek, I fear you,' she replied calmly. 'No, I do not want to lose this fight. But listen to me carefully.' She leaned forward, stabbing the board with her finger. 'The Sleepless One is not gone, Mesek. She is here, now, with us, giving her orders and positioning her powers. All is built around you failing to see what is happening.'

'Why would you trust me?'

'Because the Sleepless One is also counting on me not to. Listen to me, Mesek.' She lowered her voice, forcing him to lean forward to hear her clearly. 'I do not like you. You are savage and you are brutal. But you are honest. You are tired of failed overlordships and you want them ended. I can understand and respect this. I ask you to believe me; you are being used, and your men stand a good chance of dying if you remain here.'

Mesek did not answer, but his face began to flush red from suppressed fury. His hand clutched his leather belt, trying not to reach for his knife. Across the hall, one of his men saw them there, and touched his fellow's arm, pointing. All of them fell silent and that silence grew and spread until it smothered all the voices in the hall.

Slowly, Mesek forced himself to breathe. He took both his meaty hands and spread them out flat on the table. Gradually, the flush faded to two red spots high on his cheeks. Faces turned away and voices filled the hall once more, but not without both Mesek's men and Peran's casting many a worried glance towards the high table.

'Kings. Sorcerers. Madmen,' he said through gritted teeth. 'Is there no release from these creatures?'

'I do not know, Mesek. I only know this: whatever else

you think of Guinevere and Arthur, they have been open in their dealings with us. They have never asked from us but what is lawful of a lord from his liege man.'

He regarded her for a long time, a dozen different emotions shifting across his face. His old, bluff defiance at last settled into place, and Mesek stuck his thumb back into his belt. 'You speak of openness,' he said flatly. 'Prove what you mean. What is the power of this place?'

Laurel did not even blink. 'Birth and blood, right and heritage, the same as any other old place of lordship. My mother came from the sea to be with my father, and she bequeathed some of the sea's spirit to us when we were birthed. There was a mirror too, with a spirit servant within it, but that is in my sister's hands now, not here.'

Mesek waited, to see, Laurel thought, if she would add any other word, or if she would flinch. She did not. The tides of his emotion swirled around her, a thousand separate currents with anger the strongest of all. She could catch and hold his gaze, she knew. She could take all he poured out and force her own feeling, her own will, back upon him. She did not. Mesek must make his choice freely. If he did not, it was she, the one who stood there for his liege, who would be the traitor.

The anger grew, and so did the undercurrent of despair in his keen eyes, but neither came from weakness. Mesek was a strong man, head of his clan by right and reason as well as by the strength of his arm. All his rage was against the fact that he stood surrounded by powers that were greater than his, and there was nothing he could do.

'What would you of me?'

'Go home, Mesek,' said Laurel quietly.

His head snapped up. 'What?'

'Go home,' she repeated. 'Take yourself and your men out of here.'

'Are you mad?' The strain in his voice cracked on the last word. 'Peran will say we have rejected the law and he'll unleash his people on us. We are not yet ready for war.'

'I know,' said Laurel hollowly. 'I know. You must move your people up into the woods and wait. Camelot is gone to Tintagel to rally Mark, or to replace him. They come here next, or we will get word to them. I swear, they or we will come to your defence within three days.'

'I thought you wanted to keep the peace.'

'I do, but Morgaine has used our very desire for peace against us. She counts on us to try to move secretly and carefully even to the bitter end. So, that is what we cannot do. Go home, Mesek. Ready your men. Help will come, I swear it before God and on my mother's grave.'

Slowly, he shook his head. 'Not enough.'

'What then?'

'You.' His eyes flashed as he spoke the word.

Slowly, Laurel drew back. 'What?' she asked, even though the meaning had already begun to form itself as a cold lump in the centre of her throat.

'Never again will my clan face ignominy,' said Mesek, looking directly into her eyes. 'Never again will we hide, landless and claimless, waiting for our enemy to come and slaughter us. I am with you in your desire to end the Sleepless One's hold and cut off her reach, but I will not leave my people with only our spears and cattle at the end of it.'

'You wish to marry me,' said Laurel slowly, as if trying to explain it to herself.

'You or your sister, I care not.' Mesek shrugged. 'I would rather it was you, as you are the elder.'

'I thought you had a wife already.' Her thoughts were drifting away from her, and she could not seem to drag them back.

He shrugged. 'She is a reasonable creature and our contract

is clear. Her seven years are up and she may leave me freely at any time, with her goods, her chattels and price. When I explain the case to her, I believe she will wish to go.'

It was as if a door had closed. 'I am not the lady of this place,' she tried. 'It is Guinevere's prerogative to make such an agreement.'

'You are here and she is not. You may not wear the queen's torque yet, but you are heir to rank, wealth, land and fortress. In their turn, our sons will be heirs through you, and so will my clan. That,' he laid his broad, rough hand flat on the table cloth, 'is my price for this thing, lady.'

Laurel found her mouth had gone very dry and her heart seemed to be fluttering. What he said made excellent sense. It was not, in fact, far different from the negotiations that might have taken place outside her hearing had her father lived. But somehow, her reason could not prevent her from struggling against the idea. It was unreal that she should be having this conversation with the babble and activity of the hall swirling around her. 'If you do nothing, you will die with nothing,' she pointed out to him.

'But so will you,' Mesek reminded her. 'And then who will stand between Cambryn and the Sleepless One?'

It was as if a key slipped into a lock and closed a chest tightly. She asked him for a sacrifice, perhaps of the lives of his kin. She could not refuse to make a sacrifice in return. 'Very well, Mesek. You have my promise. I will make my oath before a witness if you require. But by stone and sea and before God and Mary, I swear, if you leave and take your men, and do not appear before Queen Guinevere when her court sits, I will be your wife.'

Mesek nodded. 'That is enough for me, Lady Laurel,' he said. She expected some word of triumph, or at the very least one of his wide grins. But Mesek remained serious. 'I ask you, of your courtesy, to try not to hate me for this,' he said, with something as close to gentleness as she had ever heard from him. 'We are both of us victims of power, and I too must protect my people however I can.'

'I understand, Master Mesek.'

'Very good.' He pushed his chair back and stood up. 'I will need to go tell my men what has happened, or some of it at least. Wish me luck.' A grim twinkle shone in his black eyes.

'God be with you,' replied Laurel gravely.

He took her hand then and bowed over it, a strange and courtly gesture for such a rough chieftain. 'And with you, lady.'

She watched him as he strode down the length of the hall to his clutch of followers, leaning close and speaking softly. They stiffened. They set down their cups and their bread. Behind them, Peran's men watched wide-eyed and afraid. It was they who stood up first, and all the hall watched them leave, including Mesek.

He looked back at her, and she raised her brows at him. *I have your promise, Master Mesek, as you have mine.* Mesek nodded as if he understood. He would not start trouble here. He would go. He slapped the shoulder of the nearest man, and all of them got to their feet to follow their chief out of the hall.

Laurel stood up. The serving women and men were beginning to clear the meal away, and the tinners had long since left for the river. There was nothing she could do now but return to her weaving and wait for Meg to bring her another message. Laurel moved between her people, calm and collected. If marriage to Mesek kept them, and her, free of Morgaine, it would be worth it. If it kept the land and the home of her father and mother together, it would be worth it. Her life had always been for barter and alliance anyway. She was luckier than some in that she entered into this with her eyes wide open.

It would take a while, but she would accept it. She must.

Laurel reached the end of the hall where her wooden loom with its inch of blue cloth waited. She picked up her shuttle and slipped another thread into the warp of the cloth. She wove steadily, facing the cloth, and no one saw the single tear leave its track on her white cheek.

'Treanhal! Treanhal!'

Peran lifted his head. The men around him frowned and shifted uneasily. He could hear them thinking *What now?* because he was thinking it himself. The only difference was that where their anger was plain on their faces, his fear was thinly concealed.

Seleven topped the earthen wall, running full tilt, with all the guardsmen of Cambryn staring after him. He skidded to a halt in front of Peran. Seleven was as thin and gangly as a beardless boy, although he'd been a man five years and more and fathered the children to prove it. His Adam's apple bobbed up and down as he gulped in air trying to catch his breath.

'What is it, man?' demanded Red Kole before Peran could get his mouth opened. Named after the colour of his hair and beard which stuck out in every direction, and his tendency to flush scarlet at the slightest change of emotion, he was the eldest among Peran's men, and, Peran had thought, one of the most loyal. But it was Red Kole who had brought him out here, and Red Kole who asked what he intended to do now that Laveen had left them.

Seleven finally drew in enough breath to form words. 'Mesek is leaving,' he said. 'I heard him tell his men. They're going home.'

'*What!*' roared Peran. At the same moment, inside he wailed *No!*

'Even now. They've gone down to the stables to get their horses.'

'So,' said Red Kole in a low voice full of calm and menace. 'They've heard of Laveen's desertion, and they have called your bluff.'

Your bluff, not ours. Yours. Panic, burning hot and unfamiliar, rose in Peran like bile.

'I will see this for myself,' he said, fighting to keep his voice even. 'Kole, you'll get as many of us as you can inside the earthworks. Use any pretence, visit any sentry post you need. Seleven, get back inside and make sure we're following Laurel Carnbrea at all times. If they mean to start a war, we will begin it here.'

He strode off as quickly as he could without breaking into a run. He left them there not knowing whether they would obey him, or if they could. They did not matter. What mattered was that Mesek stayed, that the Lady's plan be carried through, and that he be the one to present her the victory. It must be done, and it must be done by him. It was the only way he would see his son Tam again.

By the time he reached the stables, his hands and neck were sweating, and the burn scar on his face pulled and itched painfully. Seleven made no mistake. Mesek sat on his squat, sturdy horse. His men clustered about him, their pole-arms in their hands, waiting with at least an outward semblance of patience while their chieftain had a last word with Cambryn's fat stablemaster.

'Mesek!' Peran bellowed. One of the men stepped into his path. Heedless of caution, Peran shoved him aside. Mesek watched this impassively.

'What are you doing?' Peran demanded. 'You gave your oath that you would wait for the queen's judgement!'

'As you gave yours,' replied Mesek, absolutely unperturbed. 'And we both know that was the first lie.'

'Oath-breaker!' he shouted. The stablemaster fell back, but made no move to call help. The man closest to Mesek shifted his grip on his pole-arm, but Mesek touched his shoulder. That calm gesture stabbed straight to Peran's heart.

'If you go now, I will bring all the might of Treanhal down on your neck, Mesek Kynhoem! I will hunt you down wherever you hide. You will not walk away from what you have done!'

Mesek touched his heel to the pony's side, urging the beast forward so he could tower directly over Peran. 'Come then,' he said softly. 'Bring any who will still follow you, Peran Treanhal. You will not find me and mine unready.'

Now he kicked the pony's sides in earnest, moving the beast into an amble that his men had to march smartly to keep up with. Peran stood there, mouth agape, hands dangling at his side, and watched his enemy leave.

Kole would see it too. If Kole was still there. Peran felt his hands begin to shake.

What do I do? What do I do?

He felt the stablemaster's gaze on him. He could not stay here. His fists knotted at his sides, he walked away as quickly as he could. His legs had gone weak somehow, and his vision blurred. He did not know where he was going and he did not much care. Every direction was the same, for he was surrounded by his failure, and deserted by his people and his lady.

There must be a way out of this.

Perhaps Kole had not left him. Perhaps Seleven was still on guard. If they still held the Lady Laurel, her death would split Cambryn's fragile shell open.

But then, if he killed her, he would be killed at once by her men, and who would there be to ask for Tam's life in return for the victory?

He found himself on the threshold of the old tower. He stared at the closed door in front of him, distantly aware that he swayed on his feet. He put out one hand against the warm stone wall to steady himself. His hand was still shaking.

He clenched his teeth but he had no will left. He could not even feel the strength of Morgaine's expectation and promise that he had carried so closely since she kissed him. He was alone, and sick with that knowledge, because it meant all he had done had come to nothing, and made him less than nothing, since he now had no clan to return to.

It was not possible that Kole was still there.

Peran saw Tam's face before him, his bright blue eyes closed off and cold, his disapproval at having to wait so long for his return to life shining in them so plain.

He had to do something, had to bring this madness to some good end. But how could he act alone? His head ached. His throat ached as if the Lady had never worked her healing on him. Perhaps his uselessness had revoked the balm she had bestowed on him, as his failure to watch over Tam had revoked the life she had returned to him.

I should go after Mesek. Kill him outright. Kill Lady Laurel before she can warn her sister . . .

And hold the whole of Cambryn alone against its men who will rise up and slaughter me if my own don't do it first.

Someone was going to come out of this door soon. Someone was going to come looking for him. If not Seleven, then one of Laurel's men. She was not fool enough to let him wander about her place unwatched. But he could not make himself move. The reality of his circumstances wrapped around him, seizing hold of his thoughts, twisting them mercilessly into new shapes, leaving head and gut cramped and sour. The woman he had held hostage now had but to reach out and strike him down and all would be over.

Then, slowly, another thought, a hazy dream of a memory, came to him. He remembered Laurel's eyes as they stood together on the watchtower. He remembered pity. Not hatred or anger as one would expect from an enemy, just a bottomless empathy, an expression of understanding that made him want to weep like a woman. He could not, no matter how he tried, remember what he had done to earn pity from her, but he remembered that it had been there.

What if she also remembered that pity? He had done her no real wrong. He had failed in that as he had in all other things. What if he went to her now and begged forgiveness and asylum? Mesek swore she had power that could thwart even Morgaine, and Mesek was a far more honest man than he.

The world bent and swam in front of him, and Peran felt that his skull would split in two. He bowed his head and clenched his eyes shut.

Please, he prayed as the tears began to run down his face. *Please, Mother Mary, I beg you, I beg you, release me from this bewilderment. Please. Find me forgiveness, show me the way. Please, Holy Mother of Mercy, show me what to do!*

In that painful, private darkness he suddenly saw the Lady Laurel. She stood at her loom as she had stood day after day with his men uselessly watching her. Unchanged by what had happened, infinitely patient, she waited. He saw again the sympathy in her green eyes. The trembling eased in his hands.

He straightened and opened his eyes. His vision had cleared and he could once more see the door in front of him. Laurel was there inside, unafraid and carrying within her all the power of her line, more than he would ever understand. That calm, white lady whose eyes had shone with sympathy for him. Laurel would know what to do.

But as he moved his hand to push open the portal, his heart filled with terrible hope, a harsh croak made him turn his head.

In the branches of the crooked apple tree that had been planted for luck near the tower door, crouched a raven. Little

more than a patch of darkness in the greening branches, it
looked at him with one eye.

I'm watching you. The thought entered his mind unbidden.
I'm always watching you. And in the gleam of that black eye,
he saw Tam, and Tam told him what he must do.

Then, the raven took wing. Ignoring the rain, it soared up,
and for a moment its black wings blotted out the sun. Then
it was gone, carrying his son away with it.

A kind of numbness overtook Peran. Despair, bottomless
and endless, swallowed him whole and it left no room for
any other sensation. For he understood the truth now. God
did not condemn him, nor had He abandoned him. God
simply was not there. The Holy Spirit was nothing at all.
There was only Morgaine, and nothing human or Divine
stood before her. All his tiny struggles, all his fear and even
this despair that slowed his heartbeat and drove his chest to
heave like a bellows, was nothing at all. She was the raven
and the nightmare, and God was the illusion, and there was
nothing to be done.

'I understand, Morgaine,' he told her. 'I understand.'

Silent and solemn, Peran pushed open the door, but instead
of walking towards the new hall where Laurel waited, he
climbed the stairs and walked the long corridor with its closed
doors concealing Roman-style apartments, until he reached
the far end where a pair of Cambryn guards stood before the
last door.

'I am come from the lady,' he said, without thinking. The
words just came to him and he spoke them. He had no will,
no volition left at all. 'I am to try to talk some sense into
her brother, to try to get him to tell what he knows.'

The men blinked, a little sleepily, and swayed on their feet
as indecision took hold of them. Peran looked from one to
the other, and then stepped between them and pushed open
the door.

He walked into the damp and chill room, and Colan Carnbrea turned towards him.

'I am sorry about this, Peran,' he said as Peran closed the door securely behind him. 'But my sister has managed to build a good defence against my lady and does not mean to let me live much longer. I must go now, and I need your help.'

'As our lady commands,' said Peran, his voice as steady as his hands. The pain in his throat had vanished, a sign that her grace had returned.

'Good.' Colan nodded. 'Then give me your hand.'

Peran reached out and Colan seized on him with an unexpected strength. A wave of pain coursed through him. It seemed that all his bones were being swiftly broken, crushed and compacted. His throat constricted so tightly that he could not even cry out. His skull squeezed down and his hands stretched and lengthened. His ribs shrank against his lungs and every fibre of him burned as if flesh and muscle melted away. He could not move, and the agony shot lightning before his eyes. He saw Colan Carnbrea begin to stretch and change; his skin darkening, his beard thickening, and the right half of his face turning to the pebbled hide of a healing burn.

The pain and the vision were too much. Peran toppled over. The thing that had been Colan caught him gently and swung him up onto the bed. From there, Peran watched himself stride out of the door. Weakly he pushed himself up. He could scarcely move. It was as if all his fibres had become chains for his broken bones. But he managed to stumble to the window and lean against the wall, breathing harsh and hard against the agony within him.

After a little time, he saw himself down in the yard, leading a great black mare by a simple halter. The mare tossed her head playfully, jerking the halter out of his hands. Peran down below made no move to retrieve it. He just bowed to the mare, and mounted onto her bare back. Horse and man looked up to him there in the window, and Peran saw the horse had a woman's eyes.

We will need to find Mesek first, the nightmare told Colan. *He is too dangerous to leave wandering about.*

She pawed the ground once, wheeled herself around and trotted easily away. No one would stop them, Peran knew that. No one would even see them if she did not want them to.

Peran slid down to the floor. It was done then. His heart pounded against his new, narrower ribcage and his blood pressed hard against his skull. Peran Treanhal gave himself over to that pain and slowly let himself die.

TWENTY-THREE

The pale dawn light seeped slowly into the queen's pavilion. Lynet watched it with eyes gone dry from their sleepless staring. For hours she had prayed for daylight to come and wipe away the shadows. Now that it was here, she was too tired to do more than render dull and silent thanks.

Queen Guinevere was the first to wake. She shifted and rolled over, rising without protest or hesitation from her bed.

She had kept the mirror in her girdle. Lynet could feel the sick nagging weight of it as the queen stood and stretched. Queen Guinevere turned and saw Lynet's open eyes. She nodded in greeting, and Lynet returned the gesture, glad to be spared the necessity of speech. She was cold. She ached, yet again. She lifted her face in hopes that the pale light would spare her some hint of warmth to move her sluggish blood and ease her dry eyes.

Around the queen, the ladies stirred, aware that something was happening, but wishing to deny it and sleep just a little longer.

'Come, my women,' said Queen Guinevere gently, but firmly. 'It is the morning, and we must make ready to enter Tintagel.'

As the women began to mutter and blink their eyes, waking reluctantly but obediently, Lynet saw a stranger behind the queen; a woman with black hair and startlingly bright blue eyes.

Morgaine! Lynet jerked backward.

'What is it, Lynet?' Queen Guinevere asked quickly. Behind her, the blue-eyed Morgaine was holding hands with a second Guinevere. The two of them spoke soft and low, and both had tears rolling down their cheeks. Then Lynet knew that this was Morgause – Morgaine's sister, Guinevere's dear foster sister, Gareth's mother – and that this was the last time Queen Guinevere had seen this woman alive.

It was a shadow, a shadow walking in daylight and drifting behind the queen.

'Lynet?' Guinevere lifted her hand as Daere scrambled to her feet, blinking hard, trying to clear her own mind.

'It is nothing,' Lynet said, closing her eyes and breathing deeply. 'It was a pain in my arm.'

'These bandages should be changed and washed at once,' said Guinevere to Daere. 'And mind her for fever.'

'Yes, Majesty,' the maid replied. The queen believed. For the moment. Her mind was taken up with her plans and her memories. Lynet opened her eyes. The shadow was gone and she was able to breathe more easily.

It was nothing, a remnant of the night and of her folly. As the light grew stronger, surely there would be no more. She let Daere help her to sit up. *Surely there will be no more.*

The preparations to enter Tintagel began. The queen gave herself entirely over to her waiting women, not even delaying for breakfast to be served. She was bathed. Her long, rich hair was taken down from its simple plait and brushed. Then it was twined with gold thread and pearls before being rebound again beneath a veil of snow-white silk. Her under-dress was also white as snow and over this was draped a robe of scarlet embroidered with swans that swam on a river of pearls. Gold rings ornamented her fingers and her arms. Her girdle was made of gold as well, each link shaped to resemble a different summer flower and studded with a different jewel.

Lastly, her crown was placed upon her head, and Guinevere stood, so rich and regal in her bearing that all her ladies made their curtsies to her, and Lynet with them.

Like all the other ladies, Lynet had been dressed in her finest. Her clothing was yet another gift from the queen and it weighed heavily on her. Her soft grey under-dress was overlaid by a robe of deep blue silk. Her silver girdle was in the shape of sea birds, their wings spread wide, and a silver band enamelled with bluebells and hyacinths held her grey veil in place. It was more wealth and finery than she had ever worn at one time, and yet somehow it gave the appearance of grave modesty.

She stepped outside to breathe the morning air and to give those remaining more room to make their own preparations. She looked at the chaotic dance that was the process of decamping and of making ready for a grand procession, and blinked hard. It was as if she was seeing not double, but triple. Each human form had a shadow following it – one or more figures playing out some scene from the past. It was like seeing a thousand different mummers wandering about amidst the soldiers. Their voices whispered to her, trying to tell her their stories, explain their secrets, all at once.

Stop. Lynet closed her eyes. *Stop!*

She stood like that for a long moment, praying Daere would stay inside. She did not want her maid to see. She did not want anyone near her. She felt as if her self had been hollowed out and refilled with some alien element that stretched her so tightly she would burst if touched by a careless hand.

Slowly, she opened her eyes, and now she saw only the mortal around her. The shadows were gone again, removed by some shifting of light or awareness. Lynet tried to breathe, but could not draw in enough air.

It is only shadows, she told herself. *You have seen enough of shadows now. It is nothing to fear. They are gone.*

Fortunately, the whole company was so busy with their own tasks, no one noticed her standing there trying not to see. The wagons that had carried the ceremonial trappings all this way were unloaded. The horses were brushed and combed, their harnesses hung with coloured ribbons. The men polished their armour and weapons and scrubbed and cleaned their shields and themselves.

One group of men assembled the queen's litter chair. Lynet had never seen anything like it. It was, Daere said, a conveyance used by empresses of Rome. It was like a gilded throne, cushioned with silk. Pearls, garnets, amethysts and rubies studded the dragons and swans carved in sharp relief. The platform beneath the chair was fitted with stout poles so that eight strong men could lift the queen onto their shoulders and bear her forward. Lynet herself was to ride with the other ladies. Her palfrey was blanketed in blue and grey to match her clothing, and its reins hung with blue ribbons.

As they readied themselves, worry flitted perceptibly through the entire encampment. They had spent the night openly on Tintagel's doorstep. They now made great and noisy preparation, and not one person from Tintagel had come to speak with them; not a shepherd nor a cotholder, let alone any soldier or other representative from the *castell*.

The queen would not be deterred. They would go forward as planned. Lynet looked up the rise ahead. As if dazzled by sunlight, she saw flashes of colour in front of her eyes. They became quick glimpses of Tintagel's folk huddled nervously in their cots, near their fires. She saw the grim hall of the fortress, empty and cold. She saw the brown-robed monks in their chapel, prostrating themselves in prayer.

'My lady?' whispered Daere in her ear. 'My lady, you must come with us now.'

Lynet forced her gaze outward again. Her head and feet both had begun to ache as if she had travelled too far in even that brief glimpse. The queen and the other ladies were pressing past her through the pavilion's doorway, ready to take their places for the procession.

Leave me be, prayed Lynet silently as she lifted her hems and followed. *Let it fade, and leave me be.*

But this prayer went unanswered. Her head hurt and her vision was dim. Each step forward prepared the way for her to arrive in the one place she had never thought to walk again. With all this came the sick and creeping knowledge that in her spirit's flight she had opened herself wide to the invisible country, and not even the curtain of her flesh could close her off again. Looking out across the open headland filled her with memory, of the times she had ridden here at her father's side to pay court visits to Mark, of the time she had seen it with new eyes riding to begin her fosterage, of the times she had come out with Queen Iseult to take the air, and perhaps to meet Sir Tristan.

The memories sent sparks of light across her eyes, and brought the shadows gathering close at the edges of her field of vision. She bit the inside of her cheek, trying to use the pain as an anchor, but instead, she saw Queen Iseult racing away over the headland, her green skirts and red hair flying out behind her.

Lynet stumbled and cried out. Hands caught her and she looked up into Gareth's eyes.

He said nothing as he steadied her. She could not even have told where he came from. Then she saw he held her horse's reins.

'Thank you, Squire,' said Daere stonily, taking Lynet's hand from his. 'I will assist my lady.'

Gareth backed away. But she could not fail to see the worry in his eyes, the wish that he could be beside her. The intensity of that wish dizzied Lynet and she clutched at Daere's hand, but at the same time, the pain and the shadows receded, and she was able to mount her horse without difficulty.

Queen Guinevere settled onto her gilded throne, stern and distant. All around them, banners were unfurled, rippling with colour on the morning breeze. Arthur's gold and scarlet dragon rose beside the queen's own blue and white swan. Gareth carried Sir Lancelot's banner with its three broad blue stripes on a pure white field. He sat straight and proud on his red stallion, enjoying the pomp.

And Lynet saw him in the midst of battle, that stern face stretched and mad with fear and desperation, hacking out with his sword, trying to stay alive, bellowing his curses up to God in Heaven and down to the depths of Hell.

She squeezed her eyes shut, biting both her lips. Was that the past or the future she saw? She didn't know. She couldn't tell.

A blast upon a hunting horn brought Lynet back to the daylight world before her. The standard-bearers raised their banners high, and the procession began to move.

They rode across the rolling country, overflowing the narrow rutted track that was the only road to the *castell*. The trumpeters blew their horns, and the drummers sounded the beat as their royal procession came on, slowly. But all the countryside was empty of any to see their display. The cold sea wind blew uninterrupted, causing their banners to snap and their skirts to flow and flutter. Up ahead, beyond the few trees, the world was misty blue and white, and the terns and gulls cried out in surprised greeting to see the queen come to visit them.

In all their pomp they rode through the unguarded earthworks and into the *castell* of Tintagel, and only the sheep in the yards and the pigs in their pens lifted their heads to see Queen Guinevere and all her train enter. Tintagel was a small place. Out on the distant headland, the walls of the great fortress could barely be seen. The croft was older than Cambryn, but the homes huddled closer together, and clung more tightly to the earth. They had long houses for the storage of common goods, and for meetings and shelter from the ordinary storms, and the high house towered over all. A far simpler edifice than Cambryn's, it was a single hall with a roof of slate. No door or shutter opened there. No fire burned anywhere Lynet could see and the smell of smoke was nowhere on the constant wind. But the people were not gone. Not truly. Lynet could see them in their darkness. She could feel them crowded together and waiting. Nothing was to be hidden from her anymore, she realized with despair. She was to be permitted no respite from shadows and secrets.

The queen's procession marched through the rough huddle of the houses. Lynet found herself wondering if the queen meant to turn directly for the fortress island, but even as the thought came, the queen cried, 'Halt!'

All obeyed, and her bearers set the litter chair gently onto the ground. Guinevere looked about her at the silent houses, the empty yards and the dumb, disinterested animals left to fend for themselves.

'Where will they be, Lynet?' Queen Guinevere asked abruptly.

Lynet's dry tongue pressed against the top of her mouth and her mare shifted uneasily underneath her. She saw them and she felt them, with their eyes shining in the darkness, hunched among the sacks and casks, their fear emanating up through the stones. But she did not need any such vision. They were where her people would have been, and where, she suspected, Queen Guinevere knew they were. 'In the cellars, Your Majesty, those that are not in the caves below the cliffs.'

'Sir Lancelot!' called the queen. Lancelot dismounted immediately and knelt before her.

'You will send a man into the cellars,' Queen Guinevere ordered. 'Lady Lynet will show you how they may be found. I would speak with one of the people here, so use who you find gently.'

'Majesty.' Lancelot bowed. 'Gareth, Lionel, with me. If you please, my lady . . . ?' He bowed to Lynet, and there was something strange in his voice, something ever so slightly mocking.

Lynet slipped off her horse. Fear rose in a cloud around her with each step she took. Gareth's worry had sharpened and she could not even spare a smile for him. With the three men following her, she circled the long house. She felt Gareth most strongly behind her, and was sure she could discern his breath and his heartbeat. She shrank away from this, fearing to raise yet more shadows.

On the far side of the long house she found a standing stone that stuck out at an angle from the fresh spring grass. To one who did not know, it might be taken as some ancient monument, or a place to tether horses, and the great, flattened rock beside it as just one more grey and black boulder, no different from any other that dotted this land.

'There.' She pointed to the boulder. 'They will be beneath that.' *Huddled close in the darkness, straining to hear footsteps and voices the earth and stone keep from them.* 'The cellar will be bow shaped, and you must be careful, there will be a lintel set into the ground where the walls bend most sharply.'

'Why?' asked Lionel, already fingering his sword hilt nervously.

Lynet gave a small smile. 'To trip up any attempting what

we do now.' The Eirc-landers, the Saxons, the men of the next heath . . . the bloody shadows flitted across the surface of the stone, and the men beneath clutched their makeshift weapons, trying to ready themselves to spill blood one more time. 'I will go down first,' she said abruptly.

Both squires looked uneasily at their knight. Sir Lancelot frowned. 'That charge is not yours, lady,' he reminded her.

'The queen bid you proceed gently, my Lord Lancelot,' she said. 'Can you speak the tongue of this land?'

'I cannot,' he admitted.

'And I can tell you the headman beneath us cannot speak the tongue of Arthur's court. It may be I can coax him out with a good word and a promise they will not be harmed.' But they were so afraid down there, their eyes so wide and shining. There was a babe crying and its mother trying frantically to get it to suckle at her breast to quiet it.

She did not say that those who hid below all knew her and what she had done. They might well turn away for that reason alone. But she had to try.

The world swam in front of her, and Lynet stiffened her knees so that she would not sway.

'Very well,' growled the knight. 'But do not, please, get yourself killed. I have no wish to explain that to our queen. Gareth keep watch,' he went on briskly. 'Lionel, help me here.'

Lancelot and Lionel scrabbled at the stone. Gareth stood, hand on sword, deliberately not looking at her. She wanted to reach out to him, to say something, to tell him she was all right, even if that was a lie. A woman stood beside him, a woman with brown hair and brown eyes. She laughed and leaned down to tousle the hair of a scrawny little boy who grinned up at her with a child's sweet mischief. Tania was her name and this was Gareth's sister, and his heart was breaking for her all over again.

Lancelot grunted. He and Lionel had found the trick of the stone, and straining their arms managed to heave it onto its end and let it drop aside with a loud thump. Where it had been a rough, round hole was now opened. A ladder's rungs ran down one side of its wall, and beneath that a narrow stairway had been carved out of the hard-packed dirt.

Sir Lancelot walked up to the hole and stood for a moment, listening. He would hear nothing. They were all clustered at the far end of the cellar, and the babe was sucking peacefully now.

Lynet drew a deep breath. 'Halloo!' she cried out. Ignoring the shocked and sudden anger on Sir Lancelot's face, she went on. 'I am Lynet Carnbrea of Cambryn, daughter to Kenan the Steward. I come in peace. Who will speak with me?'

Silence, deep and frightened. She saw them, stirring, straining, wishing. They whispered to one another, but they did not move. The men drew close, not daring to answer.

'I will go down,' she said.

'Not alone,' announced Gareth abruptly.

'They are terrified,' Lynet tried to explain. 'God alone knows what they have been told. They may attack out of sheer panic.'

'So you will not go alone,' Gareth repeated.

'If you pair are finished planning our strategy . . .' drawled Lancelot. Gareth blanched and bowed deeply, murmuring his apologies. His knight smirked, and Lynet did not dare look into his eyes, for fear she might understand what flashed through his mind.

'If you are so anxious, Gareth, to bear the lady company, you may,' Sir Lancelot went on. 'I just remind you not to give me something else I must explain to our king and all the court, most especially your brothers.'

She saw the three men clustered around Gareth, so alike

and yet so different, all watching him, all full of love and also of fear for their youngest sibling.

Gareth bowed, and somehow that motion wiped the shadows away.

Lionel, streaked with sweat from his efforts, fetched a light, an open brazier with a sputtering flame.

'I am coming down!' Lynet called. 'And Squire Gareth with me!'

No answer. They all shrank back. The babe stirred restlessly and its mother clutched it close.

Gareth started down the ladder rungs. When he neared the bottom, Lionel handed him down the light and stood back so Lynet could begin her own climb. Her arms cried out in pain as her hands strained to grip ladder rungs worn smooth as ivory from years of use. When her slippers touched the earth, they turned together towards the steps. Gareth handed her the brazier. It was heavy as lead in her hands. Gareth drew his sword. The roof was low enough she had to duck, and Gareth bent almost double as she led him down the tunnel. The way was so narrow both her elbows brushed the walls of hard packed earth that gave way to stone. How in God's name would he swing that sword he held before him? She could not tell if that was her own thought or if it leaked to her from Gareth himself.

The sunlight did not fall past the mouth of the stair, so there was only the dim flicker of the brazier's flame to see by. Their footsteps made no noise. It was their breath that echoed harshly off the damp, confining walls.

Ahead of them, the stone walls widened and curved, as Lynet had known they would. These places were old when the druids and their kind still reigned here, and they followed a pattern that had proven more than once of good use. What Lynet did not understand was why the people of Tintagel should hide here now.

She could hear them with the ears of her body, breathing in the darkness, shuffling and shifting even as they tried to be still. Behind her, Gareth was taut as a bowstring. Lynet touched his arm, and he knew what she meant. He did not like it anymore than he liked that she had come down here, but he did not argue and he did not stop her. 'Where is the good man PenHarrow?' she called in the homely tongue, pressing close to the wall, holding the light well before her and as far to the side as she could, in case she had misjudged those who waited beyond. 'Good PenHarrow, how is your leg that I set? Does it trouble you at all?'

In the darkness, something snapped.

'Leave us, lady! Leave us alone!'

Leave me be! she heard her own voice echo.

'I cannot,' she answered back, and she felt shadows stirring and pressing close in the back of her mind. 'Good PenHarrow, I beg you, come speak with me.'

Cloth rustled and feet shuffled, and the sound of many voices hissing and murmuring came out of the darkness. Lynet stood with her sputtering light before her and Gareth at her back, every nerve and muscle straining, trying not to see and wishing desperately that she could. Panic and shadows pressed at her, digging claws into her vision to tear it apart.

Then, slowly, some of that shuffling drew nearer. A sallow, dirt-streaked face came around the corner. Seth PenHarrow had changed little in the past two years. Labour had stooped him a bit more, and his brown beard was a little thicker and a little longer. He came forward, hesitating, but, she was perversely pleased to note, not limping. He did clutch a cudgel in his hand. Gareth sucked in a breath, but otherwise held still.

'Go away, lady,' PenHarrow said huskily. 'Tell the queen . . . Just . . . go away.'

He licked his lips, and his gaze strayed to Gareth, and Gareth's naked sword. Gareth did not move, nor did he lower the blade from its ready position. Lynet knew he could understand next to nothing of what was said, but he also knew enough to hold back until attacked.

'Who brought you down here, PenHarrow?'

PenHarrow's hands trembled hard enough to shake his cudgel. 'The king, Lady Lynet. When he knew you were coming, he sent word down that any who welcomed you, any who spoke to you . . . they would be driven into the sea.'

'There are those in the fortress who would do this thing?'

PenHarrow hunched his shoulders. 'I think he would do it himself, my lady,' he whispered. 'His madness has gripped him wholly. We . . . we did not know what else to do.'

A shadowed flash broke her thoughts, and she saw Mark, huddled on his seat of stone, his great hands hanging between his knees, fear and fury warring in his eyes. Her stomach churned and for a moment she truly feared she would be sick.

'Where are the lords? Where are your chieftains?' She did not know what was worse, this vision of a king destroyed, or the fact that these people were left to fend for themselves by those who should have protected them.

'They've gone to the caves and the moors, my lady, with all the rest who could make it that far.' For the first time, anger touched PenHarrow, and his hand ceased to tremble. 'Those that could not get away . . . they are in the fortress, and all their women and children with them.'

Cold flooded Lynet. 'What does King Mark say he will do to them?'

'What he would do to us, lady, if any came out to welcome the queen.'

'I understand.' She did, and in her heart she howled out

against the horror and the wrong of it all. She touched PenHarrow's hand. 'Thank you, PenHarrow. Take care of your people now.'

Suddenly, he caught her hand, holding it hard. Gareth sucked in a breath, but Lynet waved him back.

'Help us, lady,' whispered PenHarrow hoarsely. 'Tell the queen. Help us.'

Softly, she laid her hand over his. 'We will. You must wait and trust, but tell them all, we will help you.'

His lips moved. She thought he said 'bless you', but his throat would make no sound. Instead, he raised her hand, touching it to his brow, and she accepted the gesture, trying her hardest to impart the blessing she had no right to give. PenHarrow straightened, his eyes full of mute thanks, and he walked back into the darkness, vanishing as surely as Ryol in his garden of shadow.

'Let us go,' said Lynet as she turned to Gareth. 'The queen needs to know how it is here.'

'Let me say one thing first, Lynet.'

She looked up at him. He was close to her. She could feel his warmth against her skin, feel his breath on her face. He smelled sweet and musky at the same time. 'I don't know when I will see you alone again,' he murmured. 'It feels . . . I don't know, but I'm afraid of what will happen to you in this place. I looked at you there and you were so far away . . .'

'Don't Gareth.' She stopped him. What reassurance could she give when she did not know herself? How could she say anything of the shadows that could carry her away at a moment's notice. Then, she remembered how those same shadows faded away when he looked at her. 'I promise you, somehow I will find my way back to you,' she murmured. 'I don't know how far I will have to go, or what will happen, but let you be my anchor. You will bring me back.'

His hand curled around hers, and it was warm and strong and the touch was as sweet as the scent of him. For that moment, all the pain she felt vanished. How so much could come from the handful of moments they had shared and the few touches they had exchanged, she did not know, but it was true and it was real. While he held her hand there was only warmth and heart's deep ease. 'Your anchor, then,' he said. 'Until I can be your heart's home.'

With those words, something changed inside her. If Lynet had ever dared to think at all about a moment of true redemption, she had thought she would weep when it came. She had poured out so many tears over the nature of her life and her transgressions, it was natural to believe that in this final moment, more would fall. But there were no more tears, no last extreme of feeling to transport her. There was only a quiet wonder filling her to the brim, overflowing the dams of her soul and causing all she had clenched so tightly to flow freely away. Gareth lifted her hand and laid it against his breast. A simple, wondrous movement. Lynet found she was all air and light. Light enough to fly, free enough to move, to reach forward, to touch her lips to Gareth's in a gentle kiss that passed to her the life and longing that belonged wholly to another being, and knowing that he felt all of hers.

The moment could not have lasted more than a handful of heartbeats, but it was enough to change the world, and it was with her heart full of song and strength that Lynet mounted the steps and climbed the ladder into the sunlight with Gareth, her anchor, her shelter, her promise, close behind.

One glance at Lancelot's stern and impatient visage was enough to bring her wholly back to the grim reality waiting before them both.

Lancelot looked Gareth up and down. Lynet could not tell

whether he was pleased or disappointed to find his squire unhurt. 'How many down there?' he barked. 'What are their arms?'

'I could not make a direct count, my lord,' Gareth answered promptly. 'But from the size of the cellar and the sounds that I heard, I would say there were perhaps two dozen men and boys, with as many again women and girls. There are children and infants as well. They are husbandmen and serfs with only such things as they were able to carry from their homes to arm themselves.'

It was all Lynet could do not to gape. She could not have been more surprised if Gareth had revealed he could see in the dark. Yet he spoke with absolute confidence, and Sir Lancelot nodded judiciously, accepting Gareth's assessment.

'I do not think they are minded to attack us, my lord,' Gareth continued. 'They are more interested in hiding from their king.'

Lancelot scratched his chin, eyeing the hole, the ladder and the stone. 'That's as may be, but we will put a guard on this place anyway. Perhaps our Lady Lynet will be so good as to tell us if this rabbit warren has any other runs.' He glanced over his shoulder. 'Though I think our queen would command your attention first.' He smiled fondly as he spoke and Lynet felt the hairs rise on the back of her neck in sudden warning. Her brittle mind began to break open yet again, and she forced herself into motion before the blurring of her vision could coalesce into some unnatural sight.

With Sir Lancelot beside them, Gareth and Lynet returned to the litter where the queen waited. Queen Guinevere listened gravely to what they had to say, ripples of anger passing repeatedly across her visage, although she made no move to interrupt Lynet's recitation.

When Lynet was finished, the queen glowered across the headland to the fortress island. 'Is there nothing left of you,

Mark?' she murmured in the Dumonii tongue. 'Where did the man I knew go?'

'What now, Majesty?' asked Sir Lancelot.

'We go on,' said Queen Guinevere calmly.

Sir Lancelot scowled at the distant island. 'We will not gain entrance to that fortress with what we have here.' It clearly pained the knight to admit this, but it was a plain fact.

'You will not,' replied the queen. 'But I will. Move on!' she cried out to the procession waiting behind her.

And so they had no choice but to mount their horses once more and obey.

The fortress island was not a true island, for a narrow spit of land connected it to the shore. But this land bridge rendered the place only slightly more accessible. The pass they must now take was a narrow track that sloped sharply down to the sea between two towering cliffs. In better times those cliffs would be well patrolled, as they provided excellent views of both land and sea for miles. Lancelot set the men to watch all around the procession as it descended the steep, narrow way. The watchmen looked about nervously, but they saw nothing but sky, sea and birds. Neither did the runners Lancelot sent out before and behind. There was no reassurance in this. It only made the unnatural silence press more closely about their ears, until the rushing of the sea began to fill it in. The sea where King Mark said he would drown his people. The sea that had birthed Lynet's mother, and the fae cousins who would murder her if she gave them the chance.

Only the queen betrayed no hint of worry as her bearers stepped onto the causeway. She rode in her chair with her head erect and her hands still.

Tintagel's fortress was in no way welcoming. It was a place of first defence from the sea and last defence from land. Lynet had never lived there. No one who had a choice would. King

Mark and Queen Iseult's high house stood within the *castell*. That Mark had retreated to this place was one more sign of how badly things had gone.

The narrow strip of stony beach opened out before them. The bright blue waters rolled back and forth, washing the sands. Lynet looked at the foam-laced waves and heard them mutter, telling the *morverch* she was come, calling them to lift up their heads and reach out for their revenge. Then she saw something else. She saw a man's body stretched out on the stones, blood staining his golden hair black.

Tristan! she heard a woman cry, and knew no one else heard that broken voice.

Lynet made herself look up as those around her did, straining to see the palisades and parapets of the fortress above. They saw the forms of men looking back down at them. One, two, three, four, silhouettes black against the grey sky. They did not move up there. They just looked down, counting those who counted them.

'Well, Majesty?' asked Lancelot, resting his fist against his hip. 'What shall we do?'

Queen Guinevere regarded the heights mildly for a moment. 'You will take the men back up the cliffs a safe distance,' she said. 'Set what watch you think good.' The queen held out her hands for her ladies to help her down from her chair. 'The Lady Lynet and I will go to greet King Mark.'

TWENTY-FOUR

'What?' The word rose in a staggered chorus from a dozen throats. More than one voice cried out wordlessly and men and ladies both crossed themselves. Lynet felt her face turn white but found she could make no sound. Gareth had already taken a step closer to her, and she saw on his face the last thing she expected – anger, pure and plain.

'Your Majesty, I cannot permit this,' cried Sir Lancelot over the din. 'Even if it were not madness, the king will have my head when he hears.'

'I will make it plain to him that you were carrying out my commands,' replied Guinevere. She had already ascended beyond all their objections. Lynet had seen Laurel like this often enough to know that not one of the verbal bolts shot now would reach her. She was already gone. And she would take Lynet with her.

'Majesty . . .' Sir Lancelot began again.

'Peace, my Lord Lancelot.' Queen Guinevere held up her hand. 'Listen to me.' She lifted her voice, and Lynet saw shadows flit dark around her veil, but not one of them resolved. She meant this to be something the whole crowd of them heard, and to use the strength of her words to chase back those formless fears and ghosts of memory. 'Mark has lost much of his reason, but the men who are there with him have not. If they see two women approach them, alone and on foot, they will hesitate long before attacking, perhaps even before telling him what they see. If they see a force of fighting men, they may believe whatever tales of invasion and betrayal have been flooding this countryside.'

'And if he takes you hostage rather than simply killing you?' inquired the knight. It seemed to Lynet that Sir Lancelot was attempting to shock the queen. If so, he was disappointed, for she remained impassive.

'Should that come to pass, my lord, you will have the satisfaction of not only being right when your queen was wrong, but you will have the chance to make such a daring rescue that the bards will sing about it for a thousand years.' Queen Guinevere gave him a small smile. 'And I would suggest in advance of this that you send at least some of our men, and all my ladies, to the high house. It looks sore neglected and in need of a woman's firm hand.'

The knight and the queen stared at each other for a long time. Then Sir Lancelot shrugged, as if it made no difference at all to him, and strode into the disorder that had been the royal procession.

'You heard her majesty!' he bawled. 'We withdraw! Turn around you sluggards! I want us back up those cliffs before dark!'

The mounted men took up the orders, repeating them as they rode along the clot of carts and men-at-arms. The soldiers themselves shrugged and grumbled and set about obeying, because there was nothing else they could do.

Queen Guinevere's ladies, however, were not so willing to let her march into folly. They flung themselves weeping at her feet, tearing at their hair, grabbing her hands and clutching her hems. One by one Guinevere raised them up, speaking soft words of comfort to each. Lynet paid them little attention. She already understood that this was going to happen, and that she would climb the narrow way beside the queen. Her attention was all on Gareth.

He was the only still figure in the boiling crowd that was the ruins of the royal procession. Every voice was raised in question, in curse or exclamation. Instructions and the reasons for them had to be repeated two and three times before they were believed. But Gareth did not move, nor did he answer any who shouted up at him, not even Lionel. He just stared at Lynet, reaching out to her with his gaze, begging her to take care, letting her know he wanted to sweep her up beside him and gallop away from this other woman who had suddenly gone so terribly mad, and yet still had the power to command legions.

Behind him, Lynet saw herself. She stood there in her modest finery, looking up at him. This was what he had seen when he had taken her hand to lay over his heart. It was a shadow already and stood with a host of other shadows. She saw two dim silhouettes standing before each other, speaking unheard words, the thought of which made Gareth's heart both cringe and swell with anger. Behind these waited two other shadows, blurred by time and distance yet made clear in a different way by love – a brown-haired man turning towards the black-haired, blue-eyed woman Lynet had seen with the queen. The man smiled at her, a smile of love and delight, as he took her hand, and she returned that smile with silent feeling matching his measure for measure.

With all this behind him, Gareth stared at her.

Mounted again, Lancelot brought his horse alongside his squire's, saying something. Gareth blinked and only slowly looked to his knight. Lancelot looked over his shoulder at Lynet standing there alone. His lip curled up in a sneer that might have been for the queen as much as for her, and cuffed

Gareth on the shoulder. Lynet turned her back on him, so he could listen to his knight and do what he must, and so she would not have to watch him ride away from her.

'Lady?' It was Lionel. The tall, thin squire came up beside her, carrying the staff that held Guinevere's banner. 'The queen asked that you carry this, if you are able.'

'Thank you, Lionel. Would you . . . would you tell Gareth I begged him to remember my promise, and his?'

Lionel bowed. 'I will, my lady.' He was plainly curious, but it was just as plain that like the rest of them, he was frightened out of his senses by this turn of events and did not have the wit or will left to ask questions.

Lynet moved to Guinevere's side. The sea winds snapped and rattled the swan banner overhead. The staff in her hand was heavy and warm from Lionel's grip. It wobbled in her hands. Her aching arms strained to hold it even now. It would be unbearably heavy by the time they reached the top of those towering cliffs.

Sir Tristan's corpse lay on the sands, bloody and staring at the sky. Queen Iseult draped herself over him, shedding salt tears to run down to the waves that rolled endlessly in and out.

'Lady Lynet,' called the queen.

Lynet drew her shoulders back. She shifted her grip on the banner's staff, as a man might on a pole-arm, and walked to stand before Queen Guinevere. All the queen's ladies stood arrayed around her. They watched Lynet as she approached and made her curtsey. Some saw her through veils of poison anger, others with mixtures of pity and fear. Lynet let all this brush past her as if she had been a shadow herself.

'Your Majesty,' she said to the queen in the Dumonii language. 'I understand why others call this mad.'

Queen Guinevere's mouth twitched into a hint of a smile. 'As do I,' she answered in that same language. 'But we will

go on despite that.' She lifted her gaze to the cliffside, measuring its height and seeing that now they had only three
witnesses overhead. As she watched one of these vanished.
'You will have to show me the way, Lynet.'

'As Your Majesty commands.'

Holding the swan banner before her, Lynet led the queen
to the foot of the rocky cliff.

There was only one way to show her. A narrow, steep and
crooked track had been dug by generations of hands into the
cliff face of the island. No horse could climb this way. Armed
men would have had to go single file. The sea hammered at
the stone and the vibration of it thrummed through Lynet
like the low note of a single harp string.

Sir Tristan had played the harp so beautifully. Once he had
played for her alone, and she remembered how she perched
on the edge of her stool, her eyes opened as wide as they
would go. She drank in the music and the smiles of that
golden man who called her his friend and the keeper of what
was most dear to him.

She wondered if anyone could see the shadows that
followed her.

The banner staff was a huge weight now, and it slipped
again and again in her hands as she trudged upward. Her
soft slippers were no good for this sort of climb and shifted
dangerously underfoot. Pain wracked her poorly shod feet,
and burned in her still-healing arms. The winds grabbed at
her veils and skirts, trying to pull her yet further off balance.
It was no comfort at all that the queen, whose idea this had
been, struggled as much as she.

One step at a time they climbed. They breathed on the
path's short level stretches. They gritted their teeth for the
steep lengths that were worse in some ways than climbing
a ladder would have been. Lynet could now see the main-
land easily. They had climbed above those other cliffs. Most

of their former procession still struggled up the narrow track towards the *castell*, but some had ridden ahead, and stationed themselves to watch over the progress and safety of those who followed. One rider stood out from the others, alone on the rolling green clifftops. Lynet stared, hoping to see that it was Gareth, but it was not. She could make out the bright red hide of the horse. That man was Sir Lancelot, and from the lift of his head she saw he watched them as well.

She thought of those silhouettes behind Gareth, of the queen and the knight in the darkness, their words to each other unheard, as their faces were unseen. The anger and fear Gareth had felt rolled over her, and she knew precisely what betrayal it was he feared the two of them had undertaken together.

Could it be? This struggling woman gambling now with her own life as well as for the land they both shared. Could she have betrayed her husband with that blunt, sneering man who watched them?

If Lynet looked back now, would she see Iseult looking on her sister queen with sympathy?

The very thought robbed Lynet of her breath. She stumbled, and below her the waves hissed in anticipation. She leaned against the rough rock cliff, heedless of how it would snag her delicate clothing.

'Are you all right, Lynet?'

She squeezed her eyes shut. *It cannot be I'm aiding another cuckolder. Not again.*

'Lynet, look at me.' The queen's hands grasped her shoulders.

Throw myself into the sea. The morverch *will at least be quick.* Lynet opened her eyes to see the queen leaning close, searching her for hurt or fever. Reflexively, Lynet looked over her shoulder. Only one shadow waited there now. It was Arthur, the tall, proud, greying man whom Lynet had last seen standing on the steps of Camelot's keep, watching regally as their procession started away. He watched Guinevere now, suffused with a love that was strong and gentle, and absolutely secure. There was no one else waiting for her.

'You must stay with me,' called the queen over the roar of the ocean and the endless wind.

Lynet used the banner staff as a support to push herself away from the cliff. 'Yes, Majesty,' she said, drinking in a deep breath of harsh salt air. 'All the way to the end.'

There was nothing more to be said. They turned together and they continued up the steep and jagged path.

At last, when Lynet's legs shook and her feet cracked and cringed each time she set them down, they found themselves standing amid the heather and stones of the clifftop. The wind blew harsh and hard and the leaden sky overhead seemed so close Lynet wondered that the staff's tip did not tear the clouds. A few yards ahead waited the black-timbered gates and unforgiving grey walls of Tintagel's fortress.

Like so much that belonged to the Dumonii, this had been many things in the past. It had begun as a monastery, she remembered being told, before it was realized what an unassailable fortress it made. God's house and all his servants were moved to another cliff, and these walls were raised to protect chieftains and their more earthly concerns. Bishop Austell had had his learning at that monastery, Lynet remembered as she gazed across at those other walls. She wondered if they had said mass for him there. She would ask later. If she lived. Her vision sparked and wavered, and her mind was too weary to hold the shadow plays back. She saw a man in a robe of the roughest wool hold aloft a wooden cross and give thanks to God. She saw wizened brown people clinging to the cliffside, wearing clothing that was little more than skins and strings while a storm howled around them.

She saw a man with a long face and a hooked nose looking

out from the palisades. A bronze torque flashed at his throat, and he watched an army on the opposite headland, and in all that army, he saw one man whose torque was gold and he hated that other man with a passion that robbed him of reason. The hook-nosed man was named Goloris, and the man he watched for was named Uther, who had the gall to name himself the father of dragons. Goloris turned from the palisades and went down to his wife and daughters.

'Come, Lynet,' said the queen. 'We are not done yet.'

Queen Guinevere smoothed her sleeves in an incongruous and useless gesture and started down the track to the black-timbered gates. Two black-haired girls ran behind her, laughing and holding each other's hands. Lynet trudged behind them all up to the gates. It was ludicrous, standing here, exhausted and dishevelled, arms and feet burning with pain and her legs so weakened that the next gust of sea wind might blow her over. Yet here she stood, with the queen's banner flying proudly and indifferently over her head.

Queen Guinevere lifted her chin. 'King Mark!' she called out in a voice that carried itself high and strong on the battering wind. 'Mark! The High Queen Guinevere is come to your house! Lord Wellan! Lord Peder! Master Hovan! Open for your queen!'

There is no chance she'll be heard, thought Lynet with an unsteady mix of hope and fear. They'd be left standing out here among the wind and shadows, and have to turn around and walk all that long, treacherous way down again. She did not dare look out at the water. She would cry out if she saw the *morverch* waiting.

Then, slowly, impossibly, the little door beside the gates creaked open. In the gap between door and arch stood a small man. His head had long since gone bald, but his beard and grey moustache flowed rich and full. His blue tunic was belted with knots of bronze and blue enamel and hung down to his knees over his brown trousers, but both had seen hard use of late, and were rumpled and stained as if he had had no others to wear over the past days.

Lynet remembered Lord Wellan from other times. He'd been a sturdy ox then. He had a laugh like a goat's bleating and a demeanour that could be deceptively rough and foolish, until he was ready to finish the argument he'd drawn the listener into. His wife was a stout grandmother, a full hand span taller than her husband. He had hauled Lynet by the hair to throw her out of the high house. He had called her such foul names her ears still burned with shame.

'God be with you, Lord Wellan,' said the queen, as calmly and regally as if she sat on her throne in Camelot.

Lord Wellan stood there, shifting from foot to foot, uncertain of what to do. It might have been ridiculous had the old man not looked so genuinely terrified. His keen eyes were watery and the shadows under them deepened as he lifted his gaze to meet the queen's. His knees bobbed for a moment as he tried to keep himself from kneeling. He looked wearily at Lynet, clearly seeing just one more nightmare to plague his home

'What are you doing, Majesty?' he whispered.

The queen blinked. 'I am come to visit your king, my lord, who is my neighbour and is liege man to my husband, Arthur. What are you doing, Lord Wellan?'

He was not a small man, but he had hunched in on himself, tired and uncertain. His square-boned hand gripped the edge of the door.

'You can do nothing here, Majesty,' he whispered. 'Please, go before the worst happens.'

'An army is occupying your *castell* even now, and it is waiting for a reason to call for reinforcements to begin a siege,' said the queen. 'The worst has already happened.'

'Again.'

'Why are you doing this, Wellan?'

For the first time, his voice was steady and held some of the strength Lynet remembered. 'He is my king, Majesty.'

Queen Guinevere nodded once, acknowledging the strength of that simple statement. Mark was the king, and he had held this place under constant assault for long years. He was generous to those who followed him and the families of those who fell in his wars. He understood the power God had granted him, and he had used it well, before he had been betrayed and broken. It would be a hard thing to be the one to break such a man again.

The queen reached out and touched Wellan's trembling shoulder. 'I will enter here, Wellan,' she said gently. 'I will come now, in peace, or I will come after you have all fallen to our siege. The season of war is upon us, and we already hold the *castell*. Do not let it come to that.'

He licked his lips and glanced at Lynet. *Why have you brought her?* She heard the question as plainly in his thoughts as she did in her own, and she still did not know the answer. 'Will you help him, Majesty?' Wellan asked huskily.

'I will do all I can, Wellan, I promise.'

Lord Wellan looked up at the queen who stood so calmly before him and in him Lynet saw a little child, not daring to believe the storm might be ending. Without another word, Wellan stepped aside, and knelt down.

The queen touched his head briefly in blessing, and with Lynet still holding her banner, she walked into the fortress of Tintagel. Wellan stayed where he was, watching them go.

It was a small place, not much more than a watchtower. From the top of the walls one could see the country for miles around, but those grey walls closed in and the heavy sky hung low. The salt wind whistled around the sharpened tops of the timber palisades, and the ground beneath vibrated from the sea's pounding. There were no people busy in the yard, no animals rooting or scratching. There were only a few poorly armed men in leather and bronze, watching the queen. There was no fire to give warmth and fend off the clutch of wind and weather.

There was only one doorway to the interior from this bare court, and it was dark before them. The queen walked beneath the timbered threshold, and Lynet shuffled behind her.

It was like walking into a cave. The day's dim light snuffed out. Straining against the darkness, Lynet saw the dead. She saw her father soaked in his own blood. She saw her mother peaceful on her great bed. She saw Austell, dripping and drowned, his tinner's rough hand still holding up his crucifix.

She could not close her eyes. She could not hold them back. They flowed into her, filling her up and blotting out thought. She could only dimly see the sheen of Guinevere's gold crown as she stepped among them. Tristan and Iseult lay side-by-side, his blood on her hands and mouth. Beside them lay the hawk-faced Goloris that she had seen before. Next to him knelt the black-haired girl Morgaine had been, wailing to Heaven itself. Over him stood another man, a twin to Goloris, but only a shadow within a shadow. It was the hated man, Uther, father of dragons, and with him was a woman, Goloris's wife, Ygraine, as dark-haired as her daughters. She looked mutely up at Uther, took his hand, and led him away.

A tiny fire had been lit in one corner and she saw the hands and eyes of those who huddled around it. They watched, as silent and despairing as the dead.

Unafraid, Guinevere walked into this darkness. She could not see the dead, but she knew they were there. She knew all the deeds of this place, and all the deaths that had brought her here, yet she kept walking. Lynet both hated and loved her for that calm courage.

Finally, the queen halted. 'God be with you, King Mark,' she said.

The darkness before her stirred. A brown-robed monk held a burning torch that illuminated nothing. Lynet's head pounded with the sight, and the pain ran down her spine, spreading out to her arms, her legs and her feet. The dead waited behind her, so clearly visible. Why could she see all the dead and none of the living?

'Guinevere,' the darkness said. 'You come too late, Guinevere.'

'Too late for what?'

'Too late to save this place.'

'Is this place in danger? I saw only the spring rains readying themselves outside.'

There was a long pause. 'Why is *she* here?'

'She is here because I brought her, Mark.'

'You mock me, Guinevere.'

'Never.'

It was wrong that the living were trapped here in this dark and cold. This place belonged to the dead. The living should have sunlight, and warmth. Why was she here? Why had she been brought back to this land at all? There was nothing for her here. Did the queen mean to give her over to the shadows?

'She is here because you loved her family and her father came before to beg you to take up your place again. She is here because her father, whom you neglected, is dead of murder. You have wronged her, Mark, and she deserves your apology, and a price for what you have done.'

Shadows moved behind her, shadows coming to bear away the dead. Shadows come to stare. In the circle of the monk's torchlight, Lynet saw something else. It was not the dead alone who made these shadows, but the living and the betrayed as well. They flew about King Mark, draping them-

selves over him. They weighed him down. They blotted out
the torchlight and kept it from his eyes, and he knew it not.

'Well, Lynet?' he said heavily. The shadows reached out
and covered his mouth, seeking to stop his words as they
blinded his eyes. 'Do you deserve an apology and a price
from me?'

Shadows and darkness, they bound him tight, they blocked
the light, they held him on that stone seat so that he could
not move. He did not know. No one knew. No one could see
but her, and she could not see anything else.

Lynet's hands failed her, and the staff with the queen's
banner fell clattering to the floor, instantly lost in the darkness. Lynet took one, lurching step forward, then another
and another. The air was too cold and thick and full of salt
to breathe. It was drowning her as surely as the shadows
smothered Mark. She could see his shrouded form now, as
he sat on the ancient seat carved of the same grey stone as
the wall. Saw the weight of years and sorrow and shadows
pressing him down, reaching inside and squeezing his heart.

'Shall I tell you what I see, Majesty?' Her voice was too
loud, too harsh. She trembled. She felt her own shadows
behind her, pushing her forward so that she stumbled again,
though she stood still.

'You can see now, Lynet?' King Mark laughed, a sound as
cruel and cold as the smothering stone around them. 'Yes,
tell me what you see.'

The brown-robed monk held his torch a little higher, and
the light spread out, and Lynet saw. 'I see a woman with
black hair and bright blue eyes. She is young and, to you,
she is fair beyond the telling of it. She was born in this place,
but you never saw her except at Cambryn where she and
her sister lived beside the Princess Guinevere.'

The queen sucked in a breath. 'What does Morgause have
to do with this?'

Lynet barely heard the question. There were only the shadows, showing her the whole of the past. 'I see her later, in the high house of Tintagel. You and she alone. She has come to spare your feelings. She knows your passion for her runs strong. She is come to tell you that Arthur looks with favour on her marriage to Lot of Gododdin, and that this is what she wishes for as well. She tries to tell you she is sorry, but it is best for all the Britons, and that another good woman will be found for him when the Dumonii are free of the Eire-landers.

'But you do not listen. You cannot hear. You see only that she is lost to you, and you cannot let her go. This Lot, this old man from the north, will not take her from you. You forget you are king and that you owe it to God and your people to be more than a man. You will make her yours. You knock her down and smother her screams with your hand . . .'

'You forced Morgause?' cried the queen.

'Witch! Devil!' Mark heaved himself to his feet.

'But you do not say liar, Mark,' observed Queen Guinevere, her voice as hard as iron. 'Say she is a liar and I will believe you.'

Lynet swayed again, tugged this way and that by the current of the shadows Mark's sudden motion had so disturbed. 'You said you were sorry when you were done. You said you would prove a good husband, once you had told Lot and Arthur that she was yours. But she out-foxed you. She told Lot herself. In her pain and her pride, she told him what had been done.

'He believed her. He held her as she cried, and he wanted you dead more than anything in the whole of the world.

'But you were needed. No one else had forgotten you were king. Only you. There was no other Briton who could take and hold Tintagel. Lot allowed his passions to cool, and took his lady to Gododdin, and left you here, alone with your guilt.

'One year later, they sent you the child. His mother had given him birth and given him a name of sorrow. She sent him to you, for that much her husband could not do. He could not raise the son of his wife's rape.

'That is why you could not acknowledge Tristan. Even after Morgause died, you could not tell anyone who his mother had been. And you could not bring yourself to take another wife until you saw Iseult, so beautiful and so valuable to the ones who had held you bound for so long. Then Iseult betrayed you with your own bastard son.'

He could have reached out and crushed her, swatted her back against the stone. She should have been afraid, but she had no fear left. She had nothing. She was nothing, just another shadow among shadows.

Mark never raised his heavy hand. 'He knew,' Mark whispered. 'How he came to know, I cannot tell. Perhaps this place told him, as it tells you. Perhaps the stones and the sea spoke their whispers to his harp strings. But he knew and he meant to bring me down. That was why he seduced my Iseult. That was why he lied to keep you away, Guinevere. He laughed at me and taunted me, before . . . before . . .'

Tristan's shadow lay beside him, broken, battered and still triumphant, for Mark had fallen into darkness with him. She had been wrong before. It was not he who could reach out and strike her now. It was she who struck at him with her words.

'That was why you would not have killed Iseult,' she murmured. No shadow showed her this, except perhaps the monk with his torch. 'Why you would not kill me.'

'You saw him. You knew him. He shone like the sun! Man or woman, there was no one he could not make love him . . .' Mark trembled. He shook his head from side to side.

The shadows shivered and tried to cling the more tightly. 'She screamed, my Morgause. She pleaded with me to stop and she wept when I would not.'

But he wept now, tears fresh and salt, and the shadows tried to grab at them, but they could not hold, and with the king's tears, the shadows began to slip away.

'The last I saw of her was a look of hatred so pure that I knew she would have struck me dead if she could, and from that came this . . . this man who walked the world like one of the Roman gods. How could I know what was in his heart? How could I see that this child would be Morgause's revenge?' He clutched his fists, pressing them against his brow, his anger shaking the air around him.

'Morgause did not do this thing,' said the queen, her voice ringing out hard and strong. 'Do not *dare* to blame her for your crimes.'

Mark squinted up at her, trying to see in the darkness. There were only the two shadows now, only Tristan and Iseult flanking him, sad, bloody and terrible.

'Will you bring your man to kill me now?' Mark asked. It was meant to be thrown as a barb, but it was a plea. 'Will you finally make an end of this?'

'No, Mark.' The queen shook her head slowly. 'It will not go so easy for you. Your penance is this: you will come out of this hole, and you will bring your people with you. You will come to my side, and you will show the world that Tintagel and Camelot stand united. You will host my court in your great hall, and you will come with me to Cambryn and wherever else may be necessary.'

'I cannot,' he whispered, and he fell back onto his seat of shadows. He looked down. Could he see his own dead there? They could see him and they turned their faces up, hopeful, imploring. *Come to us. Come to us.*

'You will. You left yourself alive, Mark, hoping someone

else would punish you, that God would take the burden of choosing from you. Well God is not here. There is only you and I, and you have heard your penance. You may accept it and live, or you may take your own life. The cliffs are just there beyond the wall. No one will stop you. But choose now, Mark. There is no more time.'

She stood before him, tall and implacable, a figure so bright she banished all other shadows from Lynet's sight. Queen Guinevere did not waver once while she pronounced the king's doom, and with each word he diminished until it seemed there could be nothing left to lose.

'Help me, Guinevere,' he whispered.

Again she shook her head. 'I have no more help to give you.'

He sat there, gripping the stone, staring at his liege through the darkness with which he had surrounded himself. The shadows settled once more, like crows on a dead man. He was theirs. He was theirs, and they would have him. Lynet could not breathe. Her body was too heavy. There was too much pain. She could not stand here anymore, and yet she must, or the shadows would have her too. Those were her dead there, and behind his broken father, Tristan turned his bloody face towards her. He smiled his smile of gold and sunlight, and pointed at her for the benefit of Queen Iseult, who had not seen her yet.

When we have him, we will follow her next.

Terror stopped her breath in her throat. *You are not they,* she tried to say back. *You are not! You are nightmare and fear. They sleep in God's hands. You are only here because of Mark and because of me!*

She had no words, but her will rippled the air, and she remembered what it was to be a shape, to take the fear and the guilt, to turn it into strength and give it back. She looked at Mark and gave him back the strength that poured from him like blood from a wound.

And Mark met her eyes as if there was no darkness between them. Slowly, he stood. Slowly, for he was an old man and he had been sitting still for too long, he came forward, shuffling and stumbling, but still he came. He stood before her, and she could feel his breath, feel his heartbeat. Life moved in him still, and that life was stronger than the shadows.

'I forgave you, you know,' he murmured. 'Long ago. I think even while I . . . while I threw you back to your father I forgave you. It was not your fault. You loved them both. I pray . . . I pray you will find a way to forgive me.'

He took her hands then. She felt that his flesh was calloused and cold, and it made her think of Bishop Austell, how he had held her hands like this, telling her to be strong. And with the stately pace he had used to carry the host to the communion rail, Austell came to her from the ranks of the dead. He made the sign of the cross over her, and gathered Tristan and Iseult to him gently, and lifted them both away.

Lynet watched them fly, and their current caught her own shape, which was only loosely anchored by her clay flesh, and she too flew away.

TWENTY-FIVE

Colan Carnbrea slipped into the high house of Tintagel with the men from Camelot. These men were tired, and the ladies petulant with worry for their foolish queen away on the fortress island trying to coax out a madman. No one questioned an unfamiliar man who spoke their own language, as long as he came with a strong back and willing hands to shift the loads from the carts to the hall and the outbuildings. Even had he worn his own face, none of these would have known him. He lent hand and shoulder to every task; securing and grooming the horses, pitching the tents for those who could not fit in the hall for the night, finding a place to store yet one more basket or bale. 'You There' was his name today, and he answered to it with a will.

He was crossing the yard with yet another bucket of water from the well when the shout went up, and the whole company ran to point and stare.

Out on the headland there was now a splash of blue and white against the wall of the square, grey fortress. The banner of Queen Guinevere hung out beneath the clouded sky for all to see.

'God bless Queen Guinevere!' The cry rang out from some anonymous throat. 'Hurrah for Queen Guinevere!'

Soon they all took up the cheers. Many embraced, or gripped arms and slapped shoulders, with all the relief of those who found the war they had come to fight was diverted. A plump maid with roses in her cheeks grabbed Colan's hands and swung him around in a merry dance. For this, he rewarded her with a clear, smacking kiss on her pink mouth. She grinned at him and whisked away, but not without a glance over her shoulder saying she'd be glad to see him again.

After that, the work picked up speed. Now everyone was readying the place for the queen's triumphal return. The golden Gaulish knight, Lancelot, rode out with the thinnest of his squires, a handful of men-at-arms, and spare horses, presumably to meet the queen and learn her pleasure. Colan helped with preparations for the hasty feast, finding the boards and trestles for tables, lighting fires, and wrestling iron tripods and kettles into place.

When the fresh cheering began, he ran out of doors with everyone else to see Queen Guinevere ride into Tintagel. Beside her rode King Mark, looking dazed and a thousand years older than when Colan had last seen him.

I will give the queen her due. She has managed what all the noblemen of the Dumonii could not.

But the cheering around him fell quickly to a hush, and as the little procession rounded the final turn of the earthworks, Colan saw why.

Behind the queen came the men-at-arms, bearing on their shoulders a litter laid with sheep's skins. On it, her eyes closed and her hands neatly folded, lay his youngest sister.

Colan went down on his knee with all the others around him. *What's this, sister? Have you escaped me?*

An anguished cry rang out and a black-haired man plunged forward from the crowd running up to the litter.

'No!' he cried. 'No!'

'Gareth,' growled Sir Lancelot.

But Gareth did not seem to hear. The litter-bearers set her down, and Gareth gripped Lynet's hand hard for a moment, a kind of blind panic filling his face. He swung around on his knees to face the queen on her grey mare.

'Her mirror!' Gareth cried. 'For the love of God, Majesty! Give me her mirror!'

The queen looked blankly down at the panicked man. Then, as if reaching some difficult decision within her own heart, she put her hand into her silken girdle and drew forth a shining silver circle. Gareth snatched it from her and dropped once more onto his knees at Lynet's side. He folded her unmoving hands around the pretty thing.

'Ryol!' Gareth cried. 'Ryol!'

All around him, people stirred and murmured. He heard Gareth's name and Lynet's, and the word 'lovers' repeated over and over. His brows rose as he looked at the young man clutching Lynet's still, white hands and bending his brow down to touch them.

Is it true, sister? Should I be seeking my revenge from this one for dishonouring you?

Then, ever so slowly, Lynet's chest began to move. Breath heaved in her and her eyes fluttered open. The people cried and some cringed back. Everywhere hands flew, making the sign of the cross. Colan could not remember to move this time. He just stared as Lynet raised her head and lifted her free hand to Gareth, touching his cheek briefly before she fell back, and her eyes closed once more.

A woman darted forward – a maid of some sort by the look of her dress – to grip the edge of the litter. The queen nodded to the bearers, saying something Colan could not hear. They lifted Lynet gingerly, all wearing expressions of amazement and no little fear. The man Gareth made to follow, but Sir Lancelot moved his horse into the younger man's path. Whatever the knight said, Gareth's face creased in a struggle that seemed to Colan to be similar to the one the queen had undergone in handing over the mirror.

Then Gareth bowed and walked past the knight, following the litter and leaving Sir Lancelot to stare at his back.

Well, my sister, you certainly have inspired something!

While the rest of the crowd pointed, stared, and whispered their rumours, Colan sauntered over to the paddock where the horses had been penned. The black mare trotted up to the wicker fence and ducked its head. He laid his hand on her neck.

So, now do you see? murmured Morgaine in his mind.

That I do, my lady, he answered in silence as she had taught him on their ride together.

It is for you to remove her, and put her to a good use. I will take care of all the rest.

It shall be done.

Guinevere thinks that because I have yet failed to take her home, she will have mine. She will pay for that arrogance. The horse tossed its head again and whisked around, rejoining the loose herd. Colan bowed his head once and strolled back into the hall. Amid a wealth of torches and rush lights, Queen Guinevere and King Mark sat on carved chairs while the folk of the hall moved hurriedly about them.

There, surrounded by those who would have been his enemies had they but known him, Colan squatted beside the fresh fire and waited.

Lynet spun in the darkness like a willow leaf in a gale. In the giddy, directionless motion of her soul, random flashes of sight overcame her – a battle, a love, a birth, a street in a sun-drenched city somewhere. They meant nothing to her. Guilt was gone, and fear with it, but so too was warmth and touch and self. Soon there would be nothing left but the darkness and the shadows of time, and she had left something undone. Something important lay waiting back in the clay.

If only she could remember what it was. She should ask someone: the farmer, the milking maid, the knight, the mother, the squire, the serving man in the stone hall . . .

The serving man. A dark-haired man in an ochre tunic who walked in a garden of summer and on a hill of sorrows.

Ryol?

I am here. She could not see him. She saw a woman cradling a babe in a cottage. She saw a man crouching in the bracken, his hand on a snare's thong, waiting for the partridge. She could not see Ryol.

Where am I?

You are in the high house of Tintagel. You fell. Your maid sleeps beside the fire.

I cannot find myself.

I know, he answered gently.

She had once known where she was. It seemed a long time ago. The memory was already fading, along with all the other things that came before this turbulent darkness. There had been another darkness there, but it had moved differently, she thought, and she had moved differently within it. *What happened?*

You saw too much. Mortal flesh cannot see all there is to be seen and keep its sanity. Then Ryol went silent, and she found she remembered this straining silence of his from before.

What is it?

Someone is coming, he said slowly.

Curiosity brushed weakly against her spinning self. She saw a circle of standing stones and a woman raising a knife to the moon. She saw a man holding a white staff peering from the mouth of a cave. But these were not right, not of the place or time where she had left herself. *Who is it?*

Gareth, Ryol answered.

The name froze her for the barest instant. She saw him, boy and man, she saw him, all of him all at once, and most especially she saw his smile, and his summer-brown eyes full of the wonder of love. She remembered what it was to stand beside him and know the warmth that could not reach her here. *Take me to him.*

I cannot, Ryol told her. *There is not enough of me left. You must bring yourself.*

Back to the cold. Back to the clay, to be plucked at by the shadows of the dead that surrounded Tintagel. *I don't want to.*

You must, Lynet. You must return fully to yourself, or you will not be able to anymore. I will help as I can, but you must try.

Pain, weariness, the unbearable heaviness of her own body folding around her, dragging her down into clay. The cold, dull isolation of her own senses blocking and blinding, tying her to themselves and the heavy, sluggish beating of her heart. She did not want this. She did not. She did not want to open her eyes to the ghosts and her ears to the voices that hurt so badly.

Then something reached her more gently than any of these. A sense of motion, a familiar scent, a presence moving softly in the darkness. Understanding. A name. The name Ryol had given her just a moment ago.

'Gareth?'

'I am here, Lynet.'

Here once again in the darkness, the stillness, beside the bed she lay upon. Daere – she remembered Daere now – would be livid that he was here. 'You should not be.'

'So I have been told.' There was a smile in his voice, but something had happened. She could feel it, and she could reach for it, find the shadow of it, or the shadow of it might find her. A shudder ran through her.

'The queen has sent for your sister,' he told her quickly.

Laurel. Laurel would understand. Laurel would know what to do. 'Thank God.'

His voice came closer. Did he kneel? She felt his breath on her cheek. He picked up her hand. 'What is happening, Lynet?'

She swallowed. Heart and throat constricted together as the memory of Tintagel poured forth into her thoughts. 'It is the shadows, Gareth, my shadows. They do not remain in the mirror anymore. I've brought them out with me, and now I see them everywhere.'

'Do not see them, Lynet. See me.'

'I cannot see you.'

He laid his hand, warm, rough and strong, against her cheek. He bent close, and she felt the warmth of his breath and his body before he kissed her, a long, slow, lingering kiss, gathering her close to him, wrapping his arm around her. She gave herself over to that kiss. Nothing mattered, nothing was, except the touch of his lips against hers, the strength of his arm supporting her. He laid his hand against her throat and she felt her pulse beating fast against his palm. He drew that hand down, between her breasts, across her belly.

'Do you see me now, Lynet?' he whispered.

And she opened her eyes, and she saw the faint light of the moon and the faded fire, painted eyes and solemn faces watching her, and a wooden crucifix hanging over a simple altar rail. And she saw Gareth.

'Yes,' she murmured. 'Yes, I see you now.'

He kissed her again, his caresses growing stronger, more urgent, more achingly, unbearably sweet. She found her arms again and wrapped them around him, answering his caresses with her own, her hands marvelling at the shape of his shoulders, his chest and back, his arms and thighs. There was no pain, no binding, no fear. There was only Gareth and the yearning, blissful need to bring him close, and closer still.

But it was Gareth who pulled away. 'Lynet.' He breathed her name, his lips brushing her cheek as he spoke. 'No more, Lynet. I will not be able to leave you.'

'I want you, Gareth.' There were no other words in her, no other thought.

'I want you, but it cannot be like this, not in the dark and in shame, while you are so weak.' He spoke slowly, hesitantly, as if these were new thoughts for him. 'I will not do that to your name.'

She did not want him to be right, but she knew that he was. More than that, she understood how much it meant that he spoke such words to her. 'Go then,' she whispered. But as she spoke a wave of fear overtook her. The shadows would come again. They were here now, waiting for her. Her weakened hand clutched the coverings convulsively, and found the mirror. As she gripped it she felt something else. Ryol. Ryol, back again to stand between her and the shadows. Gareth had done this. She was certain of it. He was her anchor and her shelter, as he had sworn.

He slipped away once more, moving carefully past Daere on her pallet beside the banked fire. He opened the door a bare crack, and slipped through, closing it soundlessly behind himself.

Daere snorted and turned over, and Lynet lay on her bed, her hand splayed across her belly, remembering.

Slowly, she drifted into sleep.

Gareth sat down on the corridor's stone floor. He rested his back against the door of the tiny chapel that had been given over to Lynet's use. It had been hoped that the holy oversight of the painted saints might guard her from whatever devils possessed her, or at least keep them from getting out and infecting the rest of the gathering. He laid his arms across his knees. His sword lay on the floor beside him. It was going to be a long night. It didn't matter. All that mattered was that Lynet was alive and safe. That knowledge would keep him awake as long as necessary.

What he'd do in the morning . . . well he would worry about that then. This time, Sir Lancelot was not going to forgive him.

He had looked directly into his knight's angry eyes, and he had stepped past him and walked away. A simple thing, done in front of the queen and all the court. He did not need to see the look on the great knight's face. No victory he'd brought now mattered. He had disobeyed an order. He had done it knowingly and in company. He had felt the blistering heat of Sir Lancelot's anger against his back as he walked away.

He had given away his second chance. Gareth scrubbed at his scalp. In the morning he would have to decide what to do next.

But Lynet had kissed him, and it had been achingly sweet, going straight to his heart. He had never known a touch like that, as he had never felt the lack of that final pure note of love in all the other caresses he had known. Lynet gave him of herself freely and fully, and would have given much more if she had been stronger and he had been but a little bit weaker. Even now his blood rushed at the thought of her lying just beyond the door in her woollen under-dress, her hair in its single plait, her eyes wide in the darkness, straining to see . . .

The sound of a footfall reached him and Gareth scrambled to his feet, gripping his sword. The cold, narrow corridor here made a t-junction, and coming down the other way he could see a moving light. He held back, waiting to see who it was. He'd been laughed at already for his insistence on playing armed guard to Lynet while she was surrounded by Camelot's army and all the profoundly relieved and grateful inhabitants of Tintagel. He let them laugh. They did not understand the strength of what pursued her. The queen knew, and she had not laughed, nor forbidden him this post.

The light drew closer, and Gareth saw Queen Guinevere herself walking down the corridor. She wore a garment of deep blue girdled with a simple silver chain. Her hair, unbound and uncovered, fell to her waist. For one wild moment he wondered if she came to check on Lynet. Then he saw her feet were bare. The sight of them tightened his throat uncomfortably, and he wanted to look away. She was the queen. She was his aunt. He should not see her this way. Why would the queen come barefoot to see him? He looked mutely up into her face. She smiled at him, the heavy shadows turning her eyes black.

'Where is Sir Lancelot, Gareth?' she asked. Her voice was soft, musical. He had never heard her sound like this before, as he had never seen her barefoot with her head uncovered. He had never seen her so beautiful. The blood Lynet's kiss had set to rushing surged through him even faster.

Belatedly, he remembered to kneel. 'I don't know . . . Majesty,' he stammered. 'He is much angered with me.'

She chuckled, a low, throaty sound. 'Then we must make amends between you. Come.' She held out her hand. 'We will find him together.'

Utterly dazed, Gareth grasped the queen's hand, and she raised him up. She smelled of summer and a hundred other things he could not name. Her hand was as warm and soft as a kiss. His head swimming, Gareth walked in her light and could not remember to ask a single question.

*   *   *

From the darkness, Colan watched his lady in the queen's guise lead Squire Gareth away. He wished the young man well, for he knew what it was like to be so snared.

Silent as a shadow himself, he slipped up to the chapel's unguarded door. He laid one hand on the wood, listening. When he was satisfied no one stirred within, he pushed it gently open. Its hinges creaked long and low, and he froze, but still, there was no stirring, no interruption in the deep and gentle breathing.

Your maid must be very tired, Lynet, he thought as he stepped around the form of the sleeping woman on her pallet by the banked hearth. *You should not work her so hard.*

Those last coals under their ash blanket gave him just enough light to see Lynet on her makeshift bed. Her hands were folded over her fur coverings, wrapped tight around her mirror.

Colan looked down on her and sighed. 'We are like the children in the old stories, sister, are we not?' he breathed. 'So long ago that God had not yet finished the world, there were three children. The eldest could talk to the sea. The middle child could talk to the wind, and the youngest . . . what could the youngest do, Lynet?'

He laid his hand on her brow. She did not move. 'We could have made good cause together, the two of us with our weakness, surrounded by so many with such terrible strength. We could have joined together, had you permitted it, and we might have brought them all down. But we hung separately, and now all either of us can do is serve.'

Gently, he eased his hand beneath hers. As soon as his fingers found the cool surface of the mirror, he snatched it away.

Lynet came awake at once. She held up her empty hands, staring at them in mute horror. She groped frantically among the furs. Colan lifted the mirror so it caught the faint firelight.

Lynet's head jerked up. She saw the glass in his hand.

Then she saw him.

'Peran?' she spat the word.

He smiled. 'Look again, Lynet. You have good eyes. Look hard, my sister.'

She did, and her jaw slackened. *Colan?'*

'The same. Now, Lynet, you will walk with me.'

She drew herself up, hugging the furs to her body. 'You're joking.'

He shrugged. 'As you please. But if you do not come, and quietly, I will crush this mirror you prize so much. I will be most interested to see what happens then.'

Hate and fury twisted Lynet's face. Colan shrugged it aside. He did as he must, as he had done before. He would mourn her, but he could not let her continue to hand out their lands for Camelot to pick over. She had lied to him, used his guilt against him. He would not permit her to do so again. It was her turn to serve the needs of land and lady and to pay for her sins. To let her go would be to fall into the clutch of his guilt and sin with no victory to buoy him up. He had seen Peran fall that way and he would not permit it to happen to him.

'Come, Lynet.'

One deliberate movement at a time, she pushed back the bed coverings, put one foot, then the other, on the floor. She stood. Her eyes never left his. She would kill him with those eyes if she could, but she could not. She knew this, and so did he.

Holding the mirror out of her reach, Colan walked away. Through the darkness, Lynet followed.

TWENTY-SIX

The barefoot queen led Gareth out from the hall into the
night air. The moon was near full and the heavy clouds
scudded across its surface turning the night into a place of
silver and shadows. Only the light of the queen's brazier was
gold. It caught in her hair, making her shine.

'Let us try there,' she said, soft and merry, pointing towards
a long, low building that had in other days been a barracks
like the one at Camelot. A spark of light showed beneath
one sagging shutter. 'I do believe that is where we will find
him.'

Why would Sir Lancelot take himself there? The thought swam
slowly through Gareth's mind. 'M . . . Majesty, how could
you know?'

She smiled. 'Perhaps earlier he came to me. Perhaps words
were exchanged that left him angered and wounded in his
pride. Perhaps he did not wish other men to see him so.' The
brazier's flame lit sparks in her night-blackened eyes. 'We
cannot have my Lord Lancelot angry, can we, Squire Gareth?'

Treading gracefully on her beautiful bare feet, she crossed
the yard. The wind blew back her unbound hair and it
brushed Gareth's burning skin.

As they reached the splintered door, the queen turned and winked broadly at Gareth. She handed him the brazier, and he took it. He would have done anything she said. Anything at all. At the same time, something struggled within him. Some small part of him tried to shout that this was wrong. The queen should not be here, not like this. But he could not remember why.

She reached out and rapped on the door.

'Who's there?' demanded Lancelot. His voice was slurred. He had been drinking.

'You cannot guess?' she replied, her voice deep and smooth as silk. 'I should be insulted, my Lord Lancelot.'

Boots slapped against stone and in another minute the door flew open. His face was flushed. Gareth had been right. The knight had been drinking as he did sometimes when anger or other strong feeling overtook him. Sir Lancelot leaned one hand against the stone wall to steady himself as he took in the sight of the queen standing before him.

'Will you not invite me in, my Lord Lancelot?' she inquired. 'It is not safe for me to be abroad here with only this young man for company.'

The firelight that poured past the knight showed the woman afresh. It picked out every deep curve of her form and every line of her face. Desire, so strong as to shock him, roared into Gareth's veins. It was wrong. It was horribly, perversely, sinfully wrong that he should be looking on the queen, his aunt, in this way, as wrong as the way she was looking at Sir Lancelot now.

'I thought you ordered me from you,' the knight was saying. 'You spoke of treason and how you would never betray such a man as your lord with such as me.'

She laughed, a light musical sound filled with so many promises. Lady Sabia had laughed at Gareth like that. 'You should have persisted, Lancelot. I expected a man such as you to know that a woman likes her lover best when he has proved himself in adversity.' She smiled up at him, and Gareth thought he would burst open from the horror of it. He wanted to cut out his eyes before he had to see her face for one second longer.

He wanted with every fibre in his soul for her to turn and look that way at him.

'Gareth, leave us,' said Sir Lancelot abruptly.

This is wrong. It is treason It is sin. 'M . . . my lord . . .' His mouth was dry. He could barely hear his own voice over the ringing in his ears.

'Leave us, Gareth.' Sir Lancelot took the queen's slim white hand and drew her through the door. She went lightly, easily on her bare feet, and her black eyes turned towards Gareth once before the door swung shut between them.

Gareth stared at the blank wood. Slowly, his mind reeling, he backed away until he stumbled against a stone. Then, he turned and ran.

He ran into the night, he ran without seeing where he was going or caring who saw him. He ran away from what was happening behind him, and from the lust that pounded at him.

Oh, God. Oh, God! No! It is not happening! It cannot be!

But the knight had come to her before, and she had met him in the darkness. He had gone every night to her pavilion to sit beside her, and they had exchanged so many looks, so many glances, and she had been so long beside him before she left to winkle Mark from his hole.

He scrambled up hills and slipped and stumbled down the other side, only vaguely aware that he was heading for the sea cliffs. He could hear the noise of the waves like the pounding of his blood and his heart. He ran as he had run as a child when he had heard of Tania's death.

Gareth's toe slammed against yet another stone. He went

flying and sprawled hard against the ground. He pushed himself to his knees, and all he could see before him was the queen's beauty, her unbound hair, her bare feet and her smile, and her black eyes turned towards him, so filled with obscene promise.

Gareth froze.

Black eyes. Black eyes? His breath heaved, shuddering his shoulders, rasping against his throat. *Shadows of the fire, I did not see right. No, I saw. I saw black eyes. The queen's eyes are grey.*

His fingers dug into the hard-packed dirt underneath him. The pain dragged up another memory, one that had been buried deep under his lust, under his amazement. It was ancient history, from when he was a boy. It was Geraint, kneeling beside him, trying so patiently to explain what had driven their father out of his mind.

It was not mother, nor was it her shade, Geraint told him from memory. *It was Morgaine. I promise you, Gareth. I saw her. It's the eyes, that's how you know. Be she ever so powerful, she cannot disguise her eyes.*

But as he lifted his head, filled with this new under-standing, motion caught his eyes. On the last rise before the cliff's edge, he saw two figures in the moonlight. Lynet. Lynet walking on the rise with another man. His teeth bit down hard on his tongue to silence his scream. It could not be! Not her, not with someone else! His still-dazed mind could think of nothing else, but then the moonlight flashed, and Gareth looked again.

The man held Lynet's mirror, and Lynet followed. Followed as she must because without the mirror the shadows would carry her away once more. She followed that man down the slope to the edge of the cliff.

That sight drove all other thoughts from Gareth. His mind was suddenly cold and clear as crystal. Crouching low, he moved cautiously, silently up the rise.

*   *   *

Lynet followed her brother, down the slopes and up the hills.
The mirror he held caught the silver moonlight. Her self
strained against her flesh. She could feel Ryol reaching for
her, but even this little distance was too much. The shadows
came, and she looked and saw how Morgaine held her
brother's hand, leading him on, how she smiled down at
him, so satisfied with what now happened, and how her
brother glowed with his accomplishment.

The sea. It was loud here, the rush and rumble, and the
sudden thunder-loud boom as the waves smacked the
entrance of the caves below. The silvered land ahead ended
in nothing but rushing blackness. Was that where she had
been when she had flown from herself before? In the night
over the sea?

Ryol. Ryol. Help me.

But Ryol could not answer. Was he even there, or had he
already given over the last of himself in her service? She felt
herself begin to split. She tried to clench her fists, but she
was too weak. There was only cold and pain and the rushing
of the wind, and Colan in front of her. Father stood behind
Morgaine. He stretched his hands out, but he could not touch
his son. Not anymore.

Anger burned in Lynet, tracing its lines down the wounds
of her arms and through the bones of her skull. Colan
stopped. So did she. The cliff's edge waited a bare yard away.
Below, the waves shifted and rolled, and called. Called to
their white-armed daughters, called to all the dead and
drowned. Called to her. Called to him.

Colan turned the mirror over in his hands. Her pain deepened and fear took her. She could beg. He was still her
brother.

He was still her brother, and she could not permit this to
go any further. He would not be stopped, he would not be
swayed. She met the anguished gaze of her father's shadow,

and remembered how he had held her hand as she had held the knife.

Yes, father, she said to that shadow. *I will do this too.*

'I am sorry, Lynet,' Colan said, and he did look sorry. There was grief on his face, and a little of the ocean of guilt she had felt before trickled from him now. 'I wish this could have been otherwise.'

'Oh, so do I, Colan,' she breathed.

He turned the mirror again and again, spinning it in his restless fingers, feeling how cool and light and precious it was.

Ryol? Ryol? Can you hear me? Her spirit strained at flesh. She let it go as far as she dared. She shook. She hurt. She could not find her breath. *Do you know what I mean to do, Ryol?*

Do it, lady. Mourn not for shadows. This is but the seal on the bargain I made years ago.

The effort at holding herself together made her sway. Colan watched her, mistaking utterly the reason for her weakness. 'I promised our cousins a life,' he said. 'And they are more than willing that it should be yours. Do not fear them, Lynet. It will not be long. I am sorry I must lose this pretty thing.' He held the mirror up once more. 'I think it would have been most useful in days to come.'

Now, lady!

Colan dropped the mirror to the ground, and brought his boot heel down hard on the glass. In that moment, Lynet burst free of herself. Ryol rushed free onto the wind, but with the last of his strength wrapped his ageless, endless self around her, giving her purpose to form her own shape once more. Shining with moonlight, fury, and the memory of murder and blood, Lynet stood before her brother.

'What have you done, Colan?' she whispered, knowing full well he could hear her, be wind and sea ever so loud. Nothing could keep her from him. One step at a time she walked towards Colan. 'You were right, you know. You should have kept the mirror.'

Fear spilled around her like waters in a stream. She scooped it up without pause, and she flung it back at him. He staggered. He stumbled, and she came on. It was easier than she had thought it would be. Ryol kept back the darkness for this moment, but all her anger, all her bitter desire for vengeance for all that Colan had forced on her, stolen from her, flowed from the well-spring of her freed spirit.

'You're a ghost,' Colan whispered, backing further away.

'Am I?' she replied. Another step and another. The sea roared and slammed beneath the cliff. She felt its tides surging through her. The tide knew what was happening. The sea knew and its movement changed as its children fought their strange battle above. That movement, that change, woke the sea-women

Good.

They were on the precipice now. The wind blew hard. There was nowhere else for Colan to go. He had to make his stand here. A thousand dreams and memories flashed through her. So much of life, so much childhood kindness, so much shared sorrow and fear. All the bright moments of their lives, until he turned, and he turned again, and told himself each time he had no choice.

'Lynet!' screamed a voice.

Gareth. Gareth running towards her. Did he see herself or only the clay remains? Sadness rippled through her, but she did not let herself focus on him. She needed all her attention for Colan.

Forgive me, Gareth. She made herself move forward once more.

'You cannot touch me!' Colan cried out, willing himself to believe. 'Get you gone in the name of Jesus Our Lord! Gareth! Squire Gareth help me!'

'Too late, brother. Far too late.' Lynet closed her hand around the living warmth of his wrist. She smiled at her brother as he stared at her filled with unspeakable terror.

Lynet leaned her spirit self out onto the wind above the sea, and pulled Colan behind her.

They fell together, absurdly slowly, turning and tumbling, the translucent veil of herself wrapping and encompassing him. She felt the last tatters of Ryol fall from around her, and she mourned him in the moment before the waves reached up and gathered them in. She felt their cool touch, but no shock, no change of air or place, only dimness. Colan struggled, grasping at the waves as they surged over him.

Then the *morverch* were there.

She felt their glee and their triumph. *Welcome, cousin. Welcome home.* They wound their long arms around him, dragging him down to give him the kiss of greeting, and lead him away. After a time she could feel them no more. She hung suspended in the waters, and peace suffused her. All was done. There was nothing more to hold onto or struggle against. There was a strange sorrow, but that too could be so easily let go. There was only rest now.

Lynet gave herself over to the rolling waters, and felt herself gently dissolve like foam upon the waves.

Gareth saw the man smash the mirror. He saw Lynet fall, and saw her ghost rise up. He saw the ghost drive the man from the cliff, saw them fall. He saw the arms reach up from the waves and draw them down.

He stumbled down the slope to where her corpse lay. She was sprawled on the grass, one arm pillowing her head, one flung wide. Her bandages had come loose. He knelt, mute and bewildered. Her wounds should not be exposed to the salt air. Carefully, he tucked the end of one of the cloths back into place.

She did not move.

Anger, overwhelming and unreasoning, flooded through him. 'Give her back!' he shouted to the waves. 'She is not yours! Give her back!'

But the waves only surged forward and drew back in their ancient, unbroken rhythm. No hand, no voice raised but his own.

'Give her back!'

No answer. He could not speak to the sea and make it hear. He was only flesh and blood, and he could not reach such shadows.

'Damn you!' he wailed. 'She did nothing! It is not her fault! How dare you take her!' In childish desperation he snatched the broken mirror, ignoring the pain and the blood that came instantly, and hurled the pieces into the senseless waves. 'You have no right!' he screamed at the ocean. 'You have no right!'

The blood streamed from his hand, and Gareth, alone, fell to his knees, the bitter salt tears raining down his face. He gathered Lynet into his arms. So cold. He kissed her brow. She was gone. Vanished. He threw his head back and cried out wordlessly to the distant heavens. He cradled her head in his arms and wept because he was too late, too slow, too much a fool. Because he'd let Morgaine lure him away from Lynet's door. Now she was dead, and it was his fault. He had sworn he would be shelter for her, but he had left her to sacrifice herself on these cold cliffs, and he didn't even know *why*.

Then, in the midst of his blinding, searing grief, Gareth felt something change. The winds that blew so hard fell away, leaving a ringing in his ears. The whole of the air changed. The smell of the sea grew stronger, filling his mouth with the taste of salt, like tears, like blood.

Light. Light coming towards him, moving over the cliffs.

Light like the light he had seen on the moors. Like the light Morgaine had carried in the darkness to lure him away from Lynet's door.

'No!' he shouted, clasping Lynet to him. 'No more! Get away from her!'

But still the light came on. It mellowed and spread, and Gareth could see a woman. She was not young. Long years had made a map of themselves in the lines of her face. She was tall and strong, wearing a gown of white that trailed down over her feet. She smiled as he cringed back from her. She had green eyes, he saw. Even in the moonlight that leached all colour from the world, he could tell they were green. Sea-green. But there was something about the shape of them, something in the way they looked into his.

'Lynet?' he whispered.

The lady's smile was fond. 'Her mother was my daughter.' With a gentle hand she smoothed Lynet's brow. 'I tried to tell my Morwenna of the difficulties that come when one of our kind gives her love to mortal man. But love does not have such ears to hear these cautions.' She sighed. 'I was very proud of her, my daughter. She remained true to him, as he to her.' Then she lifted her gaze to him and Gareth saw a sympathy as deep and old as the sea itself. 'I am sorry for you, Gareth, Lot's son. This has been a long, sad tale. So many fathers. So many sons. All betrayed so badly. Do you know why, Gareth?'

He licked his lips, trying to force his sluggish thoughts into some kind of order. It was so strange, so unreal that he should be kneeling here with this woman in her space of daylight with Lynet's still form lying in his lap. 'It is for love,' he said. 'Where love is strongest, the break is the hardest.'

She nodded solemnly. 'You understand then.'

'I am trying.'

The woman laid her hand on his arm. Her touch was cool

but vibrant, the feel of life held tight and close but longing to break free. 'It is enough, Gareth.'

He swallowed. It seemed irreverent, arrogant that he should question such a being as this, but even while his heart broke and he knew he knelt at the end of the world, he could not forget what he had left behind him in the dark. 'I beg your help, gracious lady. Morgaine . . .'

She held up her hand. She seemed startled, but not displeased. 'She is already gone, Gareth. Beyond my reach, and yours.'

'I left . . .'

'He has taken no lasting hurt from her, and she has done nothing other than lay with him.'

'Why? Why did she . . .' he could not finish a single sentence. He could not bring himself to truly, finally believe all he had witnessed, all he had permitted.

The lady before him sighed. 'To wound,' she said softly. 'To get what she wants. To deny that she is the one who has caused her own pain.'

They sat in silence for a moment, Gareth and the shining lady, with Lynet unmoving between them.

'Please,' he heard himself say in the voice of that small boy who had been so much with him on this horrible night. 'Where is Lynet?'

'She is with me,' said the lady simply.

'Can she return?' The words caught in his throat, caught on hope and despair.

Again the deep sympathy welled up in the Sea's eyes. 'Not alone. Not this time. She went too far.'

'Is there anything I can do, lady? Please. I will do anything. Just . . . just let her come back.'

'Anything, Gareth?'

He heard the depth of those words, felt the darkness under them. He was no more in the mortal world. This was the invisible country. In this place words bound like stone and iron. In this place any bargain made would be kept, willingly or no. He knew it from his brothers, and from the intuition of his own soul. He felt Lynet's still weight against him, felt her hair flowing loose over his hands.

'What is required?' he asked hoarsely.

'What was given, Gareth. A life.'

He would die for her. He could do it easily. He'd walk off the cliff with a full heart. He knew it. Never have to face the morning. Give his last for love and be sung about as Sir Tristan was in the countryside, and Lynet would be safe and there would be no more ghosts for either of them. No more loss. He would be the one who vanished this time.

But the Sea was looking at him sadly now, and he felt the other thing. The part of him that spoke of cowardice. It would be so easy to die, to leave all his troubles and fears behind and sleep until Judgement Day. It would take strength to find a way to live. Slowly, under the gaze of the Sea, and holding Lynet's still form, Gareth understood.

'I give her my life,' he said. 'As she gave hers. I give it in service to her. I will be hers and no one else's. My life to hers and for hers, for as long as we are granted to live. Will that be enough?'

The Sea smiled, and she stood. 'Yes, Gareth. It will be enough.'

She stepped aside, moving into the night, and for a moment he saw Lynet before him, shining, whole and well. Then, that spirit self laid down in the bed of her body. She began to breathe, naturally and deeply and he felt the warmth of her beneath his hands. In the next moment, her eyes opened as simply as if she woke from sleep.

'Gareth,' she said.

And Gareth had no words. She sat up and she smiled. 'Gareth,' she said again.

'Yes, Lynet,' he said. 'I am here.'

And he leaned forward and kissed her, and she wrapped her arms around him answering that kiss. And the light of the Sea faded away, leaving them the moonlight and the sea-wind.

It was enough.

EPILOGUE

The marriage of Lynet Carnbrea and Sir Gareth, Lot's son, took place in the great hall of Cambryn. It was the queen who gave the lady in wedlock, and Lionel who stood sentry for Sir Gareth as none of his brothers were there. Father Lucius spoke the mass in the chapel. The Lady Laurel looked on, some said lost in thought, other, more bitter tongues said in jealousy.

But what there was to be jealous of, most could not be sure. As a wedding gift, Queen Guinevere gave the whole of Cambryn over to the line of Carnbrea, and as the eldest of that line, Laurel became queen.

It was noted that Sir Lancelot stood silently at the back of the gathering, and some thought it was strange that he did not stand beside the man who, until the day before, had been his squire. Some said there had been a quarrel between the two, but none at that time was ready to say aloud what might have been the cause.

If any saw the black raven that sat in the branches of the hazel tree outside, looking in at the ceremony and celebration, none remarked on it.